SEALY & MILMAN: ANNOTATED GUIDE TO THE LEGISLATION

SUPPLEMENT TO THE TWENTY-FIFTH EDITION

SEALY & MILMAN: ANNOTATED GUIDE TO THE INSOLVENCY LEGISLATION

Supplement to the Twenty-fifth Edition

Up-to-date to 6 October 2022

David Milman LLB PhD
Professor of Law, Law School, Lancaster University, Professorial Associ-ate at Exchange Chambers

Peter Bailey LLM
In-House Author, Sweet & Maxwell

Former Editor

Len Sealy MA LLM PhD, Barrister and Solicitor (NZ)
Former SJ Berwin Professor Emeritus of Corporate Law, University of Cambridge

SWEET & MAXWELL

Published in 2022 by Thomson Reuters, trading as Sweet & Maxwell.
Thomson Reuters is registered in England & Wales, Company No.1679046.
Registered office and address for service: 5 Canada Square, Canary Wharf, London E14 5AQ.
For further information on our products and services, visit *http://www.sweetandmaxwell.co.uk*.
Computerset by Sweet & Maxwell.
Print and bound by CPI Group (UK) Ltd, Croydon, CR0 4YY
A CIP catalogue record of this book is available from the British Library.

ISBN (print): 978-0-414-11074-8

ISBN (ebook): 978-0-414-11077-9

ISBN (print and ebook): 978-0-414-11075-5

Disclaimer

PREFACE TO THE SUPPLEMENT TO THE TWENTY-FIFTH EDITION

Sealy & Milman: Annotated Guide to the Insolvency Legislation, now in its 25th edition, began life in 1987 as a single volume edition published every few years, then containing the new main legislation of the Insolvency Act 1986 (IA 1986), the Insolvency Rules 1986 (SI 1986/1925) and the Company Directors Disqualification Act 1986. The Guide progressed to two volumes in 2003, containing virtually all statutory material on insolvency, then to being an annual publication in 2008 and finally it went online with frequent updating on the Westlaw platform in 2010. The only time that we have previously published a supplement was to the 23rd edition, describing the permanent and temporary insolvency measures in the Corporate Insolvency and Governance Act 2020 (CIGA 2020) following its introduction in June 2020 in light of the COVID-19 pandemic. All this ongoing success has led our publishers to ask us to prepare a Supplement roughly half way through the life of this 25th edition, reflecting the Westlaw online update notes to date to this edition.

In one sense, timing for this first Supplement has not been the most convenient, as legislative developments in insolvency since the 25th edition was published in May 2022 have been relatively small. However this has been more than made up for with other developments such as the Insolvency Service's first five-year review of the Insolvency (England and Wales) Rules 2016 (SI 2016/1024) (IR 2016) promising a review of company voluntary liquidations (CVLs). Also the Insolvency Service has announced a review of personal insolvency law, an interim review of the permanent measures under CIGA 2020 has been published and there has been a large number of interesting cases. Most prominent amongst these, just as we were finalising the Supplement, the Supreme Court delivered the long-awaited judgment in *BTI 2014 LLC v Sequana SA* [2022] UKSC 25, primarily on directors' duty to creditors of companies in or approaching insolvency, and we have hurriedly inserted notes on this gargantuan judgment. The Supreme Court dismissed the appeal and touched on a number of provisions of IA 1986 particularly relevant to the above duty (especially ss.212, 214 and 239).

We are delighted to include in this Supplement an *Index of definitions appearing in the Insolvency Act 1986* and an *Index of definitions appearing in the Insolvency (England and Wales) Rules 2016*. These practically useful definition indexes have been recreated by Graeme Levy, a senior editor with Thomson Reuters Practical Law Restructuring and Insolvency team, drawing from material formerly reproduced in the *Annotated Guide*. They offer a labour-saving method of finding relevant meanings quickly. We are most grateful to Graeme who both suggested this inclusion and did the hard work involved in constructing the indexes.

Important case and other developments covered in this Supplement are included in the following subject areas.

Moratoriums

An interim review on permanent measures introduced by the CIGA 2020 as from 26 June 2020 reports that the standalone moratorium in Pt A1 of IA 1986 inserted by CIGA 2020 has been used successfully and has satisfied its policy objectives, but there are some significant concerns that it alters pre-existing priorities in any subsequent insolvency.

Company voluntary arrangement (CVAs)

Report on position of landlords in CVAs published.
HMRC has announced that it is to be more proactive in CVA proposal voting.

Receiverships

Denaxe Ltd v Cooper [2022] EWHC 764 (Ch) (receiver avoided liability for breach of duty by applying to the court for directions and obtaining court sanction on a sale).

Winding up

Re De Weyer Ltd (in liq.); Kelmanson v Gallagher [2022] EWHC 395 (Ch) (directors liable for preference to themselves may also be liable for a breach of duty and misfeasance).

Invest Bank PSC v El-Husseini [2022] EWHC 894 (Comm) (meaning of entering a "transaction" for purpose of avoiding transactions defrauding creditors).

Pagden v Soho Square Capital LLP [2022] EWHC 944 (Ch) (removal of liquidators considered).

Kireeva v Bedzhamov [2022] EWHC 1047 (Ch) (security of costs awarded to debtor as claimant Russian bankruptcy trustee had no assets in England and Wales against which an order for costs could be enforced).

Rushbrooke UK Ltd v 4 Designs Concept Ltd [2022] EWHC 1110 (Ch); [2022] EWHC 1416 (Ch); [2022] EWHC 1687 (Ch) (application to restrain presentation of winding-up petition struck out as solicitors acted on behalf of the applicant company without authority; costs against company but not director concerned and wasted costs order made against solicitors).

Citibank NA v Speciality Steel UK Ltd [2022] EWHC 1359 (Ch) and *Re a Company* [2022] EWHC 1690 (Ch) (coronavirus financial effect on winding-up petition).

Secretary of State for Business, Energy and Industrial Strategy v Vanguard Insolvency [2022] EWHC 1589 (Ch) (no criminal activity but companies providing IVA services wound up in public interest).

Re Edengate Homes (Butley Hall) Ltd (in liq.); Lock v Stanley [2022] EWCA Civ 626 (application by creditor against decision of liquidator must be by a person aggrieved with a legitimate interest in the relief sought).

Manolete Partners plc v Dalal [2022] EWHC 1597 (Ch) (alleged de facto director entitled to benefit of the doubt in unclear situations).

Re PGD Ltd; Manolete Partners plc v Hope [2022] EWHC 1801 (Ch) (court would not impose a cap on an assigned claim which would deprive an innocent assignee of its share of the proceeds even if other parties tainted with wrongdoing might benefit).

Glocin Ltd v Bancibo SE [2022] EWHC 1858 (Ch) (substantial dispute established to strike out winding-up petition).

Re Allied Wallet Ltd [2022] EWHC 1877 (Ch) (directions given on costs of distributing "assets pools" in the liquidation of a company subject to the Electronic Money Regulations 2011 (SI 2011/99)).

Guy Kwok-Hung Lam v Tor Asia Credit Master Fund LP [2022] HKCA 1297 (Hong Kong Court of Appeal considers application of exclusive jurisdiction clauses in determination of disputed winding-up petition debt).

Rashid v Direct Savings Ltd (unreported, 16 August 2022, County Ct) (application of limitation periods on the making of a winding-up order considered regarding insurers' liability under the Third Parties (Rights against Insurers) Act 2010).

Hamilton v Attorney-General [2022] EWHC 2132 (Ch) (freehold property held on trust by a dissolved foreign company does not escheat to the Crown, but vests in the Crown as bona vacantia subject to the trust).

Re BHS Group Ltd; Chandler v Wright [2022] EWHC 2205 (Ch) (alternative and unparticularised dates for the required increased net deficiency in wrongful trading proceedings were not fair on the defendant who needed to be able to respond to the claims).

Deposit Guarantee Fund for Individuals v Bank Frick & Co AG [2022] EWHC 2221 (Ch) (pleaded material did not contain material which justified an inference of the avoidance purpose for a transaction defrauding creditors).

BTI 2014 LLC v Sequana SA [2022] UKSC 25 (the Supreme Court has clarified and refined the common law (supported by statute) directors' duty to have regard to the interests of creditors of companies in or approaching insolvency, with further reference to the compatibility of the duty to IA 1986 provisions on wrongful trading and preferences).

The Insolvency Service is to review CVLs in light of the five-year review of IR 2016.

The deposit on the presentation of a winding-up petition increases from £1,600 to £2,600 on 1 November 2022.

Administration

Special administration regime for payment and electronic money institutions amended.

Re VTB Capital plc [2022] EWHC 1106 (Ch) (investment bank controlled by the Russian government which was subject to sanctions could be subject to an administration order).

Re Caversham Finance Ltd [2022] EWHC 789 (Ch); *Re E Realisations 2020 Ltd* [2022] EWHC 1575 (Ch) (failure to give the reasons for the extension of administrators' appointment in the notice to creditors was regarded as a procedural defect that was curable).

Re Bedford Hotel Ltd [2022] NICh 10 (order resulted in payment to fixed chargee as promoting the purpose of administration).

Fitzroy Street Capital Inc v Manning [2022] EWHC 1495 (Ch) (administrators not in breach of duty by not obtaining a court order for sale of charged property).

Re Petropavlovsk plc [2022] EWHC 2097 (Ch) (administrators' application for directions resulted in authorisation of their proposed transaction otherwise possibly subject to Russian sanctions and was not in breach of the rule on *Ex p. James* (1874) L.R. 9 Ch. App. 609).

Schofield v Smith [2022] EWCA Civ 824 (administrators could rely on a settlement agreement entered into between the company and a creditor without being parties to it).

Re Ipagoo Ltd (in admin.); Baker v Financial Conduct Authority [2022] EWCA Civ 302 (application for directions by administrators of company subject to the Electronic Money Regulations 2011 (SI 2011/99)).

Re Prime Noble Properties Ltd (in admin.) [2022] EWHC 2271 (Ch) (court sanctioned possession and sale by administrators of residential long leases where the freehold was subject to a charging order and considered payment of the administrators' fees and costs).

Personal insolvency

First major review of personal insolvency in England and Wales for 40 years has commenced.

Individual voluntary arrangements (IVAs)

Ulster Bank Ltd v Taggart [2022] NICh 8 (position of voting rights of IVA creditors with personal guarantee considered).

Bankruptcy

Howlader v Moore [2021] EWHC 3708 (Ch) (a bankruptcy order may allow the bankrupt and family to remain in possession during the marketing process of the family home).

Brittain v Ferster [2022] EWHC 1060 (Ch) (discharge from bankruptcy does not affect the continuing obligations of a bankrupt to assist the official receiver or trustee in bankruptcy).

Addison v London European Securities Ltd [2022] EWHC 1077 (Ch) (a right of appeal against refusal to set aside a statutory demand remained in the debtor, but appeal dismissed).

Shop Direct Finance Co Ltd v Official Receiver [2022] EWHC 1355 (Comm) (meaning of property in bankruptcy proceedings considered).

Hyde v Djurberg [2022] EWHC 1534 (Ch) (seizure by the trustee in bankruptcy of the bankrupt's property made where there was the real risk of his sale or dissipation of assets).

Khan v Singh-Sall [2022] EWHC 1913 (Ch) (even where a court concludes that a bankruptcy order should not have been made, it retains a discretion which it must then exercise whether to annul).

Revenue and Customs Commissioners v De Freitas [2022] EWHC 1946 (Ch) (court would not dismiss bankruptcy petition but extended period of adjournment because of debtor's mental ill health).

Hinton v Wotherspoon [2022] EWHC 2083 (Ch) (definition of what is a "transaction" defrauding creditors is "inexhaustive").

Dusoruth v Orca Finance UK Ltd [2022] EWHC 2346 (Ch) (court declined to annul a bankruptcy order of a debtor whose contested COMI was in England despite certain of his disputed debts being held not to be liquidated sums).

The Coronavirus (Recovery and Reform) (Scotland) Act 2022 amends the definition of a "qualifying creditor" who may petition for sequestration (bankruptcy) in Scotland to a minimum debt level of £5,000 as from 1 October 2022.

The deposit payable on the presentation of a bankruptcy petition increases from £990 to £1,500 on 1 November 2022.

Bankruptcy restrictions orders

Kennedy v Official Receiver [2022] EWHC 1973 (Ch) (guidance given on length of periods for BROs).

Director disqualification

Re Pure Zanzibar Ltd; Secretary of State for Business, Energy and Industrial Strategy v Barnsby [2022] EWHC 971 (Ch) (director disqualified as unfit for causing or allowing a travel agency company to operate in breach of ATOL travel legislation).

Re Arise Networks Ltd; Official Receiver v Obaigbena [2022] EWHC 1399 (Ch) (correct legal test for disqualification had been made and disqualification period was not disturbed).

First disqualifications (by undertakings) under the amending provisions in the Rating (Coronavirus) and Directors Disqualification (Dissolved Companies) Act 2021 announced concerning disqualification of directors of dissolved companies after receiving pandemic "bounce-back loans".

EU Regulation on Insolvency Proceedings 2015

Barings (UK) Ltd v Galapagos SA [2022] EWHC 1633 (Ch) (EU law and jurisdiction still apply to proceedings opened prior to Brexit completion day on 31 December 2020).

As from 30 August 2022 Ireland has belatedly signed into EU Regulation 2021/2260 replacing Annexes A and B to the 2015 Regulation.

(Retained) EU Regulation on Insolvency Proceedings 2015

Barings UK Ltd v Galapagos SA [2022] EWHC 1633 (Ch) (companies' COMI had moved to London before Brexit and the English court had jurisdiction to order winding up).

UNCITRAL Model Law on Cross-Border Insolvency

UK Insolvency Service consults on partial implementation of the Model Law on the Recognition and Enforcement of Insolvency-Related Judgments 2018.

Cross-Border Insolvency Regulations 2006

Re Astora Women's Health LLC [2022] EWHC 2412 (Ch) (US Bankruptcy Code 1978 Ch.11 protection from bankruptcy proceedings recognised as foreign proceedings by English court).

Restructuring plans

Re Houst Ltd [2022] EWHC 1765 (Ch) and [2022] EWHC 1941 (Ch) (first use of company restructure plan used by an SME and sanctioned by use of cram down).

Oceanfill Ltd v Nuffield Health Wellbeing Ltd [2022] EWHC 2178 (Ch) (plan sanctioned under which company's guarantors of landlords' debts remained outstanding for the unpaid balance).

An interim review on permanent measures introduced by CIGA 2020 as from 26 June 2020 reports that restructuring plans are seen as a success, building as they do on existing case law governing schemes of arrangements under Companies Act 2006 Pt 26, and the restructuring plan cross-class cram-down power has been used successfully in cases where previously a scheme on its own would not have been effective.

Debt Respite Scheme (Breathing Space Moratorium and Mental Health Crisis Moratorium) (England and Wales) Regulations 2020 (SI 2020/1311)

Lees v Kaye [2022] EWHC 1151 (QB) (moratorium ordered to render eviction by a landlord and sale of a flat against the leaseholder null and void).

Finally we hope that our dear old friend and mentor, the late Prof Len Sealy, would have approved of this latest development in the history of *Sealy & Milman: Annotated Guide to the Insolvency Legislation*.

David Milman
Peter Bailey
6 October 2022

HOW TO USE THIS SUPPLEMENT

This is the Supplement to the Twenty-fifth Edition of *Sealy & Milman: Annotated Guide to the Insolvency Legislation*, and has been compiled according to the structure of the main work.

Within the *Annotated Guide*, updating material is referenced to the provision number and title and the reader should either add or replace the relevant wording as instructed.

TABLE OF CONTENTS

Cases Table

The following abbreviations are used to denote the location of entries:

CBIR	Cross-Border Insolvency Regulations 2006
CDDA	Company Directors Disqualification Act 1986
DRS	Debt Respite Scheme (Breathing Space Moratorium and Mental Health Crisis Moratorium) (England and Wales) Regulations 2020
EURIP	EU Regulation on Insolvency Proceedings 2015/848
IA	Insolvency Act 1986
IR	Insolvency (England and Wales) Rules 2016
(R)ER	(Retained) EU Regulation on Insolvency Proceedings 2015/848

Volume 1

Introduction

Later legislation

Rating (Coronavirus) and Directors Disqualification (Dissolved Companies) Act 2021
Replace the note with:
This unlikely-named Act received the Royal Assent on 15 December 2021 and in a significant development from 15 February 2022 (but with retrospective effect prior to that date) extended director disqualification for unfitness to directors of companies which are dissolved without becoming insolvent. The change was partly in response to concerns that unfit company directors were avoiding scrutiny of their stewardship of a failed company by having that company dissolved without going through formal insolvency processes. This is the first time that the regime of disqualification for unfitness has applied without the company having "become insolvent" (as defined) and so closes a loophole that was particularly apparent when fraudulent companies—on which no Government checks were made—took Government loans during the COVID-19 pandemic and then dissolved the company without going through an insolvency procedure to avoid repayment and the disqualification regime. The retrospective element in the new regime may allow the Government to effect some retribution as relevant directors who can be traced may be subject not just to disqualification but also the disqualification compensation regime. The first four disqualifications under the new regime (all in relation to COVID-19 bounce back-loans) were announced on 29 July 2022.

National Security and Investment Act 2021
Add new note:
This Act, in force from 4 January 2022, is intended to protect national security risks arising from the acquisition of control over certain types of companies and assets by allowing Government intervention. It has no direct relationship with insolvency law, except that guidance published by BEIS on 19 July 2022 points out that while a company (or other qualifying entity) is in winding up or receivership (but not administration), liquidators or receivers could be in the position of a qualifying acquisition so that in specific cases (e.g. for specified types of company) may require mandatory notification, depending on whether and how the circumstances of the appointment meet the requirements of the 2021 Act. The guidance, available at *https://www.gov.uk/government/publications/national-security-and-investment-nsi-act-market-guidance-notes/national-security-and-investment-market-guidance-notes-july-2022*, outlines two scenarios where the parties need to submit a mandatory notification.

Insolvency Act 1986

GENERAL NOTE TO ss.A34–A41

Replace the note with:

The role of the monitor (originally designated as a "supervisor" in the May 2016 proposals) has undergone change in the iteration of the concept. The term "monitor" was substituted in the August 2018 proposals (para.5.25) to avoid confusion with existing office-holders (notably the CVA supervisor). It was originally suggested in the May 2016 consultation (para.7.41) that this new office should not be restricted to qualified insolvency practitioners, but this approach was dropped in the August 2018 response (para.5.63). The monitor (who now must be a qualified insolvency practitioner: see s.A6(1) and s.388(1)(a)) is an officer of the court according to s.A34. This means that the monitor is protected by the contempt of court regime, but is subject to the rule of honour in *Ex p. James; Re Condon* (1873–74) L.R. 9 Ch. App. 609. The implications of this old established principle for insolvency practice have recently been explained by the Court of Appeal in *Lehman Brothers Australia Ltd v MacNamara* [2020] EWCA Civ 321; [2020] B.C.C. 503. In *Schofield v Smith* [2022] EWCA Civ 824 the Court of appeal confirmed the conclusion of David Richards LJ that in relation to *Ex p. James* "In so far as it involves a broader test than, say, dishonourable, it reflects a development in the standards of conduct to be expected of the court and its officers.". The appointment of the monitor takes effect when the moratorium comes into operation (s.A7(2)). Joint or concurrent appointments are envisaged (see ss.A6(2) and A40).

As mentioned above, the Insolvency Service has produced "A Guide for Monitors" at *https://www.gov.uk/government/publications/insolvency-act-1986-part-a1-moratorium-guidance-for-monitors* with further additions at *https://content.govdelivery.com/attachments/UKIS/2020/12/11/file_attachments/1623466/Dear%20IP%2011 5%20December%202020.pdf*.

Section A35 explains the basic role of the monitor. The monitor oversees the moratorium—but this is a lighter touch of overview than that which operated under the former IA 1986 Sch.A1 supervision requirement for CVAs (the latter was repealed by CIGA 2020 s.2 and Sch.3 para.30). Too intensive monitoring might run the risk of a shadow directorship phenomenon arising with serious consequences for the monitor. The necessary power to obtain information from the directors to enable carrying out of the monitor's functions is provided by s.A36. Directions are available from the court under s.A37. One role of the monitor is to consider giving consent to any request from the directors to pay pre-moratorium debts of the company or to give security over its assets during the period of the moratorium—see ss.A26(2) and 28(3). In so deciding the monitor must think that this action will support the rescue of the company as a going concern. Under s.A38 the monitor *must* pull the plug on the moratorium if he *thinks that* any of the circumstances outlined in s.A38(1)(a)–(d) appear to exist. The notice must be filed "as soon as practicable after the duty to bring the moratorium to an end arises" (r.1A.23(1)(a)). These circumstances are if the monitor thinks that: it is no longer likely that the moratorium will achieve its purpose of rescuing the company as a going concern, or that said purpose has been achieved, or the directors have failed to provide information so that the monitor's functions cannot be carried out, or the company is unable to pay its due moratorium debts or pre-moratorium debts which are not covered by the payment holiday. Failure to do this might have professional disciplinary consequences for the monitor. The court in *Re*

Corbin & King Holdings Ltd; Minor Hotel Group MEA DMCC v Dymant [2022] EWHC 340 (Ch) considered the word "is" in "is unable to pay" moratorium debts that have fallen for payment under s.A38(1)(d)(i), whereby the monitor must bring the moratorium to an end. Sir Alastair Norris first noted that the Pt A1 moratorium was intended to introduce greater flexibility into the insolvency regime. He then referred to the definition in s.A54(1) of "unable to pay its debts" as having the same meaning as in s.123, in introducing an element of futurity, as the cash-flow test looks to the future as well as the present. He reasoned however that the question to be addressed by the monitor was whether the company "is unable" to pay a presently due pre-moratorium finance debt in respect of which it did not have a payment holiday: that was not the same question as whether the company "is unable to pay its debts as they fall due" for the purposes of the cash-flow insolvency test in s.123, and not the same question as whether the company was able to pay the debt within the reasonably near future. He concluded that a company "is able" to pay a presently due pre-moratorium finance obligation if (being itself unable to pay out of current cash resources) it has the immediate prospect of receiving third-party funds or owns assets capable of immediate realisation—the latter immediate realisation being a matter of commercial judgment for the monitor. This was not however the test applied by the joint monitors (unsurprisingly, in light of the new provisions raising questions not previously arising under existing insolvency regimes). The decision of the joint monitors not to bring the moratorium to an end fell on the wrong side of the line, as being one which no reasonable monitor applying the correct test could have reached.

For the procedural requirements on the monitor filing notice bringing the moratorium to an end under s.A38, see IR 2016 rr.1A.23 (and note r.1A.24 for which s.A38(1)(d) debts are to be disregarded under s.A38(2) for this purpose).

On an application to court by a monitor under s.A36 as a competent person for the enforcement of obligations on the directors to provide the monitor with any relevant information, see IR 2016 r.12.52.

The court may remove or replace a monitor or appoint an additional monitor, but only on application of the directors or the monitor (s.A39). The additional or replacement monitor must as soon as reasonably practicable after the "relevant time" that the person may act as specified in the court order notify Companies House (using Form MT08) and other relevant persons (see s.A39(8)), as must a monitor who has ceased to act (using Form MT09 for the Companies House notice): see IR 2016 r.1A.26. The court's authorisation of an additional or replacement monitor requires that person to provide a statement as to qualification and consent to act to be filed in court (for procedure see IR 2016 r.1A.25, the statement to be made within the period of five business days ending with the day on which the statement is filed with the court).

The acts of the monitor remain valid notwithstanding any defect in the appointment (s.A41). This is a standard provision in corporate insolvency law (see, e.g. IA 1986 s.232, Sch.B1 para.104).

For procedural particulars on service of documents in relation to ss.A37, A39 see IR 2016 rr.1A.28–1A.31 and Sch.4.

Despite the debtor-in-possession nature of the moratorium, the monitor has been held by the Supreme Court of New South Wales as a "foreign representative" under the UNCITRAL Model Law on Cross-Border Insolvency as the person authorised to administer the debtor's reorganisation due to moratorium constraints on the company's dealings, the monitor having the oversight role and power to terminate the moratorium: *Re Hydrodec Group plc* [2021] NSWSC 755.

One issue that was discussed in the earlier May 2016 consultation was whether the monitor could then later take up office as an insolvency office-holder with respect to the company. A strict prohibitory approach was favoured (see para.7.45). By August 2018 the modified position was reached that the monitor could not be a subsequent administrator or liquidator, but could supervise a CVA—see para.5.76. CIGA 2020 appears to be silent on this matter.

PART I

COMPANY VOLUNTARY ARRANGEMENTS

Introductory note to Part I
Replace the note with:

Part I of IA 1986, which replaces IA 1985 ss.20–26, introduced an entirely new procedure into UK company law, the "Company Voluntary Arrangement"—a term which is commonly abbreviated to "CVA".

The original CVA regime as contained in Pt I of IA 1986 had been the subject of major statutory elaboration through the mechanism of ss.1, 2 of, and Schs 1, 2 to, the Insolvency Act 2000. The effect of these changes had been to introduce a new optional CVA model with moratorium for small eligible companies. (For further guidance on eligibility see the Insolvency Act 1986 (Amendment) (No.3) Regulations 2002 (SI 2002/1990).) There are also amendments to the general CVA model.

The Cork Committee (Report, paras 400–403) considered it a weakness of the former company law that a company, unlike an individual, could not enter into a binding arrangement with its creditors for the composition of its indebtedness by some relatively simple procedure. Unless it could obtain the separate consent of every creditor, the only options previously available to a company were the formal statutory procedures of:

(1) a scheme of liquidation and reconstruction under CA 1985 s.582 (formerly CA 1948 s.287 (now IA 1986 s.110));

(2) a scheme of compromise or arrangement under CA 1985 ss.425–427 (CA 1948 ss.206–208 (now CA 2006 Pt 26)); and

(3) the little-used "binding arrangement" under CA 1985 s.601 (CA 1948 s.306 (obsolete)).

Each of these methods was too slow, cumbersome and costly to be at all useful in practice.

The present sections introduce a simpler scheme, more or less along the lines recommended by the Cork Committee. The CVA has proved to be of limited utility in practice, however, for two reasons. First, it cannot be made binding upon a secured or preferential creditor without his consent, and secondly, until the enactment of s.1A there was no provision in the Act for obtaining a moratorium while the proposal for an arrangement is being drawn up and considered (contrast the "interim order" available in the case of an insolvent individual: see ss.252–254). However, a moratorium could be achieved if a proposal for a voluntary arrangement is combined with an application to the court for the appointment of an administrator under Sch.B1: this is, of course, a more elaborate and costly procedure.

In view of these considerations, it is not surprising that the CVA procedure has been relatively little used (especially when compared with the much larger number of individual voluntary arrangements). In the first few years after the 1986 Act, the average number was under 100 per year, and although the figure has now crept up somewhat, the overall picture has been disappointing. In the light of this experience the Government suggested modifications to the CVA procedure in order to improve its effectiveness (and appeal). In particular it favoured the introduction of an optional moratorium facility for CVAs involving small eligible companies. This reform was enacted by the Insolvency Act 2000 s.1 with detailed provision being made in the accompanying Sch.A1. Unfortunately, there was a delay in bringing this reform into effect; this delay was apparently caused by concerns in the City over the impact of the new CVA moratorium on certain specialised corporate financing schemes. The new model came into force only on 1 January 2003—see the Insolvency Act 2000 (Commencement No.3 and Transitional Provisions) Order 2002 (SI 2002/2711 (C. 83)). This type of CVA was however moribund and it was of no surprise when it was abolished by the Corporate Insolvency and Governance Act 2020 (CIGA 2020). This has resulted in a number of consequential amendments in the legislation reproduced below.

Since 1 December 1994, a voluntary arrangement procedure modelled upon the CVA has been available for an insolvent partnership: see the Insolvent Partnerships Order 1994 (SI 1994/2421) art.5 and Sch.1. It is a prerequisite that the partnership be unable to pay its debts. As with a CVA, there is no provision for an interim order during which a stay of proceedings operates, although this can be achieved by applying at the same time for an administration order. Alternatively, if the partners are individuals, they may enter into individual voluntary arrangements, which will have much the same effect.

The CVA procedure has been extended to building societies by s.90A of the Building Societies Act 1986 (inserted by the Building Societies Act 1997 s.39, effective 1 December 1997). A foreign company may be permitted to use a CVA by exploiting the facility of s.426, IA 1986—*Re Television Trade Rentals Ltd* [2002] EWHC 211 (Ch); [2002] B.C.C. 807. NHS Foundation Trusts can take advantage of the CVA procedure (with or without moratorium)—the Independent Regulator of NHS Foundation Trusts is given power by s.53 of the National Health Service Act 2006 to direct foundation trustees to exploit this recovery procedure. The CVA procedure has been made available to co-operative and community benefit societies by the Co-operative and Community Benefit Societies and Credit Unions (Arrangements, Reconstructions and Administration) Order 2014 (SI 2014/229) with effect from 6 April 2014.

A question has arisen as to whether administrators of a further education college could put forward a CVA—see *Re Corp of West Kent and Ashford College* [2020] EWHC 907 (Ch). Here ICC Judge Jones confirmed this as a possibility.

The initiative in setting up a CVA is taken by the directors or, if the company is being wound up or is subject to an administration order, by the liquidator or administrator as the case may be. A "proposal" is formulated for consideration by meetings of the company's members and by its creditors using a range of decision processes: if the proposal is accepted at the respective meetings, the scheme becomes operative and binding upon the company and all of its creditors—even those who did not support the proposal. Thereafter, it is administered by a "supervisor" who must be qualified to act as an insolvency practitioner in relation to the company. The arrangement is conducted throughout under the aegis of the court, but the court itself is not involved in a judicial capacity unless there is some difficulty or disagreement.

It is not a prerequisite for the application of this Part of the Act that the company should be "insolvent" or "unable to pay its debts" within the statutory definitions of those terms.

A related reform effected by IA 1985 (see Sch.10 Pt II) was the repeal of CA 1985 s.615(2), a provision of ancient origin which stated that any general assignment by a company of its property for the benefit of its creditors was "void to all intents".

The provision which prohibits a company from giving financial assistance in the acquisition of its own shares (CA 2006 s.678) does not apply to anything done under a voluntary arrangement: see CA 2006 s.681(2)(g). The abolition of the financial assistance bar for private companies will reduce the significance of this point.

CVAs fell within the ambit of the EU Regulation on Insolvency Proceedings (2015/848) and the Cross-Border Insolvency Regulations (SI 2006/1030). The former is no longer relevant.

Although the EU Regulation on Insolvency Proceedings (2015/848) did apply to CVA cases it was held by Lloyd LJ (sitting as a Judge of the Chancery Division) in *Oakley v Ultra Vehicle Design Ltd* [2005] EWHC 872 (Ch); [2006] B.C.C. 115 that it did not apply if the CVA had been initiated prior to the coming into effect of the EC Regulation. In *Apperley Investments Ltd v Monsoon Accessorize Ltd* [2020] IEHC 523 the Irish High Court refused to allow an English CVA to be enforced against Irish landlords. Although the CVA was recognised under EU Regulation 2015/848 the public policy exception in art.33 could be engaged because inadequate attention had been given by the terms of the CVA to the rights of the Irish landlords under the Constitution of Ireland.

A CVA is not an "agreement" for the purposes of s.203 of the Employment Rights Act 1996—*Re Britannia Heat Transfer Ltd* [2007] B.P.I.R. 1038. This is because it was a statutory construct established under a specified procedure. This interpretation by HHJ Norris QC has served to protect CVAs from being avoided under s.203, thereby protecting their value as a reorganisation tool for distressed businesses. A decision of similar ilk is *Re Rhino Enterprises Properties Ltd* [2020] EWHC 2370 (Ch); [2021] B.C.C. 18 where Simon Barker J indicated that he did not regard a CVA statutory contract as falling within the Contracts (Rights of Third Parties) Act 1999. For later proceedings and further comment on the potential application of the 1999 Act see *Re Rhino Enterprises Properties Ltd* [2021] EWHC 2533 (Ch).

The concept of an "arrangement" for CVA purposes differs from an arrangement under CA 2006 Pt 26. See [163] of Zacaroli J's judgment in *Lazari Properties 2 Ltd v New Look Retailers Ltd* [2021] EWHC 1209 (Ch).

A valuable study of CVAs was undertaken on behalf of R3 by Walton, Umfreville and Jacobs—see *Company Voluntary Arrangements: Evaluating Success and Failure* (April 2018). Looking at the data produced, we find that 93% of companies using the procedure were either small or micro companies. Some 65% of CVAs were terminated without achieving their intended aims. The study identifies reforms designed to make CVAs more effective. On the Walton/Umfreville/Jacobs research project on CVAs see Sumner (2018) 11(3) C.R.I. 111. Walton and Umfreville revisit their 2018 research in [2020] Recovery (Spring) 24.

Some valuable data analysis of the CVA in practice with regard to the retail sector is to be found in the article by Addley and Milward-Oliver [2019] 12 C.R.I. 203. On retail CVAs post-*Debenhams* see also Kell [2020] (Spring) 32.

As a result of numerous challenges by landlords who believed they had been unfairly disadvantaged by CVAs, the Insolvency Service commissioned a report, published on 28 June 2022, which examines in detail the position for landlords in 59 selected CVAs initiated between and 2011 and 2020 (see *https://www.gov.uk/government/publications/company-voluntary-arrangement-cva-research-report-for-the-insolvency-service/company-voluntary-arrangement-research-report-for-the-insolvency-service*).

The fact that the successful party under an arbitration award is undergoing a CVA does not deny that party the possibility of enforcing that award by summary judgment—see *Mead General Building Ltd v Dartmoor Properties Ltd* [2009] B.C.C. 510; [2009] B.P.I.R. 516 (Coulson J). Compare *Westshield Ltd v Whitehouse* [2013] EWHC 3576 (TCC) which was concerned with whether an adjudicator's decision could be enforced by a party undergoing a CVA. Akenhead J refused to allow enforcement as the other party had raised a counterclaim which required consideration by the CVA supervisors for a possible set off under the CVA. Further consideration of the issue of enforcement of arbitral awards where one party was undergoing a CVA is to be found in *Tate Building Services Ltd v B&M McHugh Ltd* [2014] EWHC 2971 (TCC); [2014] B.P.I.R. 1560. Further consideration on the interface between adjudication processes, CVAs and insolvency procedures is to be found in the judgment of Lord Briggs in *Bresco Electrical Services Ltd v Michael J Lonsdale (Electrical) Ltd* [2020] UKSC 25; [2020] B.C.C. 906. The entry of a company into a CVA does not necessarily debar it from enforcing an adjudication award as this may help with future trading. For discussion of *Lonsdale* (in the Court of Appeal ([2019] EWCA Civ 27; [2019] B.C.C. 490)) see Cooke (2019) 32 Insolv. Int. 88. For further litigation on the interface between enforceability of an adjudicator's award and the entry of one of the parties into a CVA after the making of that award see *Indigo Projects London Ltd v Razin* [2019] EWHC 1205 (TCC); [2019] B.P.I.R. 861. The question of whether there is a real risk that summary enforcement of an adjudication award might deprive the defendant of security for a cross-claim was considered to be the determining factor in *FTH Ltd v Varis Developments Ltd* [2022] EWHC 1385 (TCC).

On the interpretation of CVA terms see *Appleyard Ltd v Ritecrown Ltd* [2009] B.P.I.R. 235 and *Tucker and Spratt v Gold Fields Mining LLC* [2009] EWCA Civ 173; [2009] B.P.I.R. 704. The latter case is an important precedent dealing with the lodging of late claims. For further consideration see *Re Energy Holdings (No.3) Ltd* [2010] EWHC 788

(Ch); [2010] B.P.I.R. 1339. In *Re TXU Europe Group plc* [2011] EWHC 2072 (Ch) Newey J held that in making any distributions to shareholders once creditor claims had been met in the supervisors must comply with requirements as to return of capital imposed by CA 2006 Pt 23. This would only be permitted if the company went into liquidation. See also *EOP II PROP Co III SARL v Carpetright Plc* [2019] CSOH 40 (contractual interpretation of notice requirements).

For further analysis of the contractual interpretation approach in the context of CVAs see the discussion of Hildyard J in *Heis v Financial Services Compensation Scheme Ltd* [2018] EWHC 1372 (Ch). This ruling went immediately on appeal and the Court of Appeal adopted a different interpretation of the terms of the CVA, with the result that the CVA could not be put into immediate operation—see [2018] EWCA Civ 1327; [2018] B.C.C. 921.

Wright v Prudential Assurance Co Ltd; Re SHB Realisations Ltd [2018] EWHC 402 (Ch); [2018] B.C.C. 712 is an important authority. It makes the point that although the CVA model rests upon a statutory contract, not every aspect of contract law (e.g. the law relating to penalties) is necessarily incorporated. The High Court upheld a CVA under which the tenant company was given a rent holiday but if the CVA was terminated the back rent would be reinstated. This was a fair commercial arrangement. For discussion of *Wright* (above) see Coverdale and Froy (2018) 11(3) C.R.I. 89.

In *Re Sixty UK Ltd* [2010] B.P.I.R. 1234 the court had to determine whether on the terms of the arrangement a party was entitled to rank as a creditor in a CVA. On the interpretation of the terms of a CVA note also the approach of Edwards-Stuart J in *Oakrock Ltd v Travelodge Hotels Ltd* [2015] EWHC 30 (TCC). Note *Re North Point Global Ltd* [2020] EWHC 1648 (Ch) where HHJ Davis White took a functional view of the CVA mechanism and sought to tie in contingent creditors as far as was possible.

For the issue of whether business rates are capable of being encompassed within a CVA see *Kaye v South Oxfordshire District Council* [2013] EWHC 4165 (Ch). Note *Re Westshield Ltd; Waldron v Waldron* [2019] EWHC 115 (Ch) at [72] where HHJ Eyre QC indicated that if a company can be treated as a quasi-partnership the fact that it enters into a CVA does not necessarily displace that classification.

For a review of the property law aspects of CVAs see the piece by Ditchburn and Tran [2019] 12 C.R.I. 137.

For the corresponding provisions relating to voluntary arrangements for insolvent individuals, see ss.252–263. There is a close parallel between the two sets of provisions, and so cases decided under the individual voluntary arrangement sections may well be relevant in CVA proceedings, and vice versa.

The Act contemplates that a system will be set up by subordinate legislation for the registration of voluntary arrangements in a register open to public inspection: see Sch.8 para.6. The rules make provision for registration with the registrar of companies: IR 2016 rr.2.38(6), 2.44(1) and 2.44(4).

For the rules relating to CVAs, see IR 2016 Pt 2. The position has been made more complicated by locating a number of key provisions in IR 2016 Pt 15—see for example rr.15.11, 15.14, 15.31, 15.34 and 15.35. Note the role of Statement of Insolvency Practice (SIP) 3 in promoting good practice. A new SIP 3 was introduced in July 2014 with SIP 3.2 being applicable to CVAs. This was upgraded in April 2021.

In 2012 there were 839 CVAs recorded for England and Wales. 767 CVAs were established in England and Wales in 2011. The 2013 figure was 577. In 2014 only 563 CVAs were recorded for England and Wales. This figure fell to 364 in 2015 and 346 in 2016. Only 292 were recorded in 2017. This figure increased to 356 in 2018 and was 351 in 2019. In 2020 there were 259 CVAs recorded. For 2021 only 115 CVAs were recorded.

Previously there were reform proposals in the air. A consultation document, a copy of which is available on the Insolvency Service website, was launched by the Insolvency Service in June 2009. Essentially it is opening up for discussion a number ideas designed to reinvigorate corporate rescue. A number of proposals are relevant to the CVA models. These include: extending the Sch.A1 procedure to larger and medium-sized companies; introducing a court-initiated moratorium for CVAs; and improving the position with regard to securing rescue finance. For a summary of these proposals see (2009) 255 Co. L.N. 1.

A further, unrelated, consultation exercise, *Proposals for a Restructuring Moratorium*, launched by the Insolvency Service on 26 July 2010, proposed a moratorium for companies restructuring their debts. This would apply to any company that could be subject to a CVA or to a scheme of arrangement under Pt 26 of CA 2006, although the company would not need to be so subject at the time of the application. Thus the directors of a company who were considering a CVA might apply for this moratorium to allow the company some breathing space while a CVA proposal was being formulated. Eligibility and qualifying conditions would apply. The moratorium as proposed would be similar to that in a small company CVA under Sch.A1. It contains some specific proposals for where a CVA is in place or where a CVA proposal is under consideration (possible to save a court hearing). For a summary of the proposal see (2010) 269 Co. L.N. 1. The consultation paper is on the Insolvency Service's website. In the end this came to nothing. But in May 2016 this area of law reform was revisited by the Insolvency Service. In its *Review of the Corporate Insolvency Framework* new proposals were put forward for a broad moratorium. These were favourably received. For discussion of this initiative see Bailey (2016) 386 Co. L.N. 1 and Umfreville (2016) 385 Co. L.N. 1. The responses to the consultation published on the Insolvency Service website in September 2016 were summarised by Bailey in (2016)

388 Co. L.N. 1. The consultation paper is on the Insolvency Service's website. In the end this came to nothing. But in May 2016 this area of law reform was revisited by the Insolvency Service. In its Review of the Corporate Insolvency Framework new proposals were put forward for a broad moratorium. These were favourably received. For discussion of this initiative see Bailey (2016) 386 Co. L.N. 1 and Umfreville (2016) 385 Co. L.N. 1. The responses to the consultation published on the Insolvency Service website in September 2016 were summarised by Bailey in (2016) 388 Co. L.N. 1. This consultation attracted (eventually) an official response in August 2018: see Insolvency and Corporate Governance: Government Response, available at *https://assets.publishing.service.gov.uk/government/ uploads/system/uploads/attachment_data/file/736163/ICG_-_Government_ response_doc_-_24_Aug_clean_ version__with_Minister_s_photo_and_signature__AC.pdf*. Among the possible changes suggested are the introduction of a new early 28-day moratorium that could be triggered pre-insolvency. This moratorium might be extended to 56 days in appropriate circumstances and is initiated by filing documents with the court. The moratorium is only available if on the balance of probabilities a rescue or arrangement with creditors can be achieved. A monitor would be responsible for overseeing said moratorium. The monitor will not be permitted to take on a subsequent role as liquidator or administrator but could act as a CVA supervisor. If this change were made the Sch.A1 moratorium for small companies would no longer be required. For full discussion see Umfreville (2018) 411 Co. L.N. 1. The new moratorium finally came about due to enactment of the CIGA 2020 in force from 26 June 2020 following a fast-track procedure through Parliament in light of the COVID-19 pandemic. This (inserting IA 1986 Pt A1) provided for a moratorium for eligible companies of 20 days, extendable (without consent) for a further 20 days and (with creditor or court consent) for up to a year in aggregate. The moratorium would be triggered (as above) by the directors filing documents in court or, if the company is subject to a winding-up petition, by application to court for an order. Overseas companies not subject to a petition may also apply to the court for a moratorium. CIGA 2020 repealed IA 1986 s.A1 and Sch.A1. As predicated in the 2018 response document, the moratorium is overseen by a monitor, who must be a qualified insolvency practitioner, and on 16 June 2020 the Insolvency Service in *Dear IP* 104 issued draft guidance to potential monitors. Companies House on 26 June 2020 published guidance on "Applying for a moratorium under the Corporate Insolvency and Governance Act 2020" and a useful series of forms relevant for the moratorium, listed in App.II in Vol.2 hereto.

Consideration and implementation of proposal

Decisions of the company and its creditors

4—

GENERAL NOTE
Replace the note with:

The terms of the scheme, when approved by the meetings, bind every member and creditor (see s.5(2)).

It appears that HMRC, by far the largest single creditor of companies in the UK, has historically not always voted on CVA proposals, to the frustration of insolvency practitioners who are trying to restructure businesses, as creditors with lower value involvement may have influenced the outcome by rejecting proposals, possibly causing the business to fail when there was an opportunity to rescue, in which case HMRC may receive a lower return that could have been achieved in a successful CVA. Thus in *Dear IP* Issue 148 (July 2022) it was announced that due to HMRC's increased creditor status following the introduction of secondary preference in some taxes in December 2020, HMRC will be more proactive in the use of its voting rights and will vote on proposals with the intention of ensuring the best return for HMRC as a creditor (although HMRC will only vote in favour if the best possible proposal is submitted). Also in *Dear IP* Issue 148 (July 2022) it was announced that the Financial Conduct Authority (FCA) has issued guidance on its approach to schemes of arrangement and other compromises for regulated firms, clarifying how the FCA approaches compromises in line with its statutory objectives to protect consumers and the integrity of markets (the guidance is available at *https://www.fca.org.uk/search-results?search_term=FG22/4*).

No provision appears to be made for any subsequent modification of the scheme unless that modification is put forward by the person who made the original proposal (see s.6(4)). The only opportunity, therefore, for any of the company's members or creditors to seek to have the proposal modified will be at the meetings themselves. Note the amendments made to subss.(4) and (7) by the Banks and Building Societies (Depositor Preference and Priorities) Order 2014 (SI 2014/3486) with effect from 1 January 2015. These changes relate to the new classification of preferential debts into ordinary preferential debts and secondary preferential debts.

Note amendment by DA 2015 s.19 and Sch.6.

Section 4 was amended by SBEEA 2015 s.126 and Sch.9 to reflect the move away from the exclusive use of meetings to determine creditor views. This amendment resulted in the addition of subs.(6A).

Section 4(4) was further amended by the Banks and Building Societies (Priorities on Insolvency) Order 2018 (SI 2018/1244) arts 1, 3, 4, 5 as from 19 December 2018 in relation to insolvency proceedings commenced on or after that date to recognise a new class of non-preferred senior debt to be issued by credit institutions.

Section 4(4A), (4B) inserted by CIGA 2020 s.2(1), Sch.3 paras 1, 4 as from 26 June 2020 subject to CIGA 2020 s.2(2), (3).

PART III

RECEIVERSHIP

Introductory note to Part III

Replace the note with:

The Companies Acts have not previously contained many provisions dealing with receivership, at least in relation to England and Wales; matters were left to the general law and the terms of the instrument under or by which the receiver was appointed. The Cork Committee (Report, Ch.8) recommended that the law should be amended so that in many respects it was placed on a statutory basis. The recommendations were broadly followed by IA 1985 Ch.IV, which is now consolidated along with a few sections of CA 1985 into the present Act.

Among the principal changes made are the introduction of the new concept of "administrative receiver" (s.29(2)), and the requirement that an administrative receiver be a qualified insolvency practitioner. The date on which a receiver takes office and the extent to which agency rules apply have been clarified, and new provisions ensure that other creditors are kept in the picture regarding the progress of the receivership. The administrative receiver is given the statutory powers set out in Sch.1, and other specific powers including power to dispose of encumbered property (s.43). In many other respects an administrative receivership is placed on a similar footing to a liquidation—e.g. in regard to a statement of affairs, the appointment of a committee of creditors, and the removal of the receiver. Some discussion of the nature of receivership is to be found in *Ventra Investments Ltd v Bank of Scotland* [2019] EWHC 2058 (Comm).

To all intents and purposes these days appointments of receivers to enforce security are effected out of court in pursuance of a contractual power vested in the debenture holder to make such an appointment. The advantage in this course of action is speed and lack of cost. There is, however, always the facility of applying to the court for such an appointment, but this is rare because of the cost and the delay—for an unusual example see *Bank of Credit and Commerce International SA v BRS Kumar Bros Ltd* [1994] 1 B.C.L.C. 211. A right to appoint a receiver will usually permit the appointment of joint receivers—*Doherty v Perrett* [2015] NICA 52. Cases decided in relation to these other forms of receiver may have a wider value. For an important statement of principle on the right of a receiver to claim remuneration from the receivership assets see *Capewell v Revenue and Customs Commissioners* [2007] UKHL 2; [2007] B.P.I.R. 678. *Capewell* (above) was followed in *Barnes v Eastenders Group* [2014] UKSC 26; [2014] B.P.I.R. 867 where the Supreme Court confirmed that the cost of the receivership falls on the person making an invalid appointment and not on the estate. Concerns were expressed about short notice appointments of receivers under the Proceeds of Crime Act 2002.

In the unusual test case of *Menon v Pask* [2019] EWHC 2611 (Ch) Mann J ruled that a receiver appointed out of court under a fixed charge could sue the mortgagor in his own name to gain possession of the charged property. But as that security encompassed a dwelling house the mortgagor could in principle seek the protection of the Administration of Justice Act 1970 s.36.

On the question of the compatibility of a receivership designed to enforce a confiscation order and the requirements of art.1 of the First Protocol ECHR see also *Hansford v Southampton Magistrates' Court* [2006] EWHC 67 (Admin); [2008] B.P.I.R. 379.

On contracting and receivers generally see *Paddy Burke (Builders) Ltd v Tullyvaraga Management Co Ltd* [2020] IEHC 170.

On the power of the court to appoint a receiver by way of equitable execution over future receipts from a defined foreign asset—see *Masri v Consolidated Contractors International UK Ltd* [2008] EWCA Civ 303; [2008] B.P.I.R. 531. The use of receivership by way of equitable execution continues to suggest its potential— see the discussion in cases such as *Fonu v Merrill Lynch Bank & Trust Co (Cayman) Ltd* [2011] UKPC 17 and *Blight v Brewster* [2012] EWHC 165 (Ch); [2012] B.P.I.R. 476 where the outcome favoured injunctive relief instead of a receivership by way of equitable execution. On whether it was appropriate to appoint receivers by way of equitable execution over foreign assets see *Cruz City 1 Mauritius Holdings v Unitech Ltd* [2014] EWHC 3131 (Comm); [2015] 1 B.C.L.C. 377. For discussion of *Masri* see *JSC VTA Bank v Skurikhin* [2019] EWHC 1407 (Comm).

Receivership orders by way of equitable execution can be used in a "non-commercial" context to facilitate the enforcement of court orders—*Behbehani v Behbehani* [2019] EWCA Civ 2301. For receivership by way of equitable execution in the wake of a successful unfair prejudice claim see *VB Football Assets v Blackpool Football Club*

(Properties) Ltd [2019] EWHC 530 (Ch); [2019] B.C.C. 896. For later proceedings in this context see *Cooper v Blackpool Football Club (Properties) Ltd* [2019] EWHC 1599 (Ch). In these later proceedings the court (Marcus Smith J) noted that its supervision of receivers by way of equitable execution was in many senses comparable to that of administrators. Accordingly, a contract made by said receivers was upheld as it was an unimpeachable exercise of their powers.

Further enlightenment on receivership by equitable execution can be found in *JSC VTB Bank v Skurikhin* [2020] EWCA Civ 1337.

A court appointed receiver is an officer of the court. For the implications flowing from this status see *Glatt v Sinclair* [2013] EWCA Civ 241; [2013] B.P.I.R. 468. This ruling is significant in terms of the receiver's claim to remuneration and expenses incurred after discharge and was applied in *Oyston v Rubin* [2021] EWHC 1120 (Ch) which concerned several matters in relation to receivers' remuneration (including whether VAT was inclusive or exclusive to the rate), fees and disbursements. *Wood v Gorbunova* [2013] EWHC 1935 (Ch); [2014] 1 B.C.L.C. 487 is worthy of note. Here Morgan J reaffirmed that a receiver appointed by the court is an officer of the court. But Morgan J then went on to consider potential liability of such a receiver in the event of the receiver instituting unsuccessful litigation. Liability for costs may arise in certain circumstances. Gloster J stressed in *Barclay Pharmaceuticals Ltd v Waypharm LP* [2013] EWHC 503 (Comm) that permission is required to sue a court appointed receiver for alleged breach of duty. But in relation to a court-appointed receiver who had vacated office it was held in *Blackpool Football Club (Properties) Ltd v Cooper* [2021] EWHC 910 (Ch) that although the court would retain a supervisory jurisdiction over such a receiver after they had left office to ensure that the receivership was properly concluded, the court's permission was not required by a claimant before issuing proceedings against the receiver who was no longer in office as the court no longer had deemed possession of the receivership estate and there was no practical or logical need for it to protect its ex-officers from interference in the performance of their duties as they would no longer have any active duties.

For another illustration of a court appointment being made in the case of a solvent firm see *BAT Industries plc v Windward Prospects Ltd* [2013] EWHC 3612 (Comm). For the use of the receivership remedy in cases where disputes have arisen as to the conduct of businesses that were solvent see *Catch a Ride Ltd v Gardner* [2014] EWHC 1220 (Ch). The courts are reluctant to appoint a receiver in respect of a solvent company because of the negative connotations associated with the term "receivership"—see Ferris J in *Jaber v Science and Info Tech Ltd* [1992] B.C.L.C. 764 at 789. The court appointed a receiver on an interim basis pending the resolution of a dispute in *Re Inter Global Surgical LLP* [2021] EWHC 2685 (Ch).

Another novel potential usage of receivership was highlighted by the Chancellor, Sir Andrew Morritt in *Re MK Airlines Ltd* [2012] EWHC 1018 (Ch) where it was pointed out at [26] that receivership could be used by administrators to enforce the charge conferred on them in respect of their claim for remuneration and expenses under IA 1986 Sch.B1 para.99.

In *Day v Tiuta International Ltd* [2014] EWCA Civ 1246 the Court of Appeal upheld the appointment of receivers who were appointed out of court to enforce an equitable security interest created by subrogation.

For a case where a receivership order made under the Senior Courts Act 1981 s.37(1) was modified (but not retrospectively) see *Shaw v Breish* [2017] EWHC 2972 (Comm).

It must be remembered that a receiver appointed to enforce a fixed charge may be subject to the old established provisions of LPA 1925. For consideration of this statutory code see *Phoenix Properties v Wimpole Street Nominees Ltd* [1992] B.C.L.C. 737; and *Sargent v C & E Commissioners* [1995] 2 B.C.L.C. 34. Note *Jumani v Mortgage Express* [2013] EWHC 1571 (Ch) (Mark Cawson QC)—an attempt to challenge the appointment of an LPA receiver and the actions of said receiver failed. In *Hyett v Wakefield Council* [2018] EWHC 337 (Admin) the court observed that, as an LPA receiver is the agent of mortgagor, it follows that the mortgagor remains liable for council tax. Note *Courtwood Holdings SA v Woodley Properties Ltd* [2018] EWHC 2163 (Ch) (Nugee J), which was concerned with the LPA power of sale and the status of receivers as agents. The court ruled that receivers cannot pass a better title than the principal had. In *Jennings v Quinn* [2018] NICh 17 the court concluded that the mortgagee can still appoint a receiver even if there was a conflict of interest (which was not so here) and any such appointment is not invalid. Specialised statutory regimes also exist for certain types of receivership involving (for example) companies incorporated by statute or as part of statutory insolvency regimes, but these are not our concern in this work. Note also *Ghai v Maymask (228) Ltd* [2020] UKUT 293 (LC) for comment on the effect of an LPA receivership on the powers of company directors.

The enforcement of security is not as a general rule prohibited by the existence of a prior freezing order over a debtor's assets—*Taylor v Van Dutch Marine Holding Ltd* [2017] EWHC 636 (Ch). On the power of the court to assist receivers to complete their task see *Beveridge v Quinlan* [2019] EWHC 424 (Ch).

The institution of receivership was unknown in Scotland until the enactment of CFCSA 1972. In the present Act the provisions of that legislation are consolidated, incorporating certain modifications made by IA 1985. Comparable provisions dealing with receivers and administrative receivers in Northern Ireland are to be found in the Insolvency (Northern Ireland) Order 1989 (SI 1989/2405) (NI 19) arts 40–59 (as amended).

Receivership enjoyed a renaissance in a niche context as a device to deal with distressed hedge funds—see *Re Cheyne Finance plc (No.1)* [2008] 1 B.C.L.C. 732; *Re Cheyne Finance plc (No.2)* [2008] B.C.C. 182 and *Re Whistlejacket Capital Ltd* [2008] 2 B.C.L.C. 683. Note also Milman (2009) 247 Co. L.N. 1.

Although the following provisions provide some statutory framework for the mechanism of an administrative receivership there is still a substantial body of rules derived from decisions of the courts. These court-derived principles continue to be important.

Part III applies to limited liability partnerships by virtue of the Limited Liability Partnerships Regulations 2001 (SI 2001/1090) reg.5(1)(a) as from 6 April 2001 subject to reg.5(2) and (3).

Many key issues are not addressed by the legislation. For example, what is the effect of the appointment of a receiver on the power of the directors to litigate on behalf of the company? Compare here *Newhart Developments v Cooperative Commercial Bank* [1978] Q.B. 814 with *Tudor Grange Holdings v Citibank* [1992] Ch. 53; the Irish High Court case of *Lascomme Ltd v United Dominions Trust (Ireland)* [1994] I.L.R.M. 227 and *Independent Pension Trustee v LAW Construction, The Times* Scots Law Report, 1 November 1996. For discussion see Doyle (1996) 17 Co Law 131. *Newhart* was followed most recently by the Court of Appeal in *Sutton v GE Capital Commercial Finance* [2004] EWCA Civ 315; [2004] 2 B.C.L.C. 662. The Court of Appeal ruled in *Mills v Birchall* [2008] B.P.I.R. 607 that a receiver who conducts litigation on behalf of a company in receivership as part of the security enforcement process does not normally do so at the risk of personal liability for costs under a third party costs order if the litigation is unsuccessful. The defendant in such proceedings is advised to seek an early security for costs order against the claimant company.

On receivers as agents see *Edenwest Ltd v CMS Cameron McKenna* [2012] EWHC 1258 (Ch) and *SNR Denton UK LLP v Kirwan* [2012] UKEAT 0158/12/1007. In *Edenwest* (above) the primary duty of the receiver to bring about a situation under which the secured creditor could be repaid was seen as critical. Again, in *International Leisure Ltd v First National Trustee Co UK Ltd* [2012] EWHC 1971 (Ch) Edward Bartley Jones QC sitting in the High Court was at pains to stress that, notwithstanding the agency provision, a receiver's primary duty was to the debenture holder who appointed him. For the meaning of "acting by the receivers" see *TBAC Investments Ltd v Valmar Works Ltd* [2015] EWHC 1213 (Ch).

The duties of a director to his company may be enforced by an administrative receiver and those duties are not discharged on the company entering administrative receivership—on this see *Simtel Communications Ltd v Rebak* [2006] 2 B.C.L.C. 571.

The question of whether a receiver owes a duty of care to the company (and those claiming through it) when managing and realising the assets has also been left for the courts to grapple with. For a generous treatment of receivers' duties by the Privy Council in this scenario see *Downsview Nominees v First City Corp Ltd* [1993] A.C. 295; [1993] B.C.C. 46. Here it was held that the responsibilities of receivers are essentially equitable in nature and there was no room for superimposing common law duties of care in negligence. This case is difficult to reconcile with earlier authorities such as *Standard Chartered Bank v Walker* [1982] 1 W.L.R. 1410 and *Knight v Lawrence* [1991] B.C.C. 411 and is best viewed as part of a general retreat on the part of the courts in the areas of economic loss and professional liability. See generally Berg [1993] J.B.L. 213 and Fealy [1994] 45 N.I.L.Q. 61. Most commentators have been critical of the approach of the Privy Council but for rare support see Rajak (1997) 21 Insolv. L. 7. Those commentators who have been critical of the aforementioned Privy Council ruling will have welcomed the subsequent clarification of the law by the Court of Appeal in *Medforth v Blake* [2000] Ch. 86; [1999] B.C.C. 771. In this case it was held that a receiver taking control of a farming business had no obligation to continue to operate the farm, but if that course of action was taken, the receiver should take reasonable steps to ensure that the business was conducted as profitably as possible and, in particular, that the customary discounts on bulk purchase of livestock feed be obtained. The Court of Appeal felt able to reconcile *Downsview* by indicating that this duty to take reasonable care could be seen as part of the obligation to act in good faith. This decision is far more in tune with prevailing professional standards. For comment see Frisby (2000) 63 M.L.R. 413. The issue of the duties owed by receivers (or mortgagees) when managing, selling or considering the sale of charged property have troubled the courts over many years—see for example *Hadjipanayi v Yeldon* [2001] B.P.I.R. 487; *Worwood v Leisure Merchandising* [2002] 1 B.C.L.C. 249; *Cohen v TSB Bank* [2002] 2 B.C.L.C. 32; and *Silven Properties Ltd v Royal Bank of Scotland* [2003] EWCA Civ 1409. At the end of the day each case does turn on its own peculiar facts and most claims alleging breach of duty tend to fail. Another vexed issue concerns both the timing of a sale and the selection of a purchaser where the mortgagor wishes to buy the property. In *Lloyds Bank v Cassidy* [2002] EWCA Civ 1606; [2003] B.P.I.R. 424 the Court of Appeal felt that these were issues in need of clarification. In *Bell v Long* [2008] B.P.I.R. 1211 the court ruled that a receiver (or a mortgagee) is entitled to choose the timing of sale even if that works to the disadvantage of the debtor. If a duty of care is owed by selling receivers that duty is owed to any party having an interest in the equity of redemption—*Raja v*

Austin Gray (a firm) [2002] EWCA Civ 1965; [2003] B.P.I.R. 725. See also *Meah v GE Money Home Finance Ltd* [2013] EWHC 20 (Ch) where there was an attempt to challenge a sale by mortgagee. The challenge failed—although some criticisms could be levelled at the sale process, the standard laid down in *Cuckmere Brick Co v Mutual Finance* [1971] Ch. 949 had not been breached. In *Aodhcon LLP v Bridgeco Ltd* [2014] EWHC 535 (Ch); [2014] 2 B.C.L.C. 237 the High Court reviewed the practicalities involved in applying the test that stated that on a sale by a mortgagee a duty to take reasonable care to obtain the best price reasonably obtainable applied. Some consideration of the duties of receivers is to be found in the judgment of the court in *Purewal v Countrywide Residential Lettings Ltd* [2015] EWCA Civ 1122. See also *PK Airfinance SARL v Alpstream AG* [2015] EWCA Civ 1318 where the comparable issue of the standard of care owed by mortgagees was revisited together with an analysis of the parties to whom a duty of care may be owed by a mortgagee. The latest review of the duties of receivers is to be found in *Ahmad v Bank of Scotland* [2016] EWCA Civ 602 at [38] of the judgment. The case provides particular analysis of the duties of a receiver when settling legal claims—there must be proof of an egregious error before the court will intervene in the decision to settle.

In *Devon Commercial Property Ltd v Barnett* [2019] EWHC 700 (Ch) HHJ Paul Matthews reviewed the duties owed to a mortgagor by an LPA receiver appointed at the request of a mortgagee. In particular HHJ Matthews undertook a thorough review of the receiver's duty to act in good faith and to exercise powers for a proper purpose. There was a duty to act in good faith, but no obligation to wait on a sale until a better price might be obtained. All that was required was that the receiver took reasonable steps to obtain the best possible price. The judgment is generally sympathetic to the operational needs of receivers. For discussion of *Devon* (above) see Davenport, Lewis and Chesher [2019] Recovery (Summer) 30. See also Williams [2019] 12(3) C.R.I. 84. There is an illuminating review of receivers' duties to be found in *Centenary Homes Ltd v Liddell* [2020] EWHC 1080 (QB). Further consideration of the duties owed by a receiver when selling assets can be found in the ruling of HHJ Cooke in *Serene Construction Ltd v Salata and Associates Ltd* [2021] EWHC 2433 (Ch) where the crux of the matter was that the receivers had only taken advice from one valuer and had only marketed the property to a specific group of potential buyers, but the court concluded that these actions did not amount to a breach of duty.

In *Davey v Money* [2018] EWHC 766 (Ch) the duties of mortgagees on sale were considered by Snowden J. In *McDonagh v Bank of Scotland* [2018] EWHC 3262 (Ch) Morgan J (at [128] et seq.) reviewed the authorities relating to the duties of receivers when conducting a sale of the mortgaged property. On the facts, Morgan J concluded that there had been no breach of duty by the receivers. This very much is in line with the bulk of authority. The duties of mortgagees on sale of a ship are no different from those generally applicable—*Close Brothers Ltd v AIS (Marine) 2 Ltd* [2018] EWHC B14 (Admlty). The judgment of the Admiralty Court neatly summarises the governing principles on a sale by a mortgagee.

One way that a receiver may avoid liability for breach of duty in the sale of the charged property is to apply to the court for directions and obtain the court's sanction as to the terms of sale: *Denaxe Ltd v Cooper* [2022] EWHC 764 (Ch) (this is a tactic used by administrators in complex cases, but the office-holder must not surrender discretion nor regard the court as a "rubber stamp": see the note to Sch.B1 para.63).

Other jurisdictions have had the foresight to address this issue through legislation—see Irish Companies Act 2014 s.439 and the New Zealand Receiverships Act 1993 s.19. In both cases a statutory duty of care when selling company assets has been imposed. In Canada the Bankruptcy and Insolvency Act 1992 s.247 requires receivers to deal with the security in a commercially reasonable manner.

The rules on set-off on receivership are also within the province of common law: *John Dee Group Ltd v W M H (21) Ltd* [1998] B.C.C. 972.

The effect of the appointment of an administrative receiver was considered by Judge Weeks QC in *Chesterton International Group plc v Deka Immobilien Inv GmbH* [2005] EWHC 656 (Ch); [2005] B.P.I.R. 1103. Here it was held that once an administrative receiver had been validly appointed by a debenture holder it would not then be possible to seek the appointment of an administrator unless that debenture holder consented. This was the position as outlined in para.39(1) of Sch.B1 to the IA 1986. Shareholders lose control on receivership—*Farnborough Airport Properties Co Ltd v Revenue and Customs Commissioners* [2019] EWCA Civ 118.

The relationship between the various corporate insolvency regimes is interesting. It has been clear from the earliest of days that the right of a secured creditor to have a receiver appointed would be protected by the law. Thus, although receivership and liquidation can run concurrently, in practice the liquidator must wait in the wings, at least so far as concerns the property covered by the charge, until the receiver has fulfilled his functions. This is so even though the agency character of the receiver's role changes: *Sowman v David Samuel Trust Ltd* [1978] 1 W.L.R. 22 or even if liquidation precedes receivership: *Re First Express Ltd* [1991] B.C.C. 782. The advent of the administration order regime posed little threat to the rights of the secured creditor in that a right of veto was created by IA 1986 s.9 in favour of a person having the power to appoint an administrative receiver (i.e. a creditor whose security includes a general floating charge) see *Re Croftbell Ltd* [1990] B.C.C. 781. However, if this veto was not exercised, the administrator did enjoy the power to interfere with the rights of the secured creditor (see IA 1986 s.15). The administration regime under EA 2002 since September 2003 offers good protection to the qualifying floating charge holder. A secured creditor who waits for a CVA to be put in place before appointing a receiver may also be in difficulties: *Re Leisure Study Group Ltd* [1994] 2 B.C.L.C. 65.

Where a receiver pursues litigation on behalf of the company as part of the security realisation process and such litigation is unsuccessful it is unlikely that the receiver will be made subject of a third party costs order pursuant to s.51 of the Supreme Court Act 1981, now rebranded Senior Courts Act 1981, according to the Court of Appeal in *Mills v Birchall* [2008] EWCA Civ 385; [2008] B.P.I.R. 607—see annotation to s.37.

Neither receivership nor administrative receivership constituted collective insolvency proceedings for the purposes of either the EU Regulation on Insolvency Proceedings (2015/848) nor the UNCITRAL Cross-Border Insolvency Regulations (SI 2006/1030). The former restriction is no longer relevant with Brexit.

Note the limitations imposed upon a receiver's power of realisation where s.430 of POCA 2002 applies.

As an institution the future of receivership is likely to be a diminished one. This is a result of the changes introduced by EA 2002 limiting the option of administrative receivership to pre-commencement floating charges and to other specialised corporate financing situations—see the note to ss.72A et seq. The relevant provisions barring administrative receivership do not apply to floating charges created before 15 September 2003—see the Enterprise Act 2002 (Commencement No. 4 and Transitional Provisions and Savings) Order 2003 (SI 2003/2093 (C. 85)). Having said that, the controversial ruling of the House of Lords in *Re Leyland DAF Ltd* [2004] UKHL 9; [2004] B.C.C. 214 to the effect that liquidation expenses could not be made payable out of assets held by receivers for the floating charge holder should maintain a degree of competitive edge for the institution of receivership, in particular when compared to administration. Note also the Crown Statement of June 2005 on this subject—see *R3 Technical Bulletin 71.2. Leyland DAF* (above) was partially reversed when s.1282 of Companies Act 2006 was brought into force in April 2008. This reversal applies only to English law and Northern Ireland—there are no signs of a reversal of *Leyland DAF* in Scots law. For an overview of the current status and future potential of the institution of receivership see Akintola and Milman [2020] 20 J.C.L.S. 99.

There were 1,222 cases of receivership recorded in England and Wales in 2012. This fell to 917 in 2013. A further decline to 724 receivership appointments was recorded for 2014. For a review of the current status of receivership in English Law see Rajak (2013) 329 Co. L.N. 1. These figures disguise the decline in administrative receivership—there were only 11 in 2015 and just five in 2016. There were two recorded in 2017. Only one was recorded for 2018. The figure for 2019 was one. This tripled to three in 2020. In 2021 only one receivership was recorded. The direction of travel (downwards) is clear.

CHAPTER I

RECEIVERS AND MANAGERS (ENGLAND AND WALES)

Receivers and managers appointed out of court

Application to court for directions

35—

S.35(1)

Replace the note with:

This allows a receiver, or his appointor, to apply to the court for directions in the event of legal uncertainty arising. The latter was only given this facility by IA 1985, as a result of the recommendations of the Cork Committee (Report, para.828). This provision is to be widely interpreted and enables guidance to be sought on remuneration: *Re Therma-Stor Ltd* [1997] B.C.C. 301; and *Munns v Perkins* [2002] B.P.I.R. 120. Such guidance may be welcome in the light of the more stringent regime ushered in by Ferris J in *Mirror Group Newspapers v Maxwell* [1998] B.C.C. 324. For an important commercial precedent delivered in response to a s.35 application for directions see *Re Cheyne Finance plc* [2007] EWHC 2402 (Ch); [2008] B.C.C. 182. Note *Bank of Ireland v Edeneast Ltd* [2013] NIQB 95 where the court took a wide view of the power to give directions. The case is unusual in that it involved a court-appointed receiver and manager.

In *Denaxe Ltd v Cooper* [2022] EWHC 764 (Ch) (in which the receiver was court appointed) the receiver obtained immunity from suit concerning the contentious sale of the charged property by applying to the court in advance for directions and obtaining its sanction for the sale on the terms agreed.

The Financial Conduct Authority or the Prudential Regulation Authority may, in an appropriate case, be heard on such an application—FSMA 2000 s.363(2).

PART IV

WINDING UP OF COMPANIES REGISTERED UNDER THE COMPANIES ACTS

CHAPTER IV

CREDITORS' VOLUNTARY WINDING UP

Introductory note to Part IV, Chapter IV
Replace the note with:

Creditors' voluntary liquidations are discussed in Totty, Moss & Segal, *Insolvency*, paras D1–22 et seq.

There were 12,661 CVLs in England and Wales in 2021, higher than 9,491 in 2020 (the first year of the coronavirus pandemic) but comparable with the 12,058 in 2019.

The *First Review of the Insolvency (England and Wales) Rules 2016*, published on 5 April 2022 (see note to IR 2016 Introductory r.7) announced that the Insolvency Service is to review the creditors' voluntary liquidation process as found to be "unhelpfully inconsistent and opaque" and this will be given initial attention.

CHAPTER V

PROVISIONS APPLYING TO BOTH KINDS OF VOLUNTARY WINDING UP

Appointment or removal of liquidator by the court

108—

GENERAL NOTE
Replace the note with:

The power of the court supplements the power of the members under s.92 (members' voluntary winding up) and that of the creditors under s.104 (creditors' voluntary winding up) to fill any such vacancy themselves. A liquidator once appointed, however, may be removed only by the court "on cause shown" under s.108(2). The case of *Re Keypak Homecare Ltd* (1987) 3 B.C.C. 558 contains a useful review of the principles upon which the court will act in exercising its power to remove a liquidator under s.108(2). In *Re Bridgend Goldsmiths Ltd* [1995] B.C.C. 226 the court exercised its powers under s.108(1) to appoint a new liquidator when the previous liquidator had ceased to be qualified to act as an insolvency practitioner. An application to remove liquidators was refused in *AMP Music Box Enterprises Ltd v Hoffman* [2002] EWHC 1899 (Ch); [2002] B.C.C. 996, where their conduct had, in the past, been open to the criticism that they had not pursued certain claims very actively but the court considered that they had more recently given the matter more attention. Other cases illustrating the exercise of the court's discretion include *Fielding v Seery* [2004] B.C.C. 315; *Re Buildlead Ltd (No.2)* [2004] EWHC 2443 (Ch); [2005] B.C.C. 138; *Sisu Capital Fund Ltd v Tucker* [2005] EWHC 2170 and 2321 (Ch); [2006] B.C.C. 463; [2006] B.P.I.R. 154 and *Re York Gas Ltd* [2010] EWHC 2275 (Ch); [2011] B.C.C. 447 (appointment of additional liquidator); *Hobbs v Gibson* [2010] EWHC 3676 (Ch); *Beattie v Smailes* [2011] EWHC 1563 (Ch); [2012] B.C.C. 205 (conflict of interest, but no such conflict was established in *Memon v Cork* [2018] EWHC 594 (Ch) where the applicant might have disagreed with the liquidators on certain proofs of debt but that did not, without more, trigger a conflict of interest requiring the liquidators' removal and there was other machinery for challenging a proof). A removal application was refused for lack of cause shown in *Re Core VCT Plc; Pagden v Fry* [2019] EWHC 540 (Ch); [2019] B.C.C. 845 but this was largely overturned on appeal as on an application for the appointment of a liquidator as here on restoration of a company to the register, the court should always consider whether, and if so how, the members should be consulted and so members' meetings should be held to determine their views: *Fakhry v Pagden* [2020] EWCA Civ 1207; [2021] B.C.C. 46. In subsequent proceedings relating to the same group of companies, liquidators argued unsuccessfully that members against whom they had issued claims were not entitled to vote on their removal: *Pagden v Soho Square Capital LLP* [2022] EWHC 944 (Ch); [2022] B.C.C. 1054.

In *Re Sankey Furniture Ltd Ex p. Harding* [1995] 2 B.C.L.C. 594 the court declined to use its power under s.108(2) to remove a liquidator (who wished to resign) where this would by-pass the statutory requirement that a meeting of creditors be called to consider whether or not to accept the resignation: the fact that this would save the expense of a meeting was not sufficient to justify the court intervening in a matter which was for the creditors to decide. However, it is now well established that where an insolvency practitioner seeks to resign from multiple offices and be replaced (usually by other members of the same firm), the court is willing to make orders without these statutory formalities: see the note to s.172(1), (2).

An application may be made under s.108 by anyone whom the court considers proper, e.g. a former liquidator who has ceased to be qualified to act in relation to the company (*Re A J Adams (Builders) Ltd* [1991] B.C.C. 62) or the recognised professional body of which such a person was once a member (*Re Stella Metals Ltd (in liq.)* [1997] B.C.C. 626). But the court will not remove the liquidator of an insolvent company on the application of a contributory: *Deloitte & Touche AG v Johnson* [1999] B.C.C. 992. For standing to bring an application (in the context of a block transfer order) see *Hunt v Down* [2020] B.P.I.R. 1141 in which ICC Judge Burton commented that the applicants were seeking relief which could only properly be sought by parties entitled to bring an application under s.108.

Save in very exceptional cases, notice of the application should be given to the liquidator whom it is sought to remove, in order to give him an opportunity to be heard: *Clements v Udal* [2001] B.C.C. 658.

For the relevant rules, see IR 2016 rr.5.4, 6.22, 7.56 (appointment), 5.7, 6.27, 7.65 (removal).

CHAPTER VI

WINDING UP BY THE COURT

Grounds and effect of winding-up petition

Definition of inability to pay debts

123—

Special note

March 2020–30 September 2021
Replace the note with:
CIGA 2020 s.10 and Sch.10 (containing temporary measures in light of the coronavirus pandemic) para.1, as amended by the Corporate Insolvency and Governance Act 2020 (Coronavirus) (Extension of the Relevant Period) Regulations 2020 (SI 2020/1031), the Corporate Insolvency and Governance Act 2020 (Coronavirus) (Extension of the Relevant Period) (No. 2) Regulations 2020 (SI 2020/1483), the Corporate Insolvency and Governance Act 2020 (Coronavirus) (Extension of the Relevant Period) Regulations 2021 (SI 2021/375) and the Corporate Insolvency and Governance Act 2020 (Coronavirus) (Extension of the Relevant Period) (No. 2) Regulations 2021 (SI 2021/718) prohibited s.123(1)(a) petitions presented on or after 27 April 2020 based on statutory demands served during the "relevant period" of 1 March 2020 to 30 September 2021. CIGA 2020 Sch.10 para.2 (as similarly) restricted presentation of petitions under s.123(1)(a)–(d) during the relevant period of 27 April 2020 to 30 September 2021 from being presented except where the creditor had reasonable grounds for believing that the coronavirus pandemic has not had a "financial effect" on the company (defined as a worsening of the company's financial position in consequence of, or for reasons relating to, coronavirus: CIGA 2020 Sch.10 para.21(3)), or the facts by reference to which the relevant ground applies would have arisen even if coronavirus had not had a financial effect on the company. See also *Insolvency Practice Direction Relating to the Corporate Insolvency and Governance Act 2020* [2020] B.C.C. 694 (reproduced as App.V to this *Guide*). Note that this system of restrictions ended on 30 September 2021 and was replaced as from 1 October 2021 by a substituted CIGA 2020 Sch.10 (see further below).

There were instances of applications to restrain the presentation of winding-up petitions being decided on the basis of the Bill which became CIGA 2020 (prior to the coming into force of the Act). *Travelodge Ltd v Prime Aesthetics Ltd* [2020] EWHC 1217 (Ch) was decided even prior to publication of the Bill but in light of Government press releases presaging its effect. Another case, decided on the basis of CIGA 2020 Sch.10, was *Re a Company (Injunction to restrain Presentation of Petition)* [2020] EWHC 1406 (Ch); [2020] B.C.C. 741. A further case, *Re a Company (Application to Restrain Advertisement of a Winding-up Petition)* [2020] EWHC 1551 (Ch); [2020] B.C.C. 773, gave a useful analysis of Sch.10 para.5 to the (then) Bill. The burden of proof on proving that it would appear to the court as to "financial effect" under para.5(1)(c) was held to be on the company, not on the petitioner, and to be intended to be a low threshold: simply that "a" financial effect must be shown and not that the pandemic was the cause of the company's insolvency. If successful, as it was, the only way then that a winding-up order could be made was under para.5(3), whereby the court may wind the company up under s.122(1)(f) (company unable to pay its dents) on the ground specified in s.123(1)(e) or (2) only if the court was satisfied that the ground would apply even if coronavirus had not had a financial effect on the company. The burden at the second stage of showing that would be on the petitioner, rather than the company, and was not discharged. These case principles on burden of proof of the "financial effect" under para.5(1)(c) and (3) were considered and applied (obiter) in *Re PGH Investments Ltd; PGH Investments Ltd v Ewing* [2021] EWHC 533 (Ch); [2021] B.C.C. 659 where the company had not discharged the burden of proving a prima facie case that coronavirus had a financial effect on the company and this could include an indirect, as well as a direct, financial effect.

Later cases have also considered the former CIGA 2020 Sch.10. In *Re a Company* [2021] EWHC 2289 (Ch) the company's relatively low first-stage threshold test was satisfied but when the burden of proof shifted at the second stage the petitioning creditor's evidence, simply comparing the company's debt levels with those from previous years, came "nowhere near establishing" that even without the impact of the coronavirus the company would be unable to pay its debts as they fell due, and the petition was dismissed. The low-level first-stage test does, however, require evidence from the debtor company to establish a prima facie case, so that a mere assertion that coronavirus prevented funding to the company was not sufficient in *Re Investin Quay House Ltd* [2021] EWHC 2371 (Ch). Further interpretation of (former) CIGA 2020 Sch.10 para.5(3) was provided by *Re a Company* [2021] EWHC 2905 (Ch), which noted that the provision made no express reference to the date at which the company's financial position should be assessed, and concluded that as the petition expressly relied on the date of the demand for payment, it was the company's failure to comply with the demand at that date—rather than the earlier due date for payment set out in a loan agreement— which formed the basis of the petitioner's pleaded reliance upon s.123(1)(e). The court should be slow to conclude that a company was unable to pay its debts from the mere fact of non-payment of a debt which had never been demanded of it (this latter point was repeated when permission to appeal the decision was later refused and it was noted that the payment date under the loan agreement had "simply passed" with no action at all then being taken: *Re a Company* [2022] EWHC 1690 (Ch)). For yet further discussion of the (former) position see *Doran v County Rentals Ltd (t/a Hunters)* [2021] EWHC 3478 (Ch) where on the facts it did not matter that the sums fell due pre-pandemic (irrespective of coronavirus) as the supposed failure to pay when the sums fell due did not go to the question of inability to pay, and the court stressed that the coronavirus test had nothing to do with the effect of the coronavirus upon the indebtedness, only with whether the company would have been insolvent apart from the effect of the coronavirus. In *Citibank NA v Speciality Steel UK Ltd* [2022] EWHC 1359 (Ch) ICC Chief Judge Briggs undertook a detailed examination as to whether coronavirus had had the required financial effect on the debtor companies and whether there was a causal link between that financial effect and the ground for winding up relied on by the creditor (and found that there was not). A petition was held not to be subject to the (former) Sch.10 restrictions in *Re a Company* [2022] EWHC 943 (Ch) where the petition debt for commercial rent arrears began in May 2018 and continued thereafter with a statutory demand sent in late 2019 (pre-pandemic) with a further demand (after negotiations failed) in February 2021 and the petition was presented in March 2021; coronavirus was held not to have had the necessary financial effect on the company and the petition was listed for hearing with the court prepared to make an immediate winding-up order.

GENERAL NOTE

Replace the note with:

The question of a company's inability to pay its debts may be determined by the court as a matter of fact (s.123(1)(e)) or settled by the application of a number of presumptions, four of which (s.123(1)(a)–(d)) turn purely on the evidence, while the fifth (s.123(2)) involves a judicial assessment of the position.

The minimum threshold figure of £750 was the same in bankruptcy and has remained unchanged in winding up since the 1986 Act came into force. Following a consultation exercise, the sum has been increased to £5,000 in bankruptcy cases from 1 October 2015 (see the Insolvency Act 1986 (Amendment) Order 2015 (SI 2015/922)), but no comparable change has been made for corporate insolvency.

On the meaning of the term "debt" in the present context, see IR 2016 r.14.1. See also the discussion of the related term "creditor" in the note to s.1(1). It is sufficient to give a creditor standing to petition that he should have a legal title to the debt, even though the beneficial interest may be in another person: *Bell Group Finance (Pty) Ltd (in liq.) v Bell Group (UK) Holdings Ltd* [1996] B.C.C. 505.

A winding-up order will not be made on the basis of a debt which is genuinely disputed: *Re LHF Wools Ltd* [1970] Ch. 27; *Re Trinity Insurance Co Ltd* [1990] B.C.C. 235; *Re Janeash Ltd* [1990] B.C.C. 250; *Re a Company (No.0010656 of 1990)* [1991] B.C.L.C. 464; *Re Richbell Strategic Holdings Ltd* [1997] 2 B.C.L.C. 429; *Re a Company (No.2634 of 2002)* [2002] EWHC 944 (Ch); [2002] 2 B.C.L.C. 591; *Re MCI WorldCom Ltd* [2002] EWHC 2436 (Ch); [2003] 1 B.C.L.C. 330; *Re UK (Aid) Ltd, Glaxosmithkline Export Ltd v UK (Aid) Ltd* [2003] EWHC 1090 (Ch); [2003] 2 B.C.L.C. 351; *Favermead Ltd v FPD Savills Ltd* [2005] EWHC 626 (Ch); [2005] B.P.I.R. 715; *Jubilee International Ltd v Farlin Timbers Pte Ltd* [2005] EWHC 3331 (Ch); [2006] B.P.I.R. 765. Contrast *Southern Cross Group plc v Deka Immobilien Investment* [2005] B.P.I.R. 1010 (prior opportunity to litigate not taken); *Tallington Lakes Ltd v Ancasta International Boat Sales Ltd* [2012] EWCA Civ 1712; [2014] B.C.C. 327; *Angel Group Ltd v British Gas Trading Ltd* [2012] EWHC 2702 (Ch); [2013] B.C.C. 265 (debt disputed in part but a sum well in excess of £750 clearly due; the case was followed in Northern Ireland in *Lagan Holdings v Lagan Developments* [2019] NICh 10 where an injunction was granted to restrain a winding up petition based upon a disputed debt); see also *Re a*

Company [2013] EWHC 4291 (Ch) and *Wolf Rock (Cornwall) Ltd v Langhelle* [2020] EWHC 2500 (Ch); [2021] B.C.C. 67. A substantial dispute was established resulting in the petition being struck out in *Glocin Ltd v Bancibo SE* [2022] EWHC 1858 (Ch) and the further substantial disagreement between the parties' expert evidence on foreign law as to liability under the contracts for the sums forming the subject matter of the petition was of itself a further reason why the matter was entirely unsuitable for disposal by way of petition. Where there is an exclusive jurisdiction clause governing the jurisdiction and law of an agreement in relation to the disputed debt, a Hong Kong Court of Appeal's detailed analysis over several jurisdictions on this area, which it described as "in a state of flux" as to whether exclusive jurisdiction clauses apply to insolvency proceedings, has concluded that there were cogent reasons for adopting the same approach to an exclusive jurisdiction clause in winding up and bankruptcy petitions as in ordinary actions, so that even in the context of insolvency proceedings the court will expect the parties to seek a determination of their dispute in accordance with their agreement on jurisdiction and a petition will not be allowed to proceed unless there are "strong reasons" otherwise (*Guy Kwok-Hung Lam v Tor Asia Credit Master Fund LP* [2022] HKCA 1297).

    This is also the case where the company has a genuine and serious cross-claim for an amount which exceeds the petition debt (or which, if successful, would reduce the company's net indebtedness below the statutory minimum of £750): *Re Bayoil SA* [1998] B.C.C. 988; *Richbell Information Services Inc v Atlantic General Investments Trust Ltd* [1999] B.C.C. 871; *Re Latreefers Inc* [1999] 1 B.C.L.C. 271; *Greenacre Publishing Group v The Manson Group* [2000] B.C.C. 11; *Orion Media Marketing Ltd v Media Brook Ltd* [2002] 1 B.C.L.C. 184; *Re Ringinfo Ltd* [2002] 1 B.C.L.C. 210; *Montgomery v Wanda Modes Ltd* [2002] 1 B.C.L.C. 289; *Re VP Developments Ltd* [2005] EWHC 259 (Ch); [2005] B.C.C. 393; *Penwith DC v VP Developments Ltd* [2005] EWHC 259 (Ch); [2005] B.P.I.R. 607. Contrast *Southern Cross Group plc v Deka Immobilien Investment* [2005] B.P.I.R. 1010; *Re a Company (No.2272 of 2004)* [2005] EWHC 422 (Ch); [2005] B.P.I.R. 1251; *R&S Fire and Security Services Ltd v Fire Defence plc* [2013] EWHC 4222 (Ch); [2013] 2 B.C.L.C. 92 (cross-claim recognised despite "pay now, litigate later" provision in contract); *Re Victory House General Partner Ltd* [2018] EWHC 1143 (Ch); [2019] B.C.C. 87 (having made an advance payment, if it paid the petition debt the company would immediately be entitled to repayment in restitution). For a Scottish court approach to proof of being a creditor and on disputed debts see *MacPlant Services Ltd v Contract Lifting Services (Scotland) Ltd* [2008] CSOH 158; 2009 S.C. 125. A person who had paid part of a company's solicitor's costs was not automatically a creditor without proof that the payment was intended as a loan (it had not been recorded as such in the company's accounts) and the substantial dispute could not be decided by the winding-up court in *Petitioner v Company* [2021] EWHC 3249 (Ch).

    It was pointed out in *Bayoil* (above) and repeated in *Re a Company* [2013] EWHC 4291 (Ch) that where the petition debt is disputed in good faith on substantial grounds the petitioner is regarded (unless there is an undisputed part of the debt in excess of £750) as not being a creditor of the company and so has no legal standing to present the petition in the first place, rather than the petition being regarded as a matter of the court's discretion; whereas the case of an undisputed debt with a genuine and serious cross-claim is treated differently, in that the dismissal or staying of the petition can only be a matter for the discretion of the court. (On this discretion see *Wilson & Sharp Investments Ltd v Harbourview Developments Ltd* [2015] EWCA Civ 1030; [2015] B.P.I.R. 1496.) A petitioner whose debt is disputed or subject to a cross-claim is not to be regarded as a contingent creditor for the purposes of presenting a winding-up petition (see *LSI 2013 Ltd v Solar Panel Co (UK) Ltd* [2014] EWHC 248 (Ch). Although the Companies Court when exercising winding-up jurisdiction has repeatedly stated that it is not the forum to resolve parties' disputes as to debts or cross-claims, in *Botleigh Grange Ltd v Revenue and Customs Commissioners* [2016] EWHC 3081 (Ch), the court was prepared to entertain a petition involving a dispute that could be determined on the documents alone, did not require further or oral evidence and was not intricate or complex. See also *Sell Your Car With Us Ltd v Sareen* [2019] EWHC 2332 (Ch); [2019] B.C.C. 1211. The dispute was "substantial" in *Craymanor Ltd v LS Power and Data Ltd* [2021] EWHC 192 (Ch) on unusual facts so that whether a creditor was entitled to present a winding-up petition against would have to be determined by a separate court and presentation of the petition was restrained. A restraining injunction was also granted in *JT Development Solutions Ltd v Secretary of State for Education acting through the Education Skills Funding Agency* [2021] EWHC 2943 (Ch) where the dispute included the construction of technical rules on "breach" in an agreement that could not properly be dealt in winding-up proceedings.

    An application to restrain presentation of a petition must be to a court with jurisdiction to wind up the company (IR 2016 r.7.24). The application to restrain must be made by the company: a director or shareholder does not have a sufficient personal interest to have standing to apply in his or her own name: *Re St Benedict's Land Trust Ltd* [2020] EWHC 1001 (Ch); [2020] B.C.C. 620. In *Re a Company* (unreported, 26 April 2017) Norris J stressed that the petitioner must establish its standing to petition as a creditor and in a complex set of facts adjourned the matter for 14 days to give the creditor time to formulate its response to the company's challenge to the petitioner's standing as such. The threshold for granting an injunction to restrain the presentation of a winding-up petition is low: the court simply has to form a view about whether the challenge to the debt is being put forward in good faith and has sufficient substance to justify it being determined in an ordinary civil action: *Mulalley & Co Ltd v Regent Building Services Ltd* [2017] EWHC 2962 (Ch). This approach that the threshold was not high (even regarded as shadowy on an application for summary judgment) was repeated in *Integral Law Ltd v Jason* [2020] EWHC 3698 (Ch).

However a petition will not be struck out or dismissed merely because the company alleges that the debt is disputed; the court must be satisfied that there is a genuine dispute founded on substantial grounds: *Re a Company (No.006685 of 1996)* [1997] B.C.C. 830; compare *Re a Company (No.001946 of 1991) Ex p. Fin Soft Holding SA* [1991] B.C.L.C. 737; *Denis Rye Ltd v Bolsover District Council* [2009] EWCA Civ 372; [2009] 4 All E.R. 1140; [2010] B.C.C. 248; *Re City Centre Resources Ltd* [2013] EWHC 4249 (Ch) (dispute whether loan repayable); *Foxholes Nursing Home Ltd v Accora Ltd* [2013] EWHC 3712 (Ch) (petition used as pressure by creditor); *Winnington Networks Communications Ltd v Revenue & Customs Commissioners* [2015] EWHC 1096 (Ch); [2015] B.C.C. 554 (mere unsubstantiated assertion that debt disputed insufficient; company's directors later heavily penalised in costs: [2015] EWHC 4287 (Ch)); *Re Company 0254/2015* [2015] EWHC 2144 (Ch) (substantial grounds shown). Similarly, the company must establish that any cross-claim is genuine. According to *GBM Minerals Engineering Consultants Ltd v Michael Wilson & Partners Ltd* [2018] EWHC 3401 (Ch) the hurdle is not high (so that even a shadowy defence will suffice) but in *Re Bayoil SA* (above) the Court of Appeal simply described the test as that the cross-claim must be genuine and serious or one of substance. The principles and cases on disputed debts and cross-claims are well summarised in *Re LDX International Group LLP* [2018] EWHC 275 (Ch), particularly at [22] (although the appeal was allowed: *Misra Ventures Ltd v LDX International Group LLP* [2018] EWCA Civ 3030; [2019] B.C.C. 739 (see below)); for comment see Chaffer (2019) 40 Co. Law. 14.

If the debt is disputed, the court will normally strike out the petition, leaving the question of its validity to be determined in other proceedings. However this is a rule of practice and not of law, and so may be departed from, in the court's discretion, in an appropriate case—e.g. where, in the case of a foreign company, the petitioner would otherwise be without a remedy; *Re Russian & English Bank* [1932] 1 Ch. 663; *Re Claybridge Shipping Co SA* [1981] Com. L.R. 107n; cf. *Re UOC Corp, Alipour v Ary* [1997] 1 W.L.R. 534; [1997] B.C.C. 377; *Jubilee International Ltd v Farlin Timbers Pte Ltd* (above); *Parmalat Capital Finance Ltd v Food Holdings Ltd* [2008] UKPC 23; [2009] 1 B.C.L.C. 274 or the circumstances are for some other reason exceptional (*Lacontha Foundation Ltd v GBI Investments Ltd* [2010] EWHC 37 (Ch); [2010] B.P.I.R. 356). The fact that the debt is based on a cheque does not exclude the court's discretion: *Re a Company* [2012] EWHC 4336 (Ch). Although it would not normally be appropriate to make a winding-up order on the basis of a judgment debt when an appeal against the judgment is pending, there are rulings to the contrary in *Re A&BC Chewing Gum Ltd* [1975] 1 W.L.R. 579; *El-Ajou v Dollar Land (Manhattan) Ltd* [2005] EWHC 2861 (Ch); [2007] B.C.C. 953 and *Re BLV Realty II Ltd* [2010] EWHC 1791 (Ch). If the parties have agreed that disputes under an agreement should go to arbitration, it has been held not appropriate for the court to decide an issue as to a debt under that agreement on a winding-up petition: the insolvency process is not to be used for debt recovery (*Rusant Ltd v Traxys Far East Ltd* [2013] EWHC 4083 (Ch): the court refused to allow the petition to proceed and the matter was to go to arbitration; compare *Salford Estates (No.2) Ltd v Altomart Ltd* [2014] EWCA Civ 1575; [2015] B.C.C. 306, where the Court of Appeal required there to be "exceptional circumstances" for the court to consider if the debt was disputed and *Re Eco Measure Market Exchange Ltd* [2015] EWHC 1797 (Ch)). Where the debt is based on the award of an arbitrator or similar adjudicator, it may be appropriate for the court to adopt a similar approach, but if the debtor has the right to appeal against the award the court may direct him to follow that course: *Towsey v Highgrove Homes Ltd* [2013] B.L.R. 45. However, the legislation relating to Value Added Tax, exceptionally, authorises the enforcement of an assessment for VAT by winding-up proceedings even though an appeal against the liability has not been disposed of: *Re D & D Marketing (UK) Ltd* [2002] EWHC 660 (Ch); [2003] B.P.I.R. 539; cf. *Re The Arena Corp Ltd* [2004] EWCA Civ 371; [2004] B.P.I.R. 415; *Hall v Poolman* [2008] B.P.I.R. 892 (Australia); and contrast *Customs & Excise Commissioners v Anglo Overseas Ltd* [2004] EWHC 2198 (Ch); [2005] B.P.I.R. 137. In *Re Enta Technologies Ltd* [2014] EWHC 548 (Ch); [2014] B.C.C. 683 it was held at first instance that the mere existence of a tax assessment creates a statutory debt, incapable of dispute and remaining extant unless and until any appeal to a tax tribunal is successful. But this view was doubted in *Re Parkwell Investments Ltd* [2014] EWHC 3381 (Ch); [2014] B.C.C. 721, and on appeal the *Enta* decision was reversed (*Revenue & Customs Commissioners v Changtel Solutions UK Ltd* [2015] EWCA Civ 29; [2015] B.C.C. 317). The court's discretion is not completely abrogated by the jurisdiction of the tax tribunal, and the question whether the appeal has a real prospect of success is likely to be a compelling factor in the court's exercise of that discretion. If a petition fails on the basis that the debt is genuinely disputed, the petitioner should pay the costs of that failure save in exceptional circumstances: *Re Sykes & Son Ltd* [2012] EWHC 1005 (Ch); [2012] B.P.I.R. 1273. Where the company is solvent, it is an abuse of the process of the court to present a petition for winding up based on a disputed debt, which the court will restrain by injunction and may penalise in costs, possibly on an indemnity basis: *Re a Company (No.0012209 of 1991)* [1992] 1 W.L.R. 351; *Re a Company (No.2507 of 2003)* [2003] EWHC 1484 (Ch); [2003] 2 B.C.L.C. 346; *Glaxosmithkline v UK (Aid) Ltd* [2003] EWHC 1383 (Ch); [2004] B.P.I.R. 528; *Re Realstar Ltd* [2007] EWHC 2921 (Ch); [2008] B.P.I.R. 1391; contrast *Frank Saul (Fashion) Ltd v Revenue and Customs* [2012] EWHC 1603 (Ch); [2012] B.P.I.R. 985 (fault on both sides; no order as to costs). Further on costs note *Helmbridge Ltd v Revenue and Customs Commissioners* [2020] EWHC 2752 (Ch). A winding-up order made on the basis of a debt which might have been disputed at the time remains in force unless and until it is rescinded by a later order: *Wilson v Specter Partnership* [2007] EWHC 133

(Ch); [2007] B.P.I.R. 649. In the case of a prospective debt which has not yet fallen due, the court may take the view that the matter should be resolved when the petition is heard rather than on an application to strike out: *Securum Finance Ltd v Camswell Ltd* [1994] B.C.C. 434. (On petitions by a prospective or contingent creditor, see further *Re a Company (No.003028 of 1987)* (1987) 3 B.C.C. 575 at 585; and *JSF Finance & Currency Exchange Co Ltd v Akma Solutions Inc* [2001] 2 B.C.L.C. 307.)

Where the company has a cross-claim against the petitioner pending in another court, the court has a discretion whether to make a winding-up order or to dismiss the petition: *Re FSA Business Software Ltd* [1990] B.C.C. 465. Note *Re LDX International Group LLP* [2018] EWHC 275 (Ch) where the High Court issued an injunction to restrain the presentation and advertisement of a winding-up petition in circumstances where the debtor appeared to have a cross claim in excess of the petition debt. On appeal (*Misra Ventures Ltd v LDX International Group LLP* [2018] EWCA Civ 3030; [2019] B.C.C. 739) the Court of Appeal, having found that the alleged cross-claim could not be substantiated, allowed the appeal. A cross-claim was not substantiated in *Agform Ltd v Fine Organics Ltd* [2018] EWHC 2211 (Ch); [2019] B.P.I.R. 461 so that the petition could continue and the application to restrain advertisement of it was refused.

A dispute as to the genuineness of a debt may also be relevant to determine the standing of a person claiming to be a creditor who seeks a winding-up order on grounds other than the company's insolvency. In this case the question is necessarily one for the court to determine: *Morrice (or Rocks) v Brae Hotel (Shetland) Ltd* [1997] B.C.C. 670 (but compare *Baker Hughes Ltd v CCG Contracting International Ltd*, 2005 S.C. 65 (petition dismissed as a serious abuse of process where standing as creditor not shown)).

Where a winding-up petition in respect of an undisputed debt is based on collateral motive, the proceedings may amount to abuse of process (i) where the petitioner does not really want to obtain liquidation but issued or threatened to issue the proceedings to put pressure on the company to take action that it was unwilling to take; and (ii) where the petitioner wants to obtain the relief sought but is not acting in the interests of his class of creditors or where the success of his petition would disadvantage the body of creditors (see *Ebbvale Ltd v Hosking* [2013] UKPC 1; [2013] 2 B.C.L.C. 204). Unfair pressure was found in *COLT Technology Services v SG Global Group Srl* [2020] EWHC 1417 (Ch), which together with a disputed debt and potential illegality in performance resulted in the petition being an abuse of process and restrained.

A petition may not be presented based on a statute-barred debt: *Re Karnos Property Co Ltd* (1989) 5 B.C.C. 14; *Bolsover District Council v Ashfield Nominees Ltd* [2010] EWCA Civ 1129; [2012] B.C.C. 803. But a judgment debt is not subject to any statutory limitation: *Ridgeway Motors (Isleworth) Ltd v ALTS Ltd* [2005] EWCA Civ 92; [2005] B.C.C. 496.

Where a company or other body is, or has been, an "authorised person" or "authorised representative" under FSMA 2000, or is or has been carrying on a "regulated activity" in contravention of s.19 of that Act, there is a special provision in s.367(4) of that Act setting out (presumably, additional) circumstances in which such a body is to be deemed unable to pay its debts.

Before Brexit, under the EU Regulation art.34, where "main" insolvency proceedings had been opened in the Member State where the debtor has his centre of main interests, his insolvency was to be taken as conclusively established for the purposes of any secondary proceedings. In such a situation it would not have been necessary or, indeed, relevant to invoke the provisions of the present section. In contrast, the CBIR art.31 states that recognition of a foreign main proceeding is, for the purpose of commencing a proceeding under British insolvency law, presumptive (but not conclusive) proof that the debtor is unable to prove his debts (or the Scottish equivalent, "apparently insolvent").

Where the term "unable to pay its debts" occurs elsewhere in the Act (as, e.g. in relation to administration in Sch.B1 para.11(a)), the s.123 tests apply: *Gas and Electricity Markets Authority v GB Energy Supply Ltd* [2016] EWHC 3341 (Ch).

Application for winding up

124—

GENERAL NOTE
Replace the note with:

Note the temporary prohibition and restrictions in CIGA 2020 s.10 and Sch.10 (originally and as substituted after 30 September 2021) against winding-up petitions presented under s.124: see the Special Note to s.123 above. See also *Insolvency Practice Direction Relating to the Corporate Insolvency and Governance Act 2020* [2020] B.C.C. 694 (reproduced as App.V to this *Guide*).

Section 124 lists the persons who have standing to present a winding-up petition; but it is not exhaustive, for the

Attorney-General or the Charity Commission may petition in the case of a charitable company or charitable incorporated organisation (Charities Act 2011 s.113), the Financial Conduct Authority and the Prudential Regulation Authority may do so in the case of various bodies carrying on investment business: FSMA 2000 s.367, and the Director of Public Prosecutions and other prosecuting authorities are empowered to petition to have a company wound up on public interest grounds following a conviction for breach of a serious crime prevention order (Serious Crime Act 2007 s.27).

The Act empowers the supervisor of an IVA (s.7(4)(b)) to apply to the court for a winding-up order and by Sch.1 para.21, states that an administrator and an administrative receiver may present a petition for winding up; but (no doubt as a result of a drafting slip) no mention is made of these office-holders in s.124(1). A partial attempt has been made to overcome this difficulty without amendment of s.124(1) by an alteration made to the rules in 1987 (now IR 2016 r.7.27(1)). This states that a petition by a "relevant office-holder" must be expressed to be the petition of the company by the office-holder. "Relevant office-holder" means an administrator, administrative receiver or the supervisor of a CVA (r.7.4(2)).

Section 124(1) was amended as from IP completion day of 11pm on 31 December 2020 to remove references to the terms "member State liquidator" and "temporary administrator" which had special meanings for the purposes of the Recast EU Regulation 2015/848, reference to which was also omitted. In particular, a "member State liquidator" was within the definition of an insolvency practitioner in most forms of insolvency proceeding (apart from receivership). An insolvency practitioner appointed under art.3(1) would have been appointed in "main" proceedings in a Member State other than the UK and, as such, was empowered by art.37(1)(a) to request the opening of secondary proceedings (i.e. apply for a winding-up order) in this jurisdiction if the debtor possessed an establishment here. The EU Regulation does however continue to apply to main proceedings opened before IP completion day, by virtue of art.67(3)(c) of the withdrawal agreement of the UK from the EU. (The "retained" EU Regulation as amended by the Insolvency (Amendment) (EU Exit) Regulations 2019 (SI 2019/146) (as amended) applies an emasculated version of the Regulation to domestic law.) Similarly, the CBIR art.9, provides that a "foreign representative" of an insolvency proceeding abroad is entitled to apply directly to a court in Great Britain (for this or any other purpose). A foreign representative (defined in art.2(j)) includes one appointed on an interim basis and is not restricted to a representative in a "main" proceeding. It is not a precondition that the foreign proceeding should have been recognised under art.15. No special formalities apply (other than a translation, where required). Article 13 of the CBIR accords to foreign creditors (including the tax and social security authorities) the same rights regarding the commencement of, and participation in, a British proceeding as creditors in Great Britain.

As a general rule, a winding-up order may only be made on the basis of a petition presented under this section: *Re Brooke Marine Ltd* [1988] B.C.L.C. 546. However, the court may in a proper case make an order of its own motion (*Lancefield v Lancefield* [2002] B.P.I.R. 1108); *Re BTR (UK) Ltd* [2012] EWHC 2398 (Ch); [2012] B.C.C. 864; *Re Marches Credit Union Ltd* [2013] EWHC 1731 (Ch) (where a petition presented by the directors was potentially defective but it was in the public interest and a matter of urgency to order the winding up), and an exception has now also been made by Sch.B1 para.13(1)(e): on an application for an administration order made under para.12 of that Schedule, the court may treat the application as a winding-up petition and make any order which the court could make under s.125. Further, the court using its wide power under Sch.B1 para.79(4)(d) on ending administration on the administrator's application has made winding-up orders without a petition: see *Re Graico Property Co Ltd* [2016] EWHC 2827 (Ch); [2017] B.C.C. 15; *Re West End Quay Estate Management Ltd* [2018] B.C.C. 1. The court in *Re Cartwright (a Bankrupt); Rendle v Panelform Ltd* [2020] EWHC 2810 (Ch) stressed that its jurisdiction to make a winding-up order without a petition was to be exercised cautiously and exceptionally and should not become a regular litigation tactic; *Lancefield* (above) was distinguished as the application was not incidental to, or a means of resolving, issues already before the court but had been specifically made by separate application notice and amounted to a creditor seeking to bypass the statutorily prescribed mechanism for obtaining a winding-up order via a petition (application refused).

For the procedure on an application for winding up, see IR 2016 rr.7.7. A deposit of £1,600 (but £5,000 for a petition under s.124A) is payable on presentation of the petition: Insolvency Proceedings (Fees) Order 2016 (SI 2016/692) art.2(c), (d) (increased to £2,600 as from 1 November 2022 by the Insolvency Proceedings (Fees) (Amendment) Order 2022 (SI 2022/929) arts 1, 2(b)). Before presenting a winding-up petition a creditor must conduct a search to ensure no petition is pending. Save in exceptional circumstances a second winding-up petition should not be presented whilst a prior petition is pending. A petitioner who presents his own petition while another petition is pending does so at risk as to costs (see the *Practice Direction: Insolvency Proceedings* [2020] B.C.C. 698 (reproduced as App.IV to this *Guide*) para.9.2).

Although a winding-up petition is a species of legal proceedings, it is not a "claim or counterclaim" within the

Arbitration Act 1996 s.9: *Best Beat Ltd v Rossall* [2006] EWHC 1494 (Comm); [2006] B.P.I.R. 1387; *Salford Estates (No.2) Ltd v Altomart Ltd* [2014] EWCA Civ 1575; [2015] B.C.C. 306.

On applications for permission to amend errors in petitions, see the *Practice Direction* [2020] B.C.C. 698, para.9.9.

Petition for winding up on grounds of public interest

124A—

GENERAL NOTE

Replace the note with:

For examples of the exercise of this jurisdiction, see *Re Walter L Jacob & Co Ltd* (1989) 5 B.C.C. 244; *Re Market Wizard Systems (UK) Ltd* [1998] 2 B.C.L.C. 282; *Secretary of State for Trade & Industry v Leyton Housing Trustees Ltd* [2000] 2 B.C.L.C. 808; *Re Equity & Provident Ltd* [2002] EWHC 186 (Ch); [2002] 2 B.C.L.C. 78; *Re Delfin International (SA) Ltd* [2000] 1 B.C.L.C. 71 (where a foreign company was ordered to be wound up under the section); *Re Drivertime Recruitment Ltd* [2004] EWHC 1637 (Ch); [2005] 1 B.C.L.C. 411; *Re UK-Euro Group plc* [2006] EWHC 2102 (Ch); [2007] 1 B.C.L.C. 812; *Re The Inertia Partnership LLP* [2007] EWHC 539 (Ch); [2007] B.C.C. 656; *Secretary of State for Business, etc. v Art IT plc* [2008] EWHC 258 (Ch); [2009] 1 B.C.L.C. 262; *Re Corvin Construction Ltd* (unreported, 21 December 2012) and of a refusal to exercise it; *Re Secure & Provide plc* [1992] B.C.C. 405; *Re Forrester & Lamego Ltd* [1997] 2 B.C.L.C. 155; *Secretary of State for Trade & Industry v Travel Time (UK) Ltd* [2000] B.C.C. 792 and *Secretary of State for Business, Innovation and Skills v KJK Investments Ltd* [2015] EWHC 1589 (Ch) (investment company with no realistic prospect of returns to investors, lack of commercial probity and of any commercial basis for the business); *Re Caledonian Ltd* [2016] EWHC 2854 (Ch) (deliberate misselling of investment products). See also *Re ForceSun Ltd* [2002] EWHC 443 (Ch); [2002] 2 B.C.L.C. 302; and *Re Alpha Club (UK) Ltd* [2002] EWHC 884 (Ch); [2004] B.C.C. 754, where the court ruled it appropriate to make a winding-up order under s.124A even though the company was already in voluntary liquidation. In *Re a Company (No.007816 of 1994)* [1997] 2 B.C.L.C. 685 and *Re Titan International Inc* [1998] 1 B.C.L.C. 102 the court declined to order the winding up of foreign companies on public interest grounds for want of evidence of a sufficient connection with the jurisdiction or of prejudice to the public interest in this country.

Note that proceedings under s.124A did not fall within the scope of the EU Regulation 2015/848, even where the company in question was insolvent: *Re Marann Brooks CSV Ltd* [2003] B.C.C. 239; or the Brussels Convention (now the Recast Judgments Regulation 1215/2012): *Re Senator Hanseatische Verwaltungsgesellschaft mbH* [1997] B.C.C. 112.

In an appropriate case, a provisional liquidator may be appointed: *Secretary of State for Business, Innovation and Skills v Hawkhurst Capital plc* [2013] EWHC 4219 (Ch); [2016] B.C.C. 125; *Revenue and Customs Commissioners v Winnington Networks Ltd* [2014] EWHC 1259 (Ch); [2014] B.C.C. 675; *Secretary of State for Business, Innovation and Skills v New Horizon Energy Ltd* [2015] EWHC 2961 (Ch); [2017] B.C.C. 629.

It may be expedient to order that a company should be wound up in the public interest even though it has not acted unlawfully: *Re Senator Hanseatische Verwaltungsgesellschaft mbH* [1997] 1 W.L.R. 515; [1997] B.C.C. 112, or even where it has not acted at all but may potentially be used for an unlawful purpose: *Secretary of State for Business, Innovation and Skills v PGMRS Ltd* [2010] EWHC 2983 (Ch); [2011] B.C.C. 368.

In *Secretary of State for Business, Energy and Industrial Strategy v Vanguard Insolvency* [2022] EWHC 1589 (Ch) the court issued compulsory winding up orders for four related companies which had been involved in providing services in relation to the conduct of IVAs but monies were paid from the IVA estates for the benefit of the owner of the business and his companies. The reasons for the payments made were deemed opaque and were most likely undisclosed benefits or commissions to the owner and associated persons from trust monies (contrary to SIP 9) and although no criminal activity could be made out it was in the interests of the public that the companies be wound up.

In *Secretary of State for Business, Innovation and Skills v PAG Management Services Ltd* [2015] EWHC 2404 (Ch); [2015] B.C.C. 720 a scheme designed to avoid the payment of business rates involved the formation of special purpose vehicles (SPVs) which took leases of the properties in question and then were immediately wound up without liquidators being appointed. Although he declined to rule that any specific provisions of IA 1986 had been infringed, Norris J held that the use of a company in liquidation as an asset shelter with an inherent bias towards prolongation of the liquidation, subverting the true purpose and function of insolvency law, justified the winding up of the companies concerned in the public interest. On the other hand, on similar facts of companies employing a scheme using SPVs to avoid business rates in *Secretary of State for Business, Energy and Industrial Strategy v PAG Asset Preservation Ltd* [2020] EWCA Civ 1017; [2020] B.C.C. 979, a difference in the scheme required payment of a determination fee, increasing the longer into the lease it was exercised, to a lessee SPV (created by the companies) which would go into MVL and thereby avoiding business rates, resulted in the determination fee being regarded as a contingent asset of the

SPV company in MVL, thereby justifying the liquidator in maintaining the liquidation in the prospect of realising the fee. and held to be a genuine insolvency process whose purpose was to collect, realise and distribute assets and so not a misuse of the insolvency legislation (or not sufficient to justify a conclusion that the activities of the companies were so clearly lacking in commercial probity or otherwise so against the public interest as to justify their being wound up on public interest grounds). The Court of Appeal agreed that the determination premium in the second scheme created a "substantial and significant difference" to the unlawful scheme used in the earlier *PAG Management Services Ltd* (above) case so that there was no subversion of the insolvency legislation in the revised scheme and, even if there had been a misuse of the insolvency process, it was not sufficient to warrant winding up under the section. In the Court of Appeal, Asplin LJ at [39] reiterated principles that Norris J had summarised in the earlier *PAG Management Services Ltd* [2015] EWHC 2404 (Ch); [2015] B.C.C. 720 case at [5] which the court should adopt in the exercise of the s.124A jurisdiction, and went on at [40] that it was then for the court to carry out a balancing exercise based upon all the circumstances. She added at [61] that the court was required to identify for itself the aspects of the public interest which would be promoted by making a winding-up order. These points were repeated in *Secretary of State for Business, Energy and Industrial Strategy v Celtic Consultancy & Enterprises Ltd* [2021] EWHC 1240 (Ch), which went on to clarify that this did not mean that in every case actual specific harm to the public was required to be established in order to found the jurisdiction.

In *Re Portfolios of Distinction Ltd* [2006] EWHC 782 (Ch); [2006] 2 B.C.L.C. 261 it was said that while in some cases the public would be seen to be affected where a company was committing offences, in others it would be expedient in the public interest to protect members of the public who had dealt with a company whose business was "inherently objectionable", i.e. that it caused members of the public inevitable loss, whether that derived from illegal activity or not. On the balance of probabilities it was held that the Secretary of State's case had not been made out.

A petition on public interest grounds may only be brought under this section and only by the Secretary of State: *Re Millennium Advanced Technology Ltd* [2004] EWHC 711 (Ch); [2004] 1 W.L.R. 2177. Where the Secretary of State decided not to pursue a petition on public interest grounds under s.124A, Harman J declined an application by contributories of the company to be substituted as petitioners: the existing evidence, he said, would not be material to the revised petition, which would be on different grounds (*Re Xyllyx plc (No.1)* [1992] B.C.L.C. 376).

A contributory may appear to oppose a public-interest petition and may file evidence in opposition, whether or not the company also appears to oppose it: *Re Rodencroft Ltd* [2004] EWHC 862 (Ch); [2004] B.C.C. 631. If the company does not appear in such a case, the court should be astute to inquire why this is so (ibid.). But the contributory has no standing unless he can show that he would have an interest in the surplus if a winding-up order were made and the company proved to be solvent: *Secretary of State for Business, Innovation and Skills v World Future Ltd* [2013] EWHC 723 (Ch), following *Re Rica Gold Washing Co Ltd* (1879) 11 Ch. D. 36.

The Financial Services and Markets Act 2000 s.367 authorises the Financial Conduct Authority or the Prudential Regulation Authority (as appropriate) to petition for the winding up of a body specified in that section on the ground (inter alia) that it is just and equitable that it should be wound up. This jurisdiction may be exercised analogously with s.124A: *Re Inertia Partnership LLP* (above).

In *Re Supporting Link Ltd* [2004] EWHC 523 (Ch); [2004] B.C.C. 764 the company had offered undertakings which, it contended, would make it unnecessary for the court to make a winding-up order, but it was held that, unless the Secretary of State was content to accept the undertakings, the court should be very slow indeed to accede to such a request, and a winding-up order was duly made. An offer of undertakings was refused in *Re London Citylink Ltd* [2005] EWHC 2875 (Ch); *Secretary of State for Business, Enterprise and Regulatory Reform v Charter Financial Solutions Ltd* [2009] EWHC 1118; [2011] 2 B.C.L.C. 788 and in *Re Corvin Construction Ltd* (unreported, 21 December 2012). In contrast, in *Secretary of State for Business, etc. v Amway (UK) Ltd* [2008] EWHC 1054 (Ch); [2008] B.C.C. 713, where the court held that the company's business was not inherently unlawful or objectionable but its merits had been oversold in its promotional material and it had used improper techniques to recruit customers, a winding-up petition was dismissed on undertakings by the company to adhere to a new business model. This ruling was affirmed on appeal [2009] EWCA Civ 32; [2009] B.C.C. 781.

In *Secretary of State for Trade and Industry v Bell Davies Trading Ltd* [2004] EWCA Civ 1066; [2005] 1 All E.R. 324; [2005] B.C.C. 564 the Court of Appeal (at [110] and [111]) gave the following guidance on the approach to be adopted on this question:

> "[110] A valuable review of the authorities on the proper approach of the court to s 124A public interest petitions, in general, and to the practice relating to the acceptance of undertakings, in particular, was carried out by the Vice-Chancellor in his judgment in *Re Supporting Link Ltd* [2004] EWHC 523 (Ch); [2004] B.C.C. 764; [2004] 1 W.L.R. 1549. The judge has a discretion whether or not to make a winding-up order. As for undertakings, the court has a discretion whether or not to accept them if they are proffered and whether or not to make the giving of them a condition of dismissing the petition. In considering the exercise of his discretion the willingness or otherwise of the Secretary of State to accept undertakings, which have to be policed by the Department of Trade and Industry, is an important factor.

[111] Thus, in the exercise of the discretion, the judge is entitled (a) to dismiss the petition on undertakings if, for example, he is satisfied that the offending business has ceased or if the undertakings are acceptable to the Secretary of State; or (b) to dismiss the petition on undertakings, even if that course is opposed by the Secretary of State, although that will be unusual; or (c) to refuse to accept undertakings and to wind the company up, if, for example, he is not satisfied that those giving the undertakings can be trusted."

A deposit of £5,000 is payable on the filing of the petition. A petition presented under this section on public interest grounds is required to be advertised in the same way as a creditor's petition, unless the court directs otherwise under IR 2016 r.7.10(1). For a discussion of the considerations affecting the exercise of the court's discretion in this respect, see *Re a Company (No.007923 of 1994), Re a Company (No.007924 of 1994)* [1995] B.C.C. 634 and 641; *Secretary of State for Business, Innovation and Skills v Broomfield Developments Ltd* [2014] EWHC 3925 (Ch); *Secretary of State for Business, Innovation and Skills v Combined Maintenance Services Ltd* (unreported, 6 November 2014) (where it was said that the court may be more inclined to dispense with advertising in the case of a petition under s.124A than in a creditors' petition, where there is a need for other creditors to be informed).

In *Secretary of State for Trade and Industry v Aurum Marketing Ltd* [2002] B.C.C. 31, where a company which had operated a swindle was ordered to be wound up on public interest grounds, its sole director was ordered to pay both the applicant's and the company's costs personally. Costs were also awarded against directors personally in *Re North West Holdings plc* [2001] EWCA Civ 67; [2002] B.C.C. 441, where the Court of Appeal held that, although it was the normal rule that directors should not be ordered to pay their company's costs, an exception should be made where the directors had no bona fide belief that the company had an arguable defence and that it was in the interests of the company to advance that defence. A similar order was made against a majority shareholder in *Secretary of State for Trade and Industry v Liquid Acquisitions Ltd* [2002] EWHC 180 (Ch); [2003] 1 B.C.L.C. 375. In *Re Broomfield Developments Ltd* (unreported, 19 June 2017), where the Secretary of State and the company agreed a consent order for dismissal of the petition subject to the company going into creditors' voluntary liquidation, the court did not have jurisdiction (under the Senior Courts Act 1981 s.51) to order the company to pay the Secretary of State's costs from its assets as expenses of liquidation but ordered costs without that priority. A non-party costs order was made against a company director in respect of the costs of public-interest winding-up proceedings of five companies involved in an investment scheme which the director had devised and was heavily involved in; the court added that the test for a costs order against a non-party on a winding-up petition was whether it was just to make such an order and not whether there was evidence of bad faith, abuse of process, procedural manipulation or improper defence of the petition (*Re Viceroy Jones New Tech Ltd* [2020] EWHC 1155 (Ch)).

Section 124A(1)(b) was substituted and s.124A(1)(bb) inserted by the Financial Services and Markets Act 2000 (Consequential Amendments and Repeals) Order 2001 (SI 2001/3649) as from 1 December 2001.

Generally on s.124A, see Keay (1999) 20 Co. Law. 296.

Commencement of winding up

Commencement of winding up by the court

129—

General Note

Replace the note with:

The effect of s.129(1), (2) is to backdate the operation of the winding-up order (for the operation of certain statutory provisions) to the time when the petition for winding up was presented (or, if the company was then already in voluntary liquidation, to the time when the resolution for voluntary winding up was passed). Note temporary deeming modification to s.129(2) by CIGA 2020 s.10 and Sch.10 paras 8, 9 if a registered or unregistered company is wound up as unable to pay its debts under ss.122(1)(f) or 221(5)(b) based on a petition presented between the relevant period of 27 April 2020 and 30 June 2021.

On the significance of the word "time", see the note to s.86.

A voluntary liquidation commences at the time of the passing of the resolution for voluntary winding up: see s.86.

The term "commencement of the winding up" is defined differently for the purposes of s.185 (effect of diligence in Scotland): see s.185(3).

Subsection (1A) was inserted by EA 2002 s.248 and Sch.17 para.16, with effect from 15 September 2003. Under Sch.B1 para.13(1)(e) the court is empowered, in hearing an application for an administration order, to treat the application as a winding-up petition and order the company to be wound up. In this case, the commencement of the winding up is not back-dated.

In the application of the EU Regulation in proceedings prior to IP completion day of 31 December 2020 at 11pm, the critical point for many purposes was the "time of the opening of proceedings", defined by art.2(8) as "the time at which the judgment opening proceedings becomes effective, regardless of whether it is a final judgment or not". This (at least prima facie) referred to the time when the court pronounced its order, except in the case where the company was already in creditors' voluntary liquidation, when it would be the time of the passing of the shareholders' resolution. However, where the issue for the court was the determination of the debtor's "centre of main interests" (COMI), it may have been necessary to examine the position at some earlier time, e.g. on the hearing of an application to serve the proceedings abroad: see the discussion of *Shierson v Vlieland-Boddy* [2005] EWCA Civ 974; [2005] B.C.C. 949 in the note to art.3(1) of the Regulation. In *Re Eurofood IFSC Ltd* [2005] B.C.C. 1,021 the Advocate General (at [93]) thought that a statutory provision equivalent to s.129, defining the "commencement of the winding up" was conclusive to fix the "time of the opening of the proceedings". However, this was to give too wide a meaning to the former phrase: in practice, the definition was applied only for the purposes of other sections of the Act which use the same expression (e.g. s.127), and not for other purposes such as the proving of debts. Moreover, the Advocate General's opinion overlooked the fact that s.129 has effect only if a winding-up order was eventually made. (The EC Court in its judgment [2006] B.C.C. 397 (at para.59) found it unnecessary to examine this question, in the light of its ruling that the appointment of a provisional liquidator (coincidentally on the same day that the petition was presented) settled the matter. But the Court would surely have considered it critical that s.129 on its own does not have the effect of divesting the company of its assets as from the presentation of the petition.)

It has been held that the periods of limitation prescribed by the Limitation Act 1980 cease to run on the making of a winding-up order, and not (except as against the petitioning creditor) at the time when the winding-up petition is presented: *Re Cases of Taff's Well Ltd* [1992] Ch. 179; [1991] B.C.C. 582; and see *Financial Services Compensation Scheme Ltd v Larnell (Insurances) Ltd* [2005] EWCA Civ 1408; [2006] B.C.C. 690 (but the latter case was distinguished in *Rashid v Direct Savings Ltd* (unreported, 16 August 2022, County Ct) so that time did not cease to run for limitation purposes in claims against liability insurers under the Third Parties (Rights against Insurers) Act 2010 relating to the liability of the insured company in winding up to the claimants for alleged negligent work). Accordingly, in the case of a six-year period of limitation, the liquidator in a winding up by the court is at liberty to distribute the assets of the company without regard to the claims of creditors which accrued more than six years before the making of the winding-up order. In the same case the judge expressed the view, obiter, that an administration order would not prevent time running against a creditor of the company.

Liquidator's powers and duties

Supplementary powers (England and Wales)

168—

GENERAL NOTE

S.168(3)
Add new note:
The power for liquidators to apply to the court for directions applies to other office-holders (see s.35 and Sch.B1 para.63) while s.112 refers to voluntary liquidators (and others) applying to the court to determine any question arising in the voluntary liquidation.

In *Re Allied Wallet Ltd* [2022] EWHC 1877 (Ch) the court gave directions in the liquidation of a company whose business was subject to the Electronic Money Regulations 2011 (SI 2011/99) about the costs of distributing "assets pools" created pursuant to the safeguarding provisions of the Regulations, which did not create a statutory trust of the relevant funds received by the liquidators. All the assets would be required to reconstitute the asset pools and the court directed that not all the fees and expenses incurred by the liquidators were costs of distributing the asset pools: costs associated with their investigations into the company's non-regulated business and dealing with trade, expense and preferential creditors and with employees were excluded from priority. The court noted, applying *Re WW Realisations Ltd* [2010] EWHC 3604 (Ch); [2011] B.C.C. 382, that some expense creditors, if tardy in pursuing their claims, may end up not being paid, but this was an acceptable price to pay in striking a proper balance.

S.168(5)
Replace the note with:
Notwithstanding the width of the words "may … make such order in the case as it thinks just", the court will not normally review the exercise by the liquidator of his powers and discretions in the management and realisation of the

corporate property. The court will only interfere with a decision of a liquidator if it was taken in bad faith or if it was so perverse as to demonstrate that no liquidator properly advised could have taken it: *Re a Debtor* [1949] Ch. 236 at 241; *Re Hans Place Ltd* [1992] B.C.C. 737 at 745–746; *Leon v York-o-Matic Ltd* [1966] 1 W.L.R. 1450; *Re Greenhaven Motors Ltd* [1997] B.C.C. 547; *Re Edennote Ltd, Tottenham Hotspur v Ryman* [1996] B.C.C. 718; *Hamilton v Official Receiver* [1998] B.P.I.R. 602; *Re Abbey Forwarding Ltd* [2010] EWHC 1644 (Ch); [2010] B.P.I.R. 1053.

On the meaning of "person aggrieved", see the remarks of Warner J (obiter) in *Re ACLI Metals (London) Ltd; AML Holdings Inc v Auger* (1989) 5 B.C.C. 749 at 754; and *Re Edennote Ltd* (above) at 721–722. Apart from creditors and contributories, those who may apply are not "any outsider" who is dissatisfied with some act or decision of a liquidator, but rather persons directly affected by a power given specifically to a liquidator, such as a landlord following the disclaimer of a lease: *Mahomed v Morris* [2001] B.C.C. 233. Environmental matters made several Welsh authorities persons aggrieved in *Counsel General for Wales v Allen* [2022] EWHC 647 (Ch) and the liquidators were ordered (subject to an indemnity) to continue the company's water supply. The Court of Appeal of the Eastern Caribbean Supreme Court in considering who is a "person aggrieved" under a BVI directly equivalent provision in *Re Fairfield Sentry Ltd (in liq.); ABN AMRO Fund Services (Isle of Man) 24 Nominees Ltd v Krys* (unreported, 20 November 2017) concluded that an "alleged debtor" was not such a person as not concerned or affected by the ultimate distribution of an estate in liquidation (and the fact that a person had "technical capacity" to be within an established category of a "person aggrieved" would also be insufficient): having a tangible interest in the liquidation was stressed. See also *Brake v Lowes* [2020] EWCA Civ 1491 where the Court of Appeal concluded on challenges to office-holders that there was no substantial difference in the effect of s.168 (liquidation) and s.303 (bankruptcy) although s.303 used the term "dissatisfied" whereas s.168 referred to "aggrieved", and the absence of the term "creditor" in s.168; case authorities applying to one section also applied to the other (trustees of a family settlement were neither contributories nor creditors in the liquidation and being without a substantial interest in the relief sought, were not persons "aggrieved"). The latter case was applied in *Re Edengate Homes (Butley Hall) Ltd (in liq.); Lock v Stanley* [2021] EWHC 2970 (Ch) where it was held that a creditor of a family company lacked standing to apply for the setting aside of an assignment by the company's liquidator to an insolvency liquidation funder as the applicant's real complaint concerned the substantive claims in the main proceedings against herself and her family, and not against the contractual arrangements between the liquidator and the funder: her interest in the outcome of the application was not aligned with the interests of the creditors as a whole. This was upheld on appeal ([2022] EWCA Civ 626) where the Court of Appeal reiterated a two-fold test for a s.168(5): (a) the applicant must be a person aggrieved, and (b) have a legitimate interest in the relief sought. Although the applicant actually was a creditor, which a person aggrieved would often be, her interest in the liquidator's assignment was as defendant to the claim assigned. The Court of Appeal also considered whether there was perversity as the court would only interfere with the act of a liquidator if it was something "so utterly unreasonable and absurd that no reasonable man would have done it". This was a "formidable" obstacle to overcome and as the liquidator was under no duty to give the applicant and her family an opportunity to acquire the claim and had no reason to think that they would have offered a better deal than the litigation funder, the liquidator's decision to assign to the funder was not perverse.

CHAPTER IX

DISSOLUTION OF COMPANIES AFTER WINDING UP

Introductory note to Part IV, Chapter IX
Replace the note with:

The dissolution of a company extinguishes its legal personality, so that it goes out of existence for all purposes. Any property and rights formerly vested in it are deemed to belong to the Crown, as bona vacantia and the Crown may disclaim it by the Crown representative (the Treasury Solicitor) giving notice within three years of the vesting date (CA 2006 ss.1012, 1013). The Crown does not hold bona vacantia property on constructive trust as it does not voluntarily assume fiduciary responsibilities in relation to the property, which is vested in it by statute as a legal convenience (*Potier v Solicitor for the Affairs of Her Majesty's Treasury Crown Nominee for Bona Vacantia* [2021] EWHC 1524 (Ch)). (Note, that in *Re Wilmott Trading Ltd* [2000] B.C.C. 321 Neuberger J held that the particular "property" in that case—a waste management licence—did not revert to the Crown on the dissolution of the company, but ceased to exist.) Note that freehold property held on trust by a foreign company that is dissolved does not escheat to the Crown, but rather vests in the Crown as bona vacantia subject to the trust (so that if the foreign company is restored, the legal title to the property will not automatically vest back in the restored foreign company but a vesting order application to the court will be necessary): *Hamilton v HM Attorney-General* [2022] EWHC 2132 (Ch).

Under the former provisions of the Companies Acts, different rules regarding dissolution applied in a compulsory winding up and a voluntary winding up, a court order being always required in the former case. The reforms in the law of insolvency which were introduced by IA 1985 dispensed with this need for a court order and so brought the various types of winding up into line. A further innovation was the provision for early dissolution now contained in s.202 below. This enables the official receiver, in a winding up by the court, to apply to the registrar of companies to have the company dissolved at an early stage in the liquidation, when the company is so hopelessly insolvent that it is pointless to proceed further. In Scotland, the liquidator is empowered to make a similar application to the court (s.204). It is possible also for a company which is in administration under IA 1986 Sch.B1 to move directly from administration to dissolution, if the administrator thinks that the company has no property which might permit a distribution to its creditors (Sch.B1 para.84).

In addition to these procedures, a company may be dissolved by having its name struck off the register under CA 2006 ss.1000–1011, on the ground that it has ceased to carry on business. The initiative may be taken by the registrar under ss.1000–1002, which provides that after he has made a preliminary inquiry and followed the prescribed procedure (including sending formal notice to the company of his intention to strike off and gazetting the notice) he may strike the company's name off the register after two (formerly three) months. Alternatively, the company itself may apply to have its name struck off (ss.1003–1011). This procedure is now available to all companies (under CA 1985 only private companies could apply). The directors who are making the application must make a declaration that neither s.1004 nor s.1005 prevents the application from being made (see the Registrar of Companies and Applications for Striking Off Regulations 2009 (SI 2009/1803, effective 1 October 2009) reg.2). Section 1004 bans a company from making an application if (inter alia) it has changed its name or carried on business within the previous three months; and s.1005 prevents an application if a scheme of arrangement under CA 2006 Pt 26 or an insolvency proceeding or moratorium is current. The registrar must first publish a notice in the Gazette inviting any person to show cause why the name should not be struck off and if there is no response he may then do so after two months. In either case, the company is dissolved by the publication in the Gazette of a further notice that the name has been struck off. The striking-off procedure is available also to LLPs (Limited Liability Partnerships (Application of Companies Act 2006) Regulations 2009 (SI 2009/1804) regs 50, 51). In light of the COVID-19 pandemic in 2020–2021, Companies House relaxed its use of the strike-off procedure from April 2020 but re-instated the procedure from 10 September 2020 (voluntary strike-off) and 10 October 2020 (compulsory strike-off). The relaxation was reintroduced from 21 January 2021 for one month but was extended to 7 March 2021 for both voluntary and compulsory strike-off procedures because of staff shortages at Companies House caused by the pandemic. This form of voluntary dissolution without an insolvency process has led to abuse, particularly in relation to director disqualification under CDDA 1986 s.6 for unfitness. This most common form of disqualification has historically only occurred following an insolvency procedure (and not on dissolution at all). During the coronavirus pandemic some unscrupulous persons took advantage of Government incentives such as "bounce-back loans" (often made to newly created companies—remarkably there were no requirements that the company had existed and traded for a minimum period and in any event checks not were made) where the company would be dissolved after the moneys disappeared. The Rating (Coronavirus) and Directors Disqualification (Dissolved Companies) Act 2021 s.2 from 15 February 2022, but with retrospective effect, by amendment has now introduced disqualification for unfitness following dissolution without an insolvency procedure: see CDDA 1986 s.6.

The Companies (Striking Off) (Electronic Communications) Order 2014 (SI 2014/1602) authorises the use of electronic means for the sending of notices and other communications in the striking off procedure.

A company which has been dissolved may be restored to the register under CA 2006 ss.1024 et seq. Under the former legislation a court order was always needed for this purpose and separate procedures with different time limits applied. The 2006 Act, following a recommendation of the Company Law Review, institutes a simpler mechanism enabling a company which has been struck off (whether or not it has also been dissolved) to be reinstated in many cases by an administrative procedure without the involvement of the court. Application must be made to the registrar by a former member or former director within six years of the dissolution (s.1024). It must be shown that:

- the company was carrying on business at the date when it was struck off,

- if any property or right has vested in the Crown as bona vacantia, the Crown representative has given his written consent to the restoration,

- the applicant has delivered to the registrar such documents as are necessary to bring up to date the records kept by the registrar and paid any outstanding penalties (s.1025).

The general effect of restoration (whether effected administratively or by the court) is that the company is deemed to have continued in existence as if it had not been dissolved or struck off (ss.1028(1), 1032(1)). In other words, reinstatement is retrospective in its effect, so that everything that has been done in the company's name while the company was struck off is automatically validated. So, in *Peaktone Ltd v Joddrell* [2012] EWCA Civ 1035; [2013] B.C.C. 112 proceedings which had been commenced against a company during the period when it was dissolved were deemed to have been effective after the company was restored to the register. This reflects the position under CA 1985 s.653 as decided in *Tyman's Ltd v Craven* [1952] 2 Q.B. 100. See also *Re Fivestar Properties Ltd* [2015] EWHC 2782 (Ch) (freehold property which had vested in the Crown as bona vacantia and subsequently been disclaimed revested in the company on restoration), and contrast *ELB Securities Ltd v Love* [2015] CSIH 67 (lease of premises disclaimed by Crown: disclaimer had the effect of bringing company's rights under the lease to an end; rights not revived by reinstatement of company). The court may give such directions and make such provision (on an application to be made within three years from the date of restoration) as seems just for placing the company and all other persons in the same position (as nearly as may be) as if the company had not been dissolved or struck off (s.1028(3)). The court's discretion under this provision is very wide—it may, for example, extend to overriding a limitation period which would normally apply: *Davy v Pickering* [2015] EWHC 380 (Ch); [2016] B.C.C. 50. (But this discretion should be sparingly exercised: *Barclays Bank plc v Registrar of Companies* [2015] EWHC 2806 (Ch); [2016] B.C.C. 64; *County Leasing Management Ltd v Hawkes* [2015] EWCA Civ 1251; [2016] B.C.C. 102 and, indeed, the Court of Appeal in *Pickering v Davy* [2017] EWCA Civ 30; [2017] B.C.C. 171 has since allowed an appeal in that case. Use of the discretion was also refused in *Housemaker Services Ltd v Cole* [2017] EWHC 753 (Ch), where the latter three cases were followed.) However, the power to grant ancillary relief may have limitations: see *Re People's Restaurant Group Ltd* (unreported, 30 November 2012), where an order was made reinstating the company but the applicant was unsuccessful in seeking to have the company placed in liquidation with backdated effect. In the *Barclays Bank* case (above) it was stressed that, although asset recovery might be the normal purpose of seeking reinstatement, there might well be other objectives, e.g. the investigation of transactions meriting examination. The effect of a termination clause in an agreement involving a company subject to restoration came to the court's attention for the first time in *Bridgehouse (Bradford No.2) Ltd v BAE Systems plc* [2019] EWHC 1768 (Comm); [2019] B.C.C. 1127 which concluded that the effect of s.1028(1) in administrative restoration is not to be interpreted as having mandatory or universal effect so as to restore in all cases the position that would have pertained had the company not been dissolved or struck off. By its terms, the clause for termination of the agreement would be triggered by the company's striking-off and the court decided that, after striking-off, the clause remained effective to terminate notwithstanding the later restoration to the register and the clause did not fall to be re-assessed retrospectively.

For the difficult position of joinder of third parties to an application for restoration, see *Welsh Ministers v Price* [2017] EWCA Civ 1768; [2018] B.C.C. 93: the court had power under CPR r.19.2(2) to join a third party to proceedings to restore a company to the register to enable that party to complain that the court was misled when making a restoration order or that there had been a breach of undertakings. Alternatively, a company that has been struck off (or dissolved or is deemed to have been dissolved) may be restored to the register by court order (s.1029(1)). For procedural requirements of a s.1029 application see *Practice Note: Claims for an Order Restoring the Name of a Company to the Register* [2012] B.C.C. 880. A refusal of an application to restore an LLP to the register under the section was upheld in *Grupo Mexico SAB de CV v Registrar of Companies for England and Wales* [2019] EWCA Civ 1673 where the purpose of the application had been to enable it to pursue an unmeritorious and dishonest claim. On disclosure requirements for restoration applications, note *Re Core VCT Plc; Pagden v Fry* [2019] EWHC 540 (Ch); [2019] B.C.C. 845 where, applying principles in *Welsh Ministers v Price* (above), errors in disclosure by the applicants were held insufficient to result in the restoration order being set aside, however on appeal the Court of Appeal allowed the appeal (distinguishing *Welsh Ministers v Price*) but did not set aside the restoration as the proper course was to convene meetings of the members to determine if they wished the liquidation to continue (*Fakhry v Pagden* [2020] EWCA Civ 1207; [2021] B.C.C. 46). Section 1029(2) lists the persons who may apply and in *Hellard v Registrar of Companies* [2020] EWHC 1561 (Ch) it was held that proposed liquidators of a company are not "any other person appearing to the court to have an interest" for the purposes of the section. The six-year time limit also applies here, but there is no limit where the purpose of the application is to bring proceedings against the company for damages for personal injury (s.1030(1)); and if the application is made where the company has been struck off and the registrar has refused reinstatement under s.1024, application may be made within 28 days from the registrar's refusal even if the six-year period has expired (s.1030(5)). The effect and consequences of the restoration are broadly the same as under s.1028 above. Sections 1033 and 1034 contain supplementary provisions dealing with problems which may arise in relation to the company's name (e.g. if another company with the same or a similar name has been registered after it was struck off) or property which was vested in the Crown as bona vacantia has been disposed of. Guidance notes on administrative striking off and restoration are available on the Companies House website.

Provision is made by the Co-operative and Community Benefit Societies Act 2014 for the dissolution of a registered co-operative or community benefit society (as defined by s.1 of that Act), either by an instrument of dissolution (ss.119–122) or, on its being wound up, in pursuance of an order or resolution made as is directed in the case of companies (s.122). A society may also be dissolved under Sch.B1 para.84 following an administration (s.125).

CHAPTER X

MALPRACTICE BEFORE AND DURING LIQUIDATION; PENALISATION OF COMPANIES AND COMPANY OFFICERS; INVESTIGATIONS AND PROSECUTIONS

Penalisation of directors and officers

Summary remedy against delinquent directors, liquidators, etc.

212—

S.212(1)

Replace the note with:

This re-enacts, with some amendments introduced by IA 1985, the traditional "misfeasance" section of successive Companies Acts, providing a summary remedy in the liquidation of a company for the restoration of property and the assessment of compensation or damages for breach of duty against its former officers and others. (On the meaning of the term "officer", see the note to s.206(3).) The section applies to de facto directors: *Holland v Revenue and Customs, Re Paycheck Services 3 Ltd* [2010] UKSC 51; [2011] B.C.C. 1. There has been some uncertainty whether shadow directors are within s.212, but the better view (now supported by Lords Hope and Collins in *Re Paycheck Services 3 Ltd*) is that they do not, since other provisions in the Act state specifically that shadow directors are included and this is not so in s.212. (See also *Mumtaz Properties Ltd v Saeed Ahmed* [2011] EWCA Civ 610; *Re Idessa (UK) Ltd* [2011] EWHC 804 (Ch); [2012] B.C.C. 315; *Re Snelling House Ltd* [2012] EWHC 440 (Ch).) The question of de facto directors was again considered in *Manolete Partners Plc v Dalal* [2022] EWHC 1597 (Ch) where a set of principles were set out based around the statement that "A de facto director is one who acts as if they were a director, although not validly appointed as such" but not merely a manager of person consulted by the decision makers and that the person in question is entitled to the benefit of the doubt in unclear situations.

As originally enacted, the section applied to administrators as well as those listed, but all references to administrators were removed by EA 2002 Sch.17 para.18, which came into effect on 15 September 2003. At the same time a separate provision dealing with misfeasance by administrators was enacted in EA 2002 Sch.16, which is now to be found in IA 1986 Sch.B1 para.75, and a saving provision, reinstating s.212 as formerly worded, came into effect under the Enterprise Act 2002 (Commencement No. 4 and Transitional Provisions and Savings) Order 2003 (SI 2003/2093 (C. 85)) art.3. This saving provision applies in cases where a petition for an administration order was presented before 15 September 2003, and also in the administration of insolvent partnerships commencing prior to 1 July 2005, limited liability partnerships and bodies which are insurers under FSMA 2000 and SI 2001/2634. There is no mention in the Order of building societies and the public utility companies listed in EA 2002 s.249, but in these cases the original s.212 will continue to apply because s.249 disapplies the new s.8 and Sch.B1 in regard to such bodies. There is also no mention of the supervisor of a CVA, but subs.(2)(c) could no doubt be invoked. The words "breach of trust" in CA 1985 have been replaced by "breach of any fiduciary or other duty", and this also has the effect of extending the coverage of the remedy, for although "breach of trust" and "breach of fiduciary duty" may be regarded as synonymous, it had been held that the former wording did not include claims based on negligence (*Re B Johnson & Co (Builders) Ltd* [1955] Ch. 634). However in *Re D'Jan of London Ltd* [1993] B.C.C. 646 Hoffmann LJ clearly accepted that the section now covers "breaches of any duty including the duty of care", and applied it in a straightforward case of negligence brought against a director. See also *Re Centralcrest Engineering Ltd* [2000] B.C.C. 727 (where a liquidator was held liable); *Re Westlowe Storage & Distribution Ltd* [2000] B.C.C. 851; *Re Pantone 485 Ltd* (below); *Re Continental Assurance Co of London plc* [2001] B.P.I.R. 733 (a lengthy judgment in which it was held that the case in misfeasance against both the executive and the non-executive directors of the company had not been made out); *Re Transocean Equipment Manufacturing & Trading Ltd* [2005] EWHC 2603 (Ch); [2006] B.C.C. 184 (where the acts of misfeasance took place while the company was dissolved); *Kinlan v Crimmin* [2006] EWHC 779 (Ch); [2007] B.C.C. 106 (where a repurchase of shares had been carried out under professional advice but without complying with all the statutory formal requirements); *Re Idessa (UK) Ltd* [2011] EWHC 804 (Ch); [2012] B.C.C. 315 and *Ingram (Liquidator of MSD Cash & Carry plc) v Singh* [2018] EWHC 1325 (Ch); [2018] B.C.C. 886 (director as a fiduciary obliged to account for propriety of payments made or of a credit note issued); *Re HLC Environmental Projects Ltd* [2013] EWHC 2876 (Ch); [2014] B.C.C. 337 (payments made in breach of fiduciary and statutory duties when director should have been aware that company was insolvent); *Madoff Securities International Ltd v Raven* [2013] EWHC 3147 (Comm) (a wide-ranging review of the duties owed by the director of a solvent company); *Re Mama Milla Ltd; Sharma v Top Brands Ltd* [2015] EWCA Civ 1140; [2016] B.C.C. 1 (nature of the duties owed by a liquidator, and whether fiduciary: liquidator held liable for negligence and failure to get in company's property; plea based on illegality rejected); *Goldtrail Travel Ltd v Aydin* [2014] EWHC 1587 (Ch) (co-defendants held liable for dishonest assistance in director's breach of fiduciary duty; plea of ex turpi causa rejected); *Re System Building Services Group Ltd; Hunt v Michie* [2020] EWHC 54 (Ch) (directors' general duties under CA 2006 ss.171–177 continue to apply notwithstanding commencement of administration or creditors' voluntary liquidation). See also *Re Snelling House Ltd* [2012] EWHC 440 (Ch). In *Re JD Group Ltd* [2022] EWHC 202 (Ch) the court held that where the respondent was liable for fraudulent trading under s.213, then fraudulent breach of duty was also established on the facts for liability under s.212. Similarly, directors who pay a preference to benefit themselves and liable under s.239 may also be liable for a breach of the duty to promote the success of the company under CA 2006 s.172 and so may accordingly be liable for misfeasance under s.212 (*Re De Weyer Ltd (in liq.); Kelmanson v Gallagher* [2022] EWHC 395 (Ch)) (it is likely that the same would apply for directors liable under s.238 for a transaction at an undervalue benefitting themselves).

In *Base Metal Trading Ltd v Shamurin* [2004] EWCA Civ 1316; [2005] 1 W.L.R. 1157; [2005] B.C.C. 325, Arden LJ observed that, in the case of a company incorporated abroad which is being wound up in this country, the content of the duties of directors will be determined by the law of the jurisdiction of incorporation, but s.212 may be invoked to enforce such duties. In *Short v Kersewell Developments Ltd* (unreported, 27 April 2018) the liability of directors of a Jersey company in respect of their duties under Jersey law was nonetheless determined by application of Jersey law. In *Hague v Nam Tai Electronics Inc* [2008] UKPC 13; [2008] B.C.C. 295 (a misfeasance claim alleging wrongdoing by a liquidator) the Privy Council ruled that, having accepted appointment as liquidator in the jurisdiction of the company's incorporation, it was not open to him to contest the competence of the courts of that jurisdiction to hear the case.

It is well settled that the section creates no new liabilities, but only provides a simpler procedure for the recovery of property or compensation in a winding up. Even here, there are limitations on its use—e.g. it is not available to enforce a contractual debt (*Re Etic Ltd* [1928] Ch. 861), and in *Re Continental Assurance Co of London plc* (above), at 855 it was said to be improper to use it to circumvent the difficulties of establishing a preference claim. Note, however, that the fact that s.212 provides a statutory remedy against a company officer does not in any way exclude the pursuit of common-law remedies in contract and tort against the same person: *A & J Fabrications (Batley) Ltd v Grant Thornton* [1999] B.C.C. 807. Necessarily, if the company is not in liquidation, neither s.212 nor any of the later sections establishing liability for wrongful trading, preference, etc. can be invoked, but such wrongdoing will normally be actionable at common law at the suit of the company (*GHLM Trading Ltd v Maroo* [2012] EWHC 61 (Ch)). While the company is solvent, breaches of this nature may be condoned by the shareholders under what is usually referred to as the *Duomatic* principle ([1969] 2 Ch. 365), but this plea is not available if the company is insolvent or approaching insolvency: *Re Finch (UK) plc* [2015] EWHC 2430 (Ch). See also *Ball (Liquidator of PV Solar Solutions Ltd) v Hughes* [2017] EWHC 3228 (Ch); [2018] B.C.C. 196 where the *Duomatic* principle above was rendered inapplicable in an insolvency case where directors' duty to have regard to the interests of creditors was also a major issue because of the company's insolvency (see CA 2006 s.172(3) and note also *Re CR and RA Eade LLP (in liq.); McTear v Eade* [2019] EWHC 1673 (Ch); [2019] B.C.C. 1155 where the *Duomatic* principle was pleaded and CA 2006 s.172(3) applied in relation to a limited liability partnership: see [138]–[148] for a useful discussion on duty to creditors, including the leading case of *BTI 2014 LLC v Sequana SA* [2019] EWCA Civ 112; [2019] B.C.C. 631). The latter case has now been subject to a rigorous appeal by the Supreme Court, with the appeal dismissed: *BTI 2014 LLC v Sequana SA* [2022] UKSC 25. The enormous judgment of over 450 paragraphs containing four separate judgments by the justices—not unanimously agreeing on all points—affirmed that company directors do have a common law duty (derived relatively recently in English law in *West Mercia Safetywear v Dodd* (1988) 4 B.C.C. 30) to consider and give appropriate weight to the interests of the company's creditors in the context of the company approaching insolvency, and this rule is supported in case law and preserved by CA 2006 s.172(3). The rule does not apply merely because the company is at a real and not remote risk of insolvency at some point in the future: the duty arises when directors know or ought to know that the company is insolvent, bordering on insolvency or when an insolvent administration or liquidation is probable. This duty is not owed directly to creditors but is part of directors' duties to the company and is not a separate duty on its own. The extent of the duty depends on the company's financial difficulties, the greater these are, then more priority should be given to the creditors' interests so that when insolvent liquidation or administration become inevitable or irreversible, the shareholders cease to retain any valuable interest in the company and creditors' interests become paramount. Failure to consider creditors in general was also stressed in *Manolete Partners Plc v Nag* [2022] EWHC 153 (Ch) where the director in breach of fiduciary duty made payments of what should have been company monies to himself and his wife and only certain creditors (such as family members) who were preferred over others.

On burden of proof for misfeasance, the initial burden is on the applicant, but once it is established that a director has received money or property belonging to the company, the evidential burden is then on the respondent director to prove that the payment or transfer was proper (*Re CSB 123 Ltd (in liq.); Reynolds v Stanbury* [2021] EWHC 2506 (Ch) at [8]; see also *Re Brookmann Home Ltd (in liq.); Green v Johnson* [2021] EWHC 2610 (Ch); [2022] B.C.C. 122 at [45]). See further on evidence and proof *Re City Build (London) Ltd (in liq.); Manolete Partners plc v Smith* [2022]

EWHC 364 (Ch) where dementia was likely to have played a significant part in a respondent's inability to remember or provide any explanation for the payments allegedly in breach of duty (no liability was ordered and the court also noted that it formed no part of the applicant's case that the respondent personally benefited from any of the payments and the applicant made no submissions regarding the respondent acting unreasonably).

Where a claim is brought under s.212 against directors alleging negligence and/or breach of duty, it is open to them to claim contribution from professional advisers on whose advice they acted, e.g. insolvency practitioners who had advised that they could continue trading before the company went into liquidation: *Re International Championship Management Ltd* [2006] EWHC 768 (Ch); [2007] B.C.C. 95. Contrast the position where the claim is brought under ss.214, 238 or 239, or where the claim is vested by statute in the liquidator (ibid.).

The question whether a claim under s.212 is statute-barred is determined on the same basis as for other claims. So, in *Re Pantone 485 Ltd* [2002] 1 B.C.L.C. 266, where a director used the company's money for his own benefit in a way which rendered him accountable to it as trustee, the claim was held to be within s.21(1)(b) of the Limitation Act 1980 and accordingly not statute-barred. See also *Re Eurocruit Ltd* [2007] EWHC 1433 (Ch); [2007] B.C.C. 916; *Re Broadside Colours and Chemicals Ltd* [2011] EWHC 1034 (Ch); [2011] 2 B.C.L.C. 597; *Burnden Holdings (UK) Ltd v Fielding* [2018] UKSC 14; [2018] A.C. 857; [2018] B.C.C. 867 (applied in relation to s.21(1)(a) in *Hellard v Macetone Ltd* [2018] EWHC 3307 (Ch) and *Pantiles Investments Ltd (in liq.) v Winckler* [2019] EWHC 1298 (Ch); [2019] B.C.C. 1003). Fraudulent breach of duty/trust in *Re JD Group Ltd* [2022] EWHC 202 (Ch) also disapplied a limitation defence under s.21(1)(a).

Sums or property recovered under this section are the product of a chose in action vested in the company prior to the liquidation and are accordingly "assets of the company" which are capable of being made the subject of a charge (*Re Anglo-Austrian Printing & Publishing Union* [1895] 2 Ch. 891), or of being assigned by it or the liquidator: *Re Oasis Merchandising Services Ltd* [1998] Ch. 170; [1997] B.C.C. 282. It was assumed by Snowden J in *Re Totalbrand Ltd* [2020] EWHC 2917 (Ch); [2021] B.C.C. 541 that an office-holder could assign the rights of action which vested in and formed part of the assets of the company at the commencement of the insolvency proceeding, such as a misfeasance claim, but for a contrary view see *Manolete Partners Plc v Hayward & Barrett Holdings Ltd* [2021] EWHC 1481 (Ch); [2022] B.C.C. 159 in which Chief ICC Judge Briggs stated at [46] that the offices of liquidator and official receiver cannot be assigned or sold (and see the notes to IA 1986 s.423 and Sch.4 para.6).

Where directors make payments in breach of duty to one or more of their number, there may be concurrent liability under this section and under such other provisions as s.214 (wrongful trading) (see, for example, *Roberts v Frohlich* [2011] EWHC 257 (Ch); [2012] B.C.C. 407) and s.239 (preference). In one such case, *Re DKG Contractors Ltd* [1990] B.C.C. 903, it was ordered that liability under the various heads should not be cumulative but that payments made under ss.212 and 239 should go to satisfy the liability under s.214. However, in a later case, *Re Purpoint Ltd* [1991] B.C.C. 121, Vinelott J made orders against the respondent for the payment of separate sums under ss.212 and 214, being satisfied that there was no injustice in the nature of overlap or "double counting" in making the orders cumulative. More recently, in *Re Idessa (UK) Ltd* [2011] EWHC 804 (Ch); [2012] B.C.C. 315, and *Re Kudos Business Solutions Ltd* [2011] EWHC 1436 (Ch), *Re DKG Contractors* has been followed in preference to *Re Purpoint* in order to obviate any risk of double counting. See also the calculations in *Re MDA Investment Management Ltd* [2003] EWHC 2277 (Ch) and [2004] EWHC 42 (Ch); [2005] B.C.C. 783. For a comprehensive discussion of this and related questions, see Goode, *Principles of Corporate Insolvency Law*, 5th edn (ed., van Zwieten, Sweet & Maxwell, 2018), at paras 14-49–14-51. See also *Re Krug International (UK) Ltd* [2008] EWHC 2256 (Ch); [2008] B.P.I.R. 1512 (s.423 claim against foreign third party held properly joined with s.212 proceedings against directors). Difficulties in establishing a wrongful trading claim, such as overcoming the test in s.214(2)(b), have resulted in a comparatively easier task for a liquidator to succeed in a claim for misfeasance: see e.g. *Re Contract Utility Services (CUS) Ltd; Jackson v Casey* [2019] EWHC 1657 (Ch) were claims under ss.214 and 244 both failed but the s.212 action succeeded.

A sum awarded against a misfeasant officer under s.212 cannot be set off against a debt due to him from the company: *Re Anglo-French Co-operative Society Ex p. Pelly* (1882) 21 Ch. D. 492; *Manson v Smith (Liquidator of Thomas Christy Ltd)* [1997] 2 B.C.L.C. 161. Both cases are discussed in *Global Corporate Ltd v Hale* [2017] EWHC 2277 (Ch); [2018] B.C.C. 306 at [58]–[64] (decision overruled by the Court of Appeal ([2018] EWCA Civ 2618) on unrelated grounds). In the latter Court of Appeal decision, Arden LJ considered the difficulty of "re-characterising" types of payments, a point applied in *Re Bronia Buchanan Associates Ltd (in liq.)* [2021] EWHC 2740 (Ch) where drawings could not be re-characterised as remuneration just because it suited the recipient to do so.

The provisions of s.212 apply to directors of building societies: see Building Societies Act 1986 s.90 and Sch.15.

S.212(3)

Replace the note with:

Although a creditor has standing to bring proceedings under s.212, the court can only make an order in favour of the company, and not the individual applicant (*Oldham v Kyrris* [2003] EWCA Civ 1506; [2004] B.C.C. 111). A liquidator owes no duty at common law (in the absence of special circumstances) to an individual creditor: *Fabb v Peters* [2013] EWHC 296 (Ch); [2013] B.P.I.R. 264. This is so even though it may well be arguable, where the defendant is a liquidator, that the duties owed by a liquidator in an insolvent liquidation are owed to the creditors as a class as well as to the company (*Hague v Nam Tai Electronics Inc* (above)). See also *Charalambous v B&C Associates* [2009] EWHC 2601 (Ch); [2013] B.C.C. 491 (no duty in tort owed by administrator to unsecured creditor). An assignee of a creditor's claim has standing: *Mullarkey v Broad* [2007] EWHC 3400 (Ch); [2008] 1 B.C.L.C. 638. A contributory's right to make an application is qualified by s.212(5). An administrator is not given standing by s.212(3), but he may initiate proceedings in the name of the company: *Irwin v Lynch* [2010] EWCA Civ 1153; [2011] 1 W.L.R. 1364.

The court has a discretion under para.(a) to order the respondent to make restitution in whole or in part, and under para.(b) to order payment of "such sum … as the court thinks just". Clearly, in relation to para.(b), the question of quantum is a matter for the discretion of the court (but even so, it does not extend to enabling the court to disregard the need to establish causation: *Re Simmon Box (Diamonds) Ltd, Cohen v Selby* [2002] B.C.C. 82). In *Re D'Jan of London Ltd* (above) the respondent was ordered to pay a sum which was less than the company's actual loss. However under para.(a) the court (although empowered to order restoration of "all or any part" of the misapplied money or property) does not have a discretion which is similarly unfettered: in particular, it will not reopen a decision as to quantum which has already been settled in the course of the liquidation or in other proceedings: *Re AMF International Ltd* [1996] B.C.C. 335. However, in *Dumville v Rich* [2019] EWHC 2086 (Ch) the High Court overturned a deputy judge's earlier decision that the effective sole director of a company was only responsible for 75% of the losses for vehicle hire transactions undertaken at the behest of another, finding that it was not for the court to grant relief under CA 2006 s.1157 (see below) where the director had not acted in a reasonable manner even if with honest intention. In *Re Shahi Tandoori Restaurant Ltd; Brown v Bashir* [2021] EWHC 337 (Ch) where a liquidator brought a claim against directors for misfeasance by under-declarations in VAT returns, it was held wrong in principle to base the measure of the directors' liability on HMRC's findings: the liquidator had sought equitable compensation and the natural relief was for the taking of an account, rather than what HMRC had assessed. In *Re Brothers Produce Ltd (in liq.)* [2022] EWHC 291 (Ch) assignments by the directors of the company's assets at an undervalue were held to be in breach of their duty to creditors (the company was clearly insolvent and a creditor's winding-up petition had been presented) and the court gave a useful discussion on valuation, particularly of goodwill, for this purpose.

Chief ICC Judge Briggs noted in *Re Glam and Tan Ltd; Barnett v Litras* [2022] EWHC 855 (Ch) that there is sparse authority on the application of the court's discretion under s.212(3) (in *Holland v Revenue and Customs; Re Paycheck Services 3 Ltd* [2010] UKSC 51; [2010] 1 W.L.R. 2793; [2011] B.C.C. 1 Lord Hope considered, obiter, at [49], [51] that s.212(3) gave the court a discretion to limit the award in light of all the circumstances, but did not provide the court with power to reduce the contribution to nil). Judge Briggs went on to order the company's sole director to be liable to pay compensation for sums paid by the company for her benefit together with unlawful dividends dressed as salary and insurance money that should have been paid to the liquidator, but concluded that it would not be just for her to be made personally liable to contribute sums wrongfully paid by the company to her violent and controlling estranged husband because her free will had been subjugated to his will under threat of violence.

Section 1157 of the Companies Act 2006 (formerly CA 1985 s.727) empowers the court, in any proceedings against an officer or auditor of a company for (inter alia) negligence, breach of duty or breach of trust, to relieve the defendant either wholly or partly from liability if he has acted honestly and reasonably and ought, in the circumstances, fairly to be excused. The Court of Appeal in *Dickinson v NAL Realisations (Staffordshire) Ltd* [2019] EWCA Civ 2146 described the section as broad in scope and not limited to personal, as opposed to proprietary, claims. This provision has been invoked in many cases brought under IA 1986 s.212 (and, indeed, it was on this provision that Hoffmann LJ relied in the *D'Jan* case). Directors who continued trading on professional advice were held not to be liable either for misfeasance under s.212 or wrongful trading under s.214 (*Re Continental Assurance Co of London plc (No.4)* [2007] 2 B.C.L.C. 287); and in *Re Ortega Associates Ltd* [2007] EWHC 2046 (Ch); [2008] B.C.C. 256 a director was held not liable under s.212 for the dishonesty of a fellow director when he had been advised by his solicitor to take no action; the deputy judge went on to hold that even if there had been any breach of duty he should be wholly relieved from liability under s.727. Note also *Hedger v Adams* [2015] EWHC 2540 (Ch); [2016] B.C.C. 390 (director held not negligent but would in any case have been granted relief). In *Re Marini Ltd* [2003] EWHC 234 (Ch); [2004] B.C.C. 172 it was said that the court would have the greatest difficulty in thinking it ever likely that a defaulting director should be granted relief if the consequence of doing so would be to leave the director enjoying benefits at the expense of creditors which he would never have received but for the default; and in *Re Loquitur Ltd* [2003] EWHC 999 (Ch); [2003] 2 B.C.L.C. 442 Etherton J said that in view of the terms of CA 1985 s.270 [now CA 2006 s.836] he had no jurisdiction to grant relief under this provision from liability for the wrongful payment of a dividend if the consequence was to leave the company insolvent or potentially so. However, rather paradoxically, his Lordship went on to observe that the court's discretion under s.212 was additional to that under the present section and was not subject to a similar limitation, and in exercise of the former thought it appropriate to limit the amount that the respondents were ordered to pay. In *Burnden Holdings (UK) Ltd (in liq.) v Fielding* [2017] EWHC 2118 (Ch) at [84] it was considered (also in a case on distributions under what is now CA 2006 s.836) that there was no invariable rule that relief should not be granted to the detriment of creditors of an insolvent company: everything depended on all the circumstances, including the nature of the breach of duty which gave rise to the claim against the directors. In another distribution case, *Re TMG Brokers Ltd (in liq.); Baker v Staines* [2021] EWHC 1006 (Ch), breach of the distribution rules amounted to breaches of CA 2006 ss.171, 172 and 174 duties so that a misfeasance application succeeded and s.1157 relief was refused as not available to misfeasant directors in respect of moneys that they had personally received. See also *Re MDA Investment Management Ltd* [2003] EWHC 2277 (Ch) and [2004] EWHC 42 (Ch); [2005] B.C.C. 783, where relief was refused to a director who had acted honestly but not reasonably (reasonableness being an issue to be determined on an objective basis); *PNC Telecom plc v Thomas (No.2)* [2007] EWHC 2157 (Ch); [2008] 2 B.C.L.C. 95. See also *Holland v Revenue and Customs, Re Paycheck Services 3 Ltd* [2010] UKSC 51; [2011] B.C.C. 1, where the Supreme Court ruled that the discretion conferred by s.212 empowers the court to reduce the amount that the defendant has to pay, but not to exonerate him altogether from liability. However, there is no similar limitation under the additional discretion conferred by CA 2006 s.1157, if the court finds that he has acted honestly and reasonably and ought fairly to be excused. A s.212 application was dismissed in *Re CSB 123 Ltd (in liq.); Reynolds v Stanbury* [2021] EWHC 2506 (Ch), but the court added that in any event it would under s.1157 have relieved the respondent from any liability (see at [583]–[590]).

The question whether a defendant should be granted relief under s.1157 is fact-sensitive and not suitable for summary determination: *Rawnsley v Weatherall Green & Smith North Ltd* [2010] B.C.C. 406; *Phillips v McGregor-Paterson* [2009] EWHC 2385 (Ch); [2010] 1 B.C.L.C. 72 and reiterated in *Burnden Holdings (UK) Ltd (in liq.) v Fielding* [2017] EWHC 2118 (Ch). In *Rawnsley* HHJ Behrens also expressed the view that it was "seriously arguable" that a liquidator was not within the ambit of s.1157. However, in *Re Powertrain Ltd* [2015] EWHC 3998 (Ch); [2016] B.C.C. 216 when the matter was more fully argued, Newey J concluded that a liquidator was an "officer" and accordingly entitled to relief.

A defendant who wishes to apply for relief under s.1157 should give notice of the intention to do so at the earliest opportunity to avoid adjournment and further evidence: *Cullen Investments Ltd v Brown* [2017] EWHC 2793 (Ch). The case also set out how applications under s.1157 should be approached and this was adopted in *Pantiles Investments Ltd (in liq.) v Winckler* [2019] EWHC 1298 (Ch); [2019] B.C.C. 1003.

Fraudulent trading

213—

GENERAL NOTE

Replace the note with:

The Companies Acts have for a long time contained provisions dealing with "fraudulent trading", making it both a criminal offence (CA 2006 s.993) and a ground for imposing personal liability upon those concerned (CA 1985 s.630, now replaced by the present section). Originally, both the criminal and the civil sanctions could be invoked only in a winding up, but the criminal provision has for some years applied without this limitation. For a useful statutory history of the civil provision, see Foxton [2018] J.B.L. 324, although Snowden J in *Bilta UK Ltd (in liq.) v NatWest Markets plc* [2020] EWHC 546 (Ch) at [191] could not agree with the author's criticism of *Banque Arabe Internationale d'Investissement* (above) as its reasoning had been endorsed by the Court of Appeal in *Bank of India* (above). At [175]–[192] Snowden J gave a useful summary of who may be liable as "outsiders" who are knowingly parties to the s.213(1) behaviour concerned and he reiterated that the section is not limited to those who have been involved in the management of the company whose business has been carried on with intent to defraud, but potentially extends to outsiders who simply deal with the company. (Note that the decision in *Bilta UK Ltd (in liq.) v NatWest Markets plc* was overturned by the Court of Appeal ([2021] EWCA Civ 680) and remitted to the High Court to be heard by another judge because of a long delay between the first-instance hearing and the judgment.)

As enacted, the fraudulent trading provision applied only in a liquidation, but SBBEA 2015 by s.117(1), (2), with effect from 1 October 2015, has extended its scope so as to apply also in an administration. This has been done, not by an amendment to s.213, but by inserting a new s.246ZA into IA 1986. As the wording of s.246ZA is virtually identical to that of s.213, the commentary which follows applies to both regimes.

The Cork Committee (Report, Ch.44) considered that the previous law in this area was inadequate to deal with irresponsible trading, mainly because the courts have always insisted on the very strict standards of pleading and proof which are invariably applied in cases of fraud. It is not enough, for "fraudulent trading", to show that the company continued to run up debts when the directors knew that it was insolvent; there has to be "actual dishonesty, involving real moral blame" (*Re Patrick and Lyon Ltd* [1933] Ch. 786). (See also *Aktieselskabet Dansk Skibsfinansiering v Brothers* [2001] 2 B.C.L.C. 324; and *Bernasconi v Nicholas Bennett & Co* [2000] B.C.C. 921.)

The Committee recommended that while this should continue to be the approach in criminal proceedings for fraudulent trading, civil liability to pay compensation could arise where loss was suffered as a result of "unreasonable" conduct, which they proposed should be termed "wrongful trading", and that for this purpose the more relaxed standard of proof appropriate to civil proceedings should apply. The former provision creating civil liability for fraudulent trading (CA 1985 s.630) could be subsumed into the new law of wrongful trading.

In the event, the legislators adopted the Committee's recommendations on wrongful trading in broad terms, but they did so by creating an *additional* new provision (s.214, below) and left the former law on fraudulent trading intact, with one or two minor amendments (the present section). There is, however, now less reason for liquidators to invoke it, since the concept of wrongful trading, with its less onerous standard of proof, is wide enough to include all cases of fraudulent trading perpetrated by directors, and for all practical purposes the consequences will be the same. However, since the decision in *Re Ralls Builders Ltd, Grant v Ralls* [2016] EWHC 243 (Ch); [2016] B.C.C. 293, although wrongful trading under s.214 may have been proved, a remedy under that provision may still not be available unless there has been an increase in the net deficiency so that a s.213 claim may still be apposite in appropriate circumstances (see the note to s.214) especially as s.213 continues to have a role to play where allegations of fraudulent trading are made against other parties, as is dramatically illustrated by the number of cases brought by the liquidators of BCCI: see *Re BCCI, Morris v State Bank of India* [1999] B.C.C. 943; further proceedings [2003] EWHC 1868 (Ch); [2003] B.C.C. 735; and *Morris v Bank of India* [2004] EWHC 528 (Ch); [2004] B.C.C. 404 (and, on appeal, [2005] EWCA Civ 693; [2005] B.C.C. 739); *Morris v Bank of America National Trust* [2000] B.C.C. 1076; *Re BCCI, Banque Arabe Internationale d'Investissement SA v Morris* [2002] B.C.C. 407. For a valuable account of the scope of "accessory liability" in relation to s.213, see Foxton [2018] J.B.L. 324, although Snowden J in *Bilta UK Ltd (in liq.) v NatWest Markets plc* [2020] EWHC 546 (Ch) at [191] could not agree with the author's criticism of *Banque Arabe Internationale d'Investissement* (above) as its reasoning had been endorsed by the Court of Appeal in *Bank of India* (above). At [175]–[192] Snowden J gave a useful summary of who may be liable as "outsiders" who are knowingly parties to the s.213(1) behaviour concerned and he reiterated that the section is not limited to those who have been involved in the management of the company whose business has been carried on with intent to defraud, but potentially extends to outsiders who simply deal with the company. Note also *Bilta (UK) Ltd v SVS Securities plc* [2022] EWHC 723 (Ch) which analysed the above cases and similarly gave a wide interpretation of who is caught by the section as knowingly parties to the fraudulent trading, which is not restricted to directors and others exercising management or control of the company's business.

In *Re Overnight Ltd* [2009] EWHC 601 (Ch); [2010] B.C.C. 787 it was ruled that for the purposes of the Statutes of Limitation a cause of action under s.213 arises when the winding-up order is made and not at any earlier date, because the appointment of a liquidator (and not a provisional liquidator) is necessary since only he is authorised to issue proceedings. It would follow that a cause of action under s.246ZA arises on the commencement of the administration.

The Supreme Court has confirmed that s.213 has extra-territorial effect, so that "any persons" resident outside the jurisdiction who are knowingly parties to the fraudulent trading may be liable, and the section is directed to recovering assets wherever they might be: *Jetivia SA v Bilta (UK) Ltd* [2015] UKSC 23; [2015] B.C.C. 343.

See also *Re Mavisat Ltd* [2018] B.C.C. 173, a procedural ruling of Registrar Barber. Here the court allowed the liquidator to re-amend particulars of claim. An appeal against this ruling was dismissed by Fancourt J in *Tradestar Ltd v Goldfarb* [2018] EWHC 3595 (Ch). During the course of the judgment Fancourt J observed that s.213 is not concerned with loss being caused to the company, but rather to its creditors as a body. An alleged fraud that causes a diminution in company assets and thereby poses a threat to creditors can fall within the scope of s.213.

At common law, the defence ex turpi causa non oritur actio prevents a person from benefiting from a fraud to which he was a party. It was held in *Jetivia SA v Bilta* (above) that this defence did not apply to a claim under s.213 where the company which (through its directors) was allegedly a party to the fraud was a victim rather than a wrongdoer. The scope of the illegality defence is the subject of some controversy and awaits further consideration by the Supreme Court: see S. Griffin (2015) 374 Co. L.N. 1.

The Fraud Act 2006, which came into force on 15 January 2007, increased the maximum penalty for contravention of CA 2006 s.993 from seven to ten years' imprisonment (s.10(1)). It also redefined various offences involving fraud or dishonesty, and in particular extended the scope of the fraudulent trading offence (CA 2006 s.993) so as to include being a party to the fraudulent carrying on of a business by a sole trader or other person who is outside the reach of s.993 (s.9).

In an action under s.213 or s.246ZA it is necessary for the liquidator to plead and prove dishonesty, which proof historically was seen as the Achilles heel of fraudulent reading and for which it was thought the provision would be surpassed by the introduction of wrongful trading (see above). In *Atkinson v Corcoran* [2011] EWHC 3484 (Ch) Bean J contrasted the provision with that in a claim to recover preferences under s.239, where it is sufficient for the liquidator to list the disputed payments and thereby impose the onus of justifying them on to the defendant directors. A modern version of dishonesty was applied in *Pantiles Investments Ltd (in liq.) v Winckler* [2019] EWHC 1298 (Ch);

[2019] B.C.C. 1003, that it was for the fact-finding tribunal to ascertain first the subjective, or actual, state of the defendant's knowledge or belief as to the facts, then to determine whether the conduct was honest or dishonest by reference to the objective standards of ordinary decent people: there was no requirement that the defendant had to appreciate that what she had done was dishonest by those standards (adopting the criminal test for dishonesty in *Ivey v Genting Casinos (UK) Ltd (trading as Crockfords Club)* [2017] UKSC 67; [2018] A.C. 391 as applied in civil proceedings in *Group Seven Ltd v Notable Services LLP* [2019] EWCA Civ 614). The modern test was also applied in *Re Vining Sparks UK Ltd* [2019] EWHC 2885 (Ch). The modern test was also used in *Re JD Group Ltd* [2022] EWHC 202 (Ch), where a director knew that the company was participating in a VAT (MTIC) fraud but he deliberately did not investigate, and the court employed the two-stage test that the liquidator had to demonstrate (a) the director's subjective state of knowledge, and then (b) that the director's conduct was dishonest applying the objective standards of ordinary decent people; the case includes discussion of the use of "blind-eye" knowledge.

The extension of the fraudulent and wrongful trading provisions so as to include administrations as from 1 October 2015 did not appear on the face of the legislation to apply to bodies other than companies, such as LLPs, insolvent partnerships and building societies. There was no clue to this poser in SBEEA 2015 itself, but eventually the Insolvency (Miscellaneous Amendments) Regulations 2017 (SI 2017/1119) from 8 December 2017 brought the regime for LLPs (by amendments to the Limited Liability Partnerships Regulations 2001 (SI 2001/1090)) and insolvent partnerships (by amendments to the Insolvent Partnerships Order 1994 (SI 1994/2421)) into line with the insolvency procedures that apply to companies. Fraudulent and wrongful trading were applied to building societies in administration by the Deregulation Act 2015, the Small Business, Enterprise and Employment Act 2015 and the Insolvency (Amendment) Act (Northern Ireland) 2016 (Consequential Amendments and Transitional Provisions) Regulations 2017 (SI 2017/400) as from 6 April 2017.

Wrongful trading

214—

General Note

Replace the note with:

For the background to this provision, see the note to s.213 above. (Ironically, some aspects of the test for wrongful trading have proved difficult to apply in practice, and particularly since the decision in *Re Ralls Builders Ltd, Grant v Ralls* [2016] EWHC 243 (Ch); [2016] B.C.C. 293 (described below) it has appeared that a positive result for the office-holder may be easier to achieve under fraudulent trading than wrongful trading, whereas the latter was introduced partly because of difficulties in proving wrongful trading!) As enacted, the wrongful trading provision applied only in a liquidation, but SBBEA by s.117(1), (2), with effect from 1 October 2015, has extended its scope so as to apply also in an administration. This has been done, not by an amendment to s.214, but by inserting a new s.246ZB into IA 1986. As the wording of s.246ZB corresponds closely to that of s.214, the commentary which follows applies to both regimes. For additional commentary on some minor points, see also the note to s.246ZB. Consequential amendments were made to s.214(2)(b) and (3), and s.214(6A) inserted, by SBEEA s.117(3) as from 1 October 2015.

On the question whether the new provision applies to bodies other than companies, such as insolvent partnerships and LLPs, see the note to s.213.

The section, according to the marginal note, is concerned with "wrongful trading"; but it is notable that the words "wrongful" and "trading" are not used in the text of the section. (The marginal note may not normally be used as an aid for the construction of the text: *Chandler v Director of Public Prosecutions* [1964] A.C. 763 (but some exceptions are noted in Halsbury, *Laws of England*, 5th edn, Vol.96, para.1113).) The section itself is singularly imprecise in defining just what conduct on the part of a director will bring him within its scope.

The Cork Committee (Report, para.1806) did put forward its own draft definition of "wrongful trading", the essential part of which read: "... at any time when the company is insolvent or unable to pay its debts as they fall due it incurs further debts or other liabilities to other persons without a reasonable prospect of meeting them in full". However, this definition was explicitly rejected by Parliament when an attempt was made to introduce it as an amendment to the Insolvency Bill 1985, and so it would be wrong to refer to it for guidance on the meaning of the present section. In particular, there may be wrongful trading under s.214 even though the company does not incur further debts: one example mentioned during the parliamentary debate was the case where a company allows its assets to be depleted, e.g. by the payment of excessive directors' fees. It was, presumably, a concern to ensure that this kind of conduct was caught that led the draftsman to omit the word "trading" from his formulation. In *Paton v Martin* [2016] SC Air 57 it was held that selling some of the company's main assets and paying the proceeds into the personal account of one of the directors was "trading" for the purposes of the section.

The Supreme Court in *BTI 2014 LLC v Sequana SA* [2022] UKSC 25 gave a brief discussion on the introduction of s.214, with reference to the Company Law Reform Steering Group's comments on the section after implementation. An argument that s.214 was incompatible with the common law rule on directors' duties to have regard to the interests of creditors of companies in (or approaching) insolvency (*West Mercia Safetywear v Dodd* (1988) 4 B.C.C. 30, now preserved by CA 2006 s.172(3): see the note to s.212) was dismissed by the Supreme Court. Lord Reed (obiter), after summarising (at [94]) several differences between the duty and s.214, stated (at [99]) that were it otherwise one would not have expected Parliament to enact s.172(3).

The amount of contribution to be ordered is left entirely to the court's discretion, and is not related by the terms of the Act either to any particular period of trading or to the loss suffered by the company or creditors. However, in *Re Produce Marketing Consortium Ltd* (1989) 5 B.C.C. 569 at 597, Knox J said:

> "In my judgment the jurisdiction under sec. 214 is primarily compensatory rather than penal. Prime facie the appropriate amount that a director is declared to be liable to contribute is the amount by which the company's assets can be discerned to have been depleted by the director's conduct which caused the discretion under sec. 214(1) to arise. However Parliament has indeed chosen very wide words of discretion and it would be undesirable to seek to spell out limits on that discretion... The fact that there was no fraudulent intent is not of itself a reason for fixing the amount at a nominal or low figure, for that would amount to frustrating what I discern as Parliament's intention in adding sec. 214 to sec. 213 in the Insolvency Act 1986, but I am not persuaded that it is right to ignore that fact totally".

In *Re Purpoint Ltd* [1991] B.C.C. 121 and *Re Kudos Business Solutions Ltd* [2011] EWHC 1436 (Ch), where the company's accounts were in disarray so that it was difficult to assess its net asset position at the relevant dates, the respondents were ordered to pay a sum equal to the aggregate of debts incurred after the date on which they ought to have concluded that insolvent liquidation was inevitable.

Although the section is silent on the question of causation, it must be shown that if the defendant had complied with his duties to the requisite standard the loss in question would not have resulted (as a matter of probability): *Lexi Holdings plc v Luqman* [2008] EWHC 1639 (Ch); [2008] 2 B.C.L.C. 725 at [40]. In that case the company's managing director, S, had defrauded it of some £60 million. The defendant non-executive directors had remained inactive and (inter alia) had not disclosed to the other directors their knowledge that S had a criminal record. They were held not liable for the loss because the likely result of disclosing this would have been nothing more than the resignation of the other directors. In *Re Ralls Builders Ltd, Grant v Ralls* [2016] EWHC 243 (Ch); [2016] B.C.C. 293 the company's financial situation had deteriorated to a position where the directors should have concluded that insolvent liquidation was inevitable, but they were excused from making a contribution under s.214 because it was held that the company had suffered no loss caused by their continuing to trade and that had not worsened the position of the creditors as a whole. The liquidators were later unsuccessful in an application for a contribution order against the directors in relation to the liquidators' increased costs by the company continuing to trade [2016] EWHC 1812 (Ch); [2016] B.C.C. 581. For critique see Moss (2017) 30 Insolv. Int. 49 and 88. This point as to a need for a causal connection between the amount of a contribution order under s.214 and the continuation of trading, albeit not mentioned in s.214 itself, was also adopted in *Brooks v Armstrong* [2016] EWHC 2893 (Ch); [2017] B.C.C. 99. A rare successful s.214 case occurred in *Biscoe v Milner* [2021] EWHC 763 (Ch) which differed from *Lexi Holdings plc v Luqman* (above, on the basis that the latter was not a s.214 application) and commented that for wrongful trading liability there was no requirement to show that the loss would not have been suffered if the person had complied with their duties; rather, it was necessary to show a causative link between the continuation of trading and an increase in the deficiency to creditors (applying *Ralls Builders*). An application to strike out parts of wrongful trading proceedings for want of detail in the pleadings as to the date when the alleged increased net deficiency (IND) for creditors began (several alternative dates were suggested) was dismissed in *Re BHS Group Ltd; Wright v Chappell* [2021] EWHC 3501 (Ch); [2022] B.C.C. 457 as the respondents knew exactly the case they had to meet; although the points of claim etc. did not provide sufficient information on what might be the relevant IND within the alternative date claims, that would be addressed by proposed expert evidence; the parties knew precisely what was being alleged on the issue of knowledge and the maximum sum sought as a compensatory payment under the section so that the pleadings were not "vague and unparticularised" and not struck out. The judge refused permission to appeal and one of the respondents applied for permission to appeal, which was granted on all four grounds of appeal advanced and the appeal allowed. Although the pleading of alternative dates was permissible, that was not so where a period of 12 months was "at large" as this would not be fair on a defendant who needed to be able to respond to the claims. The judge had asked himself the wrong questions and part of his reasoning and exercise of discretion were fundamentally flawed: *Re BHS Group Ltd; Chandler v Wright* [2022] EWHC 2205 (Ch).

In *Re Marini Ltd* [2003] EWHC 334 (Ch); [2004] B.C.C. 172, HHJ Seymour thought that the powers of the court under s.214 could not arise unless it was demonstrated that the company was, at the date of the actual liquidation, worse off than it would have been if it had ceased trading at the date when the director(s) ought to have realised that insolvent liquidation was inevitable. With respect, this view ignores the relevance of the causation factor. If this can be brought into account in order to reduce the director's liability (see *Re Brian D Pierson (Contractors) Ltd* [1999] B.C.C. 26), it must be just as relevant if the company receives an unexpected windfall which leaves it better off despite the continued wrongful trading.

For a highly critical article on the denial of contribution liability for wrongful trading where there has been no increase in the net deficiency as evinced in several of the above cases, see Moss (2017) 30 (4) Insol. Int. 49–53 and see van Zwieten (2020) 33 (1) Insolv. Int. 2–10 who thought the result principled but arguable on policy grounds.

In the light of the ruling of the Court of Appeal in *Morphitis v Bernasconi* [2002] EWCA Civ 289; [2003] Ch. 552; [2003] B.C.C. 540, it will not be appropriate to include a punitive element in the amount of contribution awarded (and it was repeated in *Brooks v Armstrong* that the award is compensatory rather than punitive): see the note to s.213(2), above.

Summary judgment on a s.214 claim was awarded in *Re Bangla Television Ltd* [2009] EWHC 1632 (Ch); [2010] B.C.C. 143. In *Re Nine Miles Down UK Ltd, Singla v Hedman* [2009] EWHC 3510 (Ch); [2010] B.C.C. 674, summary judgment was refused but a contribution order for wrongful trading was later made by Peter Smith J at the full trial (*Singla v Hedman (No.2)* [2010] EWHC 902 (Ch); [2010] B.C.C. 684).

Where a claim under s.214 is brought against a number of directors, liability is several and not joint and several, that is to say that the position of each individual has to be separately assessed, and payment by one does not discharge the liability of any other: *Re Continental Assurance Co of London plc* [2001] B.P.I.R. 733 at 846–848. However, it was also said in this case that the court may, in its discretion, order that the liability of any two or more directors should be joint and several for the whole or part of the sum which the court has assessed for contribution to the company's assets. In *Paton v Martin* [2016] SC Air 57 one of several directors who was not directly involved in the wrongful trading was held jointly and severally liable with the other directors because he was in breach of his more general responsibilities as a director.

In an appropriate case, an application may be made under s.214 against the foreign directors of a foreign company which is being wound up in this jurisdiction as an unregistered company: *Re Howard Holdings Ltd* [1998] B.C.C. 549.

On the importance of ensuring that the case is properly pleaded see *Johnson (Liquidator of Strobe 2 Ltd) v Arden* [2018] EWHC 1624 (Ch) where the court did not reject a suggestion that the company may be solvent at the relevant date chosen by the claimant as the date when the director knew or ought to have concluded that there was no reasonable prospect that the company would avoid going into insolvent liquidation or entering insolvent administration. However the liquidator's case failed because the evidence presented was not sufficiently focussed upon the requirements of s.214 and so the above comment may be regarded as obiter. The case is noted by Groves (2018) 11(5) C.R.I. 184. Note also the critique by Moss (2017) 30 (4) Insolv. Int. 49 of the way the courts have undermined the effectiveness of the wrong trading recovery mechanism.

There will plainly be cases in which claims will be made against the former director of a company both under this section and under some other provisions of the Act, e.g. s.212 (misfeasance) or s.239 (preference). In such a case there may be no injustice in making orders which impose cumulative liability on the defendant: *Re Purpoint Ltd* [1991] B.C.C. 121. However, in *Re DKG Contractors Ltd* [1990] B.C.C. 903 the court ruled that payments made under ss.212 and 239 should go to satisfy the liability under s.214, and that enforcement should be limited to what was necessary to pay the company's creditors and the costs and expenses of the liquidation. (See also *Re Idessa (UK) Ltd* [2011] EWHC 804 (Ch); *Re Kudos Business Solutions Ltd* [2011] EWHC 1436 (Ch).) On this and related questions, see the note to s.212(1).

It has been ruled that, as a matter of law, CA 2006 s.1157 [formerly CA 1985 s.727] (which empowers the court to relieve a director from liability for breach of duty where he has acted honestly and reasonably and ought fairly to be excused) is not available to a director in s.214 proceedings: *Re Produce Marketing Consortium Ltd; Halls v David* [1989] 1 W.L.R. 745; (1989) 5 B.C.C. 399.

A claim under s.214 (and, similarly, a claim under s.213) is a "claim for the recovery of a sum recoverable under any enactment" within s.9(1) of the Limitation Act 1980, and the appropriate limitation period is six years, reckoned from the date when the company went into insolvent liquidation or administration: *Re Farmizer (Products) Ltd, Moore v Gadd* [1997] B.C.C. 655. However even if proceedings are commenced within the limitation period, unreasonable delay in prosecuting the claim may justify a striking-out order (ibid.).

The provisions of ss.214–217 and 246ZB apply to the directors of building societies (Building Societies Act 1986 Sch.15 para.1(b)). In regard to limited liability partnerships, see the note preceding s.215 below.

PART VI

MISCELLANEOUS PROVISIONS APPLYING TO COMPANIES WHICH ARE INSOLVENT OR IN LIQUIDATION

Adjustment of prior transactions (administration and liquidation)

Preferences (England and Wales)

239—

GENERAL NOTE

Replace the note with:

The former law relating to "fraudulent preferences", as contained in CA 1985 s.615 and earlier Companies Acts, had long been thought unsatisfactory and, in particular, as the Cork Committee pointed out (Report, para.1244), the word "fraudulent" was both inaccurate and misleading. The Committee recommended that the term "fraudulent preference" should be replaced by "voidable preference". The draftsman, however, has rejected this suggestion (and the expression "undue preference", which is common in Australia) in favour of simply "preference", except in Scotland, for which "unfair preference" has been chosen. These differences over terminology are unimportant. The object of the change, at least in regard to England and Wales, is to remove the implication that an improper motive approaching fraud must be shown (and proved to the high standard which that charge requires), and to reflect the fact that under the redefined law it is not necessary for the liquidator even to show that the *dominant* intention of the company was to give the one creditor a preference. It need now only be established that the company was "influenced by a desire" to bring about a preference, and in some cases the burden of proof on this point is reversed (see s.239(5), (6)). The liquidator's burden may therefore be lighter than it would be if proceedings were brought under s.213 (or, arguably, s.214): *Atkinson v Corcoran* [2011] EWHC 3484 (Ch).

In the first reported case under the new section, *Re M C Bacon Ltd* [1990] B.C.C. 78, Millett J "emphatically protested" against the citation of cases decided under the old law: these, he said, could not be of any assistance in construing the language of the new statute, which had been so completely and deliberately changed.

Two new provisions inserted into IA 1986 by SBEEA 2015 have resolved certain points which were the subject of some uncertainty at common law. First, s.176ZB confirms that the proceeds of an action brought by an office-holder under s.238 or 239 fall into the insolvent estate and are not subject to any floating charge over the assets of the company. Secondly, s.246ZD(2) reverses the common-law position and empowers a liquidator or administrator to assign the right of action under these sections, and the fruits of any such action, to a third party. See the notes to those sections. On the question whether the costs of litigation under the section may be recouped from the general assets in the liquidation, see the general note to s.238.

In the context of the financial markets, no order may be made under s.239 in relation to a market contract to which a recognised investment exchange or clearing house is a party or which is entered into under its default rules, or a disposition of property in pursuance of such a market contract: see CA 1989 s.165. It is also disapplied in relation to payment and securities settlement systems by the Finality Regulations 1999 reg.17. (See the introductory notes at pp.1–3 above.) Note again the potential impact of s.427 of the POCA 2002.

For the corresponding provisions in bankruptcy, see s.340; and for the position in Scotland, see s.243.

A company may also seek redress at common law where a director has acted in breach of duty (by, e.g. advancing the interests of a particular creditor or making payments that differentiate between creditors, treating some more favourably) in circumstances analogous to a preference which do not fall within the scope of s.239: *GHLM Trading Ltd v Maroo* [2012] EWHC 61 (Ch); [2012] 2 B.C.L.C. 369. It is likely that the company will need to show (a) that it had suffered loss, (b) that the director had profited, and (c) that the transaction was not binding on the company (ibid.). Where the company is in administration or liquidation and s.239 does apply, directors who pay a preference to benefit themselves may also be liable for a breach of the duty to promote the success of the company under CA 2006 s.172 and so may accordingly be liable for misfeasance under s.212 (*Re De Weyer Ltd (in liq.); Kelmanson v Gallagher* [2022] EWHC 395 (Ch)). The position of whether the common law rule on directors' duties to have regard to the interests of creditors of companies in (or approaching) insolvency (*West Mercia Safetywear v Dodd* (1988) 4 B.C.C. 30, now preserved by CA 2006 s.172(3) was incompatible with s.239 was considered by the Supreme Court in *BTI 2014 LLC v Sequana SA* [2022] UKSC 25. Lord Reed concluded (obiter) that the duty and the section were not incompatible due to several differences between them (see [101]) and also not least in the light of s.241(4), which renders s.239 without prejudice to the availability of any other remedy (see (109)).

In *Re Parkside International Ltd* [2008] EWHC 3554 (Ch); [2010] B.C.C. 309 the insolvent company A and two other companies, B and C, were members of the same group. Shortly before A was put into administration B had assigned to C a debt owed to it by A. It was held that this was not a transaction "suffered" by A, being an act over which A had no control, and that this was so even though the three companies had common directors and, further, that although there may have been a desire to improve the position of the group as a whole, this was not the same as a desire to prefer one set of creditors over others.

Ingram (Liquidator of MSD Cash & Carry plc) v Singh [2018] EWHC 1325 (Ch); [2018] B.C.C. 886 contains a valuable review of the law on s.239 by HHJ Hodge QC in which the court also clarified the question of the limitation period for claims under s.239, which period depended upon how the claim was characterised.

In *Re Pappy Ltd* [2018] B.P.I.R. 1451 Bever DJ upheld an application under s.239 where a director had manipulated the director's loan account to prefer himself. A preference in fact had been established. The director who had thus been preferred was unable to rebut the presumption that he had been influenced by a desire to prefer.

On whether a claim under s.239 may be subject to an arbitration agreement (albeit in a cross-border context) see *Riverrock Securities Ltd v International Bank of St Petersburg* [2020] EWHC 2483 (Comm).

Power to assign certain causes of action

Power to assign

246ZD—

GENERAL NOTE

Replace the note with:

Section 246ZD was inserted by SBEEA 2015 s.118 with effect from 1 October 2015. It removes any doubt which may have existed at common law as to the power of office-holders to assign these statutory rights of action and their proceeds. The first reported case on the section, *Re Totalbrand Ltd; Cage Consultants v Iqbal* [2020] EWHC 2917 (Ch); [2021] B.C.C. 541, confirmed that an assignment of a relevant cause of action under the section does include assignment of the proceeds of the claim to the assignee. In the case a director and another argued that the claims under ss.213, 238 and 239 would result in any order against them being payable under the wording of those sections to the company for the benefit of creditors, but that as the company had been dissolved no such order could be made. Snowden J commented that s.246ZD(2) expressly refers to the proceeds of action being included in the assignment and that otherwise the power to assign a right of action in the section would not have any practical utility and the clear legislative purpose would be frustrated. On a creditor's standing to apply for an office-holder's assignment of a cause of action to be set aside, see *Re Edengate Homes (Butley Hall) Ltd (in liq.)* [2021] EWHC 2970 (Ch), where standing was denied as the applicant's interest in the outcome of the application was more intended to prevent claims against herself and her family, and thus was not aligned with the interests of the creditors as a whole. On the procedure for applications made outside the provisions referred to in s.246ZD(2), such as under ss.212 or 423, see the highly practical discussion in *Manolete Partners plc v Hayward & Barrett Holdings Ltd* [2021] EWHC 1481 (Ch); [2022] B.C.C. 159. That s.212 does not apply to assignments under s.246ZD was reiterated in *Re PGD Ltd; Manolete Partners plc v Hope* [2022] EWHC 1801 (Ch), where the court gave an interesting discussion about an attempted cap on an assigned claim, concluding that the court would not impose the cap where it would deprive an innocent assignee of its share of the proceeds even if other parties tainted with the wrongdoing might benefit. Note that s.246ZD does not apply to proceedings that commenced before 6 April 2017 in relation to bank or building society insolvency under Pt 2 of the Banking Act 2009, building society administration under Pt II of IA 1986, building society special administration under Pt 3 of the Banking Act 2009 or special administrations under the Investment Bank Special Administration Regulations 2011 (SI 2011/245) and winding up of a relevant collective investment scheme: see the Deregulation Act 2015, Small Business, Enterprise and Employment Act 2015 and the Insolvency (Amendment) Act (Northern Ireland) 2016 (Consequential Amendments and Transitional Provisions) Regulations 2017 (SI 2017/400) regs 1, 13, 16.

Section 246ZD(2) amended by CIGA 2020 s.2(1), Sch.3 paras 1, 16 as from 26 June 2020 subject to CIGA 2020 s.2(2), (3).

Decisions by creditors and contributories

Power to amend sections 246ZE and 246ZF

246ZG—

GENERAL NOTE TO SS.246ZE–246ZG

Replace the note with:

Sections 246ZE–246ZG were inserted by SBEEA 2015 s.122(1), (2) from 6 April 2017. Reference should also be made to Sch.8 para.8A and r.15.7.

These provisions introduce the "deemed consent procedure", which allows decisions which would ordinarily be made by the contributories or creditors at a meeting to be made without a physical meeting (or other equivalent procedure), simply by giving notice of the proposed decision and deeming consent to have been given unless a specified proportion (10% in value) of the contributories or creditors object within a specified time. For further details, see IR 2016 rr.15.7–15.11. The deemed consent procedure may not be used to make a decision on remuneration, or where its use is prohibited by the Act, the Rules or any other legislation, or court order (s.246ZF(1), (2)). It may be arguable whether the deemed consent procedure is available for creditors to consent to an administration pre-pack substantial disposal to connected persons as the Administration (Restrictions on Disposal etc. to Connected Persons) Regulations 2021 (SI 2021/427) reg.4(2) requires that the administrator has "sought a decision from the company's creditors". The above 10% in value proportion should not be confused with the "minimum number" of creditors/contributories who may requisition a creditors'/contributories' meeting under s.246ZE(3), (4), that number being 10% in value or number of the creditors or contributories or 10 creditors or contributories (s.246ZE(7)). It was noted in *Re Patisserie Holdings plc* [2021] EWHC 3205 (Ch); [2022] B.C.C. 401 that there was no detailed legislative indication as to how the 10% threshold stipulated in s.246ZE(7) is to be calculated, and that r.15.6(8) stated that the convenor must calculate the value of the creditor's claim by reference to r.15.31 (i.e. in that case, by reference to the amount of the claim as at the date of administration); where the convener adopted the 10% as measured by reference to the value of claim at the point of assessing whether the threshold was met, that was accepted as the correct approach. Deemed consent may not be used where actual consent is specifically required, e.g. under Sch.B1 paras 76(2)(b) and 78 for creditor consent to extension of administration (*Re Biomethane (Castle Easton) Ltd; Baker v Biomethane (Castle Easton) Ltd* [2019] EWHC 3298 (Ch); [2020] B.C.C. 111) and *quaere* whether reg.4(2) of the Administration (Restrictions on Disposal etc. to Connected Persons) Regulations 2021 (SI 2021/427) requiring an administrator to have "sought a decision from the company's creditors" before a pre-pack disposal to connected persons also disallows the deemed consent procedure. For comment on the deemed consent procedure, see Fitzgerald, Clench and Brown [2017] Recovery (Summer) 36, who engagingly refer to these confusing proportions as "single 10", "triple 10" and "hybrid 10"!

THE SECOND GROUP OF PARTS: INSOLVENCY OF INDIVIDUALS; BANKRUPTCY

Introductory note to the Second Group of Parts
Replace the note with:
Bankruptcy legislation in England can be traced back to 1542, and the system with which practitioners will be familiar was contained in BA 1914 (as amended in 1926 and 1976). This system was the product of the 1883 reforms pushed through by Gladstone and Joseph Chamberlain. For a superb historical review outlining the violent policy swings in the nineteenth century see Lester, *Victorian Insolvency* (1995). In view of the changed social conditions and altered political economy in the twentieth century it is not surprising that both the Blagden Committee (Cmnd.221) in 1957 and the Cork Committee (Cmnd.8558) in 1982 felt that major revision was long overdue. Part III of IA 1985 did put the law on a modern footing, although its changes were less radical than the Cork Committee had hoped for. IA 1986 ss.252–385 remodel the 1985 legislation mainly by fragmenting its more cumbersome provisions into several sections. Most of the provisions in the 1985 Act relating to bankruptcy never came into force. Cases under the 1914 Act still came before the courts for many years after 1986—see for example *Re Dent* [1994] 1 W.L.R. 956; *Re Dennis* [1996] Ch. 80, discussed by Tee in (1996) 55 C.L.J. 21; *Trustee of F C Jones v Jones* [1996] B.P.I.R. 644; *Re Ross* [1998] B.C.C. 29.

What were the most obvious reforms introduced by the 1985 Act and now found in the 1986 Act? The bankruptcy procedure was greatly simplified, with the abolition of the concept of the act of bankruptcy and the intermediate stage of the receiving order. An attempt was made wherever possible to harmonise bankruptcy procedures with those of company liquidations, although unlike many jurisdictions there is still a distinction between corporate and personal insolvency law. Another reform which is more symbolic than significant in practice was the abolition of the concept of reputed ownership in bankruptcy law (it did not operate on corporate insolvency). Other changes worthy of mention were the rules giving increased protection to the family home (see ss.336–338), the attempt to produce a viable alternative to bankruptcy via voluntary arrangements (ss.252–263), plus a host of minor measures designed to streamline and improve the effectiveness of bankruptcy procedures. The liberalising trend dating back to the Justice Report of 1975 and IA 1976 is again apparent, particularly with the provisions on discharge (ss.279 and 280). This trend has continued with EA 2002.

Criticisms can be made of the 1986 Act. It was heavily dependent on IR 1986. On the other hand it must be conceded that the 1914 Act was considerably supplemented by BR 1952. The drafting of the provisions of Pt III of the 1985 Act left much to be desired, and Muir Hunter QC, a leading commentator on bankruptcy law, predicted that this deficiency would lead to an increase in litigation. The drafting of the 1986 Act was much improved. In its 1994 Report entitled *Insolvency Law: An Agenda for Reform* Justice identified a number of weaknesses with the post-1986 bankruptcy regime. Concerns were expressed about the increasing use of bankruptcy to recover small debts and the considerable amount of litigation surrounding the use of statutory demands. Many of these problems could be traced back to the failure of government to implement the changes to the county court administration order procedure which were enacted in 1990.

Finally, it should be noted that ss.252–385 of IA 1986 are not the sole source of law on debt and personal insolvency. Parts XII and XIX of the Act also contain provisions that will be important in practice. Criminal bankruptcy (so far as concerns orders which are still in force: see the notes to ss.264 and 277) is dealt with by the Powers of the Criminal Courts Act 1973. The Deeds of Arrangement Act 1914 survived until repealed by DA 2015. Administration orders against judgment debtors remain governed by the County Courts Act 1984 (as amended). Indeed there are still provisions of the Debtors Act 1869 which may return to haunt debtors—see for example s.13 (offence to make a gift to defeat creditors). Thus in *Woodley v Woodley (No.2)* [1994] 1 W.L.R. 1167 a debtor (who subsequently became bankrupt on his own petition) was threatened with imprisonment by a judge under s.5 of the 1869 Act for wilfully refusing to pay a judgment debt where he had the means to do so prior to his bankruptcy. On appeal, the committal order was quashed by the Court of Appeal because there was a sufficient degree of doubt as to whether he was deliberately defying the law or had been confused as to his obligations. For a more recent case involving s.5 of the Debtors Act 1869 see *L v L* [1997] 2 F.L.R. 252. For the continued relevance of s.5 of the 1869 Act see *Prest v Prest* [2014] EWHC 3722 (Fam) which featured an application by a judgment creditor to have a judgment debtor committed for contempt. For later appeal proceedings see *Prest v Prest* [2015] EWCA Civ 714. For a rare modern example of litigation under the Debtors Act 1869 s.4 see *Hussain v Vaswani* [2020] EWCA Civ 1216 in which the Court of Appeal refused to apply s.4 and confirmed a prison sentence for failing to comply with undertakings given to the court (essentially imprisonment for contempt rather than for failure to pay the debt). For a case where the court refused to commit a debtor to prison under s.5 of the 1869 Act see *Rogan v Rogan* [2021] EWHC 2587 (Fam). The point here was that the debtor was already bankrupt and was not in control of funds so as to make a required payment. Note also Insolvent Debtors Relief Act 1729 as discussed in *Aectra Refining v Exmar* [1994] 1 W.L.R. 1634.

The personal insolvency provisions in the 1986 legislation have been amended considerably by IA 2000 and EA 2002.

The law on personal insolvency in Scotland (or sequestration, as it is termed) was formerly found in the Bankruptcy (Scotland) Act 1985 (as amended by the Bankruptcy (Scotland) Act 1993) and associated delegated legislation. The Scottish Law Commission considered the possibility of consolidating the 1985 Act. A Consultation Paper to that effect was published in August 2011. The personal insolvency reforms in EA 2002 were not made applicable to Scotland—for reform in Scotland see McKenzie Skene [2004] J.B.L. 171 and our Introduction. In November 2012 the Scottish government announced that it was planning significant reforms in personal insolvency law as applied in its jurisdiction. These reforms would include measures designed to take debtor induced bankruptcies out of the court system in Scotland. Scotland also has a procedure called the protected trust deed—the rules here were reconstituted by the Protected Trust Deeds (Scotland) Regulations 2013 (SSI 2013/318) which revoked the former 2008 rules. In addition to specific insolvency measures in Scotland readers should note related legislation such as the Home Owner and Debtor Protection (Scotland) Act 2010 (asp 6) which constrained the rights of secured creditors wishing to take action against the debtor's family home by introducing safeguards for debtors. The above legislative framework (including the 1985 Act) has been reconsolidated by the Bankruptcy (Scotland) Act 2016. The 2016 Act was modified by the Coronavirus (Scotland) (No. 2) Act 2020 as from 27 May 2020 to deal with the COVID pandemic crisis (e.g. the definition of a "qualifying creditor" who may petition for an order of sequestration was temporarily increased from a minimum debt of £3,000 to £10,000; that figure is reduced to a minimum of £5,000 by the Coronavirus (Recovery and Reform) (Scotland) Act 2022 as from 1 October 2022 and the 2022 Act makes a number of other modifications to Scottish personal insolvency law). An attempt to challenge various aspects of the Scottish system of sequestration as prescribed by legislation also came to nothing in the Sheriff Court at Airdrie in *Mond v Booth* [2019] Scot SC 64.

Comparable provisions dealing with personal insolvency in Northern Ireland are now contained in the Insolvency (Northern Ireland) Order 1989 (SI 1989/2405) (NI 19) arts 226–345 in particular. The EA 2002 reforms were introduced into the Province by SI 2005/1455 (NI 10). See note to s.441. Latest reforms to personal insolvency law in Ireland are explained by Bennett in [2014] 27 Insolv. Int. 24.

For a general review of the subject see Milman, *Personal Insolvency Law, Regulation and Policy* (2005). For a perceptive analysis of the live issues and reform options in consumer bankruptcy law in Britain (covering both English and Scots law) see McKenzie Skene and Walters (2006) 80 Am. Banky Law Jo. 477. Further illuminating insights into the broad policy issues raised by personal insolvency can be found in Ramsay (2012) 75 M.L.R. 212 and Spooner [2013] Euro Rev. of Priv. Law 747. Note also Milman [2015] 28 Insolv. Int. 37 and [2017] J.B.L. 617. Recent developments are reviewed by Milman [2021] 34 Insolv. Int. 17.

In January 2014 R3 produced an impressive overview on personal insolvency regimes entitled "The Personal Insolvency Landscape". This report represents an exemplary illustration of "joined-up" thinking in this field in which the competing interests of creditors and debtors are finely balanced.

We should also note the breathing space debt moratorium scheme which HM Treasury announced would come into effect in 2021. Full details of this scheme are to be found in *Consultation Outcome: Breathing Space Scheme – Consultation on a Policy Proposal* (HM Treasury, 19 June 2019). See also MPAS letter to HM Treasury published 26 September 2019 for further information. For comment see Leslie [2020] 13 C.R.I. 177. The scheme is in force from 4 May 2021—see the Debt Respite Scheme (Breathing Space Moratorium and Mental Health Crisis Moratorium) (England and Wales) Regulations 2020 (SI 2020/1311). A debtor does not need to be insolvent to access this scheme, which provides a 60-day moratorium in non-mental health crisis cases. It is designed to assist distressed debtors who may be struggling with unsustainable debt. In the first seven months of operation some 40,503 standard applications for a breathing space were recorded with an additional 624 mental health crisis cases listed. The 2020 Regulations are reproduced in Vol.2 and supportive amendments are provided from 4 May 2021 by the Civil Proceedings and Gender Recognition Application Fees (Amendment) Order 2021 (SI 2021/462) (amending the Civil Proceedings Fees Order 2008 (SI 2008/1053)) and the Magistrates' Courts (Amendment) Rules 2021 (SI 2021/459) (amending the Magistrates' Courts Rules 1981 (SI 1981/552)). Guidance on the scheme was updated on 6 August 2021 and is available for creditors at *https://www.gov.uk/government/publications/debt-respite-scheme-breathing-space-guidance/debt-respite-scheme-breathing-space-guidance-for-creditors* and for money advisers at *https://www.gov.uk/government/publications/debt-respite-scheme-breathing-space-guidance/debt-respite-scheme-breathing-space-guidance-for-money-advisers*. For an early case on costs under the new regime see *Axnoller Events Ltd v Brake* [2021] EWHC 1500 (Ch) with further proceedings at [2021] EWHC 2308 (Ch) in which the court refused an application by creditors to cancel a mental health crisis moratorium, where the party who had obtained the moratorium had costs orders awarded against it in the ongoing litigation, as any prejudice suffered by the applicant arose not from the moratorium itself but from the costs rules which applied to all litigation parties.

The first major review of personal insolvency in England and Wales for 40 years since the Cork Report of 1982 commenced on 5 July 2022 with a *Call for evidence: Review of the personal insolvency framework* seeking stakeholders' views and evidence on the personal insolvency framework and whether it serves the needs of debtors and creditors in the 21st century. The *Call for evidence* seeks comments on:

- The purpose of the framework, what should be the objectives for a modern insolvency framework and where should the balance fall in providing debtors with a fresh start or ensuring returns to creditors?

- Fees and funding: how should insolvency solutions be paid for, what are the wider consequential costs of insolvency and is the current burden of costs apportioned fairly?

- The current procedures within the personal insolvency framework (bankruptcy, individual voluntary arrangements (IVAs), debt relief orders (DROs)) and how they are working: it asks whether there are underlying areas of concern about the framework, what motivates debtors to seek one particular insolvency solution over another, are there barriers to entry to certain insolvency solutions and whether the framework is sufficiently flexible and does it provide the right sort of insolvency solutions for the modern day?

(Excluded from the review are statutory debt repayment plans (SDRPs), the breathing space scheme, county court administration orders and debt management plans (DMPs).) Copies of *Call for evidence: Review of the personal insolvency framework* is available at *https://www.gov.uk/government/consultations/call-for-evidence-review-of-the-personal-insolvency-framework/call-for-evidence-review-of-the-personal-insolvency-framework* and there is a dedicated online response document at *https://www.smartsurvey.co.uk/s/RKMSB1/*, although comments may be sent by email to PIR.CFE@insolvency.gov.uk. Comments are sought by 23 October 2022.

Part VIII

Individual Voluntary Arrangements

Creditors' decisions

Consideration of debtor's proposal by creditors

257—

General Note

S.257(2), (2A), (2B), (3)
Replace the note with:
These subsections identify which creditors are to participate in the decision—this will depend on whether the

debtor is an undischarged bankrupt or not. An FCA representative may attend in an appropriate case—FSMA 2000 s.357(3). On the importance of compliance with s.257(2) see *Namulas Pension Trustees Ltd v Mouzakis* [2011] B.P.I.R. 1724.

The status of creditors whose claim arises from personal guarantees was considered in *Ulster Bank Ltd v Taggart* [2022] NICh 8, where the major creditor (the bank) questioned the validity of the personal guarantees which were the basis of other creditors' claims. Those creditors supported the IVA which the bank wished to reject. Quoting from *Paget's Law of Banking*, 2014 edition the Judge considered that it was crucial for the underlying obligation to exist and the formalities to have been adhered to in order for the personal guarantee to be valid and counted in the decision.

There is no obligation to provide a creditor with a translation of the notice of meeting in another language: *Karapetian v Duffy* [2022] EWHC 1053 (Ch).

For further information, reference should be made to IR 2016 r.8.22 and Pt 15.

Part IX

Bankruptcy

Chapter I

The Court: Bankruptcy Petitions and Bankruptcy Orders

Preliminary

Who may present a bankruptcy petition

264—

General Note
Replace the note with:

This section describes the persons who may present a bankruptcy petition and authorises the court to make an order on such a petition. In *Mahmood v Penrose* [2005] B.P.I.R. 170 a petitioner in whose favour a costs award had been made jointly was held to have locus standi for the purposes of s.264(1)(a). Section 264(1)(ba) and (bb) were introduced to cater for the advent of EC Council Regulation 1346/2000 with effect from 31 May 2002 and were amended by the Insolvency Amendment (EU 2015/848) Regulations 2017 (SI 2017/702) regs 1, 2(1), Sch. paras 1, 19 in relation to proceedings opened on or after 26 June 2017 (see reg.3) when the Recast EU Regulation 2015/848 came into force. Section 264(1)(ba), (bb) omitted by the Insolvency (Amendment) (EU Exit) Regulations 2019 (SI 2019/146) reg.1(3), Sch. paras 16, 32 as from IP completion day (11pm on 31 December 2020) subject to transitional and saving provisions in reg.4 (in light of Brexit). See also Insolvency Proceedings (Fees) Amendment Order 2005 (SI 2005/544). For the "Official Petitioner" in s.264(1)(d) see s.402. The FCA and the PRA may petition in an appropriate case—for the position here see s.372 of FSMA 2000. See Peat (2006) 22 I.L. & P. 7. It may also be heard on a s.264 petition presented by any other party—see FSMA 2000 s.374(2). Creditors with separate debts can join together and present a single bankruptcy petition: *Re Allen (Re a Debtor 367 of 1992)* [1998] B.P.I.R. 319. A creditor with a non-provable bankruptcy debt is entitled to present a petition, though the court is unlikely to accede to it unless there are exceptional circumstances—*Russell v Russell* [1998] B.P.I.R. 259. Such exceptional circumstances were present in *Wheatley v Wheatley* [1999] B.P.I.R. 431. On the general issue of petitions and non-provable debts see *Levy v Legal Services Commission* [2000] B.P.I.R. 1065.

On the jurisdiction of the English courts to hear default petitions by IVA supervisors see *Loy v O'Sullivan* [2010] EWHC 3583 (Ch); [2011] B.P.I.R. 181. A default petition can be presented under s.264(1)(c) even though the specified duration for the IVA has expired—*Harris v Gross* [2001] B.P.I.R. 586. In *Clarke v Birkin* [2006] EWHC 340 (Ch); [2006] B.P.I.R. 632 Evans-Lombe J upheld a bankruptcy ruling made by a Registrar on a petition by IVA-participating creditors for the bankruptcy of the applicant pursuant to s.264(1)(c) of the IA 1986 on the grounds that the debtor had failed to comply with his obligations under the arrangement. The debtor did not deny that he had been in default in making payments, but he argued that it was not a material default. Evans-Lombe J held that as the Registrar had properly considered all relevant factors in this case when making the bankruptcy order there were no grounds for interfering with that order which was a proper exercise of his discretion. Indeed there was a term in the IVA making it clear that failure to pay instalments on time could not be remedied by subsequent payment. As to who should be appointed trustee on such a petition see *Landsman v de Concilio* [2005] EWHC 267 (Ch); [2005] B.P.I.R. 829. For a case where a bankruptcy order was made on a petition under s.264(1)(c) as a result of a failed IVA see *Varden Nuttall Ltd v Baker* [2016] EWHC 3858 (Ch) (Proudman J).

Chief Registrar Baister accepted in *Re Akaydin* [2013] B.P.I.R. 539 that for a debtor to petition within the English jurisdiction all that needed to be shown was ordinary residence at some time within the three years immediately preceding the petition.

Note prospective amendment: s.264(1)(d) and the word "or" immediately preceding it are to be repealed by CJA 1988 s.170(2) and Sch.16 as from a day to be appointed. (The power to make criminal bankruptcy orders has been abolished by s.101 of this Act, with effect from 3 April 1989 (see SI 1989/264 (C. 8)), but this and other provisions of IA 1986 and IR 2016 remain in force for the time being to govern orders already existing: see further the note to s.277.) In a paper entitled *The Fraud Landscape* (January 2015) the professional association R3 called for the return of criminal bankruptcy orders. This call did not attract a legislative response.

In the future, once s.115 of the Tribunals, Courts and Enforcement Act 2007 is commenced, the right of an unsecured creditor with a qualifying debt to petition will be restricted if the debtor has entered a debt repayment scheme under the 2007 Act. In such circumstances the creditor cannot petition for bankruptcy during the currency of such a scheme.

Note amendment made to s.264(1) involving the omission of para.(b) by ERRA 2013 Sch.19 para.6.

The fee for a creditor's petition is now £302 (see the Civil Proceedings Fees Order 2008 (SI 2008/1053) Sch.1 fee 3.1(b) as amended by the Court Fees (Miscellaneous Amendments) Order 2021 (SI 2021/985 (L.14)) art.6(1), (21)), with a debtor's adjudication fee costing £130: see the Insolvency Proceedings Fees Order 2016 (SI 2016/692). The relevant deposits for petitions presented under s.264(1) are £990 for petitions presented under para.(a), (c) and (d) (see the Insolvency Proceedings (Fees) Order 2016 (SI 2016/692); as from 1 November 2022 the fee is increased to £1,500 by the Insolvency Proceedings (Fees) (Amendment) Order 2022 (SI 2022/929) arts 1, 2(a)). The official receiver's administration fee is £2,775 for creditor petitions and £1,990 for debtor adjudications. Bankruptcy petitions (unlike winding up petitions) do not have to be advertised. See generally on the advertisement and gazetting of bankruptcy proceedings *Smeaton v Equifax plc* [2013] EWCA Civ 108.

Creditor's petition

Grounds of creditor's petition

267—

S.267(1), (2)

Replace the note with:

These provisions explain what debts can be used as the basis of a creditor's petition. Basically, the debt must be undisputed and for a liquidated sum in excess of the bankruptcy level which was surprisingly raised from £750 to £5,000 on 1 October 2015 (see note below to s.267(4)). In *Coulter v Chief of Dorset Police* [2004] EWCA Civ 1259; [2005] B.P.I.R. 62 the Court of Appeal reiterated that for the purposes of s.267 a petitioner must be a creditor who must have a debt which is payable immediately or at some future time. An unliquidated claim cannot provide the basis for a petition—*Hope v Premierpace (Europe) Ltd* [1999] B.P.I.R. 695 (considered and applied in *Dusoruth v Orca Finance UK Ltd* [2022] EWHC 2346 (Ch) where certain debts were found not to be liquidated sums, but the court still declined to exercise its discretion under s.282 to annul the bankruptcy order). On whether a debt is unliquidated or disputed see *TSB v Platts (No.2)* [1998] B.P.I.R. 284. In *Dubai Aluminium Co Ltd v Salaam* [2007] B.P.I.R. 690 Registrar Simmonds held that the reference to "debt" in s.267 must be taken to mean unsecured debt. Here it was held that where the debtor had paid the debt cited in the petition it would be wrong to allow that petition to be amended to include some other debt. The proper approach in such cases was to present a new statutory demand. The debtor must appear to be unable to pay or have no reasonable prospect of paying this debt. If an application is pending to set aside the statutory demand for payment of this debt, it falls outside the category of qualifying debts. For what constitutes an outstanding set-aside application see *Ariyo v Sovereign Leasing* [1998] B.P.I.R. 177. A statute-barred debt cannot form the basis for a statutory demand: *Jelly v All Type Roofing* [1997] B.C.C. 465; *Bruton v Inland Revenue Commissioners* [2000] B.P.I.R. 946. Compare *Times Newspapers Ltd v Chohan* [2001] B.P.I.R. 943; *Global Finance Recoveries Ltd v Jones* [2000] B.P.I.R. 1029; and *West Bromwich Building Society v Crammer* [2002] EWHC 2618 (Ch); [2003] B.P.I.R. 783. Note also *Phillips & Co v Bath Housing* [2012] EWCA Civ 1591 for a consideration of limitation issues in a non-bankruptcy case but which contains a discussion of some of the bankruptcy authorities. Note *Mittal v RP Capital Explorer Master Fund* [2014] B.P.I.R. 1537 where Deputy Registrar Briggs found that the debt was statute-barred and accordingly set aside the statutory demand.

In *Islandsbanki HF v Stanford* [2019] EWHC 595 (Ch); [2019] B.P.I.R. 876 ICC Judge Jones considered the position with regard to change of carriage/substitution of petitioner. On change of carriage see the discussion in *Hood v JD Classics Ltd* [2020] EWHC 3232 (Ch).

On the difference between a petition debt and a bankruptcy debt see the observations of Master Kelly in *ORNI v Gallagher* [2013] NIMaster 12 at [13].

In *Howell v Lerwick Commercial Mortgage Corp* [2015] EWHC 1177 (Ch); [2015] B.P.I.R. 821 Nugee J sought to clarify what was meant by a petitionable debt for the purposes of s.267(2)(c). It seems that a petition can be presented where there is a counterclaim that might reduce the debt balance to below the minimum debt—but in such a case the petition is likely to fail.

In *Regis Direct Ltd v Hakeem* [2012] EWHC 4328 (Ch) Norris J upheld a bankruptcy order notwithstanding the fact that the petition had been inadvertently presented whilst there was an extant set aside application in respect of the statutory demand. This set aside application was in fact dismissed some three days after the bankruptcy order was made; in those circumstances there was no point in setting aside the bankruptcy order. There was no injustice to the debtor. On the effect of breach of s.267(2)(d) see *Webster v Ashcroft* [2019] EWHC 2174 (Ch); [2019] B.P.I.R. 1607 where HHJ Matthews followed *Regis* (above). The retrospective issue was also covered in a very pragmatic judgment.

Where the petitioner has mixed motives in presenting the petition, that fact may not necessarily be fatal to the petition—see *Ridsdale v Bowles* [2015] B.P.I.R. 1275.

For full consideration of the requirements that must be established for the tort of malicious presentation of a bankruptcy petition see *Jacob v Vockrodt* [2007] EWHC 2403 (QB); [2007] B.P.I.R. 1568.

See also *Rio Properties Inc v Al-Midani* [2003] B.P.I.R. 128 where the court held that a foreign gaming debt which had apparently been settled via an English law compromise could form the basis of a bankruptcy petition.

See *Pace Europe Ltd v Dunham* [2012] B.P.I.R. 836 on the enforceability of foreign judgments via statutory demands in bankruptcy. Here HHJ Purle QC provides a careful analysis of the significance of the principles laid down in *Lewis v Eliades* [2003] EWCA Civ 1758. A novel point arose before District Judge Musgrave in *Sun Legend Investments Ltd v Jade Yuk Kuen Ho* [2013] B.P.I.R. 533. Here the point at issue was whether a statutory demand could be presented in respect of a foreign judgment debt. The creditor was not as such seeking to enforce the foreign judgment debt, but was using it as evidence of an inability to pay debts. The court held that the statutory demand procedure could be used.

In *Promontoria (Chestnut) Ltd v Bell* [2019] EWHC 1581 (Ch); [2019] B.P.I.R. 1241 Zacaroli J reviewed the position with regard to secured debt.

In *Klamer v Kyriakides and Braier (a firm)* [2005] B.P.I.R. 1142 Mr Registrar Simmonds held that a solicitor's bill that had not been assessed was not a liquidated debt capable of forming the basis of a statutory demand/bankruptcy petition for the purposes of s.267(2)(b) of the IA 1986. In *Truex v Toll* [2009] EWHC 396 (Ch); [2009] B.P.I.R. 692 Proudman J ruled that an untaxed solicitor's bill was not a liquidated debt for the purposes of s.267. Here it could not be said that the client had admitted liability to pay the invoice because the alleged admission was not unequivocal and was not supported by consideration. The courts have reiterated that an unassessed solicitors' bill is not a liquidated sum—*Wallace LLP v Yates* [2010] B.P.I.R. 1041. It will only become a liquidated sum if the client has accepted it or otherwise is estopped from challenging it—see *Moseley v Else Solicitors LLP* [2010] B.P.I.R. 1192. An estoppel argument failed in *Wallace LLP v Yates* (above). *Truex* was considered in the Northern Irish case of *Moore and Grimley v Williamson* [2011] NICh 20. Deputy Registrar Schaffer gave further consideration to the position where solicitors use the bankruptcy procedure to recover fees in *Orrick, Herrington and Sutcliffe (Europe) LLP v Frohlich* [2012] B.P.I.R. 169. The amount due to the solicitors must be a liquidated sum at the date of the statutory demand—the fact that it becomes liquidated by the date of the petition does not prevent the bankruptcy procedure from being defective.

As to what is a liquidated sum see the decision of HHJ Klein in *Blavo v Law Society* [2017] EWHC 561 (Ch); [2017] B.P.I.R. 909 (intervention costs not viewed as liquidated sum). In so deciding, the court refused to follow *Pyke v Law Society* [2006] EWHC 3489 (Ch). *Blavo* (above) was overturned on appeal—[2018] EWCA Civ 2250. The decision of the Court of Appeal appears to rely heavily upon policy considerations with regard to the treatment of intervention costs and on the technicalities of intervention. The Court of Appeal held that intervention costs could be regarded as a pre-ascertained liability and could therefore be for a liquidated sum within the meaning of s.267. Therefore, the statutory demands should not have been set aside.

In *Wave Lending Ltd v Parmar* [2017] EWHC 681 (Ch) the High Court held that the amount featured in the petition was not for a liquidated sum. The court considered the interplay between ss.267 and 269 in that regard. Therefore, the bankruptcy order made on the back of that petition had to be quashed. The case was remitted to the county court for further consideration. In *Sandelson v Mulville* [2019] EWHC 1620 (Ch); [2019] B.P.I.R. 1253 ICC Chief Judge Briggs found that a payment promised under a settlement was unconditional and therefore constituted a liquidated sum. Accordingly, a strike out of a bankruptcy petition was refused. An appeal against this decision was dismissed by Roth J in *Mulville v Sandelson* [2019] EWHC 3287 (Ch).

A sum due under an interim payments order made under CPR r.25.6 is a "debt" for these purposes: *Maxwell v Bishopsgate Investment Management Ltd* [1993] T.L.R. 67. In so deciding Chadwick J noted that the abolition of acts of bankruptcy had produced this change in the law—a final judgment was not necessary under the new bankruptcy code to justify a statutory demand. A taxed costs order can found a statutory demand—*Galloppa v Galloppa* [1999] B.P.I.R. 352. A debt arising under a regulated hire purchase agreement can found the basis for a statutory demand:

Mills v Grove Securities Ltd [1997] B.P.I.R. 243. A joint debt owed by a partner also falls within s.267(1) according to *Schooler v Customs and Excise Commissioners* [1996] B.P.I.R. 207. Non-provable bankruptcy debts can provide the basis for a petition—*Levy v Legal Services Commission* [2000] B.P.I.R. 1065. On the status of unpaid community charge see *Re Wood* [1994] 1 C.L. 257 (1993, Tamworth County Court). The debt can be a sum due in a foreign currency according to Morritt J in *Re a Debtor (51/SD/1991)* [1992] 1 W.L.R. 1294. In *McGuinness v Norwich & Peterborough Building Society* [2011] EWCA Civ 1286; [2012] B.P.I.R. 145 (upholding the earlier ruling of Briggs J) the Court of Appeal held on the wording of the guarantee in question the guarantor could be regarded as a principal debtor—that liability could therefore be characterised as a liquidated sum for the purposes of s.267. See also *Sofaer v Anglo Irish Asset Finance plc* [2011] EWHC 1480 (Ch); [2011] B.P.I.R. 1736 where Lewison J came to a similar conclusion. The wording of guarantees appears to be evolving to improve their enforceability and to enable the creditor to pursue the guarantor without first seeking to recover from the principal borrower. An argument that a guarantee liability was not for a liquidated sum was rejected by Chief Registrar Baister in *Dunbar Assets plc v Fowler* [2013] B.P.I.R. 46. On construction of this particular guarantee a conditional payment obligation arose, rather than generating a claim in damages. In *Francis v Solomon Taylor & Shaw* [2013] EWHC 9 (Ch) the High Court ruled that, under the terms of the guarantee under review in that case, the liability of the guarantor was for a liquidated sum within the meaning of s.267. Note *Martin v McLaren (Construction) Ltd* [2019] EWHC 2059 (Ch); [2019] B.P.I.R. 1506. Here ICC Judge Barber considered the nature of liability under a particular form of guarantee and concluded that it did not create an immediately payable debt as no demand had been made under the guarantee. A set aside was therefore granted. In *Davies v Revelan Estates (Wigston) Ltd* [2019] B.P.I.R. 1102 the court had to consider the nature of the liability arising under a guarantee. HHJ David Cooke found that the guarantee in question generated only a liability for an unliquidated sum.

In *Hurley v Darjan Estate Co plc* [2012] EWHC 189 (Ch); [2012] 1 W.L.R. 1782; [2012] B.P.I.R. 1021 sums in rent due under a lease that was defective in some respects were held to constitute contingent debts and liquidated sums.

Presumably the rule in *Re McGreavy* [1950] Ch. 269, that an unpaid rates demand is a "debt" for the purposes of a bankruptcy petition, is preserved by s.267. For confirmation that unpaid council tax arrears constitute a debt for the purposes of s.267 even if no liability order has been made see *Bolsover DC v Ashfield Nominees Ltd* [2010] EWCA Civ 1129; [2011] B.P.I.R. 7. For discussion of the position with regard to unpaid community charges see *Preston BC v Riley* [1999] B.P.I.R. 284 (an authority on county court administration orders).

The refusal of the courts to allow bankruptcy proceedings to be used to unpick tax assessments was again to the fore in *Flett v Revenue and Customs Commissioners* [2010] EWHC 2662 (Ch); [2010] B.P.I.R. 1075.

A council tax liability order is a "debt" for the purposes of s.267—see Peter Smith J in *Smolen v Tower Hamlets LBC* [2007] B.P.I.R. 448. A reduction in the amount of liability (provided the reduction does not take the liability to a sum under £750) does not affect that position. In *Yang v Official Receiver* [2013] EWHC 3577 (Ch); [2014] B.P.I.R. 826 it was confirmed by HHJ Hodge QC that a liability order made in respect of an alleged unpaid council tax bill was a liability for s.267 purposes, even if it was subsequently successfully challenged. For an example of a local council seeking to enforce a liability order via bankruptcy proceedings see *Okon v London Borough of Lewisham* [2016] EWHC 864 (Ch); [2016] B.P.I.R. 958. Here the proceedings were adjourned conditionally pending clarification of issues relating to the underlying liability order. The court gave guidance on the approach to be adopted by the parties where an appeal to the Valuation Tribunal challenging the liability as assessed was an option. In *Tower Hamlets LBC v Naris* [2019] EWHC 886 (Ch); [2019] B.P.I.R. 961 Chief ICC Judge Briggs confirmed that liability order give rise to a debt.

A statutory demand can be issued in respect of a consumer credit debt notwithstanding the provisions of s.141 of the Consumer Credit Act 1974—*Omokwe v HFC Bank Ltd* [2007] B.P.I.R. 1157. In *Brooker v Advanced Industrial Technology* [2019] EWHC 3160 (Ch) the court held that a bankruptcy petition falls within the Consumer Credit Act 1974 as an enforcement action.

A Tomlin order embodying a compromise can found a debt for these purposes. In *CFL Finance Ltd v Bass* [2019] EWHC 1839 (Ch); [2019] B.P.I.R. 1327 it was decided that such a debt could not be undermined on the basis that it was said to be unenforceable under the Consumer Credit Act 1974 or was a penalty.

See also *Jones v Sky Wheels Group Ltd* [2020] EWHC 1112 (Ch).

For guidance on preparing the petition see *Practice Direction: Insolvency Proceedings* [2020] B.C.C. 698 (see App.IV).

The criteria in s.267(2)(a) and (b) were *not* satisfied in *Dean & Dean v Angel Airlines SA* [2009] EWHC 447 (Ch) [2009] B.P.I.R. 409.

For the scope of s.267(2)(d) see *Ahmad v Commissioners of Inland Revenue* [2004] EWHC 2292 (Ch); [2005]

B.P.I.R. 541. Section 267(2)(d) must, in the opinion of Mummery J, be read as being subject to s.270: see *Re a Debtor (No.22 of 1993)* [1994] 1 W.L.R. 46 (sometimes cited as *Focus Insurance v A Debtor*).

See also *McLinden v Lu* [2021] EWHC 3171 (Ch).

Proceedings on creditor's petition

271—

GENERAL NOTE

S.271(3)
Replace the note with:
This provision states that the court may dismiss the petition if the debtor is able to meet his debts, or has made a proposal to the creditor to secure or compound the debt and it has been unreasonably refused. For discussion of the operation of this provision see *Re Gilmartin (a Bankrupt)* [1989] 1 W.L.R. 513 where Harman J concluded that the registrar had been correct in deciding that an offer had not been unreasonably refused by the petitioner and the supporting creditors. In *Re a Debtor (No.32 of 1993)* [1994] 1 W.L.R. 899; [1994] B.C.C. 438 it was held by Timothy Lloyd QC (sitting as a deputy High Court judge) that a debtor can offer to secure or compound within the meaning of s.271(3) where there is just a single creditor involved. However, in determining whether the creditor's refusal of the offer was unreasonable it must be established to the satisfaction of the court that no reasonable hypothetical creditor would have rejected the debtor's offer; the fact that some creditors might have accepted it is not conclusive. In *Inland Revenue Commissioners v A Debtor* [1995] B.C.C. 971 the court could not be persuaded that the refusal of tax officers to accept security for a debt was unreasonable. In *Evans v Clarke, Willmott & Clarke* [2007] EWHC 852 (Ch); [2008] B.P.I.R. 37 the creditor was held not to have behaved unreasonably in rejecting the debtor's offer as no clear and satisfactory offer had in fact been made. In *Revenue and Customs Commissioners v Garwood* [2012] B.P.I.R. 575 Chief Registrar Baister emphasised that the court enjoys wide discretion under s.271(3). The judgment contains a comprehensive analysis of the considerations that the court should take into account for the purposes of s.271. Some 10 points are highlighted. A mechanistic response by a creditor in the face of attempts by the debtor to settle matters does not go down well with the court; the creditor should reflect upon what is being offered. An objective test should be applied. In this case (unusually) the court held that the creditor had acted unreasonably in its response to the debtor's offers.

Shrimpton v Darby's Solicitors LLP [2011] EWHC 3796 (Ch); [2012] B.P.I.R. 631 is but one further example of an abortive attempt to argue that a creditor was acting unreasonably in rejecting the debtor's offer.

In *Dunbar Assets plc v Fowler* [2013] B.P.I.R. 46 Chief Registrar Baister ruled that the creditor had not unreasonably refused the debtor's offer of security/deferred consideration. It could not be said that refusal was beyond the range of possible actions that a reasonable creditor would take. For yet another unsuccessful attempt to challenge a creditor's refusal to accept the offer put forward by the debtor on the grounds of unreasonableness see *Cooke v Dunbar Assets plc* [2016] EWHC 579 (Ch); [2016] B.P.I.R. 576.

The creditor's refusal to compound was found not to be unreasonable by Registrar Briggs in *Barclays Bank v Atay* [2015] EWHC 3198 (Ch). The creditor was not obliged to accept an offer by the debtor involving payments by instalments over a long period of time.

On s.271(3) generally see *Re a Debtor (No.415/SD/1993)* [1994] 1 W.L.R. 917; and *King v Inland Revenue Commissioners* [1996] B.P.I.R. 414. In *Re a Debtor (No.2389 of 1989)* [1991] Ch. 326 Vinelott J held that the proposal of a voluntary arrangement by the debtor under Pt VIII of the Act cannot be regarded as an "offer" for the purposes of s.271(3) in that the decision on acceptance is not solely a matter for the petitioning creditor. The consequences of acceptance or refusal of such a proposal are dealt with exclusively by Pt VIII. For discussion, see Griffiths (1991) 135 S.J. 598.

On s.271(3) see *Sands v Layne* [2014] EWHC 3665 (Ch). In *Sahota v Singh* [2018] EWHC 2646 (Ch), Henry Carr J ruled that the creditor had not behaved unreasonably in rejecting the debtor's offer for the purposes of s.271(3). There was also no set off available to the debtor. On the facts of *Boulton v Queen Margaret's School, York* [2018] EWHC 3729 (Ch), Arnold J ruled that the creditor had acted unreasonably within s.271(3) in rejecting the debtor's offer (which offered interest payment and the provision of security in relation to the debt, but refused to include recovery costs) the debt was disputed. This is a rare outcome in that the courts normally affirm any decision by the creditor not to accept the debtor's offer.

On s.271(3) see ICC Judge Jones in *Islandsbanki HF v Stanford* [2019] EWHC 595 (Ch); [2019] B.P.I.R. 876. This ruling was confirmed by Fancourt J in [2019] EWHC 1818 (Ch) and an appeal to the Court of Appeal was dismissed in [2020] EWCA Civ 480.

Cases on dismissal of the petition under s.271(3) mainly concern the court being satisfied about the debtor's offer being unreasonably refused under s.271(3)(a)–(c), but the court in *Revenue and Customs Commissioners v De Freitas* [2022] EWHC 1946 (Ch) noted at [52] that there does not appear to be any reported case which has considered the circumstances in which the first limb of s.271(3), that "the court may dismiss the petition if it is satisfied that the debtor is able to pay all his debts", will be engaged and what relevant test requires the debtor to demonstrate cash-flow or balance sheet solvency. The court in the latter case refused to dismiss the petition but adjourned it and extended the period of adjournment bearing in mind the debtor's mental health issues. The court has discretion to adjourn the petition but this discretion must be carefully watched—*Harrison v Seggar* [2005] EWHC 411 (Ch); [2005] B.P.I.R. 583. See also *Islandsbanki HF v Stanford* [2019] EWHC 307 (Ch). On the jurisdiction to adjourn under CPR r.3.1(2)(b) see *Sekhon v Edginton* [2015] EWCA Civ 816; [2015] 1 W.L.R. 4435. The later the debtor leaves any request to adjourn the less likely it is to be granted by the court. A last minute offer to pay is unlikely to persuade the court to adjourn, unless there is clear evidence that the debtor can pay. The jurisdiction to adjourn is governed by the principles in CPR r.3.1(2)(b). This important procedural authority was applied by HHJ Behrens in *Day v Refulgent Ltd* [2016] EWHC 7 (Ch); [2016] B.P.I.R. 594. It is clear from the latter case that any appeal against a refusal by a first instance judge to adjourn faces an uphill struggle. For an unusual instance where the hearing of the petition was adjourned for a second time see *Aabar Block SARL v Maud* [2015] EWHC 3681 (Ch). A bankruptcy order was eventually made (after two adjournments of the petition) by Registrar Briggs in *Aabar Block SARL v Maud* [2016] EWHC 1016 (Ch). But on appeal ([2016] EWHC 2175 (Ch)) that bankruptcy order was quashed by Snowden J and this complex case was remitted for yet another hearing of the bankruptcy petition. The saga of this protracted piece of litigation continued with the judgment of Snowden J in *Aabar Block SARL v Maud* [2018] EWHC 1414 (Ch); [2019] Ch. 15. Where there are two petitioners pursuing a joint judgment debt the courts will be unlikely to make a bankruptcy order if the petitioners are not in agreement as to whether the petition should be adjourned or an immediate bankruptcy order sought. The saga may have come to an end with the rulings of Snowden J in *Re Maud* [2020] EWHC 974 (Ch) and [2020] EWHC 1469 (Ch).

Having made a bankruptcy order under s.271 the court has jurisdiction to stay the order if appropriate—*Emap Active Ltd v Hill* [2007] EWHC 1592 (Ch); [2007] B.P.I.R. 1228. But care must be taken when interpreting this case as its facts were very unusual. Rather it should be seen as an example of an exception proving the rule (that a stay will not normally be granted). The general reluctance of the court to grant stays save in exceptional circumstances is apparent in *Re Foster* [2012] B.P.I.R. 545—see comments of Roth J at [24] citing David Richards J.

Putative bankrupts frequently fail to turn up for the hearing of the petition against them. Provided they have been served with the petition and given appropriate notice the mere fact that the judge decides to hear the petition in their absence does not necessarily involve a contravention of ECHR art.6—*Manyan v Dewar Hogan* [2004] EWHC 3107 (Ch); [2006] B.P.I.R. 71.

Note also IR 2016 r.9.23—possibility of a debt relief order.

Note *Barker v Baxendale-Walker* [2018] EWHC 1681 (Ch) where the issues of cross-claims and adjournments were discussed.

On where a change of carriage was not appropriate under IR r.10.29 with the result that the court refused to make a bankruptcy order see *Hood v JD Classics Ltd* [2020] EWHC 3232 (Ch).

Chapter IA

Commencement and Duration of Bankruptcy

Duration

279—

General Note

S.279(3)–(5)
Replace the note with:
    These deal with the converse situation where the trustee or official receiver wish to extend the one-year period for a specified period or until a condition is satisfied. This will only happen if the bankrupt has failed to fulfil his obligations. Cases decided under the former s.279(3) will continue to be instructive—see here *Hardy v Focus Insurance Co Ltd* [1997] B.P.I.R. 77; *Holmes v Official Receiver* [1996] B.C.C. 246; *Jacobs v Official Receiver* [1999] 1 W.L.R. 619; and *Bagnall v Official Receiver* [2003] EWCA Civ 1925; [2004] B.P.I.R. 445 where the Court of Appeal adopted a purposive view on whether interim orders could in principle be made suspending discharge pending a full hearing. Late applications for such an order were not to be encouraged and the lateness of any application might persuade the court not to grant the order sought. On s.279(3) see *Hafiz v Ingram* [2012] EWHC 274 (Ch); [2012] B.P.I.R. 1116. A

12-month suspension of discharge was upheld on appeal by Norris J in *Keely v Bell* [2016] EWHC 308 (Ch); [2016] B.P.I.R. 653. The bankrupt had failed to discharge his obligations under s.291 and the suspension had been granted notwithstanding that the application by the trustee was in some respects late. Norris J considered the nature of the obligation of the bankrupt to cooperate so as to ensure that a suspension of discharge was lifted. Essentially the trustee wishing to have a suspension imposed needed to show that the bankrupt had not done all that was reasonable to comply with requests to cooperate. Late application for suspension should be avoided but the court could still grant a suspension of discharge on a late application. But late applications for suspension might be rejected—on this see *Allen v Mittal* [2022] EWHC 762 (Ch). A conditional suspension might be appropriate if there were specific things that the bankrupt should be required to do. In the case of general non-compliance a fixed term suspension of discharge was more appropriate.

On circumstances where suspension of automatic discharge might be appropriate see *Shierson v Rastogi* [2007] EWHC 1266 (Ch); [2007] B.P.I.R. 864. The court mentioned that discharge from bankruptcy does not affect the continuing obligations of a bankrupt to assist the official receiver or trustee in bankruptcy with the provision of information and the recovery of assets, reasons why suspension was granted in *Brittain v Ferster* [2022] EWHC 1060 (Ch) where the debtor had for years continued to fail to provide requested information in various regards. For an unsuccessful application for suspension of discharge see *Chadwick v Nash* [2012] B.P.I.R. 70 (Mr Registrar Nicholls). The application was refused because the evidence suggested that the bankrupt had done all he could reasonably do in terms of co-operation and to impose conditions on the grant of automatic discharge so late in the day was seen as unacceptable. One possible reason behind the application was the desire to secure an income payments agreement before discharge—but the court indicated that the matters raised on the suspension application were more appropriate for an income payments order application and no such application had been made. In *Bramston v Haut* [2012] EWHC 1279 (Ch); [2012] B.P.I.R. 672 the bankrupt (unusually) wanted the discharge suspended so as to be able to put forward an IVA to his creditors. The trustee was opposed to this course of action. At first instance the bankrupt was successful in challenging the approach of the trustee; Arnold J held that, even if the *Wednesbury* test was applied to review the actions of the trustee, that test had become more relaxed with modern developments in Public Law. But a more conservative approach was adopted in the Court of Appeal [2012] EWCA Civ 1637 where the court indicated that something amounting to perversity must be established before the court would intervene. The views of the trustee on this matter therefore prevailed. Barling J confirmed in *Tucker v Atkins* [2013] EWHC 4469 (Ch); [2014] B.P.I.R. 1359 that it was not possible for an undischarged bankrupt to invoke s.279 to obtain suspension of discharge to promote an IVA. The correct procedure was to seek an interim order under s.252 and to obtain suspension of discharge through that route. Discharge was suspended in *Hellard v Kapoor* [2013] EWHC 2204 (Ch); [2013] B.P.I.R. 745—for the costs implications see [2013] EWHC 2496 (Ch); [2013] B.P.I.R. 745 at 753. In *Mawer v Bland* [2013] EWHC 3122 (Ch) Rose J granted a suspension from discharge until the trustee could confirm full co-operation from the bankrupt. On s.279(3) see *Wilson v Williams* [2015] EWHC 1841 (Ch); [2015] B.P.I.R. 1319. Here HHJ Behrens upheld a first instance decision to suspend discharge until co-operation with the trustee could be confirmed. For the appropriate form of any order that may be made under s.279(3) see the comments of Nugee J in *Weir v Hilsdon* [2017] EWHC 983 (Ch); [2017] B.P.I.R. 1088. Nugee J stressed the importance of customising the order so as to make it appropriate to the facts of each individual case. The need to take into account the desirability of certainty had to be balanced with the necessity of supporting the trustee in securing the bankrupt's cooperation. For critique of this area of practice see Patterson [2016] 29 Insolv. Int. 22 and [2017] 30 Insolv. Int. 85. For critique of this area of practice see Patterson [2016] 29 Insolv. Int. 22 and [2017] 30 Insol. Int. 85. *OR v Cooksey* [2013] B.P.I.R. 526 is a curious case. Here an automatic discharge had been suspended for non-co-operation. The bankrupt having mended his ways was then successful in persuading the courts that he should be granted a certificate of discharge pursuant to what is now IR 2016 r.10.144/10.145.

Chief Registrar Baister refused to suspend discharge in *Bowles v Trefilov* (unreported, 29 April 2016) as the evidence before the court did not justify suspension.

On the submission of evidence where suspension is sought see *ORNI v McWilliams* [2012] NICh 28 where Deeny J deals with the equivalent provision in Northern Ireland.

For a curious case where the bankrupt was (for good reason) unaware that his discharge had been suspended see *Secretary of State for Business, Innovation and Skills v Melaris (Re Waterfall Media Ltd)* [2013] B.P.I.R. 1109 (Registrar Barber).

Note *Harris v Official Receiver* [2016] EWHC 3433 (Ch); [2017] B.P.I.R. 444 (Andrew Simmonds QC)—when a fixed term suspension order has expired that does not preclude a further indefinite suspension order being sought if cooperation is not forthcoming.

Court's power to annul bankruptcy order

282—

S.282(1), (3)

Replace the note with:

The court can annul a bankruptcy order if it should never have been made (compare here *Re a Bankrupt (No.622 of 1995), The Times,* 27 June 1996; *Henwood v Customs and Excise Commissioners* [1998] B.P.I.R. 339; and *Hope v Premierpace (Europe) Ltd* [1999] B.P.I.R. 695) and also if the bankrupt has paid all his debts and bankruptcy expenses to the extent required by the rules: see IR 2016 r.10.138. Conditional annulment is frowned upon—*Re Hagemeister* [2010] B.P.I.R. 1093. If a conditional annulment is ordered the bankruptcy remains in place until the conditions for annulment are met—*Oraki v Dean & Dean* [2017] EWHC 11 (Ch). In *Paulin v Paulin* [2009] B.P.I.R. 572 the Court of Appeal stressed that, where a wife applies for the annulment of her husband's bankruptcy and alleges that he procured his own bankruptcy as a tactic in a divorce dispute, the onus is on her to show that he was not insolvent at the time the bankruptcy order was made. The burden of proof is the ordinary burden expected in civil cases but, if she can establish he was not insolvent in terms of his balance sheet, then he falls under an evidential burden to show that he was insolvent on a commercial basis. This case is also significant with regard to the question as to whether the court can revisit its own judgment on the question of annulment. *Arif v Zar* [2012] EWCA Civ 986; [2012] B.P.I.R. 948 examines procedural aspects of the linkage between annulment proceedings and proceedings dealing with ancillary relief on divorce. The court needs to be alert to the potential abuse of annulment proceedings. The question of annulment rests upon the discretion of the court: *Askew v Peter Dominic Ltd* [1997] B.P.I.R. 163; *Re Coney* [1998] B.P.I.R. 333; *Skarzynski v Chalford Property Co Ltd* [2001] B.P.I.R. 673. Annulment is discretionary and therefore establishing grounds for annulment is no guarantee that the court will annul—*Omokwe v HFC Bank* [2007] B.P.I.R. 1157 (per Chief Registrar Baister). But the court stressed in *Royal Bank of Scotland v The Debtor* [1996] B.P.I.R. 478 that there is no inherent power of annulment beyond the statutory power. The discretion enjoyed by the court under s.282 does not permit it to refuse to annul a bankruptcy order in circumstances where it was clear that the order should not have been made in the first place due to a lack of jurisdiction—*Re Meyden* [2016] EWHC 414 (Ch); [2016] B.P.I.R. 697 per Nugee J.

In *Lambert v Forest of Dean DC* [2019] EWHC 1763 (Ch); [2019] B.P.I.R. 1220 ICC Judge Mullen stressed the discretion of the court not to annul where the court was not satisfied that the applicant was not solvent and that a further bankruptcy order appeared to be inevitable if the first order were to be annulled.

Moreover the s.375 review jurisdiction cannot be used to circumvent the stringent conditions of s.282—*Inland Revenue Commissioners v Robinson* [1999] B.P.I.R. 329. For the distinction between rescission and annulment see *Hoare v Inland Revenue Commissioners* [2002] EWHC 755 (Ch); [2002] B.P.I.R. 986. The views of Peter Smith J expressed in *Hoare* (above) were questioned in the Court of Appeal in *Yang v Official Receiver* [2017] EWCA Civ 1465. For discussion of the role of the court under these distinct jurisdictions see *Hunt v Peasegood* [2001] B.P.I.R. 76. The relationship between ss.282 and 375 was further reviewed in *Ahmed v Mogul Eastern Foods* [2005] EWHC 3532 (Ch) by Patten J. Points of similarity and areas of difference in these two jurisdictions were highlighted. In particular Patten J was disinclined to allow the rule in *Ladd v Marshall* [1954] 1 W.L.R. 1489 to intrude into the s.282 jurisdiction. For the wide power of the court under s.282(1) and its relationship with the s.375 review jurisdiction see *Snopek v Urang Ltd* [2008] B.P.I.R. 1416. On s.282 and its relationship with the s.375 review jurisdiction see also *Revenue and Customs Commissioners v Cassells* [2009] B.P.I.R. 284. On the facts here an annulment was not a realistic possibility. Another aspect of the annulment jurisdiction was considered by HHJ Hodge QC in *Yang v Official Receiver* [2013] EWHC 3577 (Ch). Once again the distinction between annulment under s.282 and rescission under s.375 was judicially reviewed. A bankruptcy order made upon the basis of liability orders which were subsequently set aside could not be annulled under s.282(1)(a) as it could not be said that the bankruptcy order was invalid when it was made. The proper course of action in such cases was a rescission granted under s.375(1). The Court of Appeal held that liability orders remain valid until set aside. If such orders are set aside the appropriate response is to rescind the bankruptcy order and not to annul it as this would imply that the liability orders never existed. The Court of Appeal explained the difference between annulment and rescission. On dissemination of information about annulment see *Smeaton v Equifax plc* [2013] EWCA Civ 108. Annulment can be granted even though discharge has occurred—though it may not be in the interests of the former bankrupt in such a case to seek annulment—*Owo-Samson v Barclays Bank (No.1)* [2003] EWCA Civ 714; [2003] B.P.I.R. 1373. The Secretary of State can appeal against an annulment order, see IR 2016 r.12.60. An annulment of a bankruptcy order was refused by Warner J in *Re Robertson (a Bankrupt)* [1989] 1 W.L.R. 1139 where there had been failure to prove all debts. See also *Artman v Artman* [1996] B.P.I.R. 511 (annulment refused). The court can annul conditionally—*Engel v Peri* [2002] EWHC 799 (Ch); [2002] B.P.I.R. 961; *Hirani v Rendle* [2004] B.P.I.R. 274; *Thornhill v Atherton* [2004] EWCA Civ 1858; [2005] B.P.I.R. 437. For general analysis of annulment see Brockman and French [2006] 19 Insolv. Int. 62 and 93.

Harman J considered the nature of the jurisdiction to annul in *Re a Debtor (No.68 of 1992)* [1993] T.L.R. 69. Here the point was made that on an annulment hearing under s.282 it was not possible for the court to consider evidence which had been unavailable to the court which had made the bankruptcy in the first place. Relevant considerations on an annulment application were discussed in *Lloyds v Waters* [2001] B.P.I.R. 698. For an unsuccessful s.282 application see *Shamash v Inland Revenue Commissioners* [2002] B.P.I.R. 189. In dealing with an annulment application the court should take into account material events occurring after the date of the bankruptcy order—see *Watts v Newham LBC* [2009] B.P.I.R. 718.

Bankruptcy is a class remedy and the court should not annul without a proper investigation of the facts—*Housiaux v Customs and Excise Commissioners* [2003] EWCA Civ 257; [2003] B.P.I.R. 858; *Leicester v Plumtree Farms* [2004] B.P.I.R. 296.

The Court of Appeal ruling in *Oraki v Dean & Dean (a firm)* [2013] EWCA Civ 1629 provides an important illustration of the annulment jurisdiction at work. Here a party was successful in having a bankruptcy annulled under s.282(1)(a) on the grounds that the bankruptcy order should not have been made. But the Court of Appeal ruled that the judge at first instance was correct in making such annulment conditional on payment of the claim for remuneration and costs submitted by the trustee in bankruptcy. There was a presumption that the trustee was entitled to be paid for work properly completed notwithstanding the later annulment. The Court of Appeal stressed the discretion enjoyed by judges at first instance in dealing with such difficult cases and underlined its reluctance to interfere with their decisions. Each case must turn on its own facts. For ongoing litigation in this case see *Oraki v Dean & Dean* [2017] EWHC 11 (Ch). In this latter stage of proceedings the judge made the important point that a bankruptcy order made without jurisdiction remains valid until annulled, as do acts performed under said order. For the latest proceedings in this difficult case see *Oraki v Bramston* [2017] EWCA Civ 403 where the Court of Appeal dismissed the appeal from Proudman J and rejected claims that the trustees in bankruptcy had failed to bring the bankruptcies to an end expeditiously. For continuing litigation in this saga see *Oraki v Hall* [2019] EWHC 1515 (Ch). See also *1st Credit (Finance) Ltd v Carr* [2013] EWHC 2318 (Ch); [2013] B.P.I.R. 1012 for comparable judicial thinking.

On going behind a default judgment for the purposes of s.282(1)(a) see *Royal Bank of Scotland v Farley* [1996] B.P.I.R. 638; and *Hunter v Lex Vehicle Finance* [2005] EWHC 223 (Ch); [2005] B.P.I.R. 586. In *Re a Debtor (No.169 of 1997)* (unreported but noted in *Current Law Week*, 14 August 1998) a county court judge annulled a bankruptcy order under s.282(1)(a) because the consent order upon which the petition has been based should never have been made. In *Ridsdale v Bowles* [2015] B.P.I.R. 1275 the county court observed that although the court can look behind a judgment on an annulment application it would not do so if the applicant had delayed unreasonably in challenging said judgment. The court also accepted the possibility of mixed motives on the part of a petitioner. The court will be unlikely to exercise its discretion to annul a bankruptcy in cases of hopeless insolvency.

An annulment application under s.282(1)(a) was allowed on appeal in *Mowbray v Sanders* [2015] EWHC 296 (Ch) because it appeared that the petition debt may have been statute-barred. The annulment was conditional on payment of certain sums by the applicant. On costs see *Mowbray v Sanders* [2015] EWHC 2317 (Ch).

In *Whig v Whig* [2007] EWHC 1856 (Fam); [2007] B.P.I.R. 1418 Munby J on the application of a wife refused to annul a bankruptcy order made against her insolvent husband on his own petition. The effect of that bankruptcy order had been to frustrate the wife's claims to ancillary relief, but the court held that, as the husband was insolvent and bad faith on his part could not be established, annulment under s.282(1)(a) was not justified. In the light of *Paulin v Paulin* [2009] EWCA Civ 221 this authority must be treated with some caution.

In *Re Ruiz* [2011] EWHC 913 (Fam); [2011] B.P.I.R. 1139 an attempt by a wife to secure the annulment of her husband's bankruptcy failed before Peter Jackson J. One reason for this failure to obtain annulment may have been that the application was made 18 months after the bankruptcy order was granted, though the wife did not become aware of the bankruptcy order immediately. The evidence indicated that the husband was insolvent and it was noted that the statutory rights of the wife under family law (and any rights under ECHR art.8) did not confer cast iron guarantees that the family home would not be sold if the husband became bankrupt. A balance had to be maintained between family rights and the rights of creditors. Leave to appeal this judgment was dismissed—see [2011] EWCA Civ 1646. The bankruptcy court is under no obligation to delay its decision on a bankruptcy petition simply because ancillary relief proceedings were ongoing.

Note *Taylor v The Macdonald Partnership* [2015] EWCA Civ 921 which shows that protracted delay in making an annulment application can prove fatal. This was an abortive application for permission to appeal against a refusal by HHJ Hodge to annul a disputed bankruptcy nine years after discharge. In *Ramsden v Official Receiver* [2018] EWHC 1226 (Ch) the delay amounted to 24 years and it was therefore not surprising that the annulment application was rejected by Deputy ICC Judge Agnello.

Where an annulment application is waiting to be heard by the court, there will be some reluctance on the part of the judiciary to restrain the exercise of powers by the duly appointed trustee in bankruptcy in the interim pending the outcome of the annulment application—see the decision of Fancourt J in *Goremsandu v Thomas* [2019] EWHC 2397 (Ch) for an insight into the appropriate approach.

On liability for the trustee's costs of the bankruptcy on an annulment application see *Tetteh v Lambeth LBC* [2008] B.P.I.R. 241. Where the annulment is made pursuant to s.282(1)(a) the starting point is that the petitioning creditor is liable for the bankruptcy costs but that presumption may be rebutted on the facts of each case. In *Redbridge LBC v Mustafa* [2010] EWHC 1105 (Ch); [2010] B.P.I.R. 893 the court reviewed the question of liability for costs on annulment under s.282(1)(a). Further consideration of this issue was provided by HHJ Pelling in the difficult case of *Re Haworth* [2011] EWHC 36 (Ch). On costs in the wake of an annulment see *Willett v Economy Power Ltd* [2012] EWCA Civ 1164; [2012] B.P.I.R. 1298. On the treatment of costs in relation to a failed annulment application see *Ardawa v Uppal* [2019] EWHC 1663 (Ch); [2019] B.P.I.R. 1086, a decision of Roth J.

In order to succeed in an annulment application under s.282(1)(a) there should be new evidence that was not before the court making the bankruptcy order—but see the flexible approach adopted by Roth J in the unusual case of *1st Credit (Finance) Ltd v Carr* [2013] EWHC 2318 (Ch); [2013] B.P.I.R. 1012.

In *Hunt v Fylde BC* [2008] B.P.I.R. 1368 the court ordered annulment under s.282(1)(a) because it uncovered circumstances not apparent at the time when the bankruptcy order was made. The bankruptcy was annulled under s.282(1)(a) in *Official Receiver v Mitterfellner* [2009] B.P.I.R. 1075 because the debtor did not have a genuine COMI in the jurisdiction so as to justify the making of the bankruptcy order by the English court. See also *Re Hagemeister* [2010] B.P.I.R. 1093. In cases such as *Re Eichler (No.2)* [2011] B.P.I.R. 1293 and *Irish Bank Resolution Corp Ltd v Quinn* [2012] NICh 1 bankruptcies were annulled because the evidence suggested that the petitioning debtors did not have their COMI within the jurisdiction at the relevant time. See *Sparkasse Hilden Ratingen Velbert v Benk* [2012] EWHC 2432 (Ch); [2012] B.P.I.R. 1258 where a bankruptcy was annulled by HHJ Purle QC on an application by a German creditor as the evidence showed that the debtor did not have COMI in the jurisdiction at the relevant time. The applicant creditor had discharged the burden of proof that on the balance of probability COMI was not within the jurisdiction at the date of the petition.

Official Receiver v Keelan [2012] B.P.I.R. 613 was another case where the bankruptcy of a debtor with foreign links was annulled under s.282(1)(a) for lack of jurisdiction. *Die Sparkasse Bremen AG v Armutcu* [2012] EWHC 4026 (Ch); [2013] B.P.I.R. 10 provides another example of a debtor-induced bankruptcy being annulled on the grounds of a lack of COMI. The annulment here was granted by Proudman J after discharge from bankruptcy had been obtained, as s.282(3) envisaged. The application was made by a secured creditor. See also *OR v Becker* [2013] B.P.I.R. 352 where District Judge Dancey reviewed the law on such applications. The case is interesting because of the use of an intermediary by the German debtor and the spotlight placed upon that feature by the court. A bankruptcy obtained by a debtor on an ex parte application was also annulled on the application of a creditor in *ACC Bank plc v McCann* [2013] NIMaster 1.

In *Commerzbank AG v Brehm* [2014] B.P.I.R. 359 Chief Registrar Baister dismissed an annulment application by a German creditor of a German debtor who had successfully petitioned for bankruptcy in the English courts. The case was marginal but the creditor had failed to convince the court that the debtor did not have COMI in the jurisdiction. For an annulment application by a German creditor in a COMI case see Registrar Briggs' ruling in *Re Riemann* [2015] B.P.I.R. 1405. The application failed because COMI within the English jurisdiction had been established and, in any case, several years had elapsed since discharge. The bankrupt had fully co-operated with the official receiver. In *Rafferty v Sealants International Ltd* [2018] EWHC 1380 (Ch) an annulment was granted. An annulment was also granted by HHJ Hodge QC on the application of a creditor in the debtor tourism case of *Re Leitzbach* [2018] EWHC 1544 (Ch); [2018] B.P.I.R. 1299. Here the court found that the supposed change of COMI from Germany to England was illusory. The judgment contains a valuable review of the use of the annulment jurisdiction in such instances.

An annulment application was dismissed in *JSC Bank of Moscow v Kekhman* [2014] B.P.I.R. 959 by Chief Registrar Baister. Although there were some errors in the information provided by the debtor to the court these did not justify annulment. On appeal ([2015] EWHC 396 (Ch)) Morgan J, whilst rejecting some of the reasoning used by Chief Registrar Baister, nevertheless confirmed that, on balance and in the exercise of discretion, this application to annul the bankruptcy should be dismissed. It clearly was a very borderline case. The judgment of Morgan J contains detailed discussion of the approach that should be taken by the court to the issues of connection to the jurisdiction and any potential benefit flowing from the order when considering any annulment application on jurisdictional grounds. See notes to ss.265 and 272. For an abortive attempt to have a bankruptcy annulled on the grounds of a lack of COMI see *Hawthorne v North West Fund for Business Loans* [2019] NIMaster 8. The court made the point that the lack of COMI argument has no weight where there is evidence that COMI may have been concealed. The decision in *Kekhman* (above) was applied in *Khan v Singh-Sall* [2022] EWHC 1913 (Ch) that even where a court concludes that a bankruptcy order should not have been made (so that s.282(1)(a) is satisfied) it nonetheless retains a discretion which it must then exercise whether to annul: the court went on further to consider COMI and in the end dismissed an appeal against a refusal to annul, including in its discretion the conduct of the bankrupt which was sustained and deliberate and negatively impacted the trustee's investigations of the bankrupt's assets and liabilities. The latter two cases were also applied in *Dusoruth v Orca Finance UK Ltd* [2022] EWHC 2346 (Ch) where, contrary to the debtor's contention, his centre of main interests was held to be in this jurisdiction and the annulment application was dismissed.

As to what must be established by the bankrupt in order to procure an annulment under s.282(1)(a) see *Flett v*

Revenue and Customs Commissioners [2010] B.P.I.R. 1075. It is not sufficient to merely raise the possibility that there may have been a defence to the debt. See *Parveen v Manchester City Council* [2010] B.P.I.R. 152 for a case of annulment under s.282(1)(a)—the bankruptcy order should not have been made as it represented a disproportionate response to council tax arrears. An application to annul pursuant to s.282(1)(a) failed in *Loy v O'Sullivan* [2010] EWHC 3583 (Ch); [2011] B.P.I.R. 181.

Although there is no fixed limitation period in which annulment must be sought the longer the bankrupt waits the more difficult it may be to ensure that the creditors can be contacted to enable them to be repaid in full for the purposes of s.282(1)(b)—*Gill v Quinn* [2004] EWHC 883 (Ch); [2005] B.P.I.R. 129. For the general principles relevant when considering whether to annul see *Harper v Buchler* [2004] B.P.I.R. 724. For later proceedings in this case see *Harper v Buchler (No.2)* [2005] B.P.I.R. 577 where the court indicated that it would be unlikely to exercise its discretion to annul a bankruptcy order made a decade ago unless statutory interest was paid. For further consideration of whether (and to what extent) statutory interest should be paid see *Wilcock v Duckworth* [2005] B.P.I.R. 682. On the issue of whether statutory interest is payable where a bankruptcy is annulled under s.282(1)(b) see *Lewis v Kennedy* [2010] B.P.I.R. 886. Registrar Jacques indicated that where there is a surplus in the estate that would be the normal expectation unless special circumstances were present (as in this case). The issue of payment of statutory interest on an annulment under s.282(1)(b) is addressed by IR 2016 r.10.138 which was derived from I(A)R 2010 (SI 2010/686). For an instructive review of these questions see Pomeroy [2005] 18 Insolv. Int. 90. On the question of solicitors' undertakings and s.282(1)(b) annulments see *Halabi v Camden LBC* [2008] EWHC 322 (Ch); [2008] B.P.I.R. 370. Here the county court practice of granting an annulment by reference to a solicitors' undertaking was ruled to be undesirable and should in future by replaced by a practice involving annulment orders conditional upon certain events occurring to the satisfaction of the official receiver. The inconvenient ruling in *Halabi* was neutralised by I(A)R 2010 (SI 2010/686) through amendments to IR 1986 and by the insertion of r.6.211(6) (now IR 2016 r.10.138(7)). There was no prospect of an annulment under s.282(1)(b) in *Dadourian Group v Simms* [2008] B.P.I.R. 508.

In *Webster v Mackay* [2013] EWHC 2571 (Ch); [2013] B.P.I.R. 1136 HHJ Purle QC dismissed an appeal from Chief Registrar Baister who had ruled that there were no grounds for annulment under s.282(1)(a) nor the exceptional circumstances required for a rescission of the bankruptcy order under s.375. The point was made that the older the order the less likely it is that the court will set it aside.

In *OR v McKay* [2009] B.P.I.R. 1061 the Court of Appeal departed from an old precedent when seeking to give a modern meaning to s.282(1)(b).

An annulment application cannot be used to relitigate issues determined in the bankruptcy proceedings—*Balendran v Law Society* [2004] EWHC 495 (Ch); [2004] B.P.I.R. 859. In *Crammer v West Bromwich Building Society* [2012] EWCA Civ 517; [2012] B.P.I.R. 963 the Court of Appeal confirmed that the annulment jurisdiction is not to be used to revisit points which had been the subject of adjudication during the bankruptcy proceedings unless there are exceptional circumstances. But there was discretion to take account of matters that were available to the bankrupt in the earlier stage of the proceedings, but which were not raised by him. In comparison, the power of rescission under s.375 only applied to new material. See *Ahmed v Mogul Eastern Foods* [2005] EWHC 3532 (Ch).

On annulment and disputed debts see *Guinan III v Caldwell Associates Ltd* [2003] EWHC 3348 (Ch); [2004] B.P.I.R. 531. The test for whether a debt is disputed is the same on an annulment application as it is on a set aside application—*Woolsey v Payne* [2015] EWHC 968 (Ch); [2015] B.P.I.R. 933. *Guinan* (above) was applied in Northern Ireland in *O'Callaghan v Clipper Holding II SARL* [2017] NICh 29 and in England in *Dusoruth v Orca Finance UK Ltd* [2022] EWHC 2346 (Ch) where the annulment application failed on several grounds, including that the debtor could not meet the low threshold for showing that the petition debts were genuinely disputed on substantial grounds.

For a case where the bankruptcy was annulled because the petitioner should have done more to explain the frailty of the debtor to the court see *Brister v Official Receiver* [2015] EW Misc B22 (CC); [2015] B.P.I.R. 1008. Here the debtor had in fact died before the bankruptcy order was made, though the creditor and court were unaware of this.

An annulment application alleging procedural unfairness was rejected in *Simmons v Mole Valley* [2004] EWHC 475 (Ch); [2004] B.P.I.R. 1022 because the bankrupt had not bothered to attend the hearing of the bankruptcy petition. In *Department of Finance v McGillion* [2018] NICh 25 annulment (and rescission) was refused as the bankruptcy order had quite properly been made against the debtor who had merely put legal nonsense before the court hearing the petition.

In *Smith v 1st Credit (Finance) Ltd* [2012] EWHC 2600 (Ch); [2013] B.P.I.R. 129 the High Court dismissed an appeal from the county court which had refused an application to annul by a person who had been bankrupted by the assignee of the original debt. The evidence showed that the debtor had been given due notice of this assignment.

In *Richards v Vivendi SA* [2017] EWHC 1581 (Ch); [2017] B.P.I.R. 1390 Morgan J quashed a decision on an annulment application and remitted it for rehearing by the High Court. The reason given was that the district judge hearing the annulment application had not given proper consideration to the fresh evidence submitted by the bankrupt who was applying for annulment.

There is no provision in s.282 requiring the annulment order to be gazetted and published in a local paper, as was necessary under BA 1914 s.29(3): now see IR 2016 r.10.139. Formerly an application for annulment had to be supplemented with a request for rescission of the receiving order under what is now s.375(1). With the abolition of receiving orders this is no longer necessary. For a Court of Appeal authority on rescission of receiving orders, which might have some impact on judicial practice in cases of annulment of bankruptcy orders, see *Re a Debtor (No.707 of 1985)*, *The Times*, 21 January 1988.

In *Cook v Revenue and Customs Commissioners* [2017] B.P.I.R. 1468 an annulment was granted by Deputy Registrar Garwood. Although it was not the case that every failure to put the full facts before the court would result in an annulment, in this instance the court making the bankruptcy order was not apprised of the full position with regard to the tax position. In granting an annulment the court should consider the interests of all creditors and not just the petitioning creditors. Here there were no other creditors. Any non-cooperation by the bankrupt could be taken into account when dealing with expenses on annulment.

For a third unsuccessful attempt to seek an annulment see *Hurst v Green* [2021] EWHC 1767 (Ch), a decision of Fancourt J. For another failed attempt at obtaining an annulment see *Magan v Wilton Management Ltd* [2021] EWHC 3393 (Ch). The annulment application here was made on the basis that the bankruptcy order should not have been made because it served no purpose as the bankrupt claimed there were no assets to realise. The High Court dismissed the application because the bankrupt had not shown that the estate was assetless.

Under BA 1914 s.29, the application for annulment had to be made by "any person interested". This requirement, which caused problems in *Re Beesley Ex p. Beesley v The Official Receiver* [1975] 1 All E.R. 385, has been dropped. See here *F v F* [1994] 1 F.L.R. 359 (application by wife of debtor). For discussion, see Miller (1994) 10 I.L. & P. 66. A similar change has been made with regard to s.375. A secured creditor may in certain circumstances be able to apply for annulment—see the comments of Proudman J in *Die Sparkasse Bremen AG v Armutcu* [2012] EWHC 4026 (Ch).

For further provisions on annulment, see IR 2016 rr.10.132–10.141. In *Howard v Savage* [2006] EWHC 3693 (Ch); [2007] B.P.I.R. 1097 Lewison J stressed the link between the requirements of s.282(1)(b) and the Insolvency Rules. For an illuminating review of this jurisdiction see Briggs and Sims [2002] Insolv. L. 2.

Local authorities which through maladministration have improperly sought the bankruptcy of a council tax defaulter are increasingly being called upon to seek a remedial annulment in the wake of an adverse ruling from local government ombudsmen.

Annulment funding agreements are generating a substantial body of case law in their own right—*Annulment Funding Co Ltd v Cowey* [2010] EWCA Civ 711; [2010] B.P.I.R. 1304; *Consolidated Finance Ltd v Hunter* [2010] B.P.I.R. 1322; *Cook v Consolidated Finance Ltd* [2010] EWCA Civ 369; [2010] B.P.I.R. 1331. On regulatory issues linked to annulment funding agreements see *Consolidated Finance Ltd v Collins* [2013] EWCA Civ 475; [2013] B.P.I.R. 543.

CHAPTER II

PROTECTION OF BANKRUPT'S ESTATE AND INVESTIGATION OF HIS AFFAIRS

Restriction on proceedings and remedies

285—

GENERAL NOTE

S.285(1)

Replace the note with:

This provision authorises the court (for definition, see s.385) to stay actions, executions, etc. where a bankruptcy petition is pending or, indeed, after the grant of the order. The Blagden Committee (Cmnd.221 (1957)), paras 19–20, called for the insertion of a provision *ex abundanti cautela* to the effect that High Court proceedings could be stayed under this provision. This has not been done, presumably because the existing language was deemed sufficiently wide. In *Re Smith (a Bankrupt) Ex p. Braintree District Council* [1990] 2 A.C. 215, the House of Lords held that this provision did enable it to stay proceedings for committal for non-payment of rates. There was no justification for excluding such proceedings from the scope of s.285. See also *Lewis v Ogwr BC* [1996] Rating Appeals 124. Compare *R. v Secretary of State for Social Security Ex p. Taylor* [1997] B.P.I.R. 505 (authorities' right to deduct benefits at source not prejudiced by s.285(3)). But *R. v Secretary of State for Social Security Ex p. Taylor and Chapman* was overruled by the Supreme Court in *Secretary of State for Work and Pensions v Payne* [2011] UKSC 60. In *Harlow District Council v Hall* [2006] EWCA Civ 156; [2006] B.P.I.R. 712 the Court of Appeal (Civil Division) held that there was no breach of s.285 of the IA 1986 where the court had ordered the surrender of a secure tenancy pursuant to s.79 of the

Housing Act 1985, such surrender of possession to be completed the day before the bankruptcy petition was presented by the debtor. At the commencement of the bankruptcy the local authority were not seeking to enforce a remedy against the property of the bankrupt under the terms of s.285. The remedy had already been granted. The court also expressed the view that the same result would probably have been arrived at had the bankruptcy order predated the ending of possession. This view seems to have been taken because it was common ground between the parties that the secure tenancy would not have vested in the trustee on bankruptcy and so there was no estate to be protected within the spirit of s.285. Roth J indicated (at [22]) in *Kemsley v Barclays Bank plc* [2013] EWHC 1274 (Ch); [2013] B.P.I.R. 839 that this provision does not apply to obstruct foreign enforcement proceedings, though the English courts can use the Senior Courts Act 1981 s.37 to achieve the same effect. The court refused to stay an application for summary judgment against a bankrupt in *Fern Advisers Ltd v Burford* [2014] EWHC 762 (QB); [2014] B.P.I.R. 581.

Registrar Barber gave detailed consideration to the exercise of discretion under s.285(1) in *Re Mireskandari* [2014] B.P.I.R. 163. Here leave was refused after a full consideration of all of the relevant factors. The decision of Registrar Barber in *Re Mireskandari* [2014] B.P.I.R. 163 went to appeal—although the appeal was dismissed (see *Hellard v Chadwick* [2014] EWHC 2158 (Ch); [2014] B.P.I.R. 1234) Charles Hollander QC appeared to take a more expansive view as to what was caught by s.285. The need to support the protective policy underpinning s.285 was emphasised.

A stay under the section is not automatic and meanwhile a judgment creditor may apply under CPR r.71.2 for a bankrupt judgment creditor to attend court and provide documents and answer questions, even though that creditor could not enforce the judgment debt, since r.71.2 was not an enforcement proceeding but an anterior information gathering process (*Hijazi v Yaxley-Lennon* [2022] EWHC 635 (QB)).

On various aspects of s.285 see also *Arnold v Williams* [2008] EWHC 218 (Ch); [2008] B.P.I.R. 247.

Note also the annotation to s.130(2) above.

CHAPTER V

EFFECT OF BANKRUPTCY ON CERTAIN RIGHTS, TRANSACTIONS, ETC.

Rights under trusts of land

Rights under trusts of land

335A—

GENERAL NOTE

Replace the note with:

This and the following three sections are part of a package to redress the balance of rights between the trustee, on the one hand, and the bankrupt and his family on the other hand, over what will probably represent the bankrupt's most valuable asset, his family home. This is a problem that has troubled the law for many years—witness the decision in *Bendall v McWhirter* [1952] 2 Q.B. 466, which created a "deserted wife's equity" capable of prevailing over the trustee's rights, and its rejection by the House of Lords in *National Provincial Bank Ltd v Ainsworth* [1965] A.C. 1175. This decision, in turn, was reversed by the Matrimonial Homes Act 1967, a piece of legislation consolidated by the Matrimonial Homes Act 1983 which in turn was replaced by the Family Law Act 1996. Notwithstanding this, it was felt that the family's right to a roof over its head required greater protection in the event of the breadwinner becoming bankrupt: see the Cork *Report*, paras 1114–1131. These provisions on the family home were a late insertion in the Insolvency Bill 1985. For the background to this legislation, see Miller (1986) 50 Conv. 393; and Cretney (1991) 107 L.Q.R. 177. For further discussion of this area see Creasey and Doyle (1992) 136 S.J. 920. For a summary of the *Joint Insolvency Committee Insolvency Guidance Paper on the family home* (2005) see [2006] 19 Insolv. Int. 42. For discussion of this area see Davey [2001] Insolv. L. 2 at 12.

Where a trustee in bankruptcy makes an application for sale under these provisions an issue will frequently arise as to the allocation of proceeds between the estate and the non-bankrupt party. In such a scenario general equitable principles governing the determination of beneficial interests will be applied, as explained by the House of Lords in *Stack v Dowden* [2007] UKHL 17; [2007] 2 W.L.R. 831—applied in *Kernott v Jones* [2010] EWCA Civ 578. For the view of the Supreme Court on the determination of relative beneficial interests see *Jones v Kernott* [2011] UKSC 53; [2012] 1 A.C. 776 where the appeal was allowed and the conclusions reached at first instance were upheld. For further discussion of the principles operating in this area see the ruling of Chief Master Marsh in *Erlam v Rahman* [2016] EWHC 111 (Ch) where the issue of determination of beneficial interests in property was a central issue.

In addition, questions may arise as to whether the trustee can invoke equitable accounting principles and charge an "occupation rent" to be paid by the non-bankrupt party. There is a body of precedent governing this scenario—see *Re*

Gorman [1990] 1 W.L.R. 616; *Re Pavlou* [1993] 1 W.L.R. 1046; *Re Byford* [2003] B.P.I.R. 1089; and *French v Barcham* [2008] EWHC 1505 (Ch). Uncertainty has crept in as a result of *Murphy v Gooch* [2007] EWCA Civ 603; [2007] B.P.I.R. 1123 where the view was taken that the common law principles of equitable accounting have been replaced by the statutory criteria listed in ss.12–15 of the TLATA 1996, but this view was questioned by Blackburne J in *French v Barcham* (above), where the residual discretion enjoyed by the court was championed. Blackburne J ruled that the principles of equitable accounting were not displaced by the House of Lords precedent of *Stack v Dowden* [2007] UKHL 17. This question is likely to be revisited in the years to come. *French v Barcham* (above) was considered in *Levy v Ellis-Carr* [2012] EWHC 63 (Ch). On equitable accounting in cases of bankruptcy where properties are co-owned or jointly owned see *Davis v Jackson* [2017] EWHC 698 (Ch); [2017] 1 W.L.R. 4005; [2017] B.P.I.R. 950 where Snowden J undertook a comprehensive review of the position.

Another incidental property-related issue that can crop up in bankruptcy cases is related to the so-called "equity of exoneration"—*Re Pittortou* [1985] 1 W.L.R. 58. *Pittortou* (above) was followed by Chief Registrar Baister in *Re Chawda* [2014] B.P.I.R. 49 where the claim by a wife of a bankrupt for an equity of exoneration was dismissed. On *Pittortou* (above) and the equity of exoneration in general in non-bankruptcy situations see the analysis of Morgan J in *Day v Shaw* [2014] EWHC 36 (Ch) at [23]. Further consideration of the equity of exoneration is to be found in *Cadlock v Dunn* [2015] EWHC 1318 (Ch). The Court of Appeal gave support to the equity of exoneration in *Armstrong v Onyearu* [2017] EWCA Civ 268; [2017] B.P.I.R. 869. The judgment of the Court of Appeal contains a comprehensive review of English and Commonwealth authorities. The court stressed that equitable accounting forms part of the law of sureties and, as the term suggests, is to be governed by principles of equity. It is not to be excluded simply because indirect benefit might accrue as a result of its application. For a valuable overview of the treatment of this consideration in the courts see Gardiner [2016] 29 Insolv. Int. 17.

Section 335A was inserted by s.25(1) of and Sch.3 para.23 to the Trusts of Land and Appointment of Trustees Act 1996 with effect from 1 January 1997. For its significance see the note to s.336 below. Early interpretation on the meaning of s.335A is provided by the Court of Appeal in *Judd v Brown* [1999] B.P.I.R. 517 where the point was made that it may be proper to order a sale even if the prime beneficiary would be a secured creditor. In *Re Raval* [1998] B.P.I.R. 389 Blackburne J was faced with the question of whether exceptional circumstances existed for the purposes of s.335A(3). Again the issue centred upon the ill-health of the wife. The registrar had decided that this did constitute an exceptional circumstance but was only prepared to delay the sale of the family home for six months to enable arrangements to be made in the light of the wife's condition. Although Blackburne J agreed with the interpretation of the registrar on whether this was an exceptional circumstance he did not feel that appropriate weight had been given to it when making the order and therefore postponed the sale for just over one year. General principles governing the s.335A jurisdiction were laid down by the High Court in *Harrington v Bennett* [2000] B.P.I.R. 630. Exceptional circumstances within s.335A(3) were present in *Claughton v Charalamabous* [1998] B.P.I.R. 558. In *Barca v Mears* [2005] B.P.I.R. 15 the High Court reluctantly followed *Re Citro* [1991] Ch. 142 but questioned whether the narrow approach used for determining "exceptional circumstances" for the purposes of s.335A(3) was consistent with the requirements of the European Convention on Human Rights and, in particular, with art.8 (right to family life).

A lucid exposition of the principles to be applied under s.335A(ii) and (iii) was provided by Lawrence Collins J in *Dean v Stout* [2005] EWHC 3315 (Ch); [2005] B.P.I.R. 1113. In particular the flexible and open-ended nature of the concept of exceptional circumstances was stressed. The fact that a wife and children will lose the family home is a normal incidence of many bankruptcies and therefore not exceptional. Simply because the proceeds of sale will be swallowed up by bankruptcy expenses does not make the circumstances exceptional. This judgment very much reflects traditional judicial attitudes.

In *Awoyemi v Bowell* [2005] EWHC 2138 (Ch); [2006] B.P.I.R. 1, yet another case on s.335A, Evans-Lombe J stressed that it was very much a matter of discretion as to whether the trustee decided to enforce a possession order granted under s.335A and the court would be reluctant to interfere with that discretion.

In *Donohoe v Ingram* [2006] B.P.I.R. 417 Stuart Isaacs QC (sitting as a Deputy Judge in the High Court) supported a ruling from the District Judge that a sale should be ordered under s.335A notwithstanding the fact that there were still children in the house. A suggestion that sale should be delayed until the youngest child reached 16 was rejected. As more than a year had elapsed since the commencement of the bankruptcy the presumption favoured sale and the mere presence of children in the family home did not constitute exceptional circumstances. Once again the issue whether a narrow construction of "exceptional circumstances" does involve an infringement of the right to family life as conferred by ECHR art.8 was left open. As a small crumb of comfort in the interests of common humanity sale was deferred for three months. An attack on the position in English law based upon ECHR art.8 was rejected by Peter Smith J in *Ford v Alexander* [2012] EWHC 266 (Ch); [2012] B.P.I.R. 528 where it was held that the exceptional circumstances test, if properly applied, maintains an appropriate balance between the competing interests of the parties so as to be consistent with art.8. But compare *Official Receiver for Northern Ireland v O'Brien* [2012] NICh 12; [2012] B.P.I.R. 826 where Deeny J felt that a long delayed sale could be resisted by combined application of ECHR arts 6 and 8. See also the comments of the court in *Hawk Recovery Ltd v Hall* [2016] EWHC 1307 (Ch); [2016] B.P.I.R. 1169 on the general relevance of ECHR art.8.

This continues to be one of the most litigated aspects of bankruptcy.

The case of *Re Karia* [2006] B.P.I.R. 1226 (which was decided in 2001) shows that the courts will not infer exceptional circumstances exist simply because the proceeds of sale will be swallowed up in meeting the expenses of the bankruptcy. Rights conferred by art.8 had to be balanced against the rights of creditors; that balance here favoured sale.

Again in *Nicholls v Lan* [2006] B.P.I.R. 1243 the High Court held that s.335A was consistent with ECHR art.8 because it sought to balance family interests against those of creditors. The order of the district judge in this case clearly did that to the extent of deferring a sale for 18 months and therefore on appeal the High Court would not interfere. For discussion see Pawlowski [2007] Conv. 78.

In *Foenander v Allan* [2006] B.P.I.R. 1392 the court took the view that even if art.8 had shifted the goalposts for the purposes of s.335A the registrar had been correct in finding no exceptional circumstances on the facts of the case. Ill-health on the part of the brother of the bankrupt who had an interest in and lived in the property did not justify a delay in the realisation of what was the estate's only real asset.

The court in *Foyle v Turner* [2007] B.P.I.R. 43 felt that there was no inconsistency between art.8 and s.335A. According to Judge Norris exceptional circumstances might arise out of prolonged and inordinate delay between initial vesting and application for sale; but in this case a delay of some 13 years was not inordinate. The point was made that the application was made within the new three year period introduced by s.283A which came into effect on 1 April 2004.

The court in *Turner v Avis* [2008] B.P.I.R. 1143 undertook a significant review of the authorities in order to explain what was meant by "exceptional circumstances". In *Everitt v Budhram* [2010] B.P.I.R. 567 Mr Justice Henderson indicated that the word "needs" in s.335A(2) was to be widely interpreted and could encompass financial, medical, emotional and mental needs. See *Grant v Baker* [2016] EWHC 1782 (Ch) where Henderson J agreed with a District Judge's ruling that the presence of a disabled adult in the property constituted an exceptional circumstance, but disagreed on the length of the sale postponement. The District Judge had imposed an indefinite period of suspension, but Henderson J felt that 12 months grace from the date of his ruling was appropriate. There was no reason why a disabled person could not live in private rented accommodation.

For discussion of recent case law on the concept of exceptional circumstances for the purposes of this provision see McPhie (2018) 11(5) C.R.I. 170.

Avis v Turner [2007] EWCA Civ 748 confirms the point that s.335A applies where s.14 of Trusts of Land and Appointment of Trustees Act 1996 would operate. Whereas in *Holtham v Kelmanson* [2006] B.P.I.R. 1422 it was held that s.335A did not apply if the applicant trustee was solely interested in the property.

The presumption in s.335A(3) was applied in *Avis v Turner* [2007] EWCA Civ 748; [2007] B.P.I.R. 663. See also *Pick v Sumpter* [2010] B.P.I.R. 638. For further review of this provision see the judgment of Warren J in *Pickard v Constable* [2017] EWHC 2475 (Ch). The provision was found by Andrew Hochhauser QC (sitting in the High Court) not to apply in *Carter & Nillson v Hewitt* [2019] EWHC 3729 (Ch)—noted by Friedman in [2020] Recovery (Spring) 14. The position of creditors was considered in *Howlader v Moore* [2021] EWHC 3708 (Ch) where on the trustee's appeal the court held that a provision in the bankruptcy order allowing the bankrupt and her family to remain in possession during the marketing process of the home, where there was no evidence that the term would be to the detriment of the creditors, was within the bounds of the wide jurisdiction given to judges in that regard, and indeed the court noted that it may assist marketing of a property if it is not empty and it may be more valuable if lived in when marketed for sale.

Full consideration was given to s.335A application by Peter Knox QC (sitting as a Deputy Judge of the High Court) in *Gostelow v Hussain* [2021] EWHC 3276 (Ch). Here the judge explained the procedural requirements for an application for sale under this provision. In considering the substance of the application the court found that a sale should be ordered. The discharge of the bankrupt did not prevent a trustee from exercising realisation powers. The one-year grace period had expired and there were no exceptional circumstances. But the sale was deferred for three months to allow the school term to be completed to minimise disruption to the education to young persons in the house.

These provisions must be read in the light of s.283A (inserted by EA 2002 from 1 April 2004).

CHAPTER VII

POWERS OF COURT IN BANKRUPTCY

Seizure of bankrupt's property

365—

S.365(1), (2)

Replace the note with:

These provisions allow the court to issue a warrant for the seizure of the bankrupt's property even though it may be in the possession of a third party. Forcing entry into premises or breaking open "receptacles" is permitted when executing such a warrant. For an example of an order being made under s.365 see *Williams v Mohammed (No.2)* [2012] B.P.I.R. 238. A s.365 order was granted by Chief Registrar Baister in *Re A Bankrupt* [2012] B.P.I.R. 469 in favour of a German insolvency administrator by applying the recognition principle formerly found in art.25 of the EC Regulation on Insolvency Proceedings 1346/2000. Chief Registrar Baister also made a s.365 order in *Nicholson v Fayinka* [2014] B.P.I.R. 692. For further guidance on the correct procedure to be used when seeking a s.365 warrant see the comments of ICC Judge Jones in *Lasytsya v Koumettou* [2020] EWHC 660 (Ch). For analysis of this decision see McPhie [2020] 13 C.R.I. 196. For a further successful application under the section by bankruptcy trustees see *Hyde v Djurberg* [2022] EWHC 1534 (Ch) in which there was the real risk of a sale or dissipation of assets and/or destruction of documentation to the detriment of creditors while the court also took into account the bankrupt's mental health issues, depression or possible suicide, and so placed safeguards for the order and its implementation.

Inquiry into bankrupt's dealings and property

366—

S.366(1)

Replace the note with:

Amended by LRO 2010 (SI 2010/18). This permits the trustee or official receiver to ask the court to examine the bankrupt privately (or his spouse, or former spouse, or third parties believed to be in possession of the bankrupt's property or of information about his affairs). Civil partners and former civil partners fall within this section by virtue of Sch.27 to the Civil Partnership Act 2004. On the meaning of "affairs", see s.385(2). The power to direct the bankrupt to attend for examination survives discharge: *Oakes v Simms* [1997] B.P.I.R. 499. On the linkage between ss.366 and 364 see *Hickling v Baker* [2007] EWCA Civ 287; [2007] B.P.I.R. 346.

This changes the previous law in a number of respects. The BA 1914 provision referred to the bankrupt's "wife", which made an assumption which can no longer be justified in an age of sexual equality. The new provision also allows the court to require affidavits from the persons mentioned in para.(a) and (b). This reform, which was recommended by the Cork Report, para.903, reverses the rule in *Ex p. Reynolds* (1882) 21 Ch. D. 601.

On the relationship between s.366 and professional privilege see *Re Murjani* [1996] 1 W.L.R. 1498; [1996] B.C.C. 278; and *Re Ouvaroff* [1997] B.P.I.R. 712. Where inquiries are made of a bank concerning a client's affairs, major issues of confidentiality can arise—*Christofi v Barclays Bank plc* [1999] B.P.I.R. 855.

It was held in *Re Tucker (a Bankrupt) Ex p. Tucker* [1990] Ch. 148 that the court had no jurisdiction under s.25(6) of BA 1914 (the precursor of the present section) over British subjects resident abroad. In *Re Seagull Manufacturing Co Ltd* [1992] Ch. 128 at 137; [1991] B.C.C. 550 at 555 Mummery J expressed the view that there was little doubt that, on the authority of *Re Tucker*, the court would construe ss.366 and 367 as subject to the same territorial limitation. In the Court of Appeal in the same case, [1993] Ch. 345; [1993] B.C.C. 241, no opinion was expressed on this point. The potential extraterritorial effect of s.366 was considered by Patten J in *Buchler v Al Midani (No.2)* [2005] EWHC 3183 (Ch); [2006] B.P.I.R. 867. The English courts would take note of the attitude of foreign courts before exercising discretion under s.366 to make a disclosure order against a party based abroad. Contrast the position in regard to a public examination under s.133: see the notes to that section and to s.236. *Re Tucker* (above) was followed by David Richards J in *Re MF Global UK Ltd* [2015] EWHC 2319 (Ch). But *MF Global* was not followed by HHJ Hodge QC in *Official Receiver v Norriss; Re Omni Trustees (No.2)* [2015] EWHC 2697 (Ch) nor by the court in *Re Carna Meats (UK) Ltd; Wallace v Wallace* [2019] EWHC 2503 (Ch) where extraterritorial application was favoured. In *Re Akkurate Ltd* [2020] EWHC 1433 (Ch) Vos C, setting aside issues tied up with the EU Insolvency Regulation, preferred the views of David Richards J in *MF Global* (above) over the views expressed in *Omni* (above) and *Carna Meats* (above). This difference of opinion on a matter of the scope of the provision will have to be resolved at some later date in a case taken to the Court of Appeal. The Supreme Court did comment upon the extraterritorial application of insolvency legislation in *R. (on the application of KBR Inc) v Director of the SFO* [2021] UKSC 2 at [60]–[65] per Lord Lloyd-Jones, but without deciding upon this particular issue. The position may be different where s.426 can be called into aid: *McIsaac, Petitioners* [1994] B.C.C. 410. Note also *Handelsveem BV v Hill* [2011] B.P.I.R. 1024 (enforcement of a s.366 order of English court by a Dutch Supreme Court using EC Regulation (1346/2000) procedures).

The provision was held to have extraterritorial effect in *Willmont and Sayers (as Joint Trustees of Shlosberg) v AS Citadele Banka* [2018] EWHC 603 (Ch). But this was very much an EU case in that the court ruled that a s.366 order fell within the ambit of what is now the EURIP 2015/848.

For the principles governing the exercise of discretion under s.366 see the comments of Rimer J in *Long v Farrer & Co* [2004] EWHC 1774 (Ch); [2004] B.P.I.R. 1218.

The case of *Hooper v Duncan Lewis (Solicitors) Ltd* [2010] B.P.I.R. 591 should be noted in this context. Here the court acceded to an application for the provision of information under s.366. The order covered disclosure of client files and an examination of the chief executive of the firm of solicitors.

For the permitted use of material obtained by compulsion under this provision see the judgment of Arnold J in *Willmont v Shlosberg; Re Webinvest Ltd* [2017] EWHC 2446 (Ch).

Examinees enjoy immunity from suit—*Al Jaber v Mitchell* [2021] EWCA Civ 1190; [2021] B.P.I.R. 1373. This was a decision under s.236 of the Act, but is applicable by analogy. Further analogies with s.236 were made in *Brittain v Ferster* [2022] EWHC 1060 (Ch) where an order under s.366 was made for the provision of a witness statement and documents. For an interesting application for disclosure of privileged Russian legal advice obtained by a bankrupt's trustees in bankruptcy, brought in the context of their s.366 application, see *Re Yurov; Thomas v Metro Bank plc* [2022] EWHC 2112 (Ch) in which the court commented that it is unusual for there to be an application for disclosure by a respondent to a s.366 application, but the application was partly successful as the court ordered some advice on the Russian law of matrimonial property to be disclosed.

On s.366 generally see *Albert v Albert* [1996] B.P.I.R. 232; and *Bird v Hadkinson* [1999] B.P.I.R. 653. Further provisions on s.366 examinations are contained in the rules: see IR 2016 rr.12.17–12.22. For an illuminating review see Frith (2005) 21 I.L. & P. 141.

THE THIRD GROUP OF PARTS: MISCELLANEOUS MATTERS BEARING ON BOTH COMPANY AND INDIVIDUAL INSOLVENCY; GENERAL INTERPRETATION; FINAL PROVISIONS

Introductory note to the Third Group of Parts

Parts XII–XIX of IA 1986 consist of a great variety of matters. Apart from the usual "mechanical" provisions (interpretation, short title, commencement, etc.), there is a group of sections, namely ss.386–387, which substantially reduced the significance of preferential claims in insolvency law. EA 2002 s.251 further reduced these by removing preferential status from Crown debts, only to have some Crown preference re-established by the Finance Act 2020 s.98 as from 1 December 2020. The provisions on the qualification of insolvency practitioners are to be found in Pt XIII. There is also reference to official receivers (happily retained for corporate and personal insolvencies), the official petitioner, the Insolvency Rules Committee, insolvency service finance, insolvent estates of deceased persons and insolvent partnerships. The connection of other sections within Pt XVII with insolvency law is more indirect—thus there are provisions dealing with Parliamentary disqualification and restrictive trade practices.

Scholars of legislative history should note ss.423–425, which revamp s.172 of LPA 1925, a provision which can trace its own ancestry back to 1571!

PART XVI

PROVISIONS AGAINST DEBT AVOIDANCE (ENGLAND AND WALES ONLY)

Transactions defrauding creditors

423—

GENERAL NOTE

Replace the note with:

The purpose of this section and those immediately following it is to revamp s.172 of LPA 1925, which was used to avoid fraudulent conveyances. The Cork Committee wanted this provision widened, and, in particular, to cover payments of money: see the Report, para.1238. This has been done. There has been a provision along these lines in English law since 1571, and ultimately it can trace its ancestry back to the Paulian action of Roman law. This provision applies to both individuals and companies alike: *Re Shilena Hosiery Co Ltd* [1980] Ch. 219. The great utility of this provision lies in the fact that no time-limit for avoidance is fixed, in contrast with the case of ss.238, 239 and 339, 340. However, this advantage may be more illusory than real in that the courts are reluctant to reopen transactions going back many years—*The Law Society v Southall* [2001] EWCA Civ 2001; [2002] B.P.I.R. 336. There may also be limitation considerations—see *Re Yates* [2005] B.P.I.R. 476 and now *Re Nurkowski* [2006] EWCA Civ 542; [2006] B.P.I.R. 789 (which is discussed below). (For further points of comparison, see the note to s.238.) See generally Milman and Parry (1997) 48 N.I.L.Q. 24; and Keay [1998] J.B.L. 515.

In *Moffat v Moffat* [2020] NICh 17; [2021] B.P.I.R. 1309 the court confirmed that this provision can apply in a non-insolvency context. Indeed many of the cases on s.423 are of that type. It can be invoked in a commercial context and even in connection with matrimonial property disputes—*Akhmedova v Akhmedov* [2021] EWHC 545 (Fam); [2021] B.P.I.R. 1077 (considered and doubted on some grounds in *Invest Bank PSC v El-Husseini* [2022] EWHC 894 (Comm)). For a more contentious usage of s.423 see the comments of ICC Judge Barber in *Hall v Nasim* [2021] EWHC 142 (Ch); [2021] B.P.I.R. 550 (a tax authority).

For guidance on various procedural aspects of a s.423 application see *Godfrey v Torpy, The Times,* 16 May 2007. In *Re Baillies Ltd* [2012] EWHC 285 (Ch); [2012] B.P.I.R. 665 HHJ Purle QC discussed further the proposition that proceedings under s.423 are not insolvency proceedings and so, for example, they do not come within the curative provision in IR 2016 r.10.64. At the end of the day the case turned on the fact that the EC Service Regulation (1393/2007) prevailed over IR 2016 r.10.64. In *Manolete Partners Plc v Hayward & Barrett Holdings Ltd* [2021] EWHC 1481 (Ch); [2022] B.C.C. 159; [2021] B.P.I.R. 1285, Chief ICC Judge Briggs, relying on *Re Taunton Logs Ltd* [2020] EWHC 3480 (Ch); [2021] B.P.I.R. 427, stated that a claim made pursuant to s.423 of the Act may be brought in any part of the High Court (including any list within the Business and Property Courts of England and Wales), but he was adamant that claims under s.423 are not "insolvency proceedings" (since they are not insolvency applications within IR 2016 r.1.35 as IR 2016 give effect to IA 1986 Pts AI–XI and s.423 is in Pt XVI) so that the claim form should be brought under the procedure in CPR Pt 7 rather than IR 2016 r.1.35, for which different procedure and fees are payable—an important warning to litigants and their legal advisors.

On the potential use of s.423 in commercial litigation generally see *Fortress Value Recovery Fund v Blue Skye Special Opportunities Fund* [2013] EWHC 14 (Comm). Here Flaux J took an expansive view of the potential range of the provision by widely defining victim and making the point that the applicant need not be the person whom the debtor had in mind when entering the disputed transaction. The extra territorial scope of s.423 was also confirmed.

Flaux J confirmed the extraterritorial potential of s.423 in *Erste Group Bank AG v JSC "VMZ Red October"* [2013] EWHC 2926 (Comm) and was emphatic that s.423 does not create a statutory tort and cannot be characterised as such. The Supreme Court has held that tortious "asset-stripping" claims which may be available in situations where a claim under s.423 is unavailable (such as intentionally causing loss by unlawful means or knowingly inducing a company to act in wrongful violation of the claimant's rights) can be brought by the company or by a creditor who is not also a shareholder (subject to any limitations on double recovery): *Sevilleja v Marex Financial Ltd* [2020] UKSC 31; [2020] B.C.C. 783.

In *Anglo-German Breweries Ltd v Chelsea Corp Inc* [2012] EWHC 1481 (Ch) instead of invoking s.423 the court decided to lift the veil of separate corporate personality in order to unravel a disputed transaction.

A warning was sent to liquidators who appeared to have attempted to "shoe-horn" their complaints into s.423 in *Hosking v Apax Partners LLP* [2018] EWHC 2732 (Ch) which seemed to Hildyard J in the surrounding circumstances to verge on an abuse of process, and he awarded indemnity costs against them. In *Farrar v Candey Ltd* [2021] EWHC 1950 (Ch), a ruling of Marcus Smith J—the s.423 claim was not pursued as the court found that an assignment was void as being champertous.

In the unusual case of *Deansgate 123 LLP v Workman* [2019] EWHC 2 (Ch) the High Court considered the interaction between a s.423 application and the rule in *Henderson v Henderson* (1843) 3 Hare 100. HHJ Eyre QC also made the perceptive observation that s.423 proceedings are not intended to be punitive. In *Lygoe v Hunt* [2019] EWHC 327 (Ch); [2019] B.P.I.R. 650 Mann J offered some procedural guidance on the formulation and handling of s.423 claims. The Court of Appeal in *Orexim Trading Ltd v Mahavir Port and Terminal Private Ltd* [2018] EWCA Civ 1660; [2019] B.C.C. 179 supported the extraterritorial nature of the s.423 jurisdiction (see further below). For procedural and jurisdictional matters arising in the context of a s.423 claim see *Lemos v Church Bay Trust Co Ltd* [2021] EWHC 1173 (Ch).

Note Banking Act 2009 ss.103 and 145.

S.423(1)–(3)
Replace the note with:

These provisions allow the court to set aside transactions at an undervalue designed to put assets out of reach of creditors. They explain what a transaction at an undervalue is. The definition is similar to that in ss.238(4) and 339(3). Section 423(1)(b) was amended by the Civil Partnership Act 2004 Sch.27. For procedural and jurisdictional matters arising in the context of a s.423 claim see *Lemos v Church Bay Trust Co Ltd* [2021] EWHC 1173 (Ch).

On identification of the relevant "transaction" see *National Westminster Bank v Jones* [2001] EWCA Civ 1541; [2002] B.P.I.R. 361. As to what is a "transaction" for s.423 purposes see *Ailyan and Fry v Smith* [2010] B.P.I.R. 289 and for detailed analysis see *Invest Bank PSC v El-Husseini* [2022] EWHC 894 (Comm) which applied the definition of "transaction" in s.436 and which considered the interesting point of whether a director of a debtor corporate director "enters into" the transaction. Similarly, the court in *Hinton v Wotherspoon* [2022] EWHC 2083 (Ch) described the definition of a "transaction" in s.423 as "inexhaustive" and referred to that in s.436 of "a gift, agreement or arrangement"; it concluded that a contractual agreement giving the bankrupt a right of restriction against any future disposition of the matrimonial home (which was legally and beneficially in his wife's name) was not a transaction within s.423 as the exercise of the restriction by the bankrupt (consenting or refusing to consent to a disposition) was not a gift, agreement or arrangement and did not fall within the inexhaustive meaning of a transaction in s.423(3) (see further below on prohibited transactions). The broad remedy which the court should have in mind is stated in s.423(2), although the specifics (including illustrations of the types of order the court may make) are detailed in s.425. Section 423(3) makes it clear that the transaction must have been intended to have a prejudicial effect.

The restitutionary (as opposed to compensatory) nature of s.423 was noted in *Johnson (Liquidator of Strobe 2 Ltd) v Arden* [2018] EWHC 1624 (Ch) (in which an application for an order against individuals who were involved in the transaction but had not benefitted from it was struck out). See also *Dormco Sica Ltd v SBL Carston Ltd* [2021] EWHC 3209 (Ch) which stressed the restitutionary nature of the remedy provided by the section, and added that the transferee who is liable may make a claim for contribution under the Civil Liability (Contribution) Act 1978 against any other person who may be liable for the same damage.

Section 423 was the basis of a successful application by a creditor in *Arbuthnot Leasing International Ltd v Havelet Leasing Ltd (No.2)* [1990] B.C.C. 636. In acceding to the application Scott J held that the fact that the debtor had acted on legal advice did not exclude the debtor having the purpose specified in s.423(3)(a). Where there is a prima facie breach of s.423 the court may lift the veil of professional privilege to ascertain motives: *Barclays Bank v Eustice* [1995] 1 W.L.R. 1238; [1995] B.C.C. 978. The status of this authority in providing an exception to the protection of legal privilege was affirmed in *Brent LBC v Kane* [2014] EWHC 4564 (Ch). See also *Re Schuppan* [1997] B.P.I.R. 271.

In *Chohan v Saggar* [1992] B.C.C. 306 (on appeal, [1994] B.C.C. 134) it was held that the requirements of subs.(3) are satisfied provided the dominant purpose of the debtor was to achieve one of the prohibited aims. This analysis sits uneasily alongside the approach the courts have taken to s.238 (see above). Indeed, in *Royscot Spa Leasing Ltd v Lovett* [1995] B.C.C. 502 the Court of Appeal was prepared to accept a test based upon substantial (rather than dominant) purpose, though it did stress that it was important to distinguish between the purpose behind a transaction and the result of it. The dominant purpose test was favoured by Lightman J in *Banca Carige v Banco Nacional de Cuba* [2001] B.P.I.R. 407. The opposite view taken by the Court of Appeal in *Hashmi v Inland Revenue Commissioners* [2002] EWCA Civ 981; [2002] B.C.C. 943 appeared to apply a "substantial purpose" test again, and that approach was noted in *Kubiangha v Ekpenyong* [2002] EWHC 1567 (Ch); [2002] 2 B.C.L.C. 597. In *4Eng Ltd v Harper* [2009] EWHC 2633 (Ch); [2010] B.C.C. 746; [2010] B.P.I.R. 1 the "substantial purpose" test was again reaffirmed. The mental state of the recipient is not relevant when trying to determine the purpose of the debtor when entering into the transaction: *Moon v Franklin* [1996] B.P.I.R. 196. The court stressed the importance of *purpose* in *Papanicola v Fagan* [2009] B.P.I.R. 320. Here it was clear that the *result* of the transaction would be to defeat creditors but the *purpose* of the transaction was to help to preserve the debtor's marriage. A detailed consideration of this provision is found in the judgment of Sales J in *4Eng Ltd v Harper* (above). Amongst the various points made was the support for the substantial purpose test. Some consideration was also given to the relevance of the state of mind of the transferee. In *JSC Mezhdunarodniy Promyshlenniy Bank v Pugachev* [2017] EWHC 2426 (Ch) there is to be found at [443] a short comment by Birss J distinguishing purpose and result and identifying the appropriate timing of purpose. The High Court in *Pathania v Tashie-Lewis* [2018] EWHC 362 (Ch); [2021] B.P.I.R. 661 emphasised that it is the purpose of the transaction which is determinative (a master had denied relief to the claimant on the basis that a sale of the property disposed of would have happened in any event, with no sale proceeds remaining for the claimant after satisfaction of a secured lender, but the High Court held that one of the statutory purposes was nonetheless established and ordered payment of the amount of the undervalue to the sole creditor accordingly). *JSC BTA Bank v Ablyazov* [2018] EWCA Civ 1176; [2019] B.C.C. 96 provides an instructive discussion of the matter of motive/purpose under s.423 by the Court of Appeal, refining the position from *Hashmi* (above), with Leggatt LJ moving away from "substantial purpose", noting at [13], that if the transaction was entered for more than one purpose, the court does not have to be satisfied that the prohibited purpose was the dominant purpose, let alone the sole purpose: it was sufficient if the statutory purpose was "*a* purpose". He went on at [14] that the word "substantial" is not actually used in s.423: and he could see "no necessity or warrant for reading this (or any other adjective) into the wording of the section. At best it introduces unnecessary complication and at worst introduces an additional requirement which makes the test stricter than Parliament intended ... there is no need to put a potentially confusing gloss on the statutory language. It is sufficient simply to ask whether the transaction was entered into by the debtor for the prohibited purpose. If it was, then the transaction falls within s.423(3), even if it was also entered into for one or more other purposes. The test is no more complicated than that.". This approach was adopted in *National Bank Trust v Yurov* [2020] EWHC 100 (Comm). In *JSC* (above) the Court of Appeal stressed that *any* purpose will suffice for s.423 to come into play. There was no need for a *substantial* purpose to be established. This point was followed by ICC Judge Barber in *Re Watkin; Wood v Watkin* [2019] EWHC 1311 (Ch); [2019] B.P.I.R. 1265. In spite of this expansive view, there was a failed application in this case due to a lack of evidence. For analysis see McPhie [2019] 12 C.R.I. 171. The above concept of not applying a gloss to the statutory wording of the section was applied, in a different context, in *Akhmedova v Akhmedova* [2021] EWHC 545 (Fam) so that there is no gateway condition in s.423 requiring that, to obtain relief, a creditor has to prove that the debtor had insufficient assets following the impugned transaction to meet the liability owed: any such condition was absent from the plain wording of the statute and binding authority deprecated reading additional words into the section.

In *Durkan v Patel* [2018] EWHC 3231 (Ch) an attempt by a trustee in bankruptcy to use s.423 to challenge the transfer of an interest in the family home some 12 years before the bankruptcy failed because the evidence did not support the view that the transfer was made with the purpose of defeating creditors. On the question of purpose see also *New Media Distribution Co Sezc Ltd v Kagalovsky* [2018] EWHC 2876 (Ch) (Marcus Smith J) and *Northampton BC v Cardoza* [2019] EWHC 26 (Ch); [2019] B.C.C. 582 and *Fox v Mohammed* [2019] EWHC 3409 (Ch). In *Deposit Guarantee Fund for Individuals v Bank Frick & Co AG* [2022] EWHC 2221 (Ch) the pleaded material did not contain material which justified an inference of the avoidance purpose in s.423(3).

In *Agricultural Mortgage Corp plc v Woodward* [1994] B.C.C. 688 a transaction falling within s.423(1)(c) was encountered. Here the Court of Appeal found that a grant of an agricultural tenancy by a farmer to his wife just before the mortgagee of the farm was intending to enforce the security was a transaction at an undervalue and should be set aside. Although a fair market rent had been charged by the husband, that rent did not take into account the fact that the wife as tenant could effectively hold the mortgagee to ransom by denying it vacant possession and thus preventing it enforcing its security. Looking at the transaction as a whole the arrangement was designed to defeat the interests of the mortgagee and the wife received real benefits outside the formal tenancy agreement that had not been paid for. In *Midland Bank v Wyatt* [1996] B.P.I.R. 288 a sham family trust established to protect assets in the event of business failure was avoided under s.423. Note also *Re Schuppan* [1997] B.P.I.R. 271 where an attempt by a wife to argue that nothing of value had been transferred was unsuccessful. A successful s.423 case was found in *Trowbridge v Trowbridge* [2003] B.P.I.R. 258. A s.423 application succeeded in *Beckenham MC Ltd v Centralex Ltd* [2004] EWHC 1287 (Ch); [2004] B.P.I.R. 1112 where a property transfer had been carried out in order to defeat the possible grant of a charging order against that property. Another successful s.423 application was exemplified by *Gil v Baygreen Properties Ltd* [2004] EWHC 1732 (Ch); [2005] B.P.I.R. 95. See also *AET v Kermanshahchi* [2003] EWHC 1939 (Ch); [2003] B.P.I.R. 1229; and *Pena v Coyne* [2004] B.P.I.R. 1286. Section 423 was successfully invoked in *Swift Advances plc v Ahmed* [2015] EWHC 3265 (Ch). A s.423 application had succeeded at first instance in *Cole v Billington* [2013] EWCA Civ 502 and the appeal by the defendant was dismissed. In *Barons Finance Ltd v Barons Bridging Finance 1 Ltd* [2018] EWHC 496 (Ch) a purported assignment of secured loans which was void under s.127 and s.238 would also have been void under s.423 (appeal dismissed: [2019] EWCA Civ 2074). For cases falling on the other side of the line see *Menzies v National Bank of Kuwait SAK* [1994] B.C.C. 119; *Pinewood Joinery v Starelm Properties Ltd* [1994] B.C.C. 569; *Re Brabon* [2000] B.P.I.R. 537; *Re Taylor Sinclair (Capital) Ltd* [2002] B.P.I.R. 203. On s.423 note also *Ashe v Mumford* [2001] B.P.I.R. 1. See *Simon Carves Ltd v Hussain* [2013] EWHC 685 (Ch) (Sir William Blackburne) for another abortive attempt to exploit s.423 in a commercial context.

In *Feakins v DEFRA* [2005] EWCA Civ 1513; [2007] B.C.C. 54; [2006] B.P.I.R. 895 the jurisdiction under s.423 came under the judicial microscope in the Court of Appeal. As is now consistent with modern authority a wide view of these provisions was adopted. In particular the concept of a "transaction" was applied flexibly to include any arrangement whether it be a formal agreement or informal understanding. The court also adopted a "commercial" view when determining any differential in consideration exchanged between the parties as part of the transaction. On the use of s.423 in commercial litigation generally see *Concept Oil Services Ltd v EN-GIN Group LLP* [2013] EWHC 1897 (Comm). Here Flaux J indicated that the word "transaction" when used in a s.423 context was capable of wide interpretation. It could in principle cover the transfer or continuation of an English company in a foreign jurisdiction. This restructuring would amount to an arrangement which constituted a transaction for s.423 purposes. This interpretation echoes that adopted by Jonathan Parker LJ in *Feakins v DEFRA* (above). *Payroller Ltd v Little Panda Consultants Ltd* [2018] EWHC 3161 (QB) provides a valuable discussion on the meaning of a "transaction" for the purposes of this provision. See also *Pathania v Tashie-Lewis* [2018] EWHC 362 (Ch); [2018] All E.R. (D) 61 (May); [2021] B.P.I.R. 661—noted in Recovery (Autumn 2018) at 8. The court here made the important point that there is no additional causation test included in the wording of s.423.

Furthermore, the Court of Appeal in *Re Nurkowski; Hill v Spread Trustee Co Ltd* [2006] EWCA Civ 542; [2006] B.C.C. 646; [2006] B.P.I.R. 789 made a number of important observations on ss.423–425. First, the Inland Revenue could be a "victim" for the purposes of these provisions where property transactions had occurred with the substantial purpose of misleading the tax authorities as to potential capital gains tax liability. The concept should be interpreted flexibly; a party could be a potential victim at one date, cease to be a victim at another and then revert to victim status at some later time. A claim under s.423 that involved a settlement of property being set aside was subject to a 12-year limitation period with time running from the date of the bankruptcy order. The Court of Appeal also took the opportunity to express the view (without finally determining the matter) that the grant of security might constitute a transaction at an undervalue, thereby doubting *Re MC Bacon Ltd* [1991] Ch. 127; [1990] B.C.C. 430 on this point.

This is interesting as a somewhat differently constituted Court of Appeal in *Feakins v DEFRA* (above) did not express such doubts. This issue is likely to be revisited in future litigation.

In *Sands v Clitheroe* [2006] B.P.I.R. 1000 further consideration was given to the question of who might invoke s.423. Here Registrar Jaques held that a party could in principle invoke s.423 to challenge a transaction entered into many years previously if the substantive requirements of the section were met. The fact that the particular claimant was not in the contemplation of the transferor at the time of the transaction was immaterial. All that was required was that the claimant was prejudiced by the transaction albeit at some later date. This, along with other rulings noted above, will expand the potential of transaction avoidance under s.423.

When assessing differences in the value of consideration the court is concerned with real economic benefits and not artificial book values—*Pena v Coyne (No.1)* [2004] EWHC 2684 (Ch); [2004] 2 B.C.L.C. 703. The curious case of *Delaney v Chen* [2010] EWCA Civ 1455; [2011] B.P.I.R. 39 should be noted with regard to the question of the burden of proving that a transaction was at an undervalue. Here it was found that there was no undervalue on the facts. The Court of Appeal judgment contains a useful discussion of the valuation rules. If "no consideration" in s.423(1) is contended it is important that the particulars of claim establish this (*Pathania v Tashie-Lewis* [2021] EWHC 526 (Ch); [2021] B.P.I.R. 681).

Further consideration of s.423 is to be found in *Kali Ltd v Chawla* [2007] EWHC 1989 (Ch); [2007] EWHC 2357 (Ch); [2008] B.P.I.R. 415. Section 423 was invoked successfully in *Griffin v Awoderu* [2008] B.P.I.R. 877, where the court (D. Phillips QC) reviewed its options in redressing the position. A s.423 claim brought on behalf of the Crown succeeded in *HM Treasury Solicitor v Doveton* [2009] B.P.I.R. 352. Here a will was found to be forged and as a result dispositions made under it were avoided and property became bona vacantia. *Barnett v Semenyuk* [2008] B.P.I.R. 1427 provides another illustration of a successful s.423 claim.

For further consideration of the interface between s.423 and the Limitation Act 1980 see *Giles v Rhind* [2008] EWCA Civ 118; [2009] Ch. 191; [2009] B.C.C. 590 where the Court of Appeal indicated that a s.423 claim involved an allegation of "breach of duty" for the purposes of s.32(2) of the Limitation Act 1980. Procedural aspects of the operation of limitation in the context of insolvency litigation were reviewed by HHJ Matthews in *Bell v Ide* [2020] EWHC 230 (Ch) and further by the Court of Appeal in *Re Ide (a Bankrupt); HH Aluminium & Building Products Ltd v Bell* [2020] EWCA Civ 1469; [2021] B.P.I.R. 113.

Note also *Stow v Stow* [2008] EWHC 495 (Ch); [2008] B.P.I.R. 673 where the potential utility of s.423 to the HMRC was commented upon. See also *Revenue and Customs Commissioners v Begum* [2010] EWHC 1799 (Ch); [2011] B.P.I.R. 59. On the potential for a s.423 claim see *Brittain v Courtway Estates* [2008] B.P.I.R. 1229.

In *Soutzos v Asombang* [2010] B.P.I.R. 960 an attempt to challenge a transaction under s.423 failed. The court also made the point that, even if the s.423 claim had been upheld, no relief could have been granted. Another abortive s.423 application featured in *Williams v Taylor* [2012] EWCA Civ 1443. Here although there were elements suggesting that the transaction was at an undervalue the court preferred to accept the evidence of the bankrupt and his wife offering an alternative explanation. A s.423 application was also dismissed by Registrar Jones in *Rubin v Dweck* [2012] B.P.I.R. 854. A number of key points were stressed in the judgment. The limitation period runs from the date of the bankruptcy order. Giving up potential rights in matrimonial proceedings could constitute valuable consideration. In *Bibby ACF Ltd v Agate* [2013] B.P.I.R. 685 Master Bowles refused to follow *Rubin v Dweck* (above) on the question of the valuation of consideration. Master Bowles found that there had been a transaction at an undervalue but the requirement of an intention to defeat creditors had not been established. The s.423 claim therefore failed. For yet another failed s.423 claim see *Withers LLP v Harrison-Welch* [2012] EWHC 3077 (QB) where the grant of security over the property had the effect of defeating a charging order granted in favour of creditor. The court held that on the evidence the grant of the security was not for the purpose of defeating the claim of the creditor.

A speculative s.423 argument failed in *Westbrook Dolphin Square Ltd v Friends Life Ltd* [2014] EWHC 2433 (Ch). The case is valuable for the in depth study of the requirements of s.423 carried out by Mann J. On the other hand, in *Re Husky Group Ltd, Watchorn v Jupiter Industries Ltd* [2014] EWHC 3003 (Ch) an assignment of a trademark was set aside by HHJ Purle QC under s.423. In *B v IB* [2013] EWHC 3755 (Fam); [2014] B.P.I.R. 331 Parker J refused to dismiss a s.423 application which sought to challenge various intra family property transfers. The wide potential usage of s.423 in non-bankruptcy situations was emphasised. A trust deed was found not to be a sham in *Ali v Bashir* [2014] EWHC 3853 (Ch) but nevertheless set aside as a contravention of s.423. An attempt to invoke s.423 was dismissed by Newey J in *Sands v Singh* [2016] EWHC 636 (Ch); [2016] B.P.I.R. 737 because as the alternative claim under s.339 was rejected there was no prospect of a successful claim under s.423. See the General Note to s.339 for further information. A TUV claim failed in *Vasdev v Bellnorth Ltd* [2017] EWHC 1395 (Ch).

In *4Eng Ltd v Harper* [2009] EWHC 2633 (Ch); [2010] B.C.C. 746 some consideration was given to the relevance of the state of mind of the transferee. By way of contrast, in *Moon v Franklin* [1996] B.P.I.R. 196 this was regarded as an irrelevant consideration. For a detailed analysis of other aspects of the decision in *4Eng Ltd v Harper* (above) (especially on the concept of "change of position") see *Bucknall v Wilson* [2021] EWHC 2149 (Ch).

This provision is capable of having extraterritorial effect—*Revenue and Customs Commissioners v Begum* [2010]

EWHC 1799 (Ch). This point was confirmed obiter by Sir Andrew Morritt in *Bilta (UK) Ltd v Nazir* [2012] EWHC 2163 (Ch) at [41]. It seems that this interpretation favouring extraterritorial application was implicitly supported on appeal sub nom. *Jetivia SA v Bilta (UK) Ltd* [2013] EWCA Civ 968; [2013] B.C.C. 655 especially at [90] per Patten LJ. Although the s.423 point was not specifically addressed when the case reached the Supreme Court (see [2015] UKSC 23; [2016] A.C. 1; [2015] B.C.C. 343) it is implicit in all of the judgments that s.423 would have extraterritorial effect. To give it such effect is to respond to the reality of modern global commerce. See also *Revenue and Customs Commissioners v Ben Nevis (Holdings) Ltd* [2012] EWHC 1807 (Ch); [2012] S.T.C. 2157 at paras [61]–[68] per HHJ Pelling QC for further consideration of the extra-territorial effect and other jurisdictional issues arising in connection with a s.423 claim. In *Erste Group Bank AG v JSC "VMZ Red October"* [2015] EWCA Civ 379; [2015] 1 B.C.L.C. 706 the Court of Appeal allowed an appeal from the first instance ruling of Flaux J ([2013] EWHC 2926 (Comm)), who had given permission for service outside the jurisdiction, but confirmed the extraterritorial application of s.423 (see [116]). That said, the Court of Appeal declined jurisdiction to allow the s.423 claim to be heard in England as there was no significant connection with the English jurisdiction—see [126]. The alleged tort had been committed in Russia and practicality suggested that the proper forum for resolution of the issue was in Russia. The question of CPR "gateways" and service outside the jurisdiction were issues considered again in *Orexim Trading Ltd v Mahavir Port and Terminal Private Ltd* [2018] EWCA Civ 1660; [2019] B.C.C. 179 where the Court of Appeal preferred the views of Flaux J in *Erste* (above) over those of HH Judge Waksman expressed at first instance in respect of the availability of the gateway for service of a s.423 claim. A s.423 claim provided a CPR gateway for service out in *China Metal Recycling (Holdings) Ltd (in liq.) v Chun Chi Wai* [2020] EWHC 318 (Ch) against defendants in Hong Kong, albeit the appropriate forum for the claim was England. The extraterritorial potential of s.423 was confirmed by Knowles J in *Akhmedova v Akhmedov* [2021] EWHC 545 (Fam); [2021] B.P.I.R. 1077. This provision's ability to apply on an extraterritorial basis was confirmed by Henshaw J in *Kazakhstan Kagazy plc v Zhunus* [2021] EWHC 3462 (Comm) at [230], but the case must have a sufficient connection with the jurisdiction in England and Wales—see [231]. On jurisdiction to hear s.423 applications note also Calver J in *Integral Petroleum v Petrogat FZA* [2021] EWHC 1365 (Comm) and Butcher J in *Suppipat v Narongdej* [2020] EWHC 3191 (Comm); [2021] B.P.I.R. 756.

On s.423 applications and the now superseded EC Regulation on Insolvency Proceedings (1346/2000) see *Byers v Yacht Bull Corp* [2010] EWHC 133 (Ch); [2010] B.C.C. 368; [2010] B.P.I.R. 535. Note *Re Phoenix Kapitaldienst GmbH* [2012] EWHC 62 (Ch); [2013] Ch. 61; [2012] B.C.C. 561 (availability of s.423 to a foreign office holder via use of comity principle at common law). One wonders about the authority of this ruling (which placed heavy reliance upon the views expressed by Lord Hoffmann in *Cambridge Gas* [2006] UKPC 26; [2007] 1 A.C. 508; [2006] B.C.C. 962) in the light of the more restrictive approach towards the comity principle in international insolvency law taken by the majority of the Supreme Court in *Rubin v Eurofinance* [2012] UKSC 46; [2013] 1 A.C. 236; [2013] B.C.C. 1. In *Singularis Holdings Ltd v PricewaterhouseCoopers (Bermuda)* [2014] UKPC 36; [2015] A.C. 1675; [2015] B.C.C. 66 Lord Collins (at [98]) went so far as to say that *Phoenix* (above) had been wrongly decided. For further discussion on a foreign office-holder seeking to use the comity principle at common law (to obtain recognition of foreign insolvency proceedings in Russia) where the court cited several of the above leading cases, see the informative judgment of Snowden J in *Kireeva v Bedzhamov* [2021] EWHC 2281 (Ch), although the actual decision to make a recognition order at common law was overruled by the Court of Appeal ([2022] EWCA Civ 35) and the point remitted to the High Court for determination (for which the court has subsequently and exceptionally granted security for costs to the debtor in the claim as the Russian bankruptcy trustee had no assets in England and Wales against which an order for costs could be enforced, there was a real risk of non-enforcement in Russia, and there was no assurance that the trustee's litigation funder would fund an adverse costs order if the application for recognition failed: [2022] EWHC 1047 (Ch)). The Court of Appeal went on (at [134]) to describe *Cambridge Gas* as "the high water mark" and that the decisions in *Rubin* and *Singularis* represented at least a retrenchment of principle and did not support the more expansive approach to modified universalism in *Cambridge Gas*.

Applications under the Northern Irish counterpart provision (art.367 of the 1989 Insolvency Order) featured in two cases which came before McCloskey J, namely *Quinn Finance v Galfis Overseas Ltd* [2012] NICh 9 and *Quinn Finance v Lyndhurst Development Trading SA* [2012] NICh 15. For a later example see the failed application in *Moffat v Moffat* [2020] NICh 17 in which the court confirmed that art.367 applies in circumstances where there is no actual or threatened insolvency, unlike ss.238 and 339 and their Northern Ireland equivalent provisions on transfers at an undervalue.

Section 423 can, in appropriate circumstances, be used to challenge the payment of a dividend to company shareholders that was otherwise lawful—see *BTI 2014 LLC v Sequana SA* [2019] EWCA Civ 112; [2019] B.C.C. 631. A dividend could not be viewed as a gift but it could constitute a transaction for the purposes of s.423. This important ruling (which also addresses the issue of the duty to creditors under s.172(3) of the Companies Act 2006) has caused some concern in the business community. A decision of the Supreme Court on this appeal was eagerly awaited but when it came ([2022] UKSC 25) the s.423 issue was not appealed, although some of the justices did refer to the section as one among a number of rules of insolvency law which provide creditors with protection against behaviour by directors which prejudices their interests (see the note to s.212 for further detail on the Supreme Court judgment). For the implications of the Court of Appeal judgment in *BTI 2014 LLC v Sequana* (above) see Smith [2019] Recovery (Summer) 32. It was applied in *Burnden Holdings (UK) Ltd v Fielding* [2019] EWHC 1566 (Ch); [2020] B.P.I.R. 1 (the necessary purpose, however, being found not to have been present). In *Burden Holdings (UK) Ltd v Fielding* (above) Zacaroli J made a number of important observations with regard to the scope of s.423. He confirmed its potential application to distributions made by companies but did not find it applicable on the facts. He considered whether it might apply to the grant of security, but again rejected that possibility—in so deciding he preferred the conclusions of Millett J in *Re MC Bacon Ltd* [1990] B.C.C. 78 to the tentative view of Arden LJ expressed in *Hill v Spread Trustees* [2007] 1 W.L.R. 2404 that it might have application in that context. Finally, he considered the issue of limitation period with respect to a s.423 claim and indicated that if the claim was essentially one of monetary recovery then a six-year limitation period applied. Note also *Stanley v Wilson* (unreported, 5 August 2016, HHJ Raeside QC) for possible linkage with s.342A. For the interface between a potential s.423 application and the freezing order jurisdiction see *Lemos v Lemos* [2016] EWCA Civ 1181. A worldwide freezing order was granted without notice in relation to an arbitration award under the section in *Integral Petroleum SA v Petrogat FZA* [2021] EWHC 1365 (Comm) with an order for service of the order out of the jurisdiction by alternative means in the special or exceptional circumstances of the case.

For an example of arbitration in s.423 proceedings, see *Deposit Guarantee Fund for Individuals v Bank Frick & Co AG* [2021] EWHC 3226 (Ch).

A transaction would include the settlement of property into a trust—*Kazakhstan Kagazy plc v Zhunus* [2021] EWHC 3462 (Comm).

Aspects of this provision were discussed by HHJ Hodge QC in *Leeds v Lemos* [2017] EWHC 1825 (Ch); [2017] B.P.I.R. 1223. The point was made that a claim to recover property under s.423 does not mean that said property is at the time of the claim property within the estate for the purposes of s.436.

Section 423 was successfully invoked in *Barons Finance Ltd v Barons Bridging Finance 1 Ltd* [2018] EWHC 496 (Ch), a decision of David Stone sitting as a deputy judge in the High Court. An appeal from this decision was dismissed without comment on s.423—see *Barons Finance Ltd v Barons Bridging Finance 1 Ltd* [2019] EWCA Civ 2074. A s.423 application also succeeded in *Northampton BC v Cardoza* [2019] EWHC 26 (Ch); [2019] B.C.C. 582. See also *Re Cartwright (a Bankrupt); Rendle v Panelform Ltd* [2020] EWHC 2655 (Ch) (HHJ Cooke) (transaction involving transfer of business assets set aside).

The difficulties of establishing the requisite "purpose", so necessary for s.423 purposes, were exemplified in *Re Farrell* [2019] EWHC 119 (Ch) where the avoidance claim was rejected.

PART XVIII

INTERPRETATION

Expressions used generally

436—

GENERAL NOTE

Replace the note with:

This is general interpretation provision for the Act. It should be read in the light of Pts VII, XI and s.435. Note that the general meaning given to words by s.436 can be excluded where the context demands this.

The "appointed day" was 29 December 1986: see the note to s.443.

The EEA State definition was inserted by the Insolvency Act 1986 (Amendment) Regulations 2005 (SI 2005/879). Note amendment by the Companies Act 2006 (Consequential Amendments, Transitional Provisions and Savings) Order 2009 (SI 2009/1941) (effective from 1 October 2009). This makes a number of changes, some of which result from the enactment of the Companies Act 2006.

Revised definition of "the Companies Acts" by the Companies Act 2006 (Commencement No.3, Consequential Amendments, Transitional Provisions and Savings) Order 2007 (SI 2007/2194 (C. 84)) art.10 and Sch.4 para.45 as from 1 October 2007, recognises the Companies Act 2006.

A definition of "distress" was added by Sch.13 para.85 of the Tribunals, Courts and Enforcement Act 2007 as activated by the Tribunals, Courts and Enforcement Act 2007 (Commencement No. 11) Order 2014 (SI 2014/768 (C. 27)) and the Tribunals, Courts and Enforcement Act 2007 (Consequential, Transitional and Saving Provisions) Order 2014 (SI 2014/600). This change took effect on 6 April 2014.

The definition of "EU Regulation" was inserted (replacing former definition to "EC Regulation") by the Insolvency

Amendment (EU 2015/848) Regulations 2017 (SI 2017/702) regs 1, 2(1), Sch. paras 1, 28 in relation to proceedings opened on or after 26 June 2017 (see reg.3) when the Recast EU Regulation 2015/848 came into force. The definition was amended by the Insolvency (Amendment) (EU Exit) Regulations 2019 (SI 2019/146) reg.1(3), Sch. paras 16, 42 as from IP completion day (11pm on 31 December 2020) subject to transitional and saving provisions in reg.4 (in light of Brexit) to refer only to the "retained" provisions of the EU Regulation (reproduced in Vol.2).

A company's interest as lessee under a lease of a chattel (an aircraft) was held to be "property" within the statutory definition contained in this section in *Bristol Airport plc v Powdrill; Re Paramount Airways Ltd* [1990] Ch. 744; [1990] B.C.C. 130. An expectation to receive a payment from the Criminal Injuries Compensation Board is not property: *Re a Bankrupt (No.145 of 1995)* [1996] B.P.I.R. 238. Compare *Re Rae* [1995] B.C.C. 102; and *Performing Rights Society v Rowland* [1998] B.P.I.R. 128. In *Official Receiver v Environment Agency* [1999] B.P.I.R. 986 the Court of Appeal held that a waste management licence was property for the purposes of s.436. In *Dear v Reeves* [2001] EWCA Civ 277; [2001] B.P.I.R. 577 a right of pre-emption was held to constitute "property" as were oc-cupational benefits in *Patel v Jones* [2001] B.P.I.R. 919. In *Re Hemming (decd)* [2009] B.P.I.R. 50 the court (Richard Snowden QC) held that the right of a residuary legatee (who had become bankrupt) to have the estate of the deceased properly administered was "property" for the purposes of s.436. This again is consistent with a broad interpretation of this pivotal concept in bankruptcy law and was applied by the Court of Appeal in *Hughes v Howell* [2021] EWCA Civ 1431. On the bankruptcy estate see generally Brown (2007) 11 J.S.P.L. 89.

In *Webster v Ashcroft* [2011] EWHC 3848 (Ch); [2012] 1 W.L.R. 1309 rights arising under a proprietary estoppel were held to be property within the meaning of s.436. In *Walden v Atkins* [2013] EWHC 1387 (Ch); [2013] B.P.I.R. 943 the court confirmed that rights arising under an estoppel could be viewed as falling within the definition of property for the purposes of insolvency legislation. See *McGann v Bisping* [2021] EWHC 704 (QB) where rights aris-ing under a contract were viewed as "property".

See also *Ward v Official Receiver* [2012] B.P.I.R. 1073 where a wide view of what might constitute property was adopted by Khan DJ in the context of sums received after the making of PPI misselling complaints. A similarly wide view was taken by the court in *Shop Direct Finance Company Ltd v Official Receiver* [2022] EWHC 1355 (Comm), where it was held that the right to bring a complaint under the FCA's Dispute Resolution: Complaints sourcebook vests in the trustee in bankruptcy and that, as a result, for the purposes of that sourcebook, the complainant in relation to PPI misselling complaints which had been lodged by the Official Receiver was the Official Receiver, and not the respective bankrupt. It followed that the limitation period prescribed by that sourcebook which is based on awareness on the part of the complainant that it has cause for complaint commenced when the Official Receiver, not the respec-tive bankrupt, became aware (or ought to have become aware) that it had cause for complaint.

Appeal rights in tax cases may be property rights within the meaning of s.436—*McNulty v Revenue and Customs Commissioners* [2012] S.T.C. 2110. Note the surprising conclusion reached by HHJ Pelling in *Re GP Aviation Group International Ltd* [2013] EWHC 1447 (Ch); [2013] B.P.I.R. 576 to the effect that a bare right of appeal would not normally constitute property. This conclusion is arrived at after a careful review of the underlying authorities. That said, it does go against the general flow of authorities in this area where an expansive view has been taken as to what could be regarded as "property". *Shlosberg v Avonwick Holdings Ltd* [2016] EWHC 1001 (Ch) raised the issue of whether a right to legal privilege constituted "property". Arnold J ruled that it was not to be so regarded. The appeal from the decision of Arnold J was dismissed in *Avonwick Holdings Ltd v Shlosberg* [2016] EWCA Civ 1138.

See *Thornhill v Atherton (No.2)* [2008] B.P.I.R. 691 (foreign property). For confirmation that foreign property is covered see *Sanders v Donovan* [2012] B.P.I.R. 219 (Chief Registrar Baister).

A piece of property that is subject to a recovery claim under s.423 is not to be regarded as "property" for the purposes of s.436—*Leeds v Lemos* [2017] EWHC 1825 (Ch); [2017] B.P.I.R. 1223.

Presumably this definition is wide enough to include cryptocurrencies (such as bitcoin) and trading items like carbon credits.

Note the unusual case of *Gwinnutt v George* [2019] EWCA Civ 656 where a barrister's unpaid, non-contractual, fees were held by the Court of Appeal (overruling first instance) to be capable of realisation and thus "property" as defined by s.436(1) for vesting purposes in the barrister's trustee in bankruptcy. This is further evidence of an expansive view of what constitutes property for the purposes of inclusion in the bankruptcy estate. The Court of Ap-peal made the point that "property" takes its meaning from the statutory context. Insolvency legislation intended the bankruptcy estate to be as wide as possible (subject to statutory carve outs) in order to protect the interests of creditors.

On the meaning of "transaction" see *Dormco Sica Ltd v SBL Carston Ltd* [2021] EWHC 3209 (Ch) and *Invest Bank PSC v El-Husseini* [2022] EWHC 894 (Comm).

SCHEDULE B1

ADMINISTRATION

Introductory note to Schedule B1
Replace this note with:

Schedule B1 was inserted into IA 1986 by EA 2002 s.248(1), (2), with effect from 15 September 2003 (see the Enterprise Act 2002 (Commencement No. 4 and Transitional Provisions and Savings) Order 2003 (SI 2003/2093 (C. 85)) art.2(1) and Sch.1), introducing a new Pt II and inaugurating a wholly new corporate administration regime. Section 248 states that the new Pt II shall "be substituted" for the original Pt II, but this does not mean that the original Pt II is repealed, for s.249, immediately following, reinstates the latter for many purposes. (See the Introductory note to the new Part II.) The original Pt II and the accompanying rules, with annotations, are to be found in the 19th edition of this *Guide*, Vol.2.

The Insolvency (Amendment) Rules 2003 (SI 2003/1730, also effective 15 September 2003) r.5 complements Sch.B1 by substituting a new Pt 2 of the Rules for the original Pt 2 of IR 1986. However, as with Pt II of the Act, the original Pt 2 of the Rules is preserved for those cases where a company or other body is put into administration under the original Pt II. There are thus two sets of rules governing corporate administrations; and, confusingly, the rules of each Pt 2 were similarly (but not correspondingly) numbered. All references to the rules in this annotation to Sch.B1 are to the substituted rules as now consolidated into the Insolvency (England and Wales) Rules 2016, unless otherwise stated.

Although Sch.B1 applies both in England and Wales and in Scotland, a company can only enter administration, by any of the statutory procedures, in the jurisdiction of its incorporation (i.e. a Scottish company must do so in Scotland): *Re Brownridge Plastics Ltd* (unreported, referred to in *Dear IP*, December 2005), and now see *Bank Leumi (UK) plc, Petitioner* [2017] CSOH 129; [2017] B.C.C. 753.

Schedule B1 applies (with modifications) to insurance companies, except that the appointment of an administrator can only be made by court order: see the Financial Services and Markets Act 2000 (Administration Orders Relating to Insurers) Order 2010 (SI 2010/3023) art.2 (replacing as from 1 February 2011 the Financial Services and Markets Act 2000 (Administration Orders Relating to Insurers) Order 2002 (SI 2002/1242) art.3) and the note to para.9.

The Insolvency Service early in 2003 issued a consultation paper proposing that the new Pt II regime should be extended to insolvent partnerships, and this was done by the Insolvent Partnerships (Amendment) Order 2005 (SI 2005/1516), operative from 1 July 2005; the Insolvent Partnerships Order 1994 (SI 1994/2421) was further amended by the Insolvency (Miscellaneous Amendments) Regulations 2017 (SI 2017/1119) as from 8 December 2017. Similar amendments to the Limited Liability Partnerships Regulations 2001 were made by SI 2005/1989 with effect from 1 October 2005 and again by SI 2017/1119 as from 8 December 2017. Thus from 8 December 2017 the relevant provisions of IR 2016 (as modified) apply to insolvent partnerships and LLPs. Building society administrations continue to be regulated by the original Pt II.

Banks and the other bodies mentioned in IA 1986 s.422(1) which are companies within the meaning of CA 2006 ss.1(1), 1171 have also been brought within the new Pt II (see the Banks (Former Authorised Institutions) (Insolvency) Order 2006 (SI 2006/3107), effective 15 December 2006). Previously the original Pt II had governed administrations relating to these bodies by virtue of the Banks (Administration Proceedings) Order 1989 (SI 1989/1276, as amended). The 2006 Order art.3 and Sch., provides that certain modifications shall be applied to Pt II in relation to the application of the administration procedure to these institutions. In particular, these modifications confer rights on the Financial Conduct Authority or the Prudential Regulation Authority (as appropriate) to participate in the proceedings. In contrast with the legislation governing insurance companies, these bodies may be put into administration without a court order (but the consent of the FCA and the PRA must be obtained and filed in court (Sch. para.5)). The Banking Act 2009 introduces a special form of administration where a bank or building society encounters financial difficulties leading to government intervention, and similar provision has been made for investment banks by the Investment Bank Special Administration Regulations 2011 (SI 2011/245). This new procedure may be put in place by court order to deal with the remaining assets where there has been a partial transfer of business from a failing bank. The Act and the Rules are extensively modified for the purposes of this legislation. See further p.6 above.

The Financial Services (Banking Reform) Act 2013 Pt 6 has introduced a "financial market infrastructure (FMI) administration" in relation to financial market "infrastructure companies". Such a company is defined as a company which is either the operator of a recognised payment system (other than a "recognised central counterparty") or a recognised Central Securities Depository which operates a securities settlement system, or which provides services to any such company and is designated as an "infrastructure company" by the Treasury. The Financial Market

Infrastructure Administration (England and Wales) Rules 2018 (SI 2018/833) from 4 August 2018 deal with FMI administrations, specifying which of the Insolvency (England and Wales) Rules 2016 apply to such administrations and setting out modifications to the 2016 Rules in their application to FMI administrations.

The Energy Act 2004 s.159 and Schs 20, 21, as extended and modified by the Energy Act 2011 ss.93–102, establishes a special administration regime for bodies licensed to supply energy under that Act, and applies the provisions of Sch.B1 (with modifications) to such bodies. This regime is designed to ensure that energy supplies are maintained where a licensee becomes insolvent. For an interesting decision on this point, involving an urgent Chancery Division hearing conducted by telephone on a Saturday evening, see *Gas and Electricity Markets Authority v GB Energy Supply Ltd* [2016] EWHC 3341 (Ch). For the relevant rules, see the Energy Administration Rules 2005 (SI 2005/2483), effective 1 October 2005 and the Energy Supply Company Administration Rules 2013 (SI 2013/1046), effective 7 June 2013. For Scotland, see the Energy Supply Company Administration (Scotland) Rules 2013 (SI 2013/1047), also effective 7 June 2013. A special insolvency regime for companies that are designated under the Postal Services Act 2011 s.35 as universal postal service providers is in force as from 31 January 2014, under the Postal Administration Rules 2013 (SI 2013/3208). The main features of postal administration are that the company enters the procedure only by a court order on application by the Secretary of State or (with his consent) by OFCOM; the order appoints a postal administrator; the objective is to secure that a universal postal service is provided in accordance with the standards set out in the universal postal service order; and in other respects the process is the same as for normal administration under IA 1986, subject to certain modifications. A modified administration regime has also been introduced to cater for public–private partnerships: see the PPP Administration Order Rules 2007 (SI 2007/3141), effective 30 November 2007 and, for a case not brought under these rules but under the Greater London Authority Act 1999 Sch.15, *Re Metronet Rail BCV Ltd* [2008] 1 B.C.L.C. 760.

The administration regime did not formerly apply to Industrial and Provident Societies: *Re Dairy Farmers of Britain Ltd* [2009] EWHC 1389 (Ch); [2010] Ch. 63; [2010] B.C.C. 637, but by the Co-operative and Community Benefit Societies and Credit Unions (Arrangements, Reconstructions and Administration) Order 2014 (SI 2014/229), which came into force on 6 April 2014, the provisions of Sch.B1 (as modified) were extended to all societies registered under the Industrial and Provident Societies Act 1965, apart from any society which was a private registered provider of social housing or registered as a social landlord. (Note that the 1965 Act was superseded by the Co-operative and Community Benefit Societies Act 2014 as from 1 August 2014, and from that date SI 2014/229 was renamed the Co-operative and Community Benefit Societies and Credit Unions (Arrangements, Reconstructions and Administration) Order. Extensive changes have been made to the wording of SI 2014/229 by the Co-operative and Community Benefit Societies and Credit Unions (Arrangements, Reconstructions and Administration) (Amendment) Order 2014 (SI 2014/1822) as from 1 August 2014.)

Private registered providers of social housing (whether companies, registered societies or charitable incorporated organisations) have now been brought within Sch.B1 (as modified) by the Housing and Planning Act 2016 (Commencement No. 9 and Transitional and Saving Provisions) Regulations 2018 (SI 2018/805), together with the Housing Administration (England and Wales) Rules 2018 (SI 2018/719) and the Insolvency of Registered Providers of Social Housing Regulations 2018 (SI 2018/728).

In total there are now over two dozen special administration regimes, including those above and even one for sixth-form and further education college corporations and companies conducting a designated further education institution in England and Wales (as from 31 January 2019: see the Technical and Further Education Act 2017 Pt 2 Ch.4 and the Education Administration Rules 2018 (SI 2018/1135)). An administration order was made under this regime in *Secretary of State for Education v Hadlow College* [2019] EWHC 2035 (Ch). A further regime was introduced from 1 August 2020 by the Smart Meter Communication Licensee Administration (England and Wales) Rules 2020 (SI 2020/629) for a special regime under the Smart Meters Act 2018 for companies acting as a smart meter communication licensee (SMCL) in Great Britain to avoid significant national disruption to consumers and industry by maintaining the smart meter services of the SMCL.

After consultation a special administration regime for payment and electronic money institutions was introduced with effect from 8 July 2021 by the Payment and Electronic Money Institution Insolvency Regulations 2021 (SI 2021/716) operative in England and Wales and Scotland. The Payment and Electronic Money Institution Insolvency (England and Wales) Rules 2021 (SI 2021/1178) as from 12 November 2021 (as amended by the Payment and Electronic Money Institution Insolvency (England and Wales) (Amendment) Rules 2022 (SI 2022/847) as from 10 August 2022) provide detailed procedural rules (in England and Wales only) for the payment institution or electronic money institution special administration process under the above Regulations.

A Department of Transport report on 9 May 2019, *Airline Insolvency Review: Final Report* (*https://assets.publishing.service.gov.uk/government/uploads/system/uploads/attachment_data/file/800219/airline-insolvency-review-report.pdf*) sought comments on recommendations to protect passengers of insolvent airlines for a special administration regime to allow an insolvent airline to continue operating for a limited period so that passengers can be repatriated and amendment of UK aviation regulation to allow airlines to operate while in administration. Although not expressly mentioned in the Queen's Speech on 19 December 2019, the Briefing Notes to the Speech confirmed plans for 2020 to include the introduction of such a regime, but this has not yet come to pass. In the Government response to the Review's final report, published on 11 July 2022, it stated that it partially accepted the recommendation for an Airline Insolvency Bill setting out a framework to handle future airline insolvencies to protect the interests of consumers, employees and taxpayers, but that balancing the interests of these stakeholders will be critical in considering the Review's recommendations, "to make sure we take forward the most appropriate package of measures". This rather ambiguous comment, noticeably without a commitment to legislation, may indicate that any legislative reform may be in doubt, and at the least remains some way off. The response document is available at *https://committees.parliament.uk/publications/22997/documents/168474/default/*.

HM Treasury on 31 May 2022 commenced a consultation exercise intended to introduce a special administration regime for the failure of systemic digital settlement asset (DSA) firms (including bitcoin), to be effected by amendment to the existing regime for Financial Market Infrastructure Special Administration. Copies of *Managing the failure of systemic digital settlement asset (including stablecoin) firms: Consultation* are available at *https://assets.publishing.service.gov.uk/government/uploads/system/uploads/attachment_data/file/1079348/Stablecoin_FMISAR_Consultation.pdf* and comments are required by 2 August 2022.

The administration regime has not only succeeded in displacing administrative receivership as the primary method available to a floating charge holder to enforce his security, but is also proving to be a popular alternative to a creditors' voluntary winding up in the insolvency of smaller companies, because of its flexibility and informality. The latest figures available for 2021 indicate that there were 796 administrations (1,527 in 2020) compared with 115 CVAs (260 in 2020), and only one administrative receivership (three in 2020).

As was to be expected when a new and complex regime was introduced, Sch.B1 has encountered a number of teething problems. These have been met, and generally resolved, by judges adopting a bold and purposive approach, as (for instance) by Blackburne J in *Re Ballast plc* [2004] EWHC 2356 (Ch); [2005] B.C.C. 96; by Lawrence Collins J in *Re Transbus International Ltd* [2004] EWHC 932 (Ch); [2004] B.C.C. 401; and by rulings on paras 83–84. However the judiciary has rather tied itself in knots in some areas, especially on the effect of failure to give notice on appointment of (or intention to appoint) an administrator: the legislation does not state what the effect of such failure is and some cases have interpreted it to be a nullity (so that the purported appointment is void) while others have held it to be a procedural defect that the court can cure, e.g. under IR 2016 r.12.64 (see Sch.B1 para.26 below). We have also had the sticking-plaster remedy of a series of temporary Practice Directions to clarify the position of filing notice in court by electronic communication, especially when attempted outside court-opening hours. It seems inevitable that a permanent Practice Direction or change in say IR 2016 will be necessary to remove these obstacles.

A considerable number of changes have been made to the law governing administrations by SBEEA 2015, which received the Royal Assent on 26 March 2015. The first tranche of reforms included the following:

- empowering an administrator to bring an action for fraudulent or wrongful trading;

- authorising an administrator to assign a cause of action (such as for fraudulent trading) vested in him by statute;

- debarring a floating charge holder from making a claim against the proceeds of an action brought by an administrator (or assignee) in exercise of specified statutory powers;

- imposing restrictions or conditions on the sale of the company's business by an administrator to connected persons;

- abolition of the requirement to hold creditors' meetings;

- allowing creditors to opt not to receive notices;

- excusing creditors with small debts from the need to submit a proof;

- increasing the period for which an administration may be extended without a court order from six months to one year.

The remaining provisions of SBEEA 2015 dealing with administrations were brought into effect by the Small Business, Enterprise and Employment Act 2015 (Commencement No. 6 and Transitional and Savings Provisions) Regulations 2016 (SI 2016/1020) as from 1 October 2016. Further changes are introduced by new IR 2016, operative from 6 April 2017. These reforms include the following:

- abandoning the use of physical meetings of contributories and creditors (in most cases) and substituting other "decision procedures";

- abolition of the requirement to hold final meetings;

- enabling creditors to opt not to receive notices;

- discontinuing the use of prescribed forms.

As well as these more substantive changes, SBEEA 2015 has made consequential and minor amendments, mostly of a purely verbal nature, to very many sections in this part of the Act. Such alterations have been made in the text which follows without detailed annotation.

These reforms do not affect administrations established under the original Pt II. Whether the changes apply to bodies other than companies (e.g. building societies) is uncertain. Curiously, although IR 2016 were originally declared not to apply to LLPs (see the Insolvency (England and Wales) Rules 2016 (Consequential Amendments and Savings) Rules 2017 (SI 2017/369) r.3(b)), although there was no similar exclusion of LLPs in the Insolvency Act itself and it was not made clear in SBEEA 2015 itself. However what may have originally been an oversight was eventually cured by SI 2017/1119 mentioned above extending IR 2016 to LLPs as from 8 December 2017.

See generally Milman (2017) 394 Co. L.N. 1.

NATURE OF ADMINISTRATION

Purpose of administration

3—

GENERAL NOTE

Para.3(1), (3)
Replace the note with:
The formula "rescuing the company as a going concern" may be contrasted with the wording under the original legislation, "the survival of *the company, and* the whole or any part of its undertaking, as a going concern". The emphasis placed on the rescue or survival of the company (as distinct from its business or undertaking) is rather curious, for the Cork Committee was firmly of the view that it was only the latter that really mattered. In *Re Rowbotham Baxter Ltd* [1990] B.C.C. 113 at 115, Harman J stated that a proposal involving the sale of a "hived down" company formed to take over part of a company's business could not be brought within the original wording, in view of the words which have been italicised above; and even more plainly it could not come within the new formulation. However, this may in fact make it easier for an administrator to conclude that it is not reasonably practicable to achieve a rescue of the company and so move on to the second statutory objective (achieving a better result for the company's creditors as a whole than would be likely under an immediate winding up).

Paragraph 3(1)(b) was relied on in *Re Logitext UK Ltd* [2004] EWHC 2899 (Ch); [2005] 1 B.C.L.C. 326, where the company had no tangible assets but stood a chance of recovering funds by pursuing claims against alleged wrongdoers. The applicant was an unsecured creditor who was prepared to put up funding to enable the administrator to investigate the case and undertake the litigation, but no similar source of funding was likely if the company were put into liquidation. In *Doltable Ltd v Lexi Holdings plc* [2005] EWHC 1804 (Ch); [2006] B.C.C. 918 the company sought an administration order with a view to preventing a secured creditor from selling the secured property (allegedly) at an undervalue. Any surplus would benefit the members. It was held that this was outside the statutory purposes and an order was refused. In *Re British American Racing (Holdings) Ltd* [2004] EWHC 2947 (Ch); [2005] B.C.C. 110 it was argued that a petition presented by a creditor which also held 89% of the company's issued share capital was an abuse of the process of the court because administration would lead to the exclusion of the minority shareholders. This contention was rejected: the applicant, as a creditor, was entitled to proceed on the basis that the company's shares were valueless and a sale of its assets by administrators was likely to achieve a better result for the company's creditors as a whole (in which the applicant would participate in the same way as any other creditor). In *Bank of Scotland plc v Targetfollow Properties Holdings Ltd* [2010] EWHC 3606 (Ch); [2013] B.C.C. 817 a floating charge holder (who had chosen to make an application to the court rather than make an out-of-court appointment) satisfied the court that it should make an order in its discretion under para.3(1) and (b): a restructuring was impracticable and there was no prospect that the business could be rescued as a going concern. In *Re Bowen Travel Ltd* [2012] EWHC 3405 (Ch); [2013] B.C.C. 182, where the supporting evidence was considered to be unreliable and misleading, the court declined to make an administration order and instead ordered the company to be wound up, so that its affairs could be properly investigated for the benefit of creditors. See also *Data Power Systems Ltd v Safehosts (London) Ltd* [2013] EWHC 2479 (Ch); [2013] B.C.C. 721 (company had not traded and was hopelessly insolvent: administration order refused); *Re Hibernia (2005) Ltd* [2013] EWHC 2615 (Ch) (order granted to avoid losing best prospect of achieving a sale); *Re Monarch Financial Services Ltd; Cooper v Monarch Financial Services Ltd* [2017] EWHC 2324 (Ch); [2017] B.C.C. 570 (order where para.3(1)(b) recovery of substantial debt owed to company was more likely to be achieved by administration than in winding up and time of the essence as others at risk of depositing money with the unregulated financial services company); *Bennett v Bosco Investments Ltd* [2018] EWHC 2901 (Ch); [2019] B.C.C. 303 (order granted on balance compared with potential cost of liquidation due to saving of ad valorem and official receiver's costs payable in winding up but certain special costs of advising on interest rate hedging claim excluded from administration costs).

In *Re VTB Capital plc* [2022] EWHC 1106 (Ch); [2022] B.C.C. 1049 the court decided that an investment bank ultimately controlled by the Russian government which was subject to sanctions imposed in the UK and the USA should be the subject of an administration order if and when a licence was issued by the US government enabling the proposed administrators to make payments (a corresponding UK licence already having been issued).

Although para.3(1)(c) refers to distribution only to "secured or preferential creditors", that final objective in the hierarchy could properly be pursued even though unsecured creditors might also receive a distribution, as the scope of the provision is not limited to distribution to secured creditors, and also that fell squarely within para.52(1)(c), under which the administrators did not need to seek a creditors' decision as to whether they approved the proposals: *Re Taylor Pearson (Construction) Ltd (in admin.)* [2020] EWHC 2933 (Ch). For the successful application of the Northern Ireland equivalent to para.3(1)(c) see *Re Bedford Hotel Ltd* [2022] NICh 10 in the context of promoting the statutory purpose under para.71(2)(b).

In considering whether the statutory purpose of administration can be achieved, the potential administrator does not have to consider the directors' motives in appointing him: *Re BW Estates Ltd* [2015] EWHC 517 (Ch); [2016] B.C.C. 475 (overruled on other grounds: [2017] EWCA Civ 1201; [2017] B.C.C. 406). The court in *Davey v Money* [2018] EWHC 766 (Ch) extensively examined the principles applicable in relation to the choice of statutory objective and held that it will not interfere unless the choice is made in bad faith or is clearly perverse.

FUNCTIONS OF ADMINISTRATOR

General powers

63

GENERAL NOTE

Replace the note with:

An unusual direction was made under this paragraph in *Re Lehman Brothers International (Europe) Ltd* [2013] EWHC 1664 (Ch); [2014] B.C.C. 132 to reassure the trustee in liquidation of the American arm of the Lehman group that the European company would perform its obligations under a settlement agreement. In *Re Nortel Networks UK Ltd* [2014] EWHC 2614 (Ch) the court approved a complex settlement (and directed that the costs of the application should be paid as an expense of the administration), but at the same time emphasised the limited extent of its role. The court must be careful in giving its blessing to a transaction clearly within the administrator's powers to ensure that the administrator was not surrendering his discretion. At the same time, the court was not a mere rubber stamp: full and frank disclosure of all material facts and circumstances was required for the court to give its approval. (A global settlement was eventually reached and approved by the court: *Re Nortel Networks UK Ltd* [2016] EWHC 2769 (Ch).) The rubber stamp analogy was also drawn in *Re Blue Co International LLP (formerly Ince & Co International LLP) (in admin.)* [2020] EWHC 2385 (Ch) where on an application for directions administrators were held to be at liberty to apply to a French court for a stay or dismissal of claims brought against them in France. Rubber stamping was also mentioned in *Re Petropavlovsk plc* [2022] EWHC 2097 (Ch) but the court authorised a transaction as the administrators had considered the matter carefully and thoroughly, were within their power to enter it, but sought court assistance as they were wary of international sanctions involved in relation to Russia. (The court added that the administrators were not in breach of the rule on *Re Condon, Ex p. James* (1874) L.R. 9 Ch. App. 609 that the court will not permit its officers to act in a way which—although lawful—would not be honourable, as there was nothing dishonourable in the administrators entering into the transaction).

Although this provision confers standing only on an administrator, it is possible that a creditor may also apply for directions under the court's general power to exercise control over administrators as officers of the court: see *Re Mirror Group Holdings Ltd* [1993] B.C.L.C. 538 at 543. An administrator may also seek a decision on any matter from the company's creditors (see para.62(b) above).

In *Re Allanfield Property Insurance Services Ltd* [2015] EWHC 3721 (Ch) it was held that the court has power under para.63 to give directions to administrators in respect of funds held by them even though they do not form part of the company's assets (e.g. trust funds). Compare *Re Worldspreads Ltd* [2015] EWHC 1719 (Ch), where the court was asked to approve a distribution of client money held on trust by a banking company which was in special administration. Although he was uncertain whether para.63 extended to companies under the special administration regime, Birss J held that he had power to authorise the payments under the court's inherent jurisdiction in relation to trusts (applied in *Hunt (Liquidator of Total Debt Relief Ltd) v Financial Conduct Authority* [2019] EWHC 2018 (Ch)). In *Re Pritchard Stockbrokers Ltd (in special admin.)* [2019] EWHC 137 (Ch) Norris J considered that an application for directions under para.63 was the appropriate vehicle but in *Re Supercapital Ltd* [2020] EWHC 1685 (Ch), concerning a proposed distribution plan for client funds held on a statutory trust by a provider of international payment services, the court had a slight preference for using its inherent jurisdiction (see at [11]–[14] and *Re MF Global UK Ltd (in special admin.)* [2013] EWHC 1655 (Ch); [2013] 1 W.L.R. 3874).

In *Re Nortel Networks UK Ltd* [2017] EWHC 1429 (Ch); [2017] B.C.C. 325 and *Re Nortel Networks SA* [2018] EWHC 1812 (Ch) the court made orders on applications for directions that administrators could inform potential claimants for expense claims in the administrations to notify the administrators by a specified "bar date" of their claim: late expense claims after that date would not be extinguished, but would only be paid to the extent that the administrators had any unreserved funds available after making distributions to unsecured creditors. Thus some expense creditors, if late in pursuing their claims, may end up not being paid, as was stated in *Re WW Realisations Ltd* [2010] EWHC 3604 (Ch); [2011] B.C.C. 382 to be an acceptable price to pay in striking a proper balance. This approach was followed in the liquidation case of *Re Allied Wallet Ltd* [2022] EWHC 1877 (Ch) where the court gave directions to liquidators of a company whose business was subject to the Electronic Money Regulations 2011 (SI 2011/99) about the costs of distributing "assets pools" under the Regulations. For an earlier complicated application for directions by administrators concerning construction of the 2011 Regulations and considered in *Allied Wallet*, see *Re Ipagoo Ltd (in admin.); Baker v Financial Conduct Authority* [2022] EWCA Civ 302.

Administrators in *Re London Bridge Entertainment Partners LLP* [2019] EWHC 2932 (Ch) sought directions on whether an obligation to top up a rent deposit, triggered by a demand served on a corporate tenant after it had entered into administration, was an administration expense.

For an interesting example of an application for directions to the Scottish court, see *Administrator of Dawson International plc, Noter* [2018] CSOH 52. Also note *Granite City Assets Ltd (Joint Administrators of)* [2018] CSOH 55.

Charged property: non-floating charge

71—

GENERAL NOTE

Replace the note with:

The disapplication provisions referred to in the note to para.70 apply also to this paragraph.

Administrators were granted an order under this provision for the sale of property subject to a fixed charge, in order to facilitate the sale of the company's business as a going concern, in *O'Connell v Rollings* [2014] EWCA Civ 639. Similarly see *Re Bedford Hotel Ltd* [2022] NICh 10 where the Northern Ireland High Court made an order resulting in the fixed chargee being paid as promoting the purpose of the administration under the equivalent to para.3(1)(c) to make a distribution to one or more secured creditors. For another successful application see *Williams v Broadoak Private Finance Ltd* [2018] EWHC 1107 (Ch) in which administrators obtained an order to dispose of a partly-developed freehold property (to be converted into apartments) free from a large number of purchasers' liens as likely to promote one or other of the administration purposes.

An application for breach of duty by administrators for not gaining a court order under para. 71 was dismissed in *Fitzroy Street Capital Inc v Manning* [2022] EWHC 1495 (Ch) where the unsecured creditors contended that entering into an exclusivity agreement and draft sale agreement without the consent of the creditors or a court order constituted acting in excess of the powers of an administrators and a breach of duty. The court found that the agreements were not a final disposal of the properties and the matter of gaining consent or a court order could have been dealt with at the actual point of transfer of the properties.

An order was made in a similar situation in *Duffy v MJF Pension Trustees Ltd* [2020] EWHC 1835 (Ch) and see also *Re Fox Street Village Ltd (in admin.)* [2020] EWHC 2541 (Ch), which applied the *Broadoak* (above) case.

An application was refused in *Re Sky Building Ltd* [2020] EWHC 3139 (Ch) where, although disposal of the property would promote the purpose of the administration under para.71(2)(b), the court could not be satisfied that the financial condition imposed by para.71(3)(b) would be met and also, importantly in considering exercise of the court's discretion under para.71(1), the majority of creditors opposed the order. (Note the court at [41] considered that para.71 does not breach the Human Rights Act 1998 because it is a provision in the general interest, but that it subsists within the context that it interferes with a right to peaceful enjoyment of possessions conferred by the First Protocol of Pt II of Sch.1 thereof.)

All proper costs, charges and expenses reasonably incurred in the preservation and realisation of the property (including the administrator's remuneration) may be deducted before payment of the realisation proceeds to the charge holder: *Townsend v Biscoe* [2010] WL 3166608. An administrator who acts unreasonably in applying for an order to sell property subject to a fixed charge may be ordered to pay the charge holder's costs personally and on an indemnity basis: *Re Capitol Films Ltd, Rubin v Cobalt Pictures Ltd* [2010] EWHC 3223 (Ch); [2011] B.P.I.R. 334. In a complex scenario, sanction was granted in *Re Prime Noble Properties Ltd (in admin.)* [2022] EWHC 2271 (Ch) in relation to possession and sale by administrators of a number of residential long leases where the freehold was subject to a charging order and an order under CPR r.73.10(c) was first necessary; the court went on to consider Sch.B1 para.71 and payment of the administrators' fees, costs and disbursements in relation to their getting possession and sale of the property and also the distribution of the net proceeds by them after discharge of the charging order.

Rule 3.49 governs the application to the court. "Market value" is defined in para.111(1).

Misfeasance

75—

GENERAL NOTE

Replace the note with:

The "misfeasance" section applicable generally in corporate insolvency proceedings is s.212. In the Act as originally drafted, an administrator was listed in s.212(1)(b) as an office-holder who could be made accountable under the section. All references to an administrator have been removed from s.212 by EA 2002 s.278 and Sch.26, and the present paragraph will now apply instead to an administrator appointed under the new regime. The main difference from s.212 is that it is not necessary that the company should be in liquidation. The only other change of significance appears to be the inclusion of a person who has purported to be an administrator. In other respects, the notes to s.212 may be treated as applicable.

The court will not order an administrator under this section to pay compensation to an individual creditor (although arguably a remedy may lie under para.74: see the note to that provision): any payment under para.75 must be for the benefit of the creditors as a class: *Re Coniston Hotel (Kent) LLP* [2013] EWHC 93 (Ch); [2015] B.C.C. 1. In later proceedings (*Re Coniston Hotel (Kent) LLP, Berntsen v Tait* [2014] EWHC 1100 (Ch); on appeal [2015] EWCA Civ 1001) the court ruled that a creditor had standing to make an application under para.75 only if he would have a pecuniary interest in the relief sought. An administrator does not owe any duty of care to an unsecured creditor of the company, unless it can be shown that a special relationship existed between them: *Charalambous v B&C Associates* [2009] EWHC 2601 (Ch); [2013] B.C.C. 491.

For the position of misfeasance liability of joint administrators, see *Re MK Airlines Ltd; Oldham v Katz* [2018] EWHC 540 (Ch); [2019] B.C.C. 48 under which proof of individual liability may be necessary.

In *Davey v Money* [2018] EWHC 766 (Ch) the principles applicable in relation to various matters, including the administrators' choice of statutory objective, their selection of property agents and their duties when selling assets, were examined extensively, against the background of a claim under this paragraph. Note also the decision of Chief ICC Judge Briggs in *Brewer (Liquidator of ARY Digital UK Ltd) v Iqbal* [2019] EWHC 182 (Ch); [2019] B.C.C. 746 for a consideration of the position where it is alleged that an administrator is in breach of both the duty to take reasonable care and certain fiduciary duties. For a detailed discussion of fiduciary duties in light of this decision see Hatton [2019] Recovery (Autumn) 10. When selling assets the administrator owes no duty to a third-party potential purchaser so as to incur liability under para.75 (or para.74): see *PJSC Uralkali v Rowley* [2020] EWHC 3442 (Ch).

In *Re One Blackfriars Ltd* [2019] EWHC 2493 (Ch) the court granted permission for liquidators to amend their particulars of claim for breach of duty against a company's former administrators to add a head of loss concerning the lost chance of a corporate rescue (the claimants were punished in costs as the loss of chance could and should have been pleaded at the outset and no real explanation was given why it had not been so). In further proceedings (*Re One Blackfriars Ltd; Hyde v Nygate* [2021] EWHC 684 (Ch)) alleging interlinked breaches of duties by the former administrators the court, in a detailed analysis of administrators' duties at [200]–[258], held amongst other things that, unlike receivers, administrators do not owe an *absolute* duty to obtain the best reasonably obtainable price (a non-delegable duty in strict liability) but as an aspect of the overall duty to take reasonable care and skill, only to take reasonable care to obtain the best price that the circumstances permit as they reasonably perceive them to be. For a successful application of the "lost chance/opportunity" concept, see the opinion of Lord Tyre in *Joint Liquidators of RFC 2021 plc, Noters* [2021] CSOH 99, where the liquidators of Rangers football club company who sought (in total) almost £47.7 million for the administrators' breach of various duties were awarded about £3.4 million, all of the latter itemised under separate lost chances of the sale of players and properties, whilst the bulk of the claim was otherwise rejected.

An application under para.75 enjoys no special status for the purpose of s.35 of the Limitation Act 1980, so that an attempt to amend such an application by way of the addition of a further claim is subject to the same limitation rules as apply to all other proceedings: *Hyde v Nygate* [2019] EWHC 1516 (Ch).

Note that under para.98(4) discharge of the administrator does not prevent the exercise of the court's powers under para.75, but under para.75(6) permission of the court is needed to bring the misfeasance application against the former administrator. The two-fold test required for such permission is whether a reasonably meritorious cause of action has been shown and whether permission would be reasonably likely to benefit the company's estate: *Katz v Oldham* [2016] B.P.I.R. 83. Permission was granted in *Re Rhino Enterprises Properties Ltd; Schofield v Smith* [2020] EWHC 2370 (Ch); [2020] B.C.C. 18 in favour of contributories of the company who had earlier voted in favour of a company voluntary arrangement (CVA) as members or creditors but, in principle, were not thereby precluded from applying under para.75: voting in favour of the CVA in other capacities did not remove their status as contributories or undermine the statutory rights afforded to them in that capacity. The administrators were subsequently found to be entitled to rely on a settlement agreement entered into between the company and a creditor, notwithstanding not being parties to it, on the basis of the Contracts (Rights of Third Parties) Act 1999: *Re Rhino Enterprises Properties Ltd* [2021] EWHC 2533 (Ch); [2022] B.C.C. 78. The court also found the principle in *Ex p. James* (1873–74) L.R. 9 Ch. App. 609 not to be applicable in relation to insolvency officers where an insolvency procedure has come to an end and the Court of Appeal has subsequently dismissed an appeal against the decision: *Schofield v Smith* [2022] EWCA Civ 824. The company itself is not listed as an applicant in para.75(2) and so cannot make an application under para.75(6) after the administrator has been discharged: *Re Glint Pay Ltd* [2020] EWHC 3078 (Ch); [2021] B.C.C. 274.

On jurisdictional matters (between England and Wales, and Scotland) concerning para.75, note *Holgate v Addleshaw Goddard (Scotland) LLP* [2019] EWHC 1793 (Ch).

For discussion of case developments under paras 74 and 75 see Oulton and Shah (2019) (32) Insolv. Int. 96.

ENDING ADMINISTRATION

Automatic end of administration

78—

Para.78(1)–(2A)
Replace the note with:

Paragraph 78(1)(b), (2)(b) substituted, para.78(3) omitted and para.78(2A) inserted by SBEEA 2015 Sch.9 paras 1, 10(25)–(27) as from 6 April 2017.

Paragraph 78 defines "consent" in various ways for the purposes of the one-off extension of an administration which can be made out of court under para.76(2)(b). The alternatives depend on whether the administrator has included in his proposals a statement under para.52(1)(b) that he thinks that the company has insufficient property to enable a distribution to be made to unsecured creditors (other than what they might be entitled to under the "prescribed part" provisions of s.176A). If he has not, and the company has unsecured creditors, the consent must be that of each secured creditor of the company and over 50% in value of the company's unsecured creditors. If he has made such a statement, the consent must be *either* that of each secured creditor of the company *or*, if the administrator thinks that a distribution may be made to the company's preferential creditors, the consent of each secured creditor and over 50% in value of the preferential creditors. There are thus three possible scenarios. In any event, the paragraph requires *actual* consent: the deemed consent procedure in s.246ZF is not available (*Re Biomethane (Castle Easton) Ltd; Baker v Biomethane (Castle Easton) Ltd* [2019] EWHC 3298 (Ch); [2020] B.C.C. 111). The debts of creditors who abstain or choose not to respond are ignored. See IR 2016 r.3.54 for the extension consent procedure. In the notice seeking creditor consent to an extension, failure to give the reasons for the extension in the notice to creditors (as required by IR 2016 r.3.54(2)) was regarded as a procedural defect in *Re Caversham Finance Ltd* [2022] EWHC 789 (Ch); [2022] B.C.C. 876 and cured under r.12.64. This was followed in *Re E Realisations 2020 Ltd* [2022] EWHC 1575 (Ch); [2022] B.C.C. 1105.

SCHEDULE 4A

BANKRUPTCY RESTRICTIONS ORDER AND UNDERTAKING

GENERAL NOTE
Replace the note with:

This was inserted by EA 2002 s.257 and Sch.20 to further supplement the rules on BROs and BRUs. See the notes to s.281A above. Details of the use of BROs and BRUs in practice are mounted on the Insolvency Service website under Press Notices. In 2015/2016 according to Insolvency Service Outcomes there were 432 cases of BROs/DRROs/BRUs/DRRUs recorded, with the vast majority being through the undertakings mode. The figures comprise both bankruptcy and debt relief restrictions, though were are informed that there are very few debt relief restrictions recorded. What is clear is that the number of restrictions, however imposed has fallen by 25% on the previous year. The average restriction lasts 5.1 years. The Insolvency Service keeps combined figures for BRRO/BRRU and DRRO/DRRU—in 2018/19 these aggregated out at 441, with the average restriction period amounting to five years. Where the court is involved the restriction tends to be for a longer period. The vast majority of restrictions are imposed through the giving of undertakings rather than as a result of court orders—see Insolvency Service Enforcement Outcomes September 2019, Tables 3 and 3A.

Cases involving bankruptcy restrictions orders are beginning to be reported. In *Randhawa v Official Receiver* [2006] B.P.I.R. 1435 the court was at pains to stress the common heritage of the BRO regime with the director disqualification procedure. Once the court had concluded that the conduct in question merited a BRO it was obliged to make such an order; this was consistent with the approach taken by the court in the director disqualification case of *Re Grayan Building Services Ltd* [1995] Ch. 241. BROs were intended both to protect the public and also to have a deterrent effect. The three-tier classification in *Re Sevenoaks Stationers Ltd* [1991] Ch. 164 governing the duration of a director disqualification could be adopted for determining the length of the BRO. The three year BRO was upheld. In concluding his judgment Launcelot Henderson QC expressed disquiet that nowhere in Sch.4A was there any indication of the consequences that would ensue if a BRO were breached. If the conduct of the bankrupt is found to fall below the required standard the court *must* impose a BRO at least for the minimum two-year period—*Official Receiver v May* [2008] B.P.I.R. 1562. Both *Randhawa* (above) and *May* (above) were distinguished in *Kennedy v Official Receiver* [2022] EWHC 1973 (Ch) which has considered the length periods for BROs (see below).

Another reported case is *Official Receiver v Merchant* [2006] B.P.I.R. 1525 where Chief Registrar Baister dismissed an application for an interim BRO. The point was made that different considerations applied to the making of an interim order. General guidance was given on procedural aspects where an application for an interim BRO was sought.

In *Official Receiver v Doganci* [2007] B.P.I.R. 87 Chief Registrar Baister refused to grant a BRO because it could not be said that the bankrupt's explanation for the loss of property, although implausible, was untruthful. The bankrupt deserved the benefit of the doubt.

In *OR v Pyman* [2007] EWHC 1150; [2007] B.P.I.R. 1150 on appeal a bankruptcy restrictions order was doubled to seven years because the trial judge had underestimated the degree of culpability of the individual concerned (who had been bankrupted previously). The fact of a previous bankruptcy experience should have alerted the defendant to his responsibilities under bankruptcy law. The advanced age of the defendant was not relevant, unless there was evidence of infirmity.

Where a bankruptcy has been annulled under s.282(1)(b) on the ground that all debts have been paid the court can still grant a BRO provided the application was made before the annulment and within a year of the commencement of the bankruptcy—*Jenkins v OR* [2007] EWHC 1402 (Ch); [2007] B.P.I.R. 740. In this case it was held that in considering whether to make a BRO the court could take into account the fact that the individual whilst an undischarged bankrupt was continuing to act as a company director without leave.

A BRO was refused in *Official Receiver v Southey* [2009] B.P.I.R. 89 because the court was not satisfied that the bankrupt when incurring the debt in question had no reasonable prospect of repaying it. It took this generous view because the bankrupt had lived a precarious financial existence in the past and had always managed to repay his credit.

The issue of the cut off period for applications for a BRO was examined in *Official Receiver v Baars* [2009] B.P.I.R. 524. Here the bankruptcy had been discharged in late 2005 but the application for the BRO was not made to the court for more than two years after that date. The justification for the late application was the allegation that the former bankrupt had not disclosed his assets and this non-disclosure had not come to light until seven months before the application. In the light of these circumstances the court allowed the application to proceed.

A further consideration of the BRO regime is to be found in the judgment of HHJ Pelling in *Official Receiver v Going* [2011] EWHC 786 (Ch); [2011] B.P.I.R. 1069. Here the bankrupt successfully appealed against an eight-year BRO on the basis that the evidence did not support the making of a BRO. The limitations of a court hearing an appeal were noted—the appellate court could not uphold a BRO on evidence that was not presented at first instance. Any evidence used to justify a BRO has to be put before the court considering the matter at first instance.

A nine-year BRO was imposed by the court in *Official Receiver v Bathurst* [2008] B.P.I.R. 1548. Here the court at first instance had imposed a three-year restriction, but this was substantially increased by Sir Andrew Morritt CVO on appeal.

In *Michael v Official Receiver* [2010] EWHC 2246 (Ch) an attempt to challenge the interim BRO procedure on the grounds that it infringed art.6 of the ECHR failed. Arnold J refused to make a declaration of incompatibility under the Human Rights Act 1998. The judgment contains a useful analysis of the interim BRO procedure.

For recent authority considering the BRO regime see *Michael v Official Receiver* [2013] EWHC 4286 (Ch); [2014] B.P.I.R. 666 where Roth J, in spite of rejecting the criticisms of the handling of the case by Chief Registrar Baister, reduced the BRO period from 8 years to 6.5 years. The litigation continues to rumble on—this case went to the Court of Appeal [2014] EWCA Civ 534 where permission to appeal the decision of Roth J was given.

A BRO was made on the facts disclosed in *OR v Lloyd* [2015] B.P.I.R. 374. For a BRO granted under the law in Northern Ireland see *OR v Gibson* [2015] NIMaster 4; [2015] B.P.I.R. 717. An attempt by the bankrupt to raise a "bucket list" defence to justify expenditure met with short shrift.

See *OR v Bayliss* [2017] EWHC 3910 (Ch) (E Johnson QC). In *OR v Baxendale-Walker* [2020] EWHC 195 (Ch); [2020] B.P.I.R. 606 ICC Judge Mullen granted a BRO where the bankrupt had failed to cooperate with his trustee in bankruptcy. In so doing, the need to protect the public was stressed. The court did not enjoy unfettered discretion in making a BRO, but as with director disqualification, that discretion had to be exercised within the legislative parameters. The three band periods used for disqualification of a director could be applied in the BRO context.

The court noted in *Kennedy v Official Receiver* [2022] EWHC 1973 (Ch) that although it was generally accepted that the Sevenoaks three-bracket approach should be used, there was some conflict in how the courts should then approach determining the exact length for a BRO, including whether the facts of earlier cases should be considered. The court noted that there have only been a few cases discussing the length of BROs and stated (at [42]) that at least until overt principles for applying a BRO have been developed by the courts, a judge should review relevant cases that have similar facts, and particularly facts which go to the culpability of the bankrupt, without disqualifying any cases which are not on appeal or which do not overtly state that they are following a particular principle. On this basis the deputy judge on appeal reduced the BRO period from eight years—in the middle *Sevenoaks* bracket—to four years, in the lowest bracket, starting at the top of that lowest bracket and deducting one year to reflect the mitigation found present.

For comment see Taylor [2007] 20 Insolv. Int. 90. For a comprehensive review see Moser [2013] J.B.L. 679.

Note a number of amendments are made to para.2 by ERRA 2013 Sch.19 para.63.

Insolvency (England and Wales) Rules 2016

Introduction to the Insolvency (England and Wales) Rules 2016
Replace the note with:

These Rules were finally published on 25 October 2016, having been scrutinised by the Insolvency Rules Committee. We had been waiting for these Rules (hereafter "the 2016 Rules" or "IR 2016") for more than a decade—see Bailey (2013) 343 Co. L.N. 1 for background to the history and policy underpinning this elephantine gestation. They entirely replace the Insolvency Rules 1986 (SI 1986/1925), which had been amended on at least 28 occasions—see Sch.1 to the 2016 Rules for the full list of amendment rules. They thus represent a fresh start in some respects, particularly so as they embody a number of reforms to the Insolvency Act 1986 generated by the Small Business, Enterprise and Employment Act 2015 which also take final effect on 6 April 2017. Modern linguistics are employed to give the terminology a contemporary feel. That said, in many respects they merely consolidate and reorder the latest version of the 1986 Rules. This reality is reflected in the fact that the Insolvency Service has produced Tables of Destination and Derivation. So we have to analyse a mixture of the old and the new.

As their full title suggests, these 2016 Rules are not applicable in Scotland or in Northern Ireland. The Scots have replaced the Insolvency (Scotland) Rules 1986 (SI 1986/1915) by two separate statutory instruments (because of devolved issues)—the Insolvency (Scotland) (Company Voluntary Arrangements and Administration) Rules 2018 (SI 2018/1082) and the Insolvency (Scotland) (Receivership and Winding up) Rules 2018 (SSI 2018/347)—as from 6 April 2019, and we await a solution in Northern Ireland. The non-application of IR 1986 to Scotland was confirmed in *Secretary of State for Trade and Industry v Frid* [2004] UKHL 24; [2004] 2 A.C. 506; [2004] B.C.C. 525 at [31].

On the basis of *St John Poulton's Trustee in Bankruptcy v Ministry of Justice* [2010] EWCA Civ 392; [2011] Ch. 1 it would seem that the 2016 Rules will not be capable of generating a private law claim for breach of statutory duty as no common law claim for breach of the Rules is recognised.

Taking an overview of the 2016 Rules *two* features stand out. Firstly, the introduction of the so-called "common Parts". This methodology makes sense in that it does avoid the duplication of similar Rules across different insolvency procedures. But in some respects it does mean that a practitioner will no longer find the Parts as self-contained as they were previously, and some lateral research will be required to find the solution to a legal question. It remains to be seen whether this will cause problems for practitioners but the court in *Cash Generator Ltd v Fortune* [2018] EWHC 674 (Ch); [2018] B.C.C. 740 at [38] was critical that the multifarious rules referred to in [9] of the judgment were "numerous, to be found in a variety of different places and feature so many requirements that they may be difficult to apply in practice" and recommended further consideration by the Insolvency Rules Committee. Secondly, the 2016 Rules were meant to signal a move away from the use of prescribed Forms and instead provide more required information detail in the Rules themselves. But that break with formality has been less than complete. Companies House has issued its own prescribed Forms for a number of situations and some "templates" particularly relevant to the activities of the Official Receiver have been produced by the Insolvency Service. HM Courts and Tribunal Service has also provided a number of court forms for use in insolvency proceedings. See App.II for a list of these forms and templates.

The 2016 Rules are generally prospective in effect, with 6 April 2017 being the key operational date. The 1986 Rules continue to apply to some extant insolvency procedures (particularly with regard to meetings) and ongoing legal proceedings—see Sch.2 to the 2016 Rules for a detailed explanation of the transitional complexities. The 19th edition of this *Guide* therefore retains some value during the transition.

Some changes to the Rules were made at the operational date of 6 April 2017. This was particularly so as several of the Rules had attracted Parliamentary criticism—see Joint Committee on Statutory Instruments, 16th Report of Session 2016/17, HL Paper 80, HC 93-xvi. The text of the legislation below contains the amendments introduced via the Insolvency (England and Wales) (Amendment) Rules 2017 (SI 2017/366) and also operational as from 6 April 2017, together with those from a correction slip. For further analysis of the 2016 Rules see Jones and Black (2016) 9 C.R.I. 221. There is also a brief but useful Explanatory Memorandum to the Rules themselves produced by the Insolvency Service.

Another important point concerning the 2016 Rules lies in the fact that they operate to supplement other secondary insolvency legislation that has been upgraded some time since the operational date—such as the Administration of

Insolvent Estates of Deceased Persons Order 1986 (SI 1986/1999), the Insolvent Partnerships Order 1994 (SI 1994/2421) and the Limited Liability Partnerships Regulations 2001 (SI 2001/1090) (and see below).

Over the course of 2017, a number of refinements were made to the matrix of provisions contained in IR 2016. For a detailed summary see Bailey [2018] 31 Insolv. Int. 7 and also the overview by Milman [2018] 31 Insolv. Int. 30.

Looking at the more important measures, firstly, there have been a number of tidying up measures. These are to be found in the Insolvency (England and Wales) and Insolvency (Scotland) (Miscellaneous and Consequential Amendments) Rules 2017 (SI 2017/1115).

Secondly, the 2016 Rules (and primary legislation) have had to take account of the arrival of the EU Recast Insolvency Regulation (2015/848). Consequential changes were thus made by the Insolvency Amendment (EU 2015/848) Regulations 2017 (SI 2017/702). With Brexit these changes have been substantially unwound by the Insolvency (Amendment) (EU Exit) Regulations 2019 (SI 2019/146) as amended.

Finally, the 2016 Rules did not extend to insolvent partnerships, insolvent LLPs or deceased insolvents. The necessary modified provisions have now been provided by the Insolvency (Miscellaneous Amendment) Regulations 2017 (SI 2017/1119).

The Insolvency Service in November 2016 set up a Blog for technical comments on the 2016 Rules. The Explanatory Memorandum para.3.1 mentions as an innovation of the 2016 Rules the use of non-legislative notes intended to assist users of the Rules: they are contained in square brackets and labelled "[Note]". These occur in the text of the Rules themselves and should not be confused with our annotations at the end of a note or a series of notes, or the bold sub-rule square bracket headings that we have inserted at the beginning of each sub-rule to assist in identification of the meaning of that sub-rule as part of the value-added process of the *Guide*.

In light of a series of conflicting cases on the effect of electronic filing of notices of appointment of administrators out of court hours, Sir Geoffrey Vos C issued guidance on 29 January 2020, reported as *Practice Note* [2020] B.C.C. 211, stating that these issues will be addressed by amendment to IR 2016 although the Insolvency Service has intimated that such amendments may not be necessary in light of the following temporary practice directions. Pending any amendments *Temporary Insolvency Practice Direction (No.5) Supporting the Insolvency Practice Direction* [2021] B.C.C. 877 (in force from 1 October 2021 until revoked or amended) superseded *Temporary Insolvency Practice Direction (No.4) Supporting the Insolvency Practice Direction* [2021] B.C.C. 731 (in force 30 June 2021–30 September 2021), replacing *Temporary Insolvency Practice Direction (No.3) Supporting the Insolvency Practice Direction* [2021] B.C.C. 199 (in force 1 April 2021–30 June 2021), replacing *Temporary Practice Direction (No.2) Supporting the Insolvency Practice Direction* [2020] B.C.C. 844 (in force 1 October 2020–31 March 2021), replacing the earlier *Temporary Practice Direction Supporting the Insolvency Practice Direction* [2020] B.C.C. 686 (in force 6 April 2020–1 October 2020), largely alleviates the problems caused by the inconsistent decisions.

The application of CIGA 2020 as from 26 June 2020 occasioned many amendments to IA 1986 and other legislation, and included temporary modified procedural rules to IR 2016 (e.g. CIGA 2020 Sch.4 Pt 3), pending permanent amendments to IR 2016. Such permanent amendments were finally carried out by the Insolvency (England and Wales) (No. 2) (Amendment) Rules 2021 (SI 2021/1028) as from 1 October 2021, subject to transitional and saving provisions, inserting a new Pt 1A containing rules applicable to moratoriums under Pt A1 of the IA 1986, and numerous other amendments were also made.

Following the UK's exit from the EU at the end of the IP completion day of 31 December 2020 at 11pm, the Insolvency (Amendment) (EU Exit) Regulations 2019 (SI 2019/146) (as amended by SI 2019/1459 and SI 2020/647) heavily amended IR 2016. These amendments are included in the text below but note that transitional arrangements in SI 2019/146 reg.4 apply to main insolvency proceedings commenced before the latter date.

The Insolvency Service on 11 March 2021 announced its first review of IR 2016 within five years of their operation as required by introductory r.7: see the note to that rule.

INTRODUCTORY RULES

Review

7—

<small>GENERAL NOTE</small>
Replace the note with:
   This rule had no counterpart in IR 1986 but follows a modern legislative drafting practice for extensive legislation: see SBEEA 2015 ss.28–32. The beginning of the first five-year review as required by r.7(3) was announced by the Insolvency Service in a call for evidence on 11 March 2021. The document notes concerns from IPs (such as the aboli-

tion of prescribed forms, the new creditor opt-out from communications, the use of electronic communications and filing of documents, changes to the procedures relating to meetings of creditors and decisions, etc.). It then provides 17 questions on the consolidation and restructuring of the Rules, implementation of primary legislation (DA 2015 and SBEEA 2015), new policy implementation and questions on specific topics. The Secretary of State was mandated to publish a report of the review before 6 April 2022 and, in light of comments to the above call for evidence the report, First Review of the Insolvency (England and Wales) Rules 2016, was published on 5 April 2022 and is available at *https://www.gov.uk/government/publications/first-review-of-the-insolvency-england-and-wales-rules-2016/first-review-of-the-insolvency-england-and-wales-rules-2016.*

The review concluded that IR 2016 as a whole are operating correctly and achieve the goals that were set for them: they provide appropriate detailed procedures to support IA 1986 as well as consolidating and modernising the preceding secondary legislation, implement policies contained in DA 2015 and SBEEA 2015 and introduce other modernisations, e.g. electronic communication between office-holders and creditors. The review does however mention numerous other issues related to IR 2016 and the insolvency regime. Some are minor technical points, while others are significant in their own right, e.g. highlighting that while IR 2016 permit office-holders to deliver documents via websites, this does not extend to directors, and that some prescribed deadlines can be very tight and so difficult to comply with. Other issues deriving from primary legislation and so falling outside the scope of the review (including the low take up of the provisions allowing creditors to opt out of receiving correspondence, which is less than 1%) have nevertheless been noted for possible change. A small number of minor and simple points will be resolved by amending secondary legislation but a longer list of more substantial items will "be reviewed in future as other work and priorities allow". Of the latter, attention will initially be given to a review of the creditors' voluntary liquidation process as a whole to ensure it remains fit for purpose and for any necessary changes and also to the scope of insolvency applications and claim forms (in light of the decision in *Manolete Partners plc v Hayward and Barrett Holdings Ltd* [2021] EWHC 1481 (Ch); [2022] B.C.C. 159). The report notes that the Insolvency Service do not intend to change the policy on the removal in IR 2016 of prescribed forms and do not intend to amend the Rules to cater for the confusion and case law on electronic filing of notices of appointments of administrators' out-of-court-hours, which is regarded in the report to have been covered by the series of Temporary Insolvency Practice Directions.

PART 1

SCOPE, INTERPRETATION, TIME AND RULES ABOUT DOCUMENTS

CHAPTER 8

APPLICATIONS TO THE COURT

Standard contents and authentication of applications to the court under Parts A1 to 11 of the Act

1.35—

GENERAL NOTE)
Replace the note with:
This covers the standard contents of court applications subject to the express exclusion for administration orders and bankruptcy and winding-up petitions. Thus an application against transactions defrauding creditors under s.423, which is in Pt XVI, is not made under r.1.35 as not within Pts A1 to XI (see r.1.35(1)) and according to *Manolete Partners plc v Hayward & Barrett Holdings Ltd* [2021] EWHC 1481 (Ch); [2022] B.C.C. 159, where the s.423 application was brought by assignees under r.1.35, is thus not an "insolvency proceeding". Chief ICC Judge Briggs came to this conclusion "with regret" as claims that are not insolvency proceedings under IR 2016 need to be issued by claim form under CPR Pt 7 (although he used the discretion under CPR r.3.10 to cure the procedural error to allow the claim to continue on payment of the relevant CPR Pt 7 fee). See also *Re Taunton Logs Ltd* [2020] EWHC 3480 (Ch). (The first five-year review of IR 2016 published on 5 April 2022 (see note to Introductory r.7) states that in light of the Manolete case the Insolvency Service is to consider whether what is an insolvency application under r.1.35 should be expanded so that applicants do not need to issue both an insolvency application and a CPR Pt 7 claim form.) On the other hand, an application under IA 1986 s.335A (in Pt IX of the Act) should plainly be under the procedure specified in r.1.35 (rather than as an application under CPR Pt 8): *Re Hussain (a Bankrupt); Gostelow v Hussain* [2021] EWHC 3276 (Ch).

On authentication in r.1.35(3) see r.1.5. Again the identification requirements in r.1.6 apply.

Heading to Ch.8 and r.1.35(1) amended by the Insolvency (England and Wales) (No. 2) (Amendment) Rules 2021 (SI 2021/1028) r.80, Sch.1 paras 1–3 as from 1 October 2021, subject to saving provisions in rr.4, 5.

PART 2

COMPANY VOLUNTARY ARRANGEMENTS (CVA)

CHAPTER 5

CONSIDERATION OF THE PROPOSAL BY THE COMPANY MEMBERS AND CREDITORS

Notice of order made under section 4A(6)

2.37—

GENERAL NOTE

Replace the note with:

The procedure for notification of court orders directing that the views of members shall prevail over creditors. Such orders are rare. See Form VAC.

Rule 2.37 heading and r.2.37(1) amended by the Insolvency (England and Wales) (No. 2) (Amendment) Rules 2021 (SI 2021/1028) r.81, Sch.2 paras 1–3 as from 1 October 2021, subject to saving provisions in rr.4, 5, to reflect the abolition of the CVA moratorium.

PART 3

ADMINISTRATION

CHAPTER 11

EXTENSION AND ENDING OF ADMINISTRATION

Moving from administration to dissolution (paragraph 84 of Schedule B1)

3.61—

GENERAL NOTE TO RR.3.53–3.61

R.3.54

Replace the note with:

The period for which the administrator's term of office may be extended under Sch.B1 para.76(2)(b) was increased from up to six months to up to one year by SBEEA 2015 s.127 as from 26 May 2015.

An application for extension must be made well ahead of time so that it can be heard by the ICC judge. On 15 October 2008 Mann J issued a warning that administrators who leave applying until a late date will have their costs disallowed by the applications judge. It is understood that in London the Companies Court ICC judge require notice to be filed six weeks in advance of the expiry date, unless the circumstances are unusual. See also the unreported case *Re Taylor Made Foods plc*, discussed in the note to Sch.B1 paras 76–77.

In *Re Caversham Finance Ltd* [2022] EWHC 789 (Ch) a defect in providing the reasons for an extension in the notice to creditors was a procedural defect only as creditors were not prejudiced where they could have read a laetter referring to an online progress report and have contacted the administrators for further clarification if necessary, so that the defect was remediable under r.12.64. A similar result occurred in *Re E Realisations Ltd* [2022] EWHC 1575 (Ch) where no reasons were given for consent which was requested less than two months after the administrators were appointed at a time when no reasons could have been given (requests for this advance "contingent consent" appear to have become common practice among insolvency practitioners).

PART 6

CREDITORS' VOLUNTARY WINDING UP

INTRODUCTORY NOTE TO PART 6

Replace the note with:

The rules contained in this Part were formerly to be found in Pt 4 of IR 1986. The most noticeable changes include the following:

- The Rules dealing with creditors' voluntary liquidation are treated separately in this Part instead of being combined with compulsory liquidations as in IR 1986. The practice by which differentiation was effected by the labelling "CVL" and "NO CVL" in the former Rules is discontinued.

- Forms are no longer prescribed: although a particular rule may require a document to be "in the prescribed form", it is not to be *on* a prescribed form. Instead the rule sets out a check-list of items which must be included in the contents of the document in question. Forms are still required for documents to be filed with the registrar of companies: these are listed in App.II.

- In the main, decisions are not to be taken by the creditors at physical meetings, convened in the traditional manner. The options available are: electronic voting, "virtual" meetings (e.g. conference calls) and the "deemed consent" procedure (see rr.15.3–15.7). A physical meeting cannot be instigated on the initiative of the company or the liquidator, but only at the request of the prescribed number or percentage of the creditors or contributories (IA 1986 s.246ZE(7)).

- Many rules formerly to be found in Pt 4 of the 1986 Rules have been moved to other Parts, where provision is made for the rules relating to several insolvency procedures to be dealt with under a single head, for instance: defined terms and form and contents of documents (Pt 1), court procedure and practice (Pt 12), creditors' claims (Pt 14), proxies and corporate representation (Pt 16), reporting and remuneration of office-holders (Pt 18), disclaimer (Pt 19) and service (Sch.4). "Liquidation committees" has a separate Part all to itself (Pt 17).

The *First Review of the Insolvency (England and Wales) Rules 2016*, published on 5 April 2022 (see note to Introductory r.7) announced that the Insolvency Service is to review the creditors' voluntary liquidation process as found to be "unhelpfully inconsistent and opaque" and this will be given initial attention.

PART 7

WINDING UP BY THE COURT

CHAPTER 3

PETITION FOR WINDING-UP ORDER

Certificate of compliance

7.12—

GENERAL NOTE TO rr.7.4–7.12

Replace the note with:

These rules deal with the filing, service, advertisement (now called notice) and verification of the petition. See generally *Practice Direction: Insolvency Proceedings* [2020] B.C.C. 698 especially at paras 9.1–9.9. Also note *Insolvency Practice Direction Relating to the Corporate Insolvency and Governance Act 2020* [2020] B.C.C. 694 (reproduced as App.V to this *Guide*) on the filing and hearing of the petition. In particular para.3.1 provides that a petition will not be accepted for filing unless it contains the statement required by r.7.5(1)(n) as to the type of proceedings in relation to the post-Brexit retained provisions of the EU Regulation 2015/848 and also draws attention to the modification in CIGA 2020 former Sch.10 para.19 (in relation to petitions presented during the relevant period 27 April 2020 to 30 September 2021) later substituted as Sch.10 para.2 (in relation to petitions presented in the relevant period 1 October 2021 to 31 March 2022) requiring extra requirements to r.7.5(1) contents of the petition where a moratorium is in force during those relevant periods.

In relation to r.7.6, *Camden LBC v Saint Benedict's Land Trust Ltd* [2019] EWHC 3370 (Ch) held that a witness statement unsigned at the time of filing of the petition, including a statement of truth, was not a nullity where it had been signed by the time of the hearing: although r.7.6(3) required that a statement of truth if endorsed on the winding-up petition it must be done before filing, but if endorsed on a separate witness statement IR 2016 did not stipulate when it must be signed.

The deposit referred to in r.7.7(2)(a) is fixed at £1,600 (but £5,000 on a petition based on s.124A) from 21 July 2016. See the Insolvency Proceedings (Fees) Order 2016 (SI 2016/692) art.2 (the fee increased to £2,600 as from 1 November 2022 by the Insolvency Proceedings (Fees) (Amendment) Order 2022 (SI 2022/929) arts 1, 2(b)). Rule 7.7(2)(b) allows alternative arrangements to be made for the payment of the deposit.

Any director, contributory or creditor of the company is entitled to a copy of the petition on payment of the appropriate fee (r.7.11).

Service of the petition under r.7.9 is now proved by a certificate of compliance rather than an affidavit in all cases (r.7.12). The gazetting of the notice of petition (r.7.10(3)) must now include the standard contents (see rr.1.10–1.12) with the further details set out in r.7.10(2). Service by a petitioner other than the company must be with a sealed copy on the company in accordance with Sch.4

In *Re Oakwood Storage Services Ltd* [2003] EWHC 2807 (Ch); [2004] 2 B.C.L.C. 404 service of a winding-up petition was effected at the company's registered office at a time when its directors were barred from attending the premises as a result of action taken by the Customs and Excise. The court held that the directors could not complain that the service was ineffective since it was up to them to have made suitable arrangements to ensure that such documents came to their notice while the ban continued. In *Re Southbourne Trading Co Ltd* [2017] EWHC 3737 (Ch); [2018] B.C.C. 604, the court dismissed HMRC's winding-up petition and criticised HMRC for failing to effect valid service under IR 1986 r.4.8(2) (now Sch.4 para.2). HMRC clearly knew that the registered office was on a particular floor of a large building but had not informed the process server who merely left the petition on the ground floor without handing to a person as required by the provision.

The court is given a discretion by r.7.10(5) to dismiss the petition if notice of it has not been duly given. It has been the practice of the court since the ruling in *Re Signland Ltd* [1982] 2 All E.R. 609 to strike out any petition where the petitioning creditor has not observed the provisions as to time set out in r.7.10(4)(b), and in particular where the petition has been advertised without giving the company the prescribed seven days' notice. This is confirmed by para.9.8.1 of the *Practice Direction: Insolvency Proceedings* [2020] B.C.C. 698 (reproduced as App.IV to this *Guide*). If the court, in its discretion, grants an adjournment instead of dismissing the petition, this will be on the condition that the petition is advertised in due time for the adjourned hearing, and no further adjournment for the purpose of gazetting will be granted.

Rule 7.12 must be complied with even if the notice is defective in any way or if the petitioner decides not to pursue the petition (e.g. on receiving payment) (ibid., para.9.8.2).

The heading to r.7.10 refers to "notice" of the petition whereas its predecessor was headed "advertisement" of the petition (although the content of the rule then used the word "notice"). The word "advertised" (and in this context, "notice") has two meanings: (1) a paid announcement in a general publication; and (2) notifying the existence of the matter in question. Where the court has made an order restraining the advertisement of a winding-up petition, the word is to be construed in a wide sense, and any communication to an unauthorised party (e.g. informing the company's bank) of the fact that the petition has been presented will be a breach of the order: see the note to r.7.31(2)(c). However in rr.7.10 and 7.12 the word "notice" refers to publication in the *Gazette*—i.e. is used in the former sense (*SN Group plc v Barclays Bank plc* [1993] B.C.C. 506), and a notification to a third party of the existence of the petition will not in itself be a breach of rr.7.10 or 7.12. The Court of Appeal in *Secretary of State for Trade and Industry v North West Holdings plc* [1998] B.C.C. 997 approved *SN Group v Barclays Bank* and held that press notices by the Department of Trade and Industry stating that a winding-up petition had been presented and provisional liquidator appointed to a company were not in breach of r.7.10, although Chadwick LJ warned the DTI that if it were in any doubt whether it was appropriate to issue a press notice then directions from the court should be sought. A communication to a third party, may, however be open to condemnation as an abuse of the process of the court, if made for an improper purpose such as putting pressure on the company: if so, the petition may be struck out for this reason (*Re Bill Hennessey Associates Ltd* [1992] B.C.C. 386).

The court has a discretion under r.7.10(1) to restrain or dispense altogether with notice, which it may do (e.g.) in order to enable presentation of an application (formerly a petition) for an administration order (*Re a Company (No.001448 of 1989)* [1989] B.C.L.C. 715) but otherwise, unless the petition is held to constitute an abuse of the process of the court, this discretion will be exercised only in exceptional circumstances: *Applied Data Base Ltd v Secretary of State for Trade & Industry* [1995] 1 B.C.L.C. 272. Conduct must be improper, and something more than pressure applied by a creditor, in order to constitute abuse: *Re a Company* [2010] EWHC 3814 (Ch); [2012] B.C.C. 289.

The factors which the court will take into account in considering whether to order a restraint on advertisement/

notice were examined in *Re a Company (No.007923 of 1994)* [1995] 1 W.L.R. 953; [1995] B.C.C. 634. In addition to satisfying the court that there was not likely to be any significant damage to the company's creditors, contributories and current trading partners, it was held that company needed to show that advertisement might cause serious damage to its reputation and financial stability. On a without-notice application to restrain advertisement of a petition, the court would normally expect evidence of the company's solvency, but the absence of such evidence was held not to be a bar where the issue was whether the debt was disputed on substantial grounds: *Global Acquirers Ltd v Laycatelcom Lda* (unreported, 2 July 2014). See also *James Dolman & Co Ltd v Pedley* [2003] EWCA Civ 1686; [2004] B.C.C. 504; *Secretary of State for Business, Innovation and Skills v Broomfield Developments Ltd* [2014] EWHC 3925 (Ch) (application refused: customers of the company, as contingent creditors, needed to know the position). On the courts' approach to litigants in person (such as a director) acting for the company at the hearing to restrain advertisement of the petition, see *EDF Energy Customers Ltd v Re-Energized Ltd* [2018] EWHC 652 (Ch). Snowden J had no hesitation in dispensing with notice under r.7.10(1) in *Re British Steel Ltd* [2019] EWHC 1304 (Ch); [2019] B.C.C. 974 due to the urgency of the situation of ordering an insolvency process and the "inevitability and desirability" of making an immediate winding-up order.

The court is more likely to dispense with the advertisement (now notice) of a s.124A petition than a creditor's petition under s.124 (unless the members might thereby be prejudiced): *Secretary of State for Business, Innovation and Skills v Combined Maintenance Services Ltd* (unreported, 6 November 2014).

By virtue of r.7.4, modifications to the procedure in Ch.3 on a petition presented by contributories or a relevant office-holder (administrator, administrative receiver or CVA supervisor: r.7.4(2)) are set out in Ch.4 (rr.7.25 et seq.).

Service of documents is now covered by IR 2016 Sch.4. Service of the winding-up petition on the company is provided for by Sch.4 para.2, of which para.2(3), (4) enables service to be effected more easily on a company which has ceased trading.

Rules 7.5(1)(n) and 7.6(8) amended by the Insolvency (England and Wales) and Insolvency (Scotland) (Miscellaneous and Consequential Amendments) Rules 2017 (SI 2017/1115) rr.1(1), (2), 22, 30(15), (16) as from 8 December 2017. Rules 7.5(1)(n), 7.6(8) and 7.9(3) amended by the Insolvency (Amendment) (EU Exit) Regulations 2019 (SI 2019/146) reg.1(3), Sch. paras 46, 71, 72 and 73 respectively as from IP completion day (11pm on 31 December 2020) subject to transitional and saving provisions in reg.4 (in light of Brexit). Rules 7.5 and 7.11 amended by the Insolvency (England and Wales) (No. 2) (Amendment) Rules 2021 (SI 2021/1028) r.34, 35, and r.7.8 amended by SI 2021/1028 r.81, Sch.2 paras 1–3, as from 1 October 2021, subject to saving provisions in rr.4, 5, to accommodate the new moratorium.

On what IR 2016 r.7.5 requires see ICC Judge Mullen in *BUJ Architects v Investin Quay House Ltd* [2021] EWHC 2371 (Ch).

Injunction to restrain presentation or notice of petition

7.24—

GENERAL NOTE TO RR.7.14–7.24

R.7.24
Replace the note with:
This rule envisages that the application for an injunction to restrain a winding-up petition will be made by the debtor company and *Re St Benedict's Land Trust Ltd; Harper v Camden LBC* [2020] EWHC 1001 (Ch); [2020] B.C.C. 620 confirmed that a director or shareholder of the company does not have a sufficient personal interest to have standing to apply for the injunction personally. In *Rushbrooke UK Ltd v 4 Designs Concept Ltd* [2022] EWHC 1110 (Ch) an application to restrain presentation was struck out on company-law grounds as the solicitors purporting to act on behalf of the applicant company had been instructed by only one of its directors holding half of the company's shares who acted without authority as he had not consulted with or obtained agreement for the application from his equal co-director-shareholder (on costs in the latter case see [2022] EWHC 1416 (Ch) where the court made a costs order against the applicant company but would not make the director concerned jointly liable for those costs as he would not benefit personally from the application and had not actually been joined to the proceedings, but in separate proceedings made a wasted costs order against the solicitors who acted unauthorised: [2022] EWHC 1687 (Ch); [2022] B.C.C. 1135). The court will grant an injunction to prevent presentation of a winding-up petition where it considers that the petition would be an abuse of process and/or that the petition is bound to fail (to the extent they are different). See the guidance given in *Coilcolour Ltd v Camtrex Ltd* [2015] EWHC 3202 (Ch); [2016] B.P.I.R. 1129 at [32] et seq. On the grounds for applications to restrain a petition based on the commonly pleaded inability to pay the company's debts, see the note to s.123.

On r.7.24 see *Sell Your Car With Us v Sareen* [2019] EWHC 2332 (Ch); [2019] B.C.C. 1211.

CHAPTER 5

Termination of appointment

7.39—

GENERAL NOTE TO RR.7.33–7.39
Replace the note with:

These rules set out the procedure governing an application to the court for the appointment of a provisional liquidator under IA 1986 s.135, and the associated questions of furnishing a deposit (where the official receiver is appointed) or security (where the provisional liquidator is an insolvency practitioner), and the liquidator's remuneration.

The Insolvency Service indicated in Dear IP Issue 146 (May 2022) that the copies of the application and witness statement required to be delivered to the Official Receiver by r.7.33(3) may be sent to the Public Interest Unit at PIU.OR@insolvency.gov.uk.

The order of appointment must be sent to Companies House under r.7.35(5) attached to Form WU02.

The court may in an appropriate case refer the fixing of remuneration under r.7.38 to one or more assessors: *Re Independent Insurance Co Ltd* [2002] EWHC 1577 (Ch); [2003] EWHC 51 (Ch); [2004] B.C.C. 919. In the judgment the principles for the fixing of remuneration and making of interim payments are discussed in detail. The judgment of Peter Smith J in *Jacob v UIC Insurance Co Ltd* [2006] EWHC 2717 (Ch); [2007] B.C.C.167 discusses many issues relating to the review of the remuneration of provisional liquidators, including (i) the procedure for an appeal under r.12.59 against an assessment made by a registrar; (ii) the reasons for disallowing claims for remuneration on the basis of over-management, the use of staff of too high a grade and of consultants; (iii) the justice of re-opening claims settled or agreed in the past; and (iv) the irrelevance of the fact that the provisional liquidation was successful. (For further proceedings, see *Re UIC Insurance Co Ltd (No.2)* [2007] B.P.I.R. 589.) See also the *Practice Direction* [2020] B.C.C. 698 (reproduced as App.IV to this *Guide*) Pt 6.

There is no provision in the rules governing the priority in which the remuneration and expenses of a provisional liquidator should be paid, either vis-à-vis the company's debts or in relation to each other; but in *Re Grey Marlin Ltd* [2000] B.C.C. 410 and *Smith v UIC Insurance Co Ltd* [2001] B.C.C. 11 the rules governing a liquidator's remuneration and expenses were applied by analogy.

In *Re Beppler & Jacobson Ltd* [2016] EWHC 20 (Ch) an agreement to "advance" the funding of a provisional liquidator was held to have connoted a loan with a right of recourse out of the assets to reimburse the outlay in accordance with r.7.38(3). The appeal was allowed in *Leibson Corp v TOC Investments Corp; Re Beppler and Jacobson Ltd* [2018] EWCA Civ 763; [2018] B.C.C. 839. The Court of Appeal judgment contains some general discussion of the statutory predecessor of r.7.38(3) (IR 1986 r.4.30(3)).

The provisions in rr.7.37 and 7.38 are directory, although subject to the overall discretion conferred by r.7.39(2); and so a court will not normally make an order that an unsuccessful petitioner should pay the remuneration of a provisional liquidator: *Re Walter L Jacob & Co Ltd* (1987) 3 B.C.C. 532. (See, however, *Re Secure & Provide plc* [1992] B.C.C. 405, where such an order was made against the Secretary of State following the failure of a petition under s.124A; and compare *Re Xyllyx plc (No.2)* [1992] B.C.L.C. 378.)

The court has power under r.7.39(2) to direct that a provisional liquidator who has been discharged before the hearing of the petition shall be paid remuneration out of the company's assets: see *Re UOC Corp, Alipour v UOC Corp* [1998] B.C.C. 191.

Rules 7.36(3) and 7.39(3)–(5) prescribe in detail the required contents of the notice of the provisional liquidator's appointment and its termination. On the standard contents for gazetted notices, see rr.1.10–1.12. The notice of termination to be sent to Companies House under r.7.39(3), (4)(a) is in Form WU03.

A provisional liquidator is listed in Annex B to the (now retained) Recast EU Regulation 2015/848 as an "insolvency practitioner" referred to in art.2(5) of the Regulation.

Rule 7.33(1)(g) amended by the Insolvency (England and Wales) and Insolvency (Scotland) (Miscellaneous and Consequential Amendments) Rules 2017 (SI 2017/1115) rr.1(1), (2), 22, 26 as from 8 December 2017.

Rule 7.33(2)(f) inserted by the Insolvency Amendment (EU 2015/848) Regulations 2017 (SI 2017/702) regs 1, 2(1), Sch. paras 32, 39 in relation to proceedings opened on or after 26 June 2017 (see reg.3) when the Recast EU Regulation 2015/848 came into force. Rule 7.33(1)(g) omitted and (2)(f) amended by the Insolvency (Amendment) (EU Exit) Regulations 2019 (SI 2019/146) reg.1(3), Sch. paras 46, 81(b), (c) as from IP completion day (11pm on 31 December 2020) subject to transitional and saving provisions in reg.4 (in light of Brexit).

Rule 7.35(1)(e)(ii) amended by the Insolvency (England and Wales) and Insolvency (Scotland) (Miscellaneous and Consequential Amendments) Rules 2017 (SI 2017/1115) rr.1(1), (2), 22, 30(21) as from 8 December 2017. Rule 7.35(1)(e)(ii) amended by the Insolvency (Amendment) (EU Exit) Regulations 2019 (SI 2019/146) reg.1(3), Sch. paras 46, 82 as from IP completion day (11pm on 31 December 2020) subject to transitional and saving provisions in reg.4 (in light of Brexit).

Rules 7.33(2)(d)(zi), 7.35(4A) inserted and r.7.39(4)(a) substituted by the Insolvency (England and Wales) (No. 2) (Amendment) Rules 2021 (SI 2021/1028) r.37, 38, 39 as from 1 October 2021, subject to saving provisions in rr.4, 5, to accommodate the new moratorium.

Part 10

Bankruptcy

Chapter 1

The statutory demand

Application to set aside statutory demand

10.4—

General Note

Replace the note with:

The debtor can apply to the court to have the statutory demand set aside. He has 18 days after service to make such an application. If an application is made, the three weeks' deadline for compliance with the demand ceases to run. In *Revenue and Customs v Soor* [2005] EWHC 3080 (Ch); [2006] B.P.I.R. 429 Warren J rejected a later application to set aside a statutory demand. There were no grounds for allowing an application for the late setting aside of the statutory demand. The liability, established by court judgment, could not be disputed.

The courts will be reluctant to accede to a set aside application where the alleged debt which is the basis of the demand is being contested in ongoing court proceedings—*Central Bridging Loans Ltd v Anwer* [2019] EWHC 1602 (Ch). Adjournment of the set aside application may be appropriate until those other proceedings are resolved.

A set aside application made by a debtor facing a statutory demand is covered by an Extended Civil Restraint Order granted against that debtor and therefore requires permission—*Webster v Ashcroft* [2019] EWHC 2174 (Ch); [2019] B.P.I.R. 1607. The court in this case indicated that such permission will often be given.

See also *Practice Direction: Insolvency Proceedings* [2020] B.C.C. 698 (reproduced as App.IV of this *Guide*); and *Morley v Inland Revenue Commissioners* [1996] B.P.I.R. 452 and *Makki v Bank of Beirut SAL* [2022] EWHC 733 (Ch) (in which latter case the court would have extended time for the application if necessary and considered para.11.4.2 of the *Practice Direction* on extension of the 18-day time limit). The Northern Irish court refused to exercise its discretion to extend time to set aside a statutory demand in *McFarland v Burnside* [2022] NICh 5. On the need for proper formal requirements to be satisfied see *Ariyo v Sovereign Leasing* [1998] B.P.I.R. 177.

Hearing of application to set aside

10.5—

General Note

Replace the note with:

This rule outlines the hearing procedure for an application made under r.10.4. If the application succeeds, the court's order should contain the details in r.10.5(6). If the application fails the court can permit the immediate presentation of the bankruptcy petition. The leading case on former IR 1986 r.6.5(4) (now IR 2016 r.10.5(5)) is *Re a Debtor (No.1 of 1987)* [1989] 1 W.L.R. 271 where the Court of Appeal held that a document purporting to be a statutory demand was to be treated as such until set aside. In cases of setting aside under r.10.5(5)(d) the debtor must not merely convince the court that the demand was perplexing but also prove what the true position was between himself and the creditor. See the general note after s.268. For a useful comparison between the rules relating to set aside of statutory demands in corporate and personal insolvency law see *Re A Debtor (544/SD/98)* [2001] 1 B.C.L.C. 103 (also reported as *Garrow v The Society of Lloyds* [1999] B.P.I.R. 885).

A set aside is most likely to succeed where the statutory demand was served by a person who was neither a creditor nor appointed agent of the creditor—*Agilo Ltd v Henry* [2010] EWHC 2717 (Ch).

For the purposes of r.10.5 it is not necessary to state the date of the petition—*Vaidya v Wijayawardhana* [2010] B.P.I.R. 1016.

A set-aside application is not a trial on the merits and fresh evidence can be adduced: *Royal Bank of Scotland v Binnell* [1996] B.P.I.R. 352; *Norman Laurier v United Overseas Bank* [1996] B.P.I.R. 635; *Salvidge v Hussein* [1999] B.P.I.R. 410. These cases confirm that the rule in *Ladd v Marshall* [1954] 1 W.L.R. 1489 does not apply. For further discussion in the context of appeals from decisions on set-aside applications see *AIB Finance Ltd v Alsop* [1998] B.C.C. 780. Such appeals are true appeals and subsequent events should not be taken into account—*Cozens v Customs and Excise Commissioners* [2000] B.P.I.R. 252.

The jurisdiction to set aside statutory demands is permissive; the court is under no obligation to act, as was stressed in *Re a Debtor (No.106 of 1992), The Independent,* 20 April 1992. See also *Khan v Breezevale SARL* [1996] B.P.I.R. 190 (failure to refer to security). The fact that a statutory demand may be defective does not guarantee that it will be set aside under r.10.5(4)—*Coulter v Chief of Dorset Police* [2004] EWCA Civ 1259; [2005] B.P.I.R. 62. For a continuation of this saga see *Coulter v Dorset Police (No.2)* [2005] EWCA Civ 1113; [2006] B.P.I.R. 10. *Coulter (No.2)* was followed in *Vaidya v Wijayawardhana* [2010] B.P.I.R. 1016. For procedural requirements under r.10.5(4) to be followed by the court when hearing a set aside application see *Black v Sale Service and Maintenance Ltd* [2018] EWHC 1344 (Ch); [2018] B.P.I.R. 1260.

The court in *Addison v London European Securities Ltd* - [2022] EWHC 1077 (Ch) considered the question of appeals against the refusal to set-aside and whether the debtor had the standing to make the appeal. The court found that the debtor did have the standing to appeal as it is extremely unlikely that the trustee in bankruptcy would risk funds on such an appeal and right to appeal was retained by the debtor as a personal right relating to their status and did not vest with the rest of the estate. However, the grounds of appeal were ultimately dismissed.

The court cannot make a conditional order on a set-aside application. Either the demand must be set aside or the application rejected: *Re a Debtor (No.90 of 1992)* [1993] T.L.R. 387; and *Re Debtor (No.32 of 1991) (No.2)* [1994] B.C.C. 524. Equally the courts will not allow a petition to be presented and then adjourned simply in order to trigger time periods for transactional avoidance. Thus if the debtor has an arguable cross claim the proper course of action is to set aside the demand and not to allow this issue to be reserved for trial of the petition—*Garrow v The Society of Lloyds* [1999] B.P.I.R. 885. If a set-aside application fails the same issues cannot normally be relitigated on the hearing of the petition—*Turner v Royal Bank of Scotland* [2000] B.P.I.R. 683; *Atherton v Ogunlende* [2003] B.P.I.R. 21. See also *Coulter v Dorset Police (No.2)* [2005] EWCA Civ 1113; [2006] B.P.I.R. 10. See also *Roseoak Investment Ltd v Network Rail* [2010] B.P.I.R. 646, where the point was re-emphasised that failed arguments on a set aside application cannot be reopened.

An application to set aside a statutory demand based upon former IR 1986 r.6.5(4)(a) failed in *Ghadami v Donegan* [2014] EWHC 4448 (Ch).

A statutory demand was set aside by Registrar Barber in *Dowling v Promontoria (Arrow) Ltd* [2017] EWHC B25 (Ch); [2017] B.P.I.R. 1477. Multiple reasons were given for the setting aside of this large demand which was based upon an alleged guarantee liability.

On r.10.5(5)(a) see *Hofer v Strawson* [1999] B.P.I.R. 501; and *Re A Debtor (No.87 of 1999)* [2000] B.P.I.R. 589, which offer guidance on cross-claims. The requirements of former IR 1986 r.6.5(4)(a) (now IR 2016 r.10.5(5)(a)) were found to be satisfied in *Stone v Vallance* [2008] B.P.I.R. 236. For the meaning of a cross demand within r.10.5(5)(a) see *Popely v Popely* [2004] EWCA Civ 463; [2004] B.P.I.R. 778. In determining whether to set aside a statutory demand because of the existence of a potential cross claim the court should ask itself whether there was a "genuinely triable issue" as to the existence of the cross claim. That test was, in effect, the same as that used in the Civil Procedure Rules, where the requirement was for a "real prospect of success"—*Ashworth v Newnote Ltd* [2007] EWCA Civ 793; [2007] B.P.I.R. 1012. See *Abernethy v Hotbed Ltd* [2011] EWHC 1476 (Ch); [2011] B.P.I.R. 1547 where Newey J equates the genuinely triable issue with the test applied to summary judgment applications. There was a genuinely triable issue in *Slowikowsa v Rogers* [2021] EWHC 192 (Ch) where the debtor contested as a potential penalty a 65% interest rate on the bankruptcy debt of a loan from her solicitor and the court added that where a debtor was facing bankruptcy and its many debilitating consequences, and it was finely balanced as to whether a defence was sustainable, the court should lean in favour of the debtor. In *Darjan Estate Co plc v Hurley* [2012] EWHC 189 (Ch); [2012] 1 W.L.R. 1782 the High Court confirmed a decision of the deputy district judge that there were no substantial grounds for disputing the debt (which consisted of rent arrears) featured in the statutory demand. The court refused to extend the full protective rules embodied in cases such as *RBS v Etridge (No.2)* [2002] 2 A.C. 773 to wives signing standard contracts, as opposed to contracts of surety. A set aside was granted in *Welsh v Bank of Ireland* [2013] NIMaster 6 as the debt was disputed on *Etridge* grounds. The court made the point that the test to be applied was whether the debtor had raised a good arguable case in respect of the dispute. See also *Logue v Bank of Ireland* [2012]

NIMaster 10 for a similar approach. An attempt to seek a set aside on the basis of a dubious cross claim failed in *Gustavi v Moore* [2004] B.P.I.R. 268. Any counterclaim must be legally enforceable—*Re A Debtor (No.35 of 2000)* [2002] B.P.I.R. 75. Where there is a counterclaim within r.10.5(5)(a) there appears to be a mutuality requirement—*Hurst v Bennett* [2001] EWCA Civ 182; [2001] B.P.I.R. 287; *Southward v Banham* [2002] B.P.I.R. 1253. In *Chan Sui v Appasamy* [2005] EWHC 3519 (Ch); [2008] B.P.I.R. 18 the court set aside a statutory demand under IR 1986 r.6.5(4)(a) where there were a series of interlocking cross-claims producing a situation that could not be resolved by the court on a summary set aside application. HHJ Weeks QC in this case explains the residual role played by r.10.5(5)(d). In *Vaidya v Wijayawardhana* [2010] B.P.I.R. 1016 the court was quite liberal on the background to the cross-claim which was being raised—it need not relate to the debt featured in the statutory demand. On cross-claims see also *Bush v Bank Mandiri (Europe) Ltd* [2011] B.P.I.R. 19. In *Ahmed v Landstone Leisure Ltd* [2009] B.P.I.R. 227 the statutory demand was set aside under IR 1986 r.6.5(4)(a) (now IR 2016 r.10.5.(5)(a)) by HHJ Purle QC because the debtor may have had a counterclaim. For comment see V. Cocks (2009) 22 Insolv. Int. 108. An appellate court is unlikely to overturn a finding at first instance that a debt is not disputed on substantial grounds—*Macpherson v Wise* [2011] EWHC 141 (Ch); [2011] B.P.I.R. 472. A Northern Ireland example of failure to establish a counterclaim occurred in *McFarland v Burnside* [2022] NICh 5. For a discussion on several of the above points, including genuine triable issue, counterclaims etc., see *Makki v Bank of Beirut SAL* [2022] EWHC 733 (Ch) in which the court also rejected an argument that for a claim to comprise a "counterclaim, set-off or cross demand" under r.10.5(5)(a), there must be mutuality between the parties: such was not a requirement.

Note also *Hayes v Hayes* [2014] EWHC 2694 (Ch); [2014] B.P.I.R. 1212 where Nugee J undertook an in depth review of the position on disputed debts and cross-claims. In upholding the decision of the Registrar to dismiss the creditor's petition the point was made that in some situations the court hearing the petition could revisit arguments made on an abortive set aside application if new evidence had come to light.

A statutory demand was set aside by Registrar Jones in *Ryan v Tiuta International Ltd* [2015] B.P.I.R. 123 in view of a dispute as to the alleged underlying liability on a guarantee. See also *Baker v LSREF III Wight Ltd* [2016] B.P.I.R. 509 on the test to be applied as to whether there is a bona fide dispute on substantial grounds.

In *Inbakumar v United Trust Bank Ltd* [2012] EWHC 845 (Ch); [2012] B.P.I.R. 758 the court indicated that the fact that a debtor may have a claim against a third party in connection with the transaction from which the debt arose was no justification in itself for setting aside a statutory demand served by a creditor. In [41] of his judgment Vos J confined his observations to the facts of the present case.

An attempt to rely on former IR 1986 r.6.5(4)(b) (now IR 2016 r.10.5.(5)(b)) was rejected by Nugee J in *Knight v APS Recycling Ltd* [2014] EWHC 4620 (Ch).

In *Re a Debtor (No.960/SD/1992)* [1993] S.T.C. 218 Mummery J refused to set aside a statutory demand under former IR 1986 r.6.5(4)(c) (now IR 2016 r.10.5.(5)(c)) in a case where a tax assessment was being challenged by the taxpayer; the case did not appear to be covered by this provision. See *Fagg v Rushton* [2007] EWHC 657 (Ch); [2007] B.P.I.R. 1059 for the meaning of "security" in r.10.5(5)(c). On the valuation of security see *Ludsin Overseas Ltd v Maggs* [2014] EWHC 3566 (Ch). On the interpretation of r.10.5(5)(c) see the ruling of Floyd J in *White v Davenham Trust* [2010] EWHC 2748 (Ch); [2011] B.P.I.R. 280. Note also *1st Credit (Finance) Ltd v Bartram* [2010] EWHC 2910 (Ch); [2011] B.P.I.R. 1. The fact that a creditor enjoys security *granted by a third party* does not preclude a creditor from pursuing bankruptcy proceedings against a person properly determined as a debtor—*White v Davenham Trust Ltd* [2011] EWCA Civ 747; [2011] B.P.I.R. 1193. This ruling is important in the context of guarantees given by company directors where the lender has security over the company's assets. On r.10.5(5)(c) see *Cahillane v National Asset Management Ltd* [2014] EWHC 1992 (Ch); [2014] B.P.I.R. 1093.

A set-aside application also proved unsuccessful in *Re a Debtor (No.415/SD/1993)* [1994] 1 W.L.R. 917. Here the debtor was seeking to set aside the demand by arguing that he had made a reasonable offer of security to the creditor. In discussing the meaning of "other grounds" in IR 1986 r.6.5(4)(d) Jacob J made it clear that set-aside applications were designed to deal with procedural flaws in the demand and were not meant to raise substantive issues of reasonableness—these issues could be considered when the petition was heard. Equally in *Platts v Western Trust and Savings Ltd* [1996] B.P.I.R. 339 the court indicated that it would not investigate such questions as whether the creditor was secured or not as these were issues best dealt with when the petition was heard. However see the comments of the Court of Appeal on IR 1986 r.6.5(4)(d) (now IR 2016 r.10.5(5)(d)) in *Budge v Budge (Contractors) Ltd* [1997] B.P.I.R. 366. *Budge* (above) was followed in *Mahon and Mahon v FBN Bank (UK) Ltd* [2011] EWHC 1432 (Ch); [2011] B.P.I.R. 1035. In *Re a Debtor (No.90 of 1997), The Times,* 1 July 1998, the High Court considered the position with regard to setting aside under IR 1986 r.6.5(4)(d) (now IR 2016 r.10.5(5)(d)) when there were parallel bankruptcy and civil proceedings afoot. The importance of the general discretion vested in the court by r.10.5(5)(d) was clearly illustrated in *City Electrical Factors v Hardingham* [1996] B.P.I.R. 541 where a statutory demand based upon a debt slightly in excess of £750 was set aside. In *Turner v Turner* [2006] EWHC 2023 (Ch); [2006] B.P.I.R. 1531 the court dealt with the factors relevant to the exercise of discretion under r.10.5(5)(d). The factors taken into account should have some relevance/proximity to the statutory demand. A statutory demand was set aside under IR r.10.5(5)(d) in *Jones v Sky Wheels Group Ltd* [2020] EWHC 1112 (Ch).

Note *Howell v Lerwick Commercial Mortgage Corp Ltd* [2015] EWHC 1177 (Ch); [2015] B.P.I.R. 821. This case features a valuable analysis by Nugee J of the situation where the debtor seeking set aside has a cross-claim or counterclaim that might reduce the amount of the debt to below the prescribed amount (then £750). According to Nugee J this would not require the court to accede to the set aside application; this conclusion was arrived at by examination of the statutory provision and after taking soundings from the bankruptcy registrars. Nugee J noted that the position might be different where there was a disputed element in the debt—r.10.5(5)(d) might then be engaged. Nugee J did note that if a bankruptcy petition did proceed where the debt was less than the minimum amount then the petition would be likely to fail.

Harvey v Dunbar Assets [2013] EWCA Civ 952; [2013] B.P.I.R. 722 is a case on guarantee liability that bucks the trend. The statutory demand here was set aside because the alleged guarantee liability did not arise. The guarantee was a composite guarantee and as there was not a valid signature from each of the guarantors, no liability arose. *Josife v Summertrot Holdings Ltd* [2014] EWHC 996 (Ch); [2014] B.P.I.R. 1250 featured an abortive attempt to set aside a statutory demand on the basis of an allegation that the debtor lacked mental capacity when signing up to the guarantee producing the underlying debt. The court also made the general point that set aside will not be granted simply because the debtor might come up with a defence before any bankruptcy petition is heard. In *Harvey v Dunbar Assets plc* [2015] EWHC 3355 (Ch) HHJ Kaye QC warned about allowing arguments to be rerun by a debtor on a set aside application where these same arguments had been unsuccessful at an earlier hearing. This point was stressed even though the doctrine of res judicata might not apply.

Some further consideration was given to the criteria governing the exercise of discretion under former IR 1986 r.6.5(4)(d) (now IR 2016 r.10.5(5)(d)) in *TS&S Global Ltd v Fithian-Franks* [2007] EWHC 1401 (Ch). For an interesting discussion on whether it was appropriate to set aside a statutory demand served on a guarantor of a tenant see *Octagon Assets Ltd v Remblance* [2009] B.P.I.R. 1129.

For the utility of the "other grounds" basis for set aside which is located in r.10.5(5)(d) see *Maud v Libyan Investment Authority* [2015] EWHC 1625 (Ch); [2015] B.P.I.R. 858. The set aside decision in this case was set aside on appeal in *Libyan Investment Authority v Maud* [2016] EWCA Civ 788 with the Court of Appeal basing its decision on its interpretation of a range of grounds in the former IR 1986 r.6.5(4). But for later developments in this long running saga see *Re Maud* [2020] EWHC 974 (Ch) and [2020] EWHC 1469 (Ch).

The broad r.10.5(5)(d) "other grounds" approach succeeded in *Jones v Sky Wheels Group Ltd* [2020] EWHC 1112 (Ch) to set aside a statutory demand that had been employed for the purpose of obtaining a bankruptcy order to avoid unfairly prejudicial conduct proceedings against the creditor which if successful would result in value to the debtor probably far in excess of that claimed in the statutory demand. For a successful set aside application based upon "other grounds" see *May v Ulster Bank Ltd* [2021] NICh 11.

If the creditor bases his petition upon a judgment debt the court will not on a set-aside application look behind the earlier judgment: see Ferris J in *Re a Debtor (657/SD/1991)* [1993] B.C.L.C. 1280 applying *Practice Direction* [1987] 1 W.L.R. 119. Note also *Neely v Inland Revenue Commissioners* [1996] B.P.I.R. 473; and *Practice Direction: Insolvency Proceedings* [2020] B.C.C. 698, para.11.4.4 in App.IV of this *Guide*.

For the position where the debt is disputed within the context of r.10.5(5)(b), see *Re a Debtor (No.11 of 1987), The Independent,* 28 March 1988; *Re a Debtor (No.10 of 1988)* [1989] 1 W.L.R. 405; and *Cale v Assiudoman KPS (Harrow) Ltd* [1996] B.P.I.R. 245. On the standard of proof see *Kellar v BBR Graphic Engineers Ltd* [2002] B.P.I.R. 544. Another interesting case involving a disputed debt was *Re a Debtor (No.49 and 50 of 1992)* [1995] Ch. 66. Here part of the debt upon which the statutory demand was based was disputed by the debtor. The undisputed element was for an amount less than the statutory minimum upon which a creditor could petition for bankruptcy. In those circumstances the Court of Appeal held that although the demand could not be set aside in its entirety under former IR 1986 r.6.5(4)(b) (now IR 2016 r.10.5(5)(b)) the court could set aside the whole demand using its residual discretion under the previous IR 1986 r.6.5(4)(d) (now IR 2016 r.10.5(5)(d)). In *Interframe Ltd v Brown* [2005] EWHC 3527 (Ch); [2008] B.P.I.R. 49 Lawrence Collins J indicated that an overstated debt will not normally justify the setting aside of a statutory demand. For the dangers as to costs of a creditor using a statutory demand in cases where a trial of the action is pending see *Re a Debtor (No.620 of 1997), The Times,* 18 June 1998.

On r.10.5(5)(c) see *Promontoria (Chestnut) Ltd v Bell* [2019] EWHC 1581 (Ch); [2019] B.P.I.R. 1241 where Zacaroli J based his decision upon the provision in IR 1986, but his reasoning applies to the 2016 regime. In *Harrling v Midgley* [2019] EWHC 3278 (Ch) ICC Judge Jones set aside a statutory demand under r.10.5(5)(c) because there was a substantial dispute concerning the validity of the personal guarantee under which liability was said to arise. See also *Hancock v Promontoria (Chestnut) Ltd* [2020] EWCA Civ 907 where a set aside application made on the basis of a disputed debt failed.

In *Feldman v Nissim* [2010] B.P.I.R. 815 the court discussed the requirements of success under former IR 1986 r.6.5(4)(b) (now IR 2016 r.10.5(5)(b))—substantial grounds must be established in order to show that a debt was disputed. Note also *Crossley-Cooke v Europanel (UK) Ltd* [2010] B.P.I.R. 561 for discussion of the appropriate test to be applied where a debt is said to be disputed within the meaning of r.10.5(5)(b). On the test as to whether a debt is to be treated as disputed see *Alexander-Theodotou v Michael Kyprianou & Co LLC* [2016] B.P.I.R. 1114. On r.10.5(5), see *Wagner v White* [2018] EWHC 2882 (Ch). The court dismissed an appeal against a failed set aside application under IR 2016 r.10.5(5)(b) in *Swallow v Masreqbank PSC* [2021] EWHC 3265 (Ch). The onus was on the debtor when disputing a debt to show that there was a genuinely triable issue as to said dispute.

See *MFP Foundations v Shaw* [2010] B.P.I.R. 397 where the point was reiterated that the fact a debtor could have afforded to pay the statutory demand was not in itself grounds for dismissing the debtor's set aside application.

On the exercise of discretion under r.10.5(8) see *Everard v Lloyds* [2003] B.P.I.R. 1286. In *Davies v Barnes Webster & Sons Ltd* [2011] EWHC 2560 (Ch); [2012] B.P.I.R. 97 the court deferred the earliest date before which a petition could be presented.

On the predecessor IR 1986 r.6.5(6) (now IR 2016 r.10.5(8)) see *Darbyshire v Turpin* [2013] EWHC 954 (Ch); [2013] B.P.I.R. 558—if a set aside application is dismissed, the creditor can present a petition immediately unless court has set a date for presentation.

Note the unusual case of *Pace (Europe) Ltd v Dunham* [2012] EWHC 852 (Ch); [2012] B.P.I.R. 836 where the court allowed an appeal against a decision to set aside a statutory demand based upon a foreign judgment debt. In his judgment HHJ Purle undertakes a comprehensive analysis of the enforcement of foreign judgment debts.

An appeal against a decision to set aside a statutory demand where *Etridge* issues had been raised by the debtor was unsuccessful in *O'Neill v Ulster Bank Ltd* [2015] NICA 64.

There is authority that the remedial IR 1986 r.7.55 (now IR 2016 r.10.64) cannot apply in the context of defects in the statutory demand: *Re a Debtor (No.190 of 1987), The Times*, 21 May 1988.

See *Woolsey v Payne* [2015] EWHC 968 (Ch); [2015] B.P.I.R. 933 where the court made the point that the same test is to be applied on both a set aside application and an annulment application as to whether a debt is to be regarded as disputed.

A set aside application was dismissed in *Maud v Aabar Block SARL* [2015] EWHC 1626 (Ch); [2015] B.P.I.R. 845 as there were no arguable grounds for disputing the underlying liability. For later proceedings as to whether the bankruptcy petition should be adjourned for a second time—see the ruling of Registrar Briggs reported in [2015] EWHC 3681 (Ch). Eventually Registrar Briggs made a bankruptcy order (see [2016] EWHC 1016 (Ch) but the appeal to Snowden J succeeded [2016] EWHC 2175 (Ch)) and the issue therefore remained unresolved. Note also S. Najib (2016) 9 C.R.I. 214. See note to s.271(3). For the latest instalments in this saga see *Re Maud* [2020] EWHC 974 (Ch) and [2020] EWHC 1469 (Ch).

Note also *Diamond v Holding* (unreported, 2 November 2017). See also the views of Barling J in *Dunhill v Hughmans (a firm)* [2017] EWHC 2073 (Ch).

Set aside was considered by the Court of Appeal in *Doherty v Fannigan Holdings Ltd* [2018] EWCA Civ 1615; [2018] B.P.I.R. 1266. The Court of Appeal reviewed the contractual obligations existing between the parties as clarification on this point was essential before a decision could be made on whether bankruptcy proceedings could go ahead. The issue was whether those obligations were independent or dependent. *Doherty* (above) was distinguished on the facts by ICC Chief Judge Briggs in *Sandelson v Mulville* [2019] EWHC 1620 (Ch); [2019] B.P.I.R. 1253. An appeal against this ruling of Chief ICC Judge Briggs was dismissed by Roth J—see [2019] EWHC 3287 (Ch).

See also *Re Fulton* [2018] NICh 9 and *Fulton v AIB Group (UK) plc* [2018] NICh 10.

See also *Philbin v Davies* [2018] EWHC 3472 (Ch) where the statutory demand was set aside by Barling J because the debtor had a reasonable prospect of establishing a cross-claim which could overtop the amount featured in the statutory demand. A statutory demand was set aside in *Slowikowsa v Rogers* [2021] EWHC 192 (Ch).

Compare *Pearse v Revenue and Customs Commissioners* [2018] EWHC 3422 (Ch), where an attempt to have a statutory demand set aside by challenging the liability of the debtor under a guarantee failed before Rose J. There was also a failed set aside application recorded in *Re Brennan* [2018] NICh 29. An argument in a set-aside application that a guarantee was not binding on the debtor as not personally signed by him was dismissed in *Tatishev v Zimmerz Management LP* [2021] EWHC 2611 (Ch) where it was held that a settlement agreement acknowledging the debt was binding up on him and there was no mistake or misrepresentation involved; having dismissed the application the court referred to its duty under r.10.5(8) to order the creditor to present a petition as soon as practicably practicable, and ordered this to be done after 14 days. A similar outcome was the result in *Kerkar v Investment Opportunities IV PTE Ltd* [2021] EWHC 3255 (Ch) where ICC Judge Burton found that the debtor had no realistic grounds of challenging the liability stated in the statutory demand.

An attempt by a debtor to set aside a statutory demand served by an assignee of the original creditor failed before Mann J in *Nicoll v Promontoria (Ram 2) Ltd* [2019] EWHC 2410 (Ch); [2019] B.P.I.R. 1519. The attempt to challenge the assignment of the debt was rejected. A similar outcome prevailed in *Hancock v Promontoria (Chestnut) Ltd* [2019]

EWHC 2646 (Ch) with HH Judge Hodge QC upholding the dismissal of the set aside application as the debt (which had also been assigned) could not be disputed on serious grounds. For the unsuccessful appeal in this case see *Hancock v Promontoria (Chestnut) Ltd* [2020] EWCA Civ 907.

See also *Martin v McLaren Construction Ltd* [2019] EWHC 2059 (Ch); [2019] B.P.I.R. 1506.

PART 12

COURT PROCEDURE AND PRACTICE

CHAPTER 11

COURT ORDERS, FORMAL DEFECTS AND SHORTHAND WRITERS

Formal defects

12.64

GENERAL NOTE

Replace the note with:

This rule appears to have been based on BA 1914 s.147(1), but is made to apply to all forms of insolvency proceedings. For its relevance in the context of setting aside a statutory demand, see *Re a Debtor (No.1 of 1987)* [1988] 1 W.L.R. 419. In the later case of *Re a Debtor (No.190 of 1987), The Times,* May 21, 1988, Vinelott J held that IR 1986 r.7.55 (now IR 2016 r.12.64) did not apply to cure defects in the statutory demand. He thereby followed *Re Cartwright* [1975] 1 W.L.R. 573, which was decided under the old law. In *Re Awan* [2000] B.P.I.R. 241 Boggis J refused to allow IR 1986 r.7.55 to be invoked to justify failure to provide proof of service of petition as this was regarded as such a fundamental flaw. See also *Ardawa v Uppal* [2019] EWHC 456 (Ch). The courts have stated repeatedly that this provision cannot be used to validate the defective appointment of an administrator out of court where there has been a significant procedural defect—see Henderson J in *Re Frontsouth (Witham) Ltd* [2011] EWHC 1668 (Ch); [2011] B.C.C. 635; [2011] B.P.I.R. 1382. But the test today is to ask whether the flaw is so fundamental as to render the appointment a nullity. The law is evolving here (see Norris J in *Re Euromaster Ltd* [2012] EWHC 2356 (Ch); [2012] B.C.C. 754 and Zacaroli J in *Re Statebourne (Cryogenic) Ltd* [2020] EWHC 231 (Ch)) and there is therefore a question of degree engaged depending upon the procedural defect in each case under scrutiny. In *Re Anderson Owen Ltd* [2009] EWHC 2837 (Ch); [2010] B.P.I.R. 37 it was held by Norris J that IR 1986 r.7.55 (now IR 2016 r.12.64) could be invoked to cure any defective service of proceedings instituted under IA 1986 s.212. Unusually, in *Re Brickvest Ltd; Lumineau v Berlin Hyp AG* [2019] EWHC 3084 (Ch) the court used its own discretion to disregard a defect of non-compliance with the articles without a r.12.64 application, but suggested that similar situations would in future be better cured under r.12.64 through an application on notice to affected parties.

Rule 12.64 only applies in the context of "insolvency proceedings"—this phrase had in the past been somewhat narrowly defined by the courts so as to exclude the appointment of an administrator out of court pursuant to Sch.B1 para.22—*Re Blights Builders Ltd* [2006] EWHC 3549 (Ch); [2007] B.C.C. 712. This provision can only come into play if there are insolvency proceedings afoot—see *Pui-Kwan v Kam-Ho* [2015] EWHC 621 (Ch). Here the Chancellor refused to apply it to the appointment of an administrator where there was no decision ever taken by the directors to make such an appointment—see [75] per Sir Terence Etherton. IR 1986 r.7.55 (now IR 2016 r.12.64) was also held not to be applicable in exactly the same circumstances in *Re G-Tech Construction Ltd* [2007] B.P.I.R. 1275. However, later decisions have adopted a more expansive approach—see *Re Frontsouth (Witham) Ltd* [2011] EWHC 1668 (Ch); [2011] B.C.C. 635 and *Re Euromaster Ltd* [2012] EWHC 2356 (Ch); [2012] B.C.C. 754 at [37] per Norris J. This view that administration activated outside court is a form of insolvency proceeding reflects reality and is consistent with its treatment under the Recast EU Insolvency Regulation 2015/848. But on the specific point of determining the appropriate relief to excuse the defective appointment out of court of administrators the observations of Norris J in *Euromaster* (above) were not followed by Andrew Hochhauser QC (sitting in the High Court) in *Re Eiffel Steelworks Ltd* [2015] EWHC 511 (Ch); [2015] 2 B.C.L.C. 57. Although the irregularity was excused because no one was prejudiced, the court also flatly refused to make a retrospective order validating the appointment. The Northern Irish decision of Deeny J in *Cavanagh v Dolan* [2015] NICh 14 adds weight to the uncertainty as to the applicability of IR 1986 r.7.55 to defective out of court appointments of administrators.

In *Re a Debtor (No.340 of 1992)* [1996] 2 All E.R. 211 it was held that IR 1986 r.7.55 did not validate an improperly executed writ of fieri facias as in the circumstances of the case the irregularity was so serious as to mean that the writ could not be said to have been served at all. Here apart from knocking on a debtor's door the bailiff had left the premises without any serious attempt to gain access.

IR 1986 r.7.55 did, however, come into play in *Re a Debtor (No.22 of 1993)* [1994] 1 W.L.R. 46 (sometimes cited as *Focus Insurance v a Debtor*) where an omission by a creditor to state in his petition that there was an extant set-aside application by the debtor was waved through by Mummery J. See also *Re Continental Assurance Co of London plc (in liq.) (No.2)* [1998] 1 B.C.L.C. 583, where an application had been made in the wrong form but no prejudice had occurred. See also *Oben v Blackman* [2000] B.P.I.R. 302.

In *Foenander v Allan* [2006] B.P.I.R. 1392 the potential usage of this rule in addressing complaints about the constitution of the creditors' committee was noted.

Rule 12.64 could be used to correct a slip in a block transfer order that had incorrectly suggested that there was jurisdiction under IR 1986 r.6.132(5) (now IR 2016 r.10.80) to make an appointment of a trustee in bankruptcy— *Donaldson v O'Sullivan* [2008] EWHC 387 (Ch); [2008] B.P.I.R. 288 which was confirmed on other grounds—see [2008] EWCA Civ 879. But see now IR 2016 rr.12.35–12.39.

This provision was deployed to excuse a possible defect in the service of a bankruptcy petition in *Gate Gourmet Luxembourg IV SARL v Morby* [2015] EWHC 1203 (Ch); [2015] B.P.I.R. 787. On whether that was necessary on the facts of the case see the appeal before Edward Murray in [2016] EWHC 74 (Ch), where useful observations are made on when IR 2016 r.12.64 should come into play. In *Canning v Irwin Mitchell LLP* [2017] EWHC 718 (Ch); [2017] B.P.I.R. 934, however, improper service of a statutory demand was found not to be a defect that could be cured and the *Gate Gourmet* case (above) was distinguished. For a similar decision on service of a bankruptcy petition see *Ardawa v Uppal* [2019] EWHC 456 (Ch).

The potential application of this remedial rule to errors in a bankruptcy order relating to the application of what was EU Insolvency Regulation 2015/848 was also confirmed in *Loy v O'Sullivan* [2010] EWHC 3583 (Ch); [2011] B.P.I.R. 181. There was no evidence that such errors had caused prejudice to the debtor.

IR 1986 r.7.55 (now IR 2016 r.12.64) was used by Norris J to cure the procedural defect in the appointment of administrators in *Re Euromaster Ltd* [2012] EWHC 2356 (Ch); [2012] B.C.C. 754 (appointment made one day after notice of intention to appoint had expired). But compare *Re Eco Link Resources Ltd* [2012] B.C.C. 731 where the court refused to deploy this provision to cure the defect (failure to notify prior charge holder). See also *Re MTB Motors Ltd* [2010] EWHC 3751 (Ch); [2012] B.C.C. 601 (IR 1986 r.7.55 validation refused where appointment of administrator was defective).

In *Re Baillies Ltd* [2012] EWHC 285 (Ch); [2012] B.C.C. 554; [2012] B.P.I.R. 665 HHJ Purle QC discussed this provision in the context of a failure to comply with the requirements of the EC Service Regulation (1393/2007) and doubted whether IR 1986 r.7.55 could operate in this context to override the Regulation.

In *Re Care People Ltd* [2013] EWHC 1734 (Ch); [2013] B.C.C. 466 HHJ Purle QC used this provision to validate an irregular appointment of an administrator made under Sch.B1 para.14. The qualifying floating charge holder had not allowed the debtor company adequate time to meet the demand but it was crystal clear that the company could not have met the repayment even if such time had been granted. The interests of creditors generally dictated the validation of the appointment of the administrator. The potential utility of this provision was raised in *Kasumu v Arrow Global (Guernsey) Ltd* [2013] EWHC 789 (Ch); [2013] B.P.I.R. 1047 where there had been a failure to comply with the requirements of IR 1986 r.6.26 (now IR 2016 r.10.26). See also *Quinn v Cloughvalley Stores (NI) Ltd* [2018] NICh 4 (where a record of the directors' decision was not filed with the notice of intention to appoint, as required by the Northern Irish rule corresponding (now) to IR 2016 r.3.23). For later proceedings see [2019] NICA 5. This relieving jurisdiction was utilised by the court (HHJ Klein QC) in *Ross v Fashion Design Solutions; Re NJM Clothing Ltd* [2018] EWHC 2388 (Ch); [2018] B.C.C. 875 in a case where there was a dispute as to the validity of the appointment of the administrator in view of uncertainty as to the stated time of appointment. The whitewash procedure was also thought to be available on similar facts in *Re Towcester Racecourse Ltd* [2018] EWHC 2902 (Ch); [2019] B.C.C. 274 and *Re Spaces London Bridge Ltd* [2018] EWHC 3099 (Ch); [2019] B.C.C. 280—but in both instances it did not need to be applied because the appointment of the administrators was found to be valid.

A series of cases in 2019/2020 considered whether para.8.1 of *Practice Direction: Insolvency Proceedings* [2020] B.C.C. 698 (PD:IP) precludes electronic filing in court of notice of appointment of administrators out of usual court hours. Paragraph 2.1 of *Practice Direction 51O: Electronic Working Pilot Scheme* allows the filing of documents "in court online 24 hours a day every day all year round, including during out of normal Court office opening hours and on weekends and bank holidays", and PD:IP para.8.1 states that the latter para.2.1 of PD 51O shall not apply to "*any* filing of a notice of appointment of an administrator" outside court hours and that IR 2016 rr.3.20–3.22 shall apply, but this confuses matters as rr.3.20–3.22 only apply in the case of appointment by a qualifying floating charge holder and not by the company or its directors. In the first of the cases, *Wright v HMV Ecommerce Ltd* [2019] EWHC 903 (Ch); [2019] B.C.C. 887, concerning e-filing of appointment of administrators by directors out of court hours, Barling J found it uncertain whether para.8.1 of PD:IP precluded such an appointment, but regarded it as a defect that the court cured under r.12.64. *Re Skeggs Beef Ltd* [2019] EWHC 2607 (Ch); [2020] B.C.C. 43 concerned filing of notice out of hours of an appointment by a qualifying floating charge holder and was held to be invalid (but distinguishing *HMV*

Ecommerce (above)) and the court again considered that this amounted to a purely formal defect which did not cause any substantial injustice to anyone and could be declared valid under r.12.64. The court in *Re Keyworker Homes (North West) Ltd; Woodside v Keyworker Homes (North West) Ltd* [2019] EWHC 3499 (Ch); [2020] B.C.C. 223 agreed with the curing of the defect under r.12.64 as above. Those cases must be contrasted with *Re SJ Henderson & Co Ltd* [2019] EWHC 2742 (Ch); [2020] B.C.C. 52 in which e-filing of out-of-hours appointment of administrators by directors was held by ICC Judge Burton to be invalid at the time of purported appointment, and that until such time as the legislature created an express power for appointments to be made out of hours they simply could not be made at all, whether in a curably defective manner (under r.12.64) or otherwise (but the court allowed the appointment to take effect when the court counter next formally opened for business: in London at 10am but that may be different in the various District Registries). In *Causer v All Star Leisure (Group) Ltd* [2019] EWHC 3231 (Ch); [2020] B.C.C. 100 the defect in out of hours e-filing by directors of notice of appointment was validated by the court (as being at the purported time of appointment, out of court hours), noting that no injustice was caused, where again the court referred to the differing opening hours of different courts. Zacaroli J in *Re Statebourne (Cryogenic) Ltd* [2020] EWHC 231 (Ch) adopted a similar approach in the case of an appointment of administrators made in this instance not out of usual court hours but on the day after expiry of the 10-day period allowed by Sch.B1 para.28(2), holding that the defect was an irregularity for the purposes of r.12.64 and could be validated as it had not caused substantial injustice. The majority of these cases (except *SJ Henderson*) thus did allow validation under r.12.64 but in any event the IR 2016 are to be amended at some stage (see *Practice Note* [2020] B.C.C. 211) in an attempt to avoid the confusion of the above differing approaches. In the first case after that *Practice Note*, Zacaroli J in *Re Symm & Co Ltd* [2020] EWHC 317 (Ch); [2020] B.C.C. 425 concluded that an appointment by a company or its directors by way of electronic filing outside court hours is not permissible but that r.12.64 enables the court to declare the appointment effective as from the time when the court office next opens, provided that the irregularity has caused no substantial injustice. The problems of e-filing notices in relation to the appointment of administrators out of court hours have been alleviated a series of Temporary Practice Directions (from 6 April 2020) the latest one being *Temporary Insolvency Practice Direction (No.5) Supporting the Insolvency Practice Direction* [2021] B.C.C. 877, paras 5, 6 (in force from 1 October 2021 until amended or revoked and reproduced as App.VII to this *Guide*).

For a lucid account of the rationale behind this provision and comparison with IR 1986 r.7.55 see Baister [2018] 31 Insolv. Int. 3. Also see *Re A.R.G. (Mansfield) Ltd; Gregory v A.R.G. (Mansfield) Ltd* [2020] EWHC 1133 (Ch); [2020] B.C.C. 641 for an exhaustive analysis of many of the above cases on curable defects compared with defects resulting in a nullity of appointment (which analysed the cases as resulting in the breach of procedure as either (i) fundamental; (ii) not fundamental but causing no injustice; or (iii) not fundamental but causing substantial injustice), and a comparison of r.12.64 with IA 1986 Sch.B1 para.104. For a further summary of High Court cases see the appendix to the judgment in *Re Tokenhouse VB Ltd (formerly VAT Bridge 7 Ltd); Strategic Advantage SPC v Rutter* [2020] EWHC 3171 (Ch); [2021] B.C.C. 107. See also *Re Zoom UK Distribution Ltd* [2021] EWHC 800 (Ch); [2021] B.C.C. 735 (applied in *Re Patisserie Holdings Plc; Costley-Wood v Rowley* [2021] EWHC 3205 (Ch); [2022] B.C.C. 401). Several of the above cases were followed in *Re Caversham Finance Ltd* [2022] EWHC 789 (Ch) where failure to provide full reasons in the notice to creditors for an extension to an administration as required by r.3.54(2) was a procedural defect only, the creditors were not prejudiced, and the defect was cured under r.12.64 (but failure to obtain the creditors' consent to the extension would have been a nullity). In *Re E Realisations 2020 Ltd* [2022] EWHC 1575 (Ch) the question of failure to provide reasons was considered in the light of a consent that was obtained on a contingency basis nine months before the notice of extension was filed. However, the court found that the situation was analogous to the *Caversham* case and it was still a procedural irregularity and not a matter of fundamental validity and there was no substantial injustice created by the validation of the extension under r.12.64.

The Court of Appeal reiterated in *Islandsbanki HF v Stanford* [2020] EWCA Civ 480 that this whitewash provision cannot be exploited to whitewash fundamental procedural errors. For further judicial comment on r.12.64 see *Moorgate Industries UK Ltd v Mittal* [2020] EWHC 1550 (Ch) and *Kirker v Holyoak Investments Inc; Re SMU Investments Ltd* [2020] EWHC 875 (Ch). Rule 12.64 was utilised again in *Re NMUL Realisations Ltd* [2021] EWHC 94 (Ch) where Deputy ICC Judge Frith found that failure to give notice under Sch.B1 para.15 did not invalidate the appointment of an administrator as this was not deemed to be a fundamental irregularity.

An attempt to use IR 2016 r.12.64 to cure what was an ordinary debt application and which could not therefore be viewed as an "insolvency application" within the meaning of IR 2016 r.1.35 was rejected by HH Judge Cawson QC in *Re Taunton Logs Ltd* [2020] EWHC 3480 (Ch); [2021] B.P.I.R. 427. But the matter was saved by the court allowing the "Insolvency Act application" to be cured under CPR r.3.10. See also *Manolete Partners plc v Barrett Holdings* [2021] EWHC 1481 (Ch); [2022] B.C.C. 159 for further discussion of similar procedural issues where Chief ICC Judge Briggs took an equally narrow view of insolvency proceedings in the context of what have become known as hybrid claims (in this case pursued by an assignee). These two decisions, although undoubtedly correct, pose difficulties for practitioners and a reconsideration of the meaning of insolvency applications in IR 2016 might be required. On the other hand, note *Gostelow v Hussain* [2021] EWHC 3276 (Ch) where an application by trustee for sale under IA 1986 s.335A was found to be an insolvency application.

PART 15

DECISION MAKING

CHAPTER 3

NOTICES, VOTING AND VENUES FOR DECISIONS

Notices to creditors of decision procedure

15.8—

GENERAL NOTE

Replace the note with:

This delineates in great detail various notice requirements for the full range of insolvency procedures. This rule is drawn from numerous predecessors in IR 1986. Note the special provision made in r.15.8(3)(f), (g) (moratoriums subsequently excepted) for opted-out creditors and creditors with small debts (instances not covered under the former regime). A "blank proxy" (see r.16.3) must accompany the notice where the decision procedure is a meeting (r.15.8(5)). Giving of notices is not required where the court allows notice of decision procedures by advertisement under r.15.12 (r.15.8(6)).

It seems that if strict adherence to the statutory requirement of the contents of a notice is unnecessary in the circumstances, e.g. as the information is redundant or simply not applicable, then the notice will not be regarded as defective (see *Re Caversham Finance Ltd* [2022] EWHC 789 (Ch) where there were no creditors under r.15.8(3)(f), (g) so that per Michael Green J at [25] "Parliament cannot have intended that redundant information should be included on the notice").

Rule 15.8(3)(f), (g) amended by the Insolvency (England and Wales) (No. 2) (Amendment) Rules 2021 (SI 2021/1028) r.66 as from 1 October 2021, subject to saving provisions in rr.4, 5.

CHAPTER 8

CREDITORS' VOTING RIGHTS AND MAJORITIES

Procedure for admitting creditors' claims for voting

15.33—

GENERAL NOTE

Replace the note with:

This offers guidance to conveners/chairs. There of course is a right to appeal against any decision by the convener/chair—see IR 2016 r.15.35. In relation to an earlier version of this rule, Harman J in *Re a Debtor (No.222 of 1990), Ex p. Bank of Ireland* [1992] B.C.L.C. 137 established a practical test: "The scheme is quite clear … the chairman must look at the claim; if it is plain or obvious that it is good he admits it, if it is plain or obvious that it is bad he rejects it, if there is a question, a doubt, he shall admit it but mark it as objected". This was followed by the Northern Ireland High Court in the IVA case of *Ulster Bank Ltd v Taggart* [2018] NIMaster 7, which concluded that a creditor was not to be deprived of his right to vote unless it was "plain or obvious" that it was bad (and as the disputed debt was not plainly or obviously good but could not be said to be plainly or obviously bad, the only decision the chair could make was to admit the proof to vote marked as objected to). ICC Judge Mullen made it clear in *Karapetian v Duffy* [2022] EWHC 1053 (Ch) that it is for the creditor to put the claim forward, together with such evidence as may be appropriate. Note also *Re Rochay Productions Ltd* [2020] EWHC 1737 (Ch).

Appeals against decisions under this Chapter

15.35—

GENERAL NOTE

Replace the note with:

This right to appeal applies to matters covered by IR 2016 rr.15.28–15.35 above. Similar provisions existed under IR 1986. Note the longer leeway for appeals in the case of proposed voluntary arrangements.

A judge hearing an appeal under r.15.35(1) should form his or her own view, based on the evidence and arguments advanced in court, and not merely review the decision of the convenor or chair of the decision procedure: *Revenue and Customs Commissioners v Maxwell* [2010] EWCA Civ 1379; [2012] B.C.C. 30. In this administration case under IR 1986, the Court of Appeal stated that the characterisation and quantification of a debt under what is now r.15.31 should be effected at the date when the company went into administration rather than the date of the meeting (now decision procedure: see r.15.31(1)), but the chair's powers of quantification under what are now rr.15.31(2) and 15.35 should be exercised taking into account events which had occurred since the date of the administration. The test to be applied by the court is whether the indebtedness is owed on a balance of probabilities: *Re McNally* [2013] EWHC 1685 (Ch); *Karapetian v Duffy* [2022] EWHC 1053 (Ch).

Note the case of *Ulster Bank Ltd v Taggart* [2018] NIMaster 7 where the court comments upon a number of issues relating to appeals (based upon alleged material irregularity) against decisions of nominees on voting rights. In particular, the court observed that a creditor with a statute-barred debt was not automatically disqualified from voting. Also in relation to voting rights and an unsuccessful challenges to a CVA, see *Re Dealmaster Ltd* [2021] EWHC 2892 (Ch); [2022] B.C.C. 252 for an overlap between r.15.35 and IA 1986 s.6, which should not be used in a fishing expedition for information. For a successful appeal based on material irregularity against a chairman's decision to accept certain votes in favour of an IVA proposal see *Elser v Sands* [2022] EWHC 32 (Ch) where the decision of the meeting was thereby reversed under r.15.35(3).

For a case that arose in the context of r.15.35 see *Barton v Gwyn-Jones* [2019] EWCA Civ 1999.

The chair or convener of a creditors' meeting will only be personally liable for the costs of an appeal under r.15.35 against that person's decision to admit or reject a proof of debt in special circumstances, such as where the decision was self-interested, irrational or unreasonable, or there was otherwise good reason to impose personal liability (*Re Rochay Productions Ltd (in liq.)* [2020] EWHC 1737 (Ch)). Where the appeal is unsuccessful and a party was joined who was, nonetheless, not involved in any matter in dispute, the costs of the convenor or chairperson should not be awarded against such a party: *Re McCarthy* [2022] EWHC 1419 (Ch).

The court refused to extend the 21-day period for an appeal in *Edwards v Tailby* [2021] EWHC 2819 (Ch); [2022] B.C.C. 10 and rejected an argument that an appeal against an administrator's valuation of a proof for voting purposes could be made under r.14.8: a decision of administrators valuing a creditor's debt for voting purposes could only be challenged under r.15.35.

To allow for appeals against moratorium decisions, r.15.35(3) amended and (3A), (3B) inserted by the Insolvency (England and Wales) (No. 2) (Amendment) Rules 2021 (SI 2021/1028) r.78, and r.15.35(5)(a) amended by SI 2021/1028 r.81, Sch.2 paras 1–3, as from 1 October 2021, subject to saving provisions in rr.4, 5.

Corporate Insolvency and Governance Act 2020

General features of the Act

Replace the note with:

CIGA 2020 is a complex piece of legislation for a variety of reasons.

First of all, it contains a mixture of temporary and more permanent measures. There are also modifying and transitional provisions. The temporary measures often have "sunset" dates, but the legislation enables the Government to extend these, and this has been taken full advantage of with at least four extensions to some of the temporary provisions, so that they were well over a year old by the end of the latest extension. The legislation is also a composite of free-standing sections, provisions that amend the Insolvency Act 1986 (IA 1986) (and other legislation) and insertions into the Companies Act 2006 (CA 2006).

Secondly, there are specific provisions introduced for Northern Ireland. These often mirror the provisions designed for England and Wales, but with appropriate adaptation, and we do not discuss them further in this *Guide*.

Thirdly, as the short title of the Act suggests, this legislation is not solely concerned with corporate insolvency *stricto sensu*. There are a few provisions applicable to companies in general by offering concessions on the holding of annual general meetings (AGMs) and with regard to filing obligations. For example, CIGA 2020 ss.39 and 40(e) led to the temporary extension of the permitted time for registering particulars of company charges—see the Companies etc. (Filing Requirements) (Temporary Modifications) Regulations 2020 (SI 2020/645) reg.18. These concessions are time limited. Most importantly of all for our readers, is the introduction of a new CA 2006 Pt 26A, which offers a new restructuring tool with a cross-class cram down capability binding dissenting creditors.

Fourthly, the provisions are not all of general application throughout the corporate population. The moratorium provisions apply only to "eligible" companies only (as defined by new IA 1986 Sch.ZA1, as amended). There are carve outs for firms operating in the financial services sector. See s.A49 for special rules applicable to "regulated companies". Overseas companies also attract special treatment in some instances. Relief from some of the restrictive provisions on discontinuing supplies is only applied to small firms (see CIGA 2020 s.15 for instance).

Fifthly, this legislation is not all about adding to the existing legislative structure. It *repeals* the company voluntary arrangement (CVA) cum moratorium regime contained in IA 1986 s.1A and Sch.A1. This regime, which was introduced via the Insolvency Act 2000 but not brought into force until April 2003, has been an almost complete failure in that it was little used in practice. Few will lament its passing. But, in fairness, the new moratorium does draw upon it for inspiration in terms of a number of its provisions. Having said that, there has been little publicised take-up of the new moratorium to date (and certainly no concluded litigation on it).

Finally, the Bill, which was pushed through using curtailed Parliamentary procedures, contained some extraordinarily wide legislative powers enabling amendment, etc., by ministers, including some permitted exceptions from the affirmative resolution requirement. Henry VIII would have been familiar with this law-making technique. However the democratic institutions of this country do remain strong. The House of Lords Delegated Powers and Regulatory Reform Committee's *14th Report of Session 2019–21* (HL Paper 74) published on 10 June 2020 severely criticised the Bill as although "an extraordinary Bill for extraordinary times" the report went on that "we have found many aspects of the Bill deeply troubling". This was so particularly in relation to the Henry VIII powers.

The House of Lords Select Committee on the Constitution, *7th Report of Session 2019–21* (HL Paper 76) on 12 June 2020 was also critical of several aspects of the Bill:

- while temporary measures to respond to the pandemic may meet the threshold of urgency and exceptional circumstances to warrant fast-tracking, it was "inappropriate" for the permanent changes proposed in the Bill to be fast-tracked;

- the Bill included provisions which apply retrospectively: such provisions are generally regarded as inconsistent with the rule of law and are "inherently constitutionally suspect"; and

- the cl.18 Henry VIII power in the Bill to modify all "corporate insolvency or governance legislation" using the affirmative resolution procedure should be constrained so to be used only when urgency was justified and then the power should expire and not be renewed repeatedly.

The Government's response (reproduced as an Appendix to the House of Lords Delegated Powers and Regulatory Reform Committee, *15th Report of Session 2019–21* (HL Paper 82) published on 22 June 2020) agreed to amend the Bill particularly to remove some of the Henry VIII powers. Accordingly, after such criticism the affirmative resolution procedure was restored (see for instance CIGA 2020 ss.26(7) and 43(1)). There are also other restrictions in ss.21–24 (e.g. by imposing time constraints) on the general power in s.20 to amend the law by secondary legislation, although an extension has been felt necessitated to extend this expiration date in s.24(1) from 30 April 2021 to 29 April 2022 by the Corporate Insolvency and Governance Act 2020 (Coronavirus) (Change of Expiry Date) Regulations 2021 (SI 2021/441) reg.2. Such is the complexity of it all that the Government appears to have been caught out by its own drafting of subordinate legislation powers as the temporary suspension of wrongful trading liability in CIGA 2020 s.12 expired on 30 September 2020 and, it seems, could not be revived by a mere amendment of that expiration date: instead a new instrument (Corporate Insolvency and Governance Act 2020 (Coronavirus) (Suspension of Liability for Wrongful Trading and Extension of the Relevant Period) Regulations 2020 (SI 2020/1349)) from 26 November 2020 repeating the whole suspension to a later date was necessary (and has itself subsequently been time extended), thereby leaving a gap between 1 October and 25 November 2020 in which, presumably in theory, liability could arise!

That said, the legislative provisions very much reflect the crisis presenting itself to the Government and country. The powers to make extensive use of delegated legislation mirror those found in the Coronavirus Act 2020 and one wonders whether CIGA 2020 would have been necessary had the Coronavirus Act 2020 anticipated the need for these changes in corporate insolvency law and had empowered ministers accordingly.

The process of using delegated legislation to fine-tune the Act began quickly and there has been a host of statutory instruments amending or modifying its provisions to date, which we hope to have covered in the text below and where relevant throughout the *Guide*.

The Act itself has seen amendments particularly to the temporary measures in Sch.4 occasioned by the Corporate Insolvency and Governance Act 2020 (Coronavirus) (Early Termination of Certain Temporary Provisions) Regulations 2020 (SI 2020/1033) as from 1 October 2020 and also by the effect of Sch.4 itself as paras 12 and 52 caused the temporary rules on moratoria in England and Wales and respectively in Scotland to "cease to have effect" at the end of the relevant period expressed in para.1(b) as 30 September 2021, after which the Insolvency (England and Wales) (No. 2) (Amendment) Rules 2021 (SI 2021/1028) amended IR 2016 to provide permanent procedural rules for the moratorium. Schedule 10 was substituted on 1 October 2021 by the Corporate Insolvency and Governance Act 2020 (Coronavirus) (Amendment of Schedule 10) (No. 2) Regulations 2021 (SI 2021/1091) as from 1 October 2021 to operate until the "relevant period" ended on 31 March 2022.

The Government committed to a review of the operation of three permanent measures introduced by CIGA 2020 into other legislation (restructuring plans under CA 2006 Pt 26A, the stand-alone moratorium under IA 1986 Pt A1 and the restriction on contractual ipso facto termination clauses under IA 1986 s.233B) within three years of their Act's commencement and as part of that review in September 2021 the University of Wolverhampton was commissioned to conduct independent research. The first stage of this review consisted of an Interim Report created by considering the data arising from a series of semi-structured interviews of various stakeholders. According to the Interim Report the permanent CIGA 2020 measures have been broadly welcomed by stakeholders and are seen as satisfying their policy objectives as follows in assisting the rescue of companies as going concerns and thus contributing to job retention in the companies concerned as follows:

- Restructure plans (RPs) are seen as a success building as they do on existing case law governing schemes of arrangements under CA 2006 Pt 26. The RP cross-class cram-down power has been used successfully in cases where previously a scheme on its own would not have been effective. The high quality of UK judges adjudicating on RPs is seen as a real strength. RPs are however seen as too costly and time-consuming for use in the small and medium-sized entity (SME) market.

- The moratorium has been used successfully and has satisfied its policy objectives, but there are significant concerns that it alters pre-existing priorities in any subsequent insolvency. The alteration of creditor priorities may have unintended consequences and there is uncertainty about how this alteration of priorities operates in relation to a number of specific types of creditor (e.g. those engaged in international trade) so that there is evidence that the measure is not being used in some cases because of it.

- The restrictions on ipso facto clauses are seen as a positive addition to the powers available to insolvency practitioners and companies who have entered a formal insolvency procedure and to satisfy the policy objectives but it remains too early to assess fully how the measure will operate in the longer term.

Copies of *Corporate Insolvency and Governance Act 2020 – Interim report March 2022* are available at *https://www.gov.uk/government/publications/corporate-insolvency-and-governance-act-2020-interim-report-march-2022/corporate-insolvency-and-governance-act-2020-interim-report-march-2022.*

Moratoriums in Northern Ireland

4–6

GENERAL NOTE

Add new note:

The moratorium system for Northern Ireland is equivalent to that in Great Britain but went into abeyance after 30 March 2022 as the permanent rules intended to replace the temporary procedural rules in CIGA 2020 Sch.8 (which had been extended to 30 March 2022) were not approved before the Northern Ireland Executive was suspended in February 2022 (and the temporary rules could not be further extended for the same reason of lack of approval). The moratorium procedure therefore is not available to companies in Northern Ireland from 31 March 2022 until a new Executive is established after the Northern Ireland Assembly elections in May 2022 and a new Executive is established to approve the permanent rules.

Volume 2

Company Directors Disqualification Act 1986

Introductory note to the Act
Replace the note with:

This Act brings together in consolidated form the whole of the law relating to the disqualification of company directors (and, in some circumstances, other persons), either by order of the court or by an undertaking accepted in lieu of a court order.

The title of the Act is somewhat misleading, in that it may be read as applying only to company directors. While it is true that some of its provisions (e.g. ss.6–8 and 9A) are restricted to persons who are or have been directors, most of the rest of the Act is not so limited; and its scope has been extended by supplementary legislation so as to include other categories of persons such as the members of insolvent partnerships.

Historically the Act has only applied to directors of insolvent (as defined) companies (and other bodies), but this was changed from 15 February 2022 by the Rating (Coronavirus) and Directors Disqualification (Dissolved Companies) Act 2021 which, to close a loophole, by amendment to the CDDA 1986 extends disqualification for unfitness to directors of companies which are dissolved without becoming insolvent. As from 15 February 2022 the relevant amending provisions of the 2021 Act have retrospective effect to apply to companies dissolved at any time before, as well as after, the passing of that Act. The measure applies to England and Wales and to Scotland and there is also amendment to the Northern Ireland equivalent legislation. Explanatory Notes to the Rating (Coronavirus) and Directors Disqualification (Dissolved Companies) Act 2021 were published on 17 January 2022 and are available at *https://www.legislation.gov.uk/ukpga/2021/34/pdfs/ukpgaen_20210034_en.pdf*. On 29 July 2022 the Insolvency Service announced the first disqualifications (all by disqualification undertakings, rather than disqualification orders: for the difference, see below) under the amending provisions in the 2021 Act to CDDA 1986 of four directors of different companies who had secured business "bounce-back" loans available during the Covid pandemic before dissolving their companies to avoid paying their liabilities back. The four disqualification undertakings ranged from seven to 12 years and the Insolvency Service is considering recovery of the bounce back loan funds by seeking compensation orders under CDDA 1986 ss.15A and 15B (see below) against the directors concerned.

There has been a power to make disqualification orders in the Companies Acts since 1947, and this power was extended in later Companies Acts, notably in CA 1976 and CA 1981; but little use was made of the sanction prior to 1985, mainly because the necessary resources were not committed to investigation and enforcement. With the enactment of the insolvency reforms of 1985, there was manifested a new resolve on the part of Government to make much greater use of the power to disqualify directors. Difficulties which had been experienced in the operation of the earlier law (e.g. as regards the heavy burden of proof required in some circumstances) were overcome by amending legislation and new grounds for disqualification introduced. These reforms were brought into force on 28 April 1986, several months ahead of the general implementation of IA 1985. The Department of Trade and Industry (now the Department for Business, Energy and Industrial Strategy) was authorised, in the name of the Secretary of State, to investigate cases of suspected breaches of the law and to institute proceedings for disqualification orders; and liquidators, administrators, receivers and other insolvency practitioners were required by law to make reports to the Department on the conduct of the directors in every case of corporate insolvency. A more recent innovation is the Disqualification Stakeholder Group, established by the Insolvency Service in 2012 as a forum for the Service, recognised professional bodies and insolvency practitioners' representatives to discuss issues relating to the duty of office-holders to report suspected cases of unfitness.

Under the legislation as originally enacted, a person could be disqualified only by order of the court, but the Insolvency Act 2000 introduced the alternative of a disqualification *undertaking*, which applies only to cases under CDDA 1986 ss.6–8, i.e. cases where the basis of the charge is that the director has shown by his conduct that he is unfit to be concerned in the management of a company. A person who is prepared to accept liability may give an undertaking to the Secretary of State that he will not be a director or otherwise concerned in the management of a company for an agreed period, with the same consequences as would follow if a court order had been made in the same terms. Since the change came into force, undertakings have displaced disqualification orders in the great majority (about 85 per cent) of cases.

The Act applies to "companies", an expression which (by s.22(2)) "includes any company which may be wound up under the Insolvency Act 1986". This means that it applies to "unregistered companies": see the note to IA 1986 s.220. As originally drafted, it did not apply to building societies or incorporated friendly societies, but it has since been extended so as to apply to the directors (or the members of the committee of management) and officers of both: see ss.22A and 22B, below. In 2004, the Act was extended to include the directors and officers (but not "shadow directors"—see below) of NHS Foundation Trusts: see s.22C. It applied also to EEIGs until Brexit and subsequently to UK EEIGs and EEIG establishments: see the European Economic Interest Grouping Regulations 1989 (SI 1989/638) reg.20 (as amended by the European Economic Interest Grouping (Amendment) (EU Exit) Regulations 2018 (SI 2018/1299) reg.18(a) as from IP completion day on 31 December at 11pm). The Co-operative and Community Benefit Societies and Credit Unions Act 2010, when it was brought into force on 6 April 2014, extended the Act to registered co-operative and community benefit societies and credit unions by the insertion of s.22E. Section 22F, inserted by the Charitable Incorporated Organisations (Consequential Amendments) Order 2012 (SI 2012/3014) art.2, effective 2 January 2013, extends the Act to include the trustees of a charitable incorporated organisation. Extension to protected-cell companies was introduced by the Risk Transformation Regulations 2017 (SI 2017/1212) reg.190, Sch.4 para.3 as from 8 December 2017 by insertion of s.22H (which contains modifications in s.22H(4)). Its application to other bodies remains uncertain: see the note to s.22(2).

Disqualification applies to directors of charitable companies but the courts are mindful of the special role of such companies and especially in the case of their non-executive directors, so in *Re Keeping Kids Co; Official Receiver v Batmanghelidjh* [2021] EWHC 175 (Ch) allegations of running an unsustainable business model in conducting a charity's operations were dismissed.

Where an insolvent partnership is wound up as an unregistered company under Pt V of IA 1986 (see the note to IA 1986 s.420), any member or former member of the partnership or any other person who has or has had control or management of the partnership business is treated in the same way as the director of a company, and ss.1, 1A, 6 to 10, 13 to 15, 17, 19(c) and 20 and Sch.1 of CDDA 1986 apply: see the Insolvent Partnerships Order 1994 (SI 1994/2421) art.16 (as amended).

The provisions of CDDA 1986 are made to apply to limited liability partnerships by the Limited Liability Partnerships Regulations 2001 (SI 2001/1090 reg.4(2)), subject to certain modifications set out in Sch.2 Pt II of the Regulations. More particularly, references in the Act to a director or officer of a company are to be taken as including references to a member or officer of an LLP, and there is a new concept of "shadow member" corresponding to "shadow director". The disqualification regime is also available to be used against any member of an LLP and is not to just designated members or managing members: *Re Bell Pottinger LLP; Secretary of State for Business, Energy and Industrial Strategy v Geoghegan* [2021] EWHC 672 (Ch); [2021] B.C.C. 675.

For the purposes of the Act, "director" includes any person occupying the position of director, by whatever name called (s.22(3)), so that it is immaterial that, in the company in question, the members of the board may be called (e.g.) "trustees" or "governors". For the purposes of ss.6–9E, the term "director" includes a "shadow director", as defined in s.22(5). A de facto director has also been held to be within s.6: see the note to s.6(1) and, on the meaning of this term, the note to s.22(5).

All sections of CDDA 1986 apply to England and Wales and to Scotland, but not (except s.11) to Northern Ireland. However, equivalent legislation has been in force in that jurisdiction since 1986. Initially, this was brought about by the Companies (Northern Ireland) Order 1986 (SI 1986/1032 (NI 6)); but this has now been replaced by the Companies (Northern Ireland) Order 2002 (SI 2002/3150 (NI 4)). (See further the note to s.24(2).)

Generally speaking, the courts of England and Wales have no jurisdiction in matters of insolvency over companies registered in Scotland, and vice versa. Most sections of the CDDA 1986 also make it plain that this separation between the two jurisdictions applies also in relation to the present Act (frequently by reference to the "court having jurisdiction to wind up the company" in question). One notable exception is s.8 (below), where the language is ambiguous and arguably would allow the Secretary of State to choose to start proceedings concerning a Scottish company in either jurisdiction; but in *Re Helene plc* [2000] 2 B.C.L.C. 249 Blackburne J held that the distinction should be observed and it was competent only to make application to the court in Scotland. However, a disqualification order made (or an undertaking given) in either England and Wales or Scotland is operative in all parts of Britain (and, indeed, has unrestricted extraterritorial effect). And an amendment introduced by IA 2000 gives force throughout these jurisdictions to a Northern Ireland disqualification order or undertaking: see the note to s.12A, below.

In a number of cases relating to director disqualification an issue has arisen based on an allegation that there has been a violation of the European Convention for the Protection of Human Rights and Fundamental Freedoms (now largely embodied in UK domestic law following the enactment of the Human Rights Act 1998), and opinions have been expressed both by the courts in England and by the European Commission on Human Rights on the applicability of the Convention to disqualification proceedings.

In *EDC v United Kingdom (Application No.24433/94)* [1998] B.C.C. 370 the director concerned had been a respondent to an application for disqualification which had begun in August 1991 and was not finally disposed of until January 1996—nearly four and a half years from the start of the proceedings and seven years after the events had occurred on which the case was based. He alleged that there had been a violation of art.6(1) of the Convention, which states that "In the determination of his civil rights and obligations or of any criminal charge against him, everyone is entitled to a fair and public hearing within a reasonable time ...". The Commission upheld his complaint, holding that the delay was in breach of the Convention (and accepting the view, incidentally, that the proceedings constituted a dispute over "civil rights and obligations").

In the later case of *DC, HS and AD v United Kingdom (Application No.39031/97)* [2000] B.C.C. 710 the European Court of Human Rights rejected an argument that disqualification proceedings constituted "criminal charges" within art.6(1): "the disqualification of directors is a matter which is regulatory rather than criminal". The applicants' main complaint was that it was unfair to base the disqualification proceedings on statements which had been obtained compulsorily under IA 1986 s.235, citing *Saunders v United Kingdom (Case 43/1994/490/572)* [1997] E.H.R.R. 313; [1997] B.C.C. 872. But this contention was rejected, one ground being that, unlike *Saunders*, this was not a criminal case. The court also ruled that the exclusion of evidence of the directors' good character was not incompatible with a fair hearing.

This ruling has been confirmed by the courts in this country. In *R. v Secretary of State for Trade and Industry Ex p. McCormick* [1998] B.C.C. 379, the Court of Appeal held that it was not unreasonable for the Secretary of State to continue to make use of compelled evidence in disqualification proceedings even though, in the light of the *Saunders* ruling, she had adopted a policy of not using compelled evidence in criminal cases. Again, in *Re Westminster Property Management Ltd, Official Receiver v Stern* [2000] 1 W.L.R. 2230; [2001] B.C.C. 121 the Court of Appeal, affirming Scott VC ruled that there had been no violation of the Convention on this ground, nor on the ground that an order would interfere with the freedom of establishment and freedom to provide services (arts 43, 49 of the Convention).

In *WGS and MSLS v United Kingdom (Application No.38172/97)* [2000] B.C.C. 719 the European Court of Human Rights held that director disqualification proceedings do not infringe art.8 of the Convention (respect for private life): in so far as the applicants' complaint was about press reporting of their case it was open to them to invoke the law of defamation. It was also ruled that no appeal could be made to the European Court until after the matter had been determined at a trial in the United Kingdom court and an order made.

It is normal practice for the Secretary of State to require that there should be attached to a disqualification undertaking a statement of the grounds on which the finding of unfitness against the director had been made: see the note to s.7. In *Re Blackspur Group plc (No.3), Secretary of State for Trade and Industry v Davies (No.2)* [2002] 2 B.C.L.C. 263 the court rejected a contention by the director that to impose such a requirement was a breach of his human rights. In another case concerning a different director of the same company, *Re Blackspur Group plc (No.3), Secretary of State for Trade and Industry v Eastaway* [2003] B.C.C. 520 a delay of over eight years was held not to have prevented the director from having a fair and public hearing of his case: the greater part of this delay was due to various unsuccessful actions taken by the applicant himself, trying to prevent the case from coming to trial. However, this issue was taken to the European Court of Human Rights (*Davies v UK* [2005] B.C.C. 401), where it was held that the Government was responsible for the greater part of the delay and was in breach of the Convention. On the strength of this ruling, the director applied to the domestic court to have the disqualification proceedings against him dismissed and his disqualification retrospectively set aside, but he was unsuccessful, both at first instance and on appeal: *Re Blackspur Group plc (No.4)* [2006] EWHC 299 (Ch); [2006] 2 B.C.L.C. 489; *Eastaway v Secretary of State for Trade and Industry* [2007] EWCA Civ 425; [2007] B.C.C. 550. See also, on the ECHR costs, *Eastaway v UK* [2006] 2 B.C.L.C. 361.

Although the Secretary of State may be compelled under IA 1986 to make disclosure of materials, this obligation is restricted to materials in his possession and does not extend to materials that could be in his possession: requirements of fairness under the Convention do not require him to interview or obtain documents from third parties (*Re Stakefield (Midlands) Ltd* [2010] EWHC 2518 (Ch)). Similarly, in *Secretary of State for Business, Innovation and Skills v Doffman* [2010] EWHC 2518 (Ch); [2011] 1 B.C.L.C. 597 it was held that neither the Convention nor his general duty to act fairly would normally extend to requiring the Secretary of State to obtain evidence or undertake investigations requested by the respondent.

Independently of the Human Rights legislation, a plea has been raised on occasion that it would be an infringement of the principle of "double jeopardy" to pursue disqualification proceedings against a defendant when he has been, or is concurrently being, faced with disciplinary proceedings by a professional body (e.g. the Financial Conduct Authority) in respect of the same charges. In *Re Barings plc (No.4)* [1999] B.C.C. 639; and *Re Migration Services International Ltd* [2000] B.C.C. 1,095 such an objection was not upheld, the court ruling that the issues in the two proceedings were materially different. An objection on the ground of "double jeopardy" was also not upheld in *Re Cedarwood Productions Ltd* [2001] EWCA Civ 1083; [2004] B.C.C. 65, where a disqualification order under CDDA

1986 s.2 had been made against the defendants as part of a criminal sentence and the Secretary of State wished to pursue civil proceedings for an order under s.6 which relied partly on the same facts. Although there was some overlap, the court in the latter proceedings would be looking at a wider picture. However, in the later case of *Secretary of State for Business, Innovation and Skills v Weston* [2014] EWHC 2933 (Ch), *Cedarwood* was distinguished and an application by the Secretary of State made after the criminal court had declined to make an order was refused: the facts in the two hearings would be identical and it would be unfair to expose the director to a second hearing on the same grounds. (See also *Re Denis Hilton Ltd* [2002] 1 B.C.L.C. 302.)

The present Act has its own definition section (s.22), but there is some cross-referencing between it and IA 1986, and also to the Companies Acts; and s.22(9) provides that any expression not specifically defined in this Act is to be interpreted by reference to the Companies Acts. The terms used in all of these Acts may therefore for the most part be taken to have the same meanings.

The Enterprise Act 2002 s.204, inserting new ss.9A–9E into CDDA 1986, introduced the regime of competition disqualification orders (CDOs) and competition disqualification undertakings (CDUs). This reform took effect from 20 June 2003: see the Enterprise Act 2002 (Commencement No. 3, Transitional and Transitory Provisions and Savings) Order 2003 (SI 2003/1397 (C. 60)) arts 1, 2(1) and Sch.1. Under s.9A the court is empowered to make a disqualification order against a person who is or has been a director or shadow director of a company which has committed a breach of competition law where the court considers that his conduct as a director, taken together with his conduct in relation to one or more other undertakings, makes him unfit to be concerned in the management of a company. Responsibility under ss.9A–9E lies with the Competition and Markets Authority and a number of named regulators, and not with the Secretary of State. See further the notes to ss.9A–9E.

The Enterprise Act 2002 s.257 also introduced the system of bankruptcy restrictions orders and undertakings (see the comment to IA 1986 s.281A and Sch.4A). The law governing these orders and undertakings closely parallels that already established by the present Act for director disqualification, and the CDDA cases are likely to be relevant. This will be the case also with debt relief restrictions orders and undertakings, a regime introduced (as IA 1986 Pt 7A) by the Tribunals, Courts and Enforcement Act 2007.

The Companies Act 2006 Pt 40 introduced (from 1 October 2009) new provisions relating to persons who are subject to restrictions similar to those imposed by a director disqualification order (or equivalent undertaking) under the law of a country or territory outside the United Kingdom. The Secretary of State is empowered to make regulations which either (a) automatically disqualify such persons from acting as director, etc. of a UK company or (b) may be disqualified by order of the court on the application of the Secretary of State; and there may be provision also in the regulations for the Secretary of State to accept a disqualification undertaking in lieu of an order. No regulations have yet been made.

The Small Business, Enterprise and Employment Act 2015 has made a number of changes and introduced some new provisions relating to director disqualification, including:

- extending the power to disqualify a person convicted of a company-related offence abroad;

- restating the matters that the Secretary of State and the court are to take into account when considering whether a person should be disqualified;

- increasing the factors to be taken into account in determining a person's "unfitness" by including his conduct in regard to overseas companies;

- making a person who influences or instructs a person to engage in unfit conduct liable to disqualification;

- extending the time limit for instituting disqualification proceedings from two to three years;

- providing for a disqualified person to be ordered to pay compensation to either the company or a specified creditor (or creditors) who has suffered loss as a result of his improper conduct, with corresponding provision where a disqualification undertaking is accepted by the Secretary of State;

- extending the definition of "shadow director";

- introducing a streamlined system of reporting of director misconduct.

The majority of these changes were brought into force on 26 May or 1 October 2015, except for the new reporting regime, which took effect from 1 April 2016. Together with the Insolvent Companies (Reports on Conduct of Directors) (England and Wales) Rules 2016 (SI 2016/180), which from 6 April 2016, revoke and replace the Insolvent Companies (Reports on Conduct of Directors) Rules 1996 (SI 1996/1909), the new provisions introduce a streamlined system for reporting of directors' conduct by insolvency office-holders using an online system, the Conduct Assessment Service, under which reports must be submitted within three months of the company's "insolvency date". The system is to be reviewed within five years. Without doubt the introduction of disqualification compensation orders by insertion of ss.15A–15C—in which the Secretary of State is empowered to apply for a court order (or accept a voluntary compensation undertaking) against disqualified directors and pay the proceeds (after deduction of a fee) to the company's assets or to individual or a class of creditors without intervention by an insolvency office-holder—appears the most radical and may involve a tension between the state functionary and office-holders.

The Deregulation Act 2015 has also made an amendment to the Act, extending the power of the Secretary of State to obtain information from third parties (s.7(4)).

Regulations relating to director disqualification were made under CA 1985 and replaced by new regulations in similar terms after the 1986 legislation became operative. Further regulations have been made subsequently. Those currently in force are:

- the Act of Sederunt (Company Directors Disqualification) 1986 (SI 1986/2296 (S.168));

- the Insolvent Companies (Disqualification of Unfit Directors) Proceedings Rules 1987 (SI 1987/2023, as amended by SI 1999/1023, 2001/765, 2003/1367 and 2007/1906);

- the Companies (Disqualification Orders) Regulations 2009 (SI 2009/2471, replacing SI 2001/967);

- the Insolvent Companies (Reports on Conduct of Directors) (England and Wales) Rules 2016 (SI 2016/180);

- the Insolvent Companies (Reports on Conduct of Directors) (Scotland) Rules 2016 (SI 2016/185 (S.1));

- the Compensation Orders (Disqualified Directors) Proceedings (England and Wales) Rules 2016 (SI 2016/890);

- the Disqualified Directors Compensation Orders (Fees) (England and Wales) Order 2016 (SI 2016/1047); and

- the Disqualified Directors Compensation Orders (Fees) (Scotland) Order 2016 (SI 2016/1048).

Comparable secondary legislation has been introduced in Northern Ireland. See the note to s.24(2).

The Insolvency Service has published Guidance Notes for the completion of statutory reports and returns under the Disqualification Act, which are available at *https://www.gov.uk/government/publications/company-directors-disqualification-act-1986-guidance-notes-completion-of-statutory-reports-and-returns* but which in some respects are now outdated.

Significant changes were made by the Rating (Coronavirus) and Directors Disqualification (Dissolved Companies) Act 2021. The purpose of these changes is to extend certain provisions in the CDDA 1986 to directors of companies that have been dissolved without going through formal insolvency procedures.

Attention should also be drawn to the *Practice Direction: Directors Disqualification Proceedings* [2015] B.C.C. 224 (reproduced as App.IX to this *Guide*).

Reference will be made at appropriate places in this section to Totty, Moss & Segal, *Insolvency* (Sweet & Maxwell, looseleaf), Ch.G1; and to Davis-White and Walters, *Directors' Disqualification & Insolvency Restrictions*, 3rd edn (Sweet & Maxwell, 2010).

In the year to 31 March 2021 there were 981 disqualifications (88% by undertakings) in total (8.5% of which were in the top "bracket" of 10 years or more: see the note to s.1(2) below), a reduction on the 1,280 in the previous year, which was the highest number for several years.

Company Directors Disqualification Act 1986

(1986 Chapter 46)

Preliminary

Disqualification orders: general

1—

GENERAL NOTE

S.1(2)
Replace the note with:
    Under the legislation as originally enacted, only s.6(4) contained provision for a minimum period of disqualification (two years), but it has now been joined by the new s.8ZA(4) (instructing director who has been disqualified on the

ground of unfitness). (Although s.9A(1) makes it mandatory for the court to make an order if unfitness is found, no minimum period is fixed.) In *Re Bath Glass Ltd* (1988) 4 B.C.C. 130 at 133, Peter Gibson J expressed the view that the fact that the legislature had imposed this minimum disqualification period for "unfitness" was relevant to deciding whether a person should be classed as "unfit": only conduct which was sufficiently serious to warrant such a period of disqualification would justify a conclusion that a person was unfit. There is no power to make an order of indefinite duration.

In *Re Sevenoaks Stationers (Retail) Ltd* [1991] Ch. 164; [1990] B.C.C. 765 (the first reported director disqualification case decided by the Court of Appeal), Dillon LJ thought that it would be a helpful guide to the courts to divide the possible periods of disqualification under s.6 into three brackets. The top period of disqualification for periods of 10–15 years should be reserved for particularly serious cases. This might include cases where a director who had already been disqualified fell to be disqualified again. The minimum bracket of two to five years' disqualification should be applied where, although disqualification was mandatory, the case was relatively not very serious. The middle bracket of disqualification for from six to ten years should apply in serious cases which did not merit the top bracket. In *R. v Goodman* [1992] B.C.C. 625 at 628 the guidelines were not applied in criminal proceedings under s.2; but they were referred to in *R. v Millard* (1993) 15 Cr. App. R. (S) 445. In *Randhawa v Official Receiver* [2006] B.P.I.R. 1435 it was considered "helpful and appropriate" to adopt the same three brackets in the context of bankruptcy restrictions orders. (See also *Official Receiver v Pyman* [2007] EWHC 2002 (Ch); [2007] B.P.I.R. 1150.)

The Court of Appeal has since given further guidance in *Re Westmid Packing Services Ltd, Secretary of State for Trade and Industry v Griffiths* [1998] B.C.C. 836. In determining the appropriate period of disqualification the court should start with an assessment of the correct period to fit the gravity of the offence, bearing in mind that the period has to contain deterrent elements, and then allow for mitigating factors (such factors not being restricted to the facts of the offence). The power to grant leave under s.17 (and the fact that the court is minded to grant leave) is, however, not relevant at this stage. Relevant matters include the director's general reputation and conduct in discharge of the office of director, his age and state of health, the length of time he has been in jeopardy, whether he had admitted the offence, his general conduct before and after the offence and the periods of disqualification meted out to any of his co-directors.

In the same case Lord Woolf MR stated that in the great majority of cases it is unnecessary and inappropriate for the court to be taken through the facts of previous cases in order to guide it on the period of disqualification: this, he said, was a jurisdiction which the court should exercise in a summary manner, using a "broad brush" approach.

In *Re Smooth Financial Consultants Ltd* [2018] EWHC 2146 (Ch) the court stated that in determining disqualification periods it was important to take into account all the relevant circumstances, including the period of time for which each defendant had been culpable, their respective roles and knowledge of the company's financial position, the impact disqualification would have on their respective career prospects, and the extent to which each had been involved in the financial administration of the company.

In *Secretary of State for Business, Innovation and Skills v Warry* [2014] EWHC 1381 (Ch) the court gave guidance on the disqualification periods that should be imposed in cases of missing trader fraud: normally, in the top bracket (10–15 years). However, in another missing trader fraud case, *Re Focus 15 Trading Ltd; Official Receiver v Duckett* [2020] EWHC 3016 (Ch), the director's conduct in failing to ensure proper maintenance of adequate accounting records placed him in the middle bracket and his egregious lies on oath and attempts to distance himself from a company that he clearly controlled caused the case to fall at the higher end of the middle bracket at 10 years, but not the top bracket. A further missing trader intracommunity (MTIC) fraud case, involving over £1 million, resulted in top bracket disqualification orders for the directors concerned (but only four years for a non-executive director not involved in the fraud but still found to be in breach of duty): *Re XE Solutions Ltd; Secretary of State for Business, Energy and Industrial Strategy v Selby* [2021] EWHC 3261 (Ch).

In *Re Arise Networks Ltd; Official Receiver v Obaigbena* [2021] EWHC 852 (Ch); [2021] 2 B.C.L.C. 474 the director of a company who allowed it to continue to trade while insolvent but with no trading revenue (and none expected) and reliant on possible loans for almost two years was in effect gambling at the expense of creditors and this fell squarely within the middle bracket so that he was disqualified for seven years. The court made some useful observations on the policy behind disqualifying unfit directors. That policy was to protect the public in the future from individuals who had shown themselves to be a danger to creditors. Mere commercial misjudgment did not denote unfitness. But here an unreasonable belief in the continued availability of external finance meant that trading had continued for too long to the detriment of creditors. An appeal against this decision was dismissed ([2022] EWHC 1399 (Ch); [2022] B.C.C. 1087: see the note to s.6) and although the seven-year disqualification period was at the upper limit of a reasonable exercise of discretion by any judge on the facts, it was not so excessive as to be beyond the ambit of the discretion of the judge who was entitled to conclude that, even absent dishonesty and a finding that the director knew or should have known that there was no reasonable prospect of avoiding insolvent liquidation, this was a serious case that fell into the middle bracket. A disqualification for unfitness was also imposed by HH Judge Halliwell in *Secretary of State for Business, Energy and Industrial Strategy v Lummis* [2021] EWHC 1501 (Ch) where the unfitness here consisted of the undertaking of transactions that exposed creditors (in particular HMRC) to risk.

In *Re Mea Corp Ltd* [2006] EWHC 1846 (Ch); [2007] B.C.C. 288 the disqualification period was increased from 7 to 11 years because the respondent was already subject to a disqualification order.

Chadwick J in *Secretary of State for Trade and Industry v Arif* [1996] B.C.C. 586 considered that the court cannot take into account in fixing the period of disqualification the fact that the person has been suspended from acting as a director or has voluntarily refrained from doing so pending the hearing, but he added that such de facto disqualification could be a relevant consideration on an application for leave to act under s.17. However, the Court of Appeal in *Re Westmid Packing Services Ltd, Secretary of State for Trade and Industry v Griffiths* [1998] B.C.C. 836 disagreed with that comment regarding the length of the disqualification period, and in the Scottish case *Secretary of State for Business, Innovation and Skills v Bloch* [2013] CSOH 57 the court took into account as a mitigating factor the fact that for several years the respondent had treated himself as de facto disqualified and had turned down a number of offers of directorships.

See *Secretary of State for Business, Innovation and Skills v Rahman* [2017] EWHC 2468 (Ch); [2018] B.C.C. 567 for a useful review of disqualification period cases and in particular the correct disqualification period "bracket". Also see *Re Pure Zanzibar Ltd; Secretary of State for Business, Energy and Industrial Strategy v Barnsby* [2022] EWHC 971 (Ch) at [190]–[207].

Section 1(2) (as amended by IA 2000) provides that the period of disqualification shall begin 21 days after the date of the order (unless the court orders otherwise). The defendant is thus given a breathing space to sort out his affairs before the order takes effect. The discretion given to the court to order otherwise will allow this period to be extended or curtailed in special circumstances—even, conceivably, to make the disqualification run from the end of a custodial sentence.

Disqualification for unfitness

Duty of court to disqualify unfit directors

6—

General Note

S.6(1)
Replace the note with:
Both the word "shall" and the use of the expression "duty" in the marginal note indicate that where unfitness is found the court is obliged to make a disqualification order. However, the court's discretion is not altogether excluded, since it is required to be "satisfied" that the director's conduct makes him "unfit to be concerned in the management of a company"; and a court which took the view that a director's conduct did not warrant the making of a disqualification order would be free to stop short of making such a finding. In *Re Bath Glass Ltd* (1988) 4 B.C.C. 133, Peter Gibson J reached such a conclusion: though the director's conduct had been imprudent and, in part, improper, it was not so serious as to justify a finding of unfitness warranting a two-year disqualification. See also *Secretary of State for Trade and Industry v Lewis* [2003] B.C.C. 611; and *Secretary of State for Trade and Industry v Walker* [2003] EWHC 175 (Ch); [2003] 1 B.C.L.C. 363, where no order was made because although incompetence was found it was not of a sufficiently high degree. In *Re Polly Peck International plc, Secretary of State for Trade & Industry v Ellis (No.2)* [1993] B.C.C. 890, Lindsay J took this factor into account in declining to grant the Secretary of State leave to issue proceedings out of time.

In *Re Polly Peck International plc, Secretary of State for Trade & Industry v Ellis (No.2)* (above) the court declined to qualify the wording of s.6(1)(b) by adding at the end the words "without the leave of the court": to do this would be to make the threshold which a claimant had to cross other than what parliament had by its language intended. In the same case it was held that "a company" in s.6(1)(b) meant "companies generally".

"Director" includes a shadow director: see ss.6(3C) and 22(4) and, for the meaning of the latter term, s.22(5). Former directors are also within the scope of the section. An order may also be made against a de facto director—i.e. a person who acts as a director without having been properly appointed, or whose appointment has expired: *Re Lo-Line Electric Motors Ltd* [1988] Ch. 477; (1988) 4 B.C.C. 415; *Re Cargo Agency Ltd* [1992] B.C.C. 388; *Re Hydrodan (Corby) Ltd* [1994] B.C.C. 161; *Re Moorgate Metals Ltd* [1995] B.C.C. 143; *Re Richborough Furniture Ltd* [1996] B.C.C. 155. For further discussion of this term and the distinction between it and "shadow director", see the note to s.22(5). In *Re Eurostem Maritime Ltd* [1987] B.C.C. 190 the court expressed the view, obiter, that it had power to disqualify a director in respect of a foreign company that was being wound up in England, and it held that in proceedings against the director of an English company his conduct in relation to foreign companies of which he was also a director could be taken into consideration. (See also *Re Dominion International Group plc (No.2)* [1996] 1 B.C.L.C. 572.) "Director" and "shadow director" also include "member" and "shadow member" respectively of an LLP (per

LLPR 2001 reg.4(2)(f), (g)), as explained in *Re Bell Pottinger LLP; Secretary of State for Business, Energy and Industrial Strategy v Geoghegan* [2021] EWHC 672 (Ch); [2021] B.C.C. 675, so that s.6 applies to any member of an LLP and is not restricted only to designated members and those who carry out management functions of the LLP.

Section 6 contains no territorial restriction. It may be applied to persons, whether British subjects or foreigners, who are out of the jurisdiction at the relevant time and in respect of conduct which occurred outside the jurisdiction. However, the court has a discretion not to order that the proceedings be served out of the jurisdiction, which it will exercise where it is not satisfied that there is a good arguable case on the requirements of s.6(1): *Re Seagull Manufacturing Co Ltd (No.2)* [1994] 1 W.L.R. 453; [1993] B.C.C. 833.

The one exception to the extraterritorial scope of the court's jurisdiction (above) is that the courts in England and Wales and those in Scotland have mutually exclusive jurisdictions and will not make disqualification orders based on a person's conduct in relation to a company incorporated in the other part of Great Britain: *Re Helene plc* [2000] 2 B.C.L.C. 249. But once jurisdiction is established, the person's conduct as a director of such companies may be taken into account in determining his "unfitness".

The phrase "has become insolvent" is explained in s.6(2).

There is no anterior time limit fixed by s.6(1)(a): the court may inquire right back into the defendant's history as a director of the company and any other companies, and also into his conduct after he has ceased to be a director, if it relates to a matter "connected with or arising out of the insolvency of that company" (s.6(2)). It should be noted that an application has to be made no later than three (previously two) years after the company "became insolvent": s.7(2).

The matters to be taken into account in determining the question of "unfitness" are dealt with by s.12C and Sch.1: see the note to s.12C. Note that the conduct relating to the unfitness need not be dishonest but can be as a result of incompetence as in *Official Receiver v Arron* [2021] EWHC 1587 (Ch). On the courts' attitude to unfitness in relation to non-executive director trustees of a charitable company see *Re Keeping Kids Co; Official Receiver v Batmanghelidjh* [2021] EWHC 175 (Ch).

For a discussion of the term "management", see the note to s.1(1).

The court may take into account a person's conduct in relation to other companies: it is not necessary that those companies should also have "become insolvent", but it is only his conduct as a director of those companies that is relevant. In the cases it has become customary to refer to the company with reference to which the disqualification proceedings are brought as the "lead company" and the other companies as "collateral companies". It is permissible to specify more than one lead company in an application (*Re Surrey Leisure Ltd* [1999] B.C.C. 847); and the court may, in its discretion, allow an amendment to add a further lead company, but this is not appropriate where to do so would alter the fundamental focus and nature of the complaint against the defendant (*Re Diamond Computer Systems Ltd* [1997] 1 B.C.L.C. 174). If there is no finding of unfitness in relation to the lead company, the court cannot proceed to consider the defendant's conduct as director of the other companies (*Secretary of State for Trade and Industry v Tillman* [1999] B.C.C. 703).

In *Re Country Farm Inns Ltd* [1997] B.C.C. 801 it was emphasised that it was not necessary that the director's conduct in relation to the collateral company should be the same as, similar to or explanatory or confirmatory of the conduct relied on in relation to the lead company, and that there was no need for a nexus of any kind between the two, over and above the fact that the respondent had been a director of both companies and that his conduct in each case tended to show unfitness. It was held, however, in *Re Bath Glass Ltd* (above), that the director's conduct in relation to other companies is to be looked at only "for the purpose of finding additional matters of complaint": in other words, it is not open to the director to adduce evidence that his conduct in relation to other companies has been impeccable in an endeavour to show that a disqualification order would be inappropriate. In determining the question of unfitness, the court will also disregard a plea that the respondent has mended his ways: the question for the court is whether disqualification is merited on the evidence relied on in the application, and not whether the future protection of the public might or might not merit a disqualification: *Re Grayan Building Services Ltd* [1995] B.C.C. 554. On similar reasoning, it was held in *Secretary of State for Trade & Industry v Dawes* [1997] B.C.C. 121 that evidence of the respondent's general good character was inadmissible (compare *Re Oakframe Construction Ltd* [1996] B.C.C. 67; and *Re Pinemoor Ltd* [1997] B.C.C. 708, where the court struck out as irrelevant evidence by accountants which purported to express expert opinions on the issue before the court). However, once unfitness has been established, evidence of a person's general conduct which relates specifically to discharging the office of director may be admitted in determining the appropriate length of the disqualification period; and it may also be relevant to the question whether the court should give leave to act under s.17: *Re Barings plc, Secretary of State for Trade & Industry v Baker* [1998] B.C.C. 583 at 590 (a point not raised on appeal, [2001] B.C.C. 273); *Secretary of State for Trade and Industry v Griffiths* [1998] B.C.C. 836.

Two Scottish cases illustrate the difficulty in trying to persuade an appeal court to overturn a finding of unfitness: *Gerard v Secretary of State for Trade and Industry* [2007] CSIH 85; 2008 S.C. 409 and *Hamilton v Secretary of State for Business, Innovation and Skills* [2016] CSIH 13A; 2016 G.W.D. 9-168.

Note also that, although matters subsequent to the initiation of disqualification proceedings are not normally relevant to the case, the conduct of the respondent in the proceedings themselves may be taken into account, as in *Secretary of State for Trade and Industry v Blunt* [2006] B.C.C. 112, where the defendant was given credit for admitting the allegations of misconduct; and in *Secretary of State for Trade and Industry v Reynard* [2002] B.C.C. 813, where the deceitful conduct of the director concerned in the witness box was held to justify a longer period of disqualification.

In *Secretary of State for Trade and Industry v Queen* [1998] B.C.C. 678 the court had regard to the fact that the respondent had been convicted of criminal offences as a director some years previously, even though these were now "spent" convictions under the Rehabilitation of Offenders Act 1974.

Procedural unfairness, such as not giving a respondent adequate notice of the charges that he has to face, may be a ground for refusing to make a disqualification order: *Re Cubelock Ltd* [2001] B.C.C. 523. (See further the note to s.7(1).) A defendant may seek clarification of the case against him by informal or formal requests or, in the last recourse, by application to the court: *Secretary of State for Business, Innovation and Skills v Chohan* [2011] EWHC 1350 (Ch); [2012] 1 B.C.L.C. 138. In *Official Receiver v Key* [2009] B.C.C. 11 the applicant had chosen to issue disqualification proceedings against only one of two directors, who in the opinion of the court could have been considered equally culpable, and had accepted without making proper inquiries the evidence of the other director: the court declined to make an order. See also *Department of Enterprise, Trade and Investment v Black* [2012] NI Master 1.

In *Re Arise Networks Ltd; Official Receiver v Obaigbena* [2021] EWHC 852 (Ch); [2021] 2 B.C.L.C. 474 a seven-year disqualification was imposed by Deputy ICC Judge Agnello QC the High Court. The court made some useful observations on the policy behind disqualifying unfit directors. That policy was to protect the public in the future from individuals who had shown themselves to be a danger to creditors. Mere commercial misjudgment did not denote unfitness. But here an unreasonable belief in the continued availability of external finance meant that trading had continued for too long to the detriment of creditors. An appeal against the finding of unfitness was dismissed ([2022] EWHC 1399 (Ch); [2022] B.C.C. 1087) as the deputy ICC judge had not erred in law by failing to apply a "legal test" of whether the director ought to have concluded that there was no reasonable prospect of the company avoiding insolvency: this legal test was not required by s.6 or by the statement of the matters alleged to make the director unfit in the official receiver's report. A disqualification for unfitness was also imposed by HH Judge Halliwell in *Secretary of State for Business, Energy and Industrial Strategy v Lummis* [2021] EWHC 1501 (Ch). The unfitness here consisted of the undertaking of transactions that exposed creditors (in particular HMRC) to risk.

In *Official Receiver v Arron* [2021] EWHC 1587 (Ch) a four-year disqualification was imposed by HH Judge Matthews under s.6. The problem here was the non-payment of VAT and the pursuit of a discriminatory policy of favouring certain creditors over the HMRC. On the issue of costs arising in this case note [2021] EWHC 1775 (Ch). This latter judgment is interesting in that there were possible discussions as to the giving of an undertaking before the case went to trial.

For a failed disqualification application see *Secretary of State for Business, Energy and Industrial Strategy v Lord* [2021] EWHC 21 (Ch). Here Deputy ICC Judge Greenwood found that the defendant had not *completely* abrogated his responsibilities as had been alleged by the authorities in seeking a disqualification. See also *Official Receiver v Atkinson; Re Kids Co* [2021] EWHC 175 (Ch) where Falk J dismissed disqualification applications alleging the operation of an unsustainable business model in relation to a high-profile charitable company.

See the ruling of HH Judge Mithani (sitting in the High Court) in *Secretary of State for Business, Energy and Industrial Strategy v Rajgor; Re Javazzi Ltd* [2021] EWHC 1239 (Ch). HH Judge Mithani offers expert insights into both the procedural and substantive aspects of the disqualification regime. The main element of unfitness here was the failure to maintain proper books and accounts. As a result a seven-year ban was imposed.

Secretary of State for Business, Energy and Industrial Strategy v Selby [2021] EWHC 3261 (Ch) is an important ruling from ICC Judge Prentis. It deals with a VAT fraud and results in disqualifications against a number of directors ranging from 14 years to 4 years. ICC Judge Prentis makes important observations with regard to the role of NEDs and their importance as watchdogs. A four-year disqualification was imposed on an NED for abrogating supervisory duties.

Disqualification orders under section 6: applications and acceptance of undertakings

7—

GENERAL NOTE

S.7(1)
Replace the note with:

The Secretary of State, or the official receiver acting at his direction, alone has standing to make an application.

The procedure is prescribed in detail by the Insolvent Companies (Disqualification of Unfit Directors) Proceedings Rules 1987 (SI 1987/2023) and by the *Practice Direction: Directors Disqualification Proceedings* issued by the Vice-Chancellor following the introduction of the Civil Procedure Rules 1998 (SI 1998/3132: the "CPR") and reported (as amended) [2015] B.C.C. 224. The *Practice Direction* incorporates, where relevant, provisions from the 1987 Rules, and is reproduced in App.IX to this *Guide*. This procedure governs disqualification applications under ss.2(2)(a), 3, 4 and 8 as well as under the present section. An application is commenced by a claim form issued in the High Court, out of the office of the companies court registrar or a chancery district registry (or, in the county court, out of a county court office), in the form annexed to the *Practice Direction*. All disqualification proceedings are multi-track. The first hearing is before a registrar. Where the application is made under ss.7 or 8, the first hearing is on a summary basis and on that hearing a disqualification order of up to five years may be imposed; but if it appears that a longer period is justified on the evidence then before the court, the matter is adjourned to a later hearing. An adjournment may also be ordered if the registrar is of opinion that questions of law or fact arise which are not suitable for summary determination. The adjourned hearing may be before a registrar or a judge, as the registrar (or, at a later stage, the court) directs. Directions may also be given as to the subsequent management of the case, e.g. as to the filing and service of further evidence, a timetable for the steps to be taken prior to the hearing, etc. A pre-trial review may also be ordered. Special rules apply if the defendant does not intend to contest his liability and it is proposed to invite the court to adopt the Carecraft procedure (see below). The procedure set out in CPR Pt 8 applies, subject to any modification of that procedure under the *Practice Direction* or the Rules.

Evidence in disqualification applications is by affidavit (or, where the applicant is the official receiver, a written report, with or without affidavits by other persons, made by him (or his deputy: *Re Homes Assured Corp Ltd* [1993] B.C.C. 573); this, under the 1987 Rules, is prima facie evidence of any matter contained in it). (Note that the Legislative Reform (Insolvency) (Miscellaneous Provisions) Order 2010 (SI 2010/18) and the Insolvency (Amendment) Rules 2010 (SI 2010/686), which abolish the use of affidavits for many purposes in insolvency proceedings, do not extend to the CDDA 1986.) The same evidential status is accorded to any documents that are annexed to the report (*Re City Investments Ltd* [1992] B.C.L.C. 956). In practice, an affidavit from the insolvency practitioner concerned is invariably filed. (For a description of a typical affidavit and its contents, see D. S. Henry (1992) 5 Insolv. Int. 1.) Guidance on the drawing up of affidavits and the official receiver's report is to be found also in *Re Pamstock Ltd* [1994] B.C.C. 264 (avoidance of excessive detail); *Secretary of State for Trade and Industry v Hickling* [1996] B.C.C. 678 (significant available evidence in favour of a respondent should not be omitted); *Re Pinemoor Ltd* [1997] B.C.C. 708 (evidence of opinion as to respondent's fitness (unless expert opinion) must be excluded); *Re Park House Properties Ltd* [1998] B.C.C. 847 (distinction to be made between matters of fact, inferences which the court is invited to draw and matters said to amount to unfitness on the part of a defendant). The office-holder's report is a public document and, subject to any question of privilege, should be made available to the defendant (*Re Barings plc (No.2)* [1998] B.C.C. 888).

There is one exception to the requirement that evidence is to be by affidavit: where an application is made within the proceedings, it is made under CPR Pt 23, and is therefore supported by a witness statement.

The defendant has 28 days after service of the proceedings to file his own affidavit evidence in reply. Again, evidence of opinion must be excluded, unless that of an expert, as must evidence of good character (*Secretary of State for Trade and Industry v Dawes* [1997] B.C.C. 121). The *Practice Direction* states that, so far as possible, all evidence should be filed before the first hearing of the application.

Deponents may be cross-examined on their affidavit evidence (*Re Dominion International Group plc* [1995] B.C.C. 303). Disclosure (formerly discovery) may be ordered in the usual way, but an order for disclosure made against the Secretary of State will not extend to documents which are not held by him personally but by the insolvency practitioner on whose report the disqualification proceedings have been based: *Re Lombard Shipping and Forwarding Ltd* [1992] B.C.C. 700. (In practice, however, disclosure is always made available: *Re Thomas Christy Ltd* [1994] 2 B.C.L.C. 527 at 529.) Nor will it extend to internal departmental memoranda: *Re Astra Holdings plc* [1999] B.C.C. 121. Witness summonses (e.g. in a case prior to the introduction of the CPR, a subpoena duces tecum) may be issued, on general principles (*Re Global Information Ltd* [1999] 1 B.C.L.C. 74); but an order requiring the Secretary of State to file replies to interrogatories (under the CPR, further information) was refused (and doubts expressed whether such an order would ever be appropriate) in *Re Sutton Glassworks Ltd* [1996] B.C.C. 174.

In *Official Receiver v Stojevic* [2007] EWHC 1186 (Ch); [2008] Bus. L.R. 641 findings of fraud had been made against the defendant director in a claim based on deceit. It was held that the judgment could be adduced as prima facie evidence in disqualification proceedings subsequently brought against him. In *Secretary of State for Business, Innovation and Skills v Potiwal* [2012] EWHC 3723 (Ch) the sole director of a company had been found by the VAT Tribunal to have been involved in VAT evasion. Briggs J refused to allow him to re-litigate this finding in subsequent disqualification proceedings.

Where a report of inspectors appointed by the Secretary of State under Pt XIV of the Companies Act 1985 is to be put in evidence, s.441 of that Act provides that a certified copy of the inspectors' report shall be admissible in all legal proceedings. [These provisions are not consolidated within CA 2006.]

Rule 3(3) of the 1987 Rules requires that in the affidavit evidence (or, where appropriate, the official receiver's report) there shall be stated the matters by reference to which the defendant is alleged to be unfit to be concerned in the management of a company. In *Re Sevenoaks Stationers (Retail) Ltd* [1991] Ch. 164 at 177; [1990] B.C.C. 765 at 774 the Court of Appeal ruled that it was improper for matters not so stated to be taken into account by the court, either in determining the question of "unfitness" or in fixing the appropriate period of disqualification, unless the court had, in a proper exercise of its discretion, allowed the altered or new allegation to be relied on. This should be done only if there was no injustice to the accused director, and might call for the giving of prior notice or the granting of an adjournment, so that he would have an opportunity to put in new evidence if he wished, and generally a fair opportunity to answer the new allegations (*Re Jazzgold Ltd* [1992] B.C.C. 587 at 594). An amendment may be refused if its effect is to shift the fundamental focus of the complaint to the defendant's conduct in relation to a different company: *Re Diamond Computer Systems Ltd* [1997] 1 B.C.L.C. 174; *Secretary of State for Trade and Industry v Gill* [2004] EWHC 175 (Ch); [2005] B.C.C. 24. The cases of *Re Finelist Ltd* [2003] EWHC 1780 (Ch); [2004] B.C.C. 877, *Secretary of State for Trade and Industry v Gill* [2004] EWHC 175 (Ch); [2005] B.C.C. 24, *Secretary of State for Business, Innovation and Skills v Chohan* [2011] EWHC 1350 (Ch); [2012] 1 B.C.L.C. 138 and *Secretary of State for Business, Energy and Industrial Strategy v Lord* [2022] EWHC 21 (Ch) emphasise the need for a respondent to disqualification proceedings to have a clear statement of the charges and the evidence in support which are brought against him, and the desirability of offering the director an opportunity before the proceedings are begun to proffer explanations for his conduct. A defendant may seek clarification of the case against him by informal or formal requests or, in the last recourse, by application to the court: *Secretary of State for Business, Innovation and Skills v Chohan* (above). In *Kappler v Secretary of State for Trade and Industry* [2006] B.C.C. 845 the allegation against the director was that he had "caused" the use by the company of fraudulent invoices, whereas the case was conducted on the basis that he knew of the fraud and had not put a stop to it. On appeal, he argued that there should have been a formal amendment of the allegation from "caused" to "allowed", but it was ruled that the lack of an amendment had not prevented the trial from being conducted fairly. The court in *Secretary of State for Business, Enterprise and Industrial Strategy v Adam* [2022] EWHC 922 (Ch) found a genuine lack of clarity in some of the disqualification case allegations against a number of non-executive directors of the collapsed Carillion plc and ordered greater particularisation as the court considered relevant.

The report of the official receiver and other evidence on the court file is confidential: it is punishable as a contempt of court to publish this information in a newspaper before the hearing of the application: *Dobson v Hastings* [1992] Ch. 394; [1992] 2 All E.R. 94.

In *Re Rex Williams Leisure plc* [1994] Ch. 350; [1994] B.C.C. 551 the respondent directors wished (a) to object to much of the evidence put forward on behalf of the Secretary of State on the ground that is was hearsay and inadmissible; (b) to file no affidavit evidence of their own before the hearing and give no evidence at all until they had had an opportunity of submitting that there was no case to answer; and (c) to have the disqualification proceedings stayed until a civil action brought against one of the respondents had been disposed of. They failed on all three counts. The court ruled (a) that evidence put forward by an examiner of the investigations division of the Department of Trade and Industry had to be treated analogously with the reports of inspectors appointed under the Companies Act 1985 s.431, and was accordingly admissible as evidence of the facts it contained, even though the examiner was reporting on matters of which he had little or no first-hand knowledge; (b) that the procedure as regards evidence on affidavit laid down in the 1987 Rules (above) should be followed as the norm; and (c) that disqualification proceedings, being a matter of public interest, should not be held up pending the outcome of parallel private litigation. Similarly, objection may not be taken to evidence in an affidavit or report by the official receiver or an officeholder (or a professional person, such as an accountant, employed to report on his behalf) on the ground that it is or contains hearsay: this may go to the weight to be attached to the evidence, but not to its admissibility (*Re Moonbeam Cards Ltd* [1993] B.C.L.C. 1,099; *Re Circle Holidays International plc* [1994] B.C.C. 226; *Secretary of State for Trade and Industry v Moffatt* [1997] 2 B.C.L.C. 16; *Secretary of State for Trade and Industry v Ashcroft* [1998] Ch. 71; [1997] B.C.C. 634; *Re Barings plc (No.3)* [1999] B.C.C. 146). The Court of Appeal considered the position more generally in *Aaron v Secretary of State for Business, etc.* [2008] EWCA Civ 1146; [2009] B.C.C. 375, where the defendant challenged the admissibility of a report by the Financial Services Authority [now the FCA] into complaints that had been made against the defendant's company, and also the decisions of the Financial Ombudsman Service in the same matter. It was held that in disqualification proceedings it was a well-established exception to the hearsay rule that material obtained under a statutory scheme for investigation was admissible as prima facie evidence and that it was a matter for the judge what weight should be given to it. Further, where the documents contained some inadmissible material (such as the recital of evidence given by complainants) this did not justify the exclusion of the documents as a whole and it would be for the judge to decide what weight should be attached to them.

Factual findings in an earlier civil case for breach of contract and wrongful dismissal are not admissible in later disqualification proceedings and the Secretary of State must make good his allegations afresh by legally admissible evidence (*Secretary of State for Trade and Industry v Bairstow* [2003] EWCA Civ 321; [2004] Ch. 1; [2003] B.C.C. 682; *Secretary of State for Trade and Industry v Arnold* [2007] EWHC 1933 (Ch); [2008] B.C.C. 119).

An order may be made in the absence of the defendant if he fails to appear. Where he has failed to file an acknowledgment of service and the time for doing so has expired, he may attend the hearing of the application but may not take part in the hearing unless the court gives permission (*Practical Direction: Directors Disqualification Proceedings* [2015] B.C.C. 224 (reproduced as App.IX to this *Guide*) para.7.3).

Disqualification proceedings are adversarial in nature. The court has no investigative function. It is up to the Secretary of State (or official receiver) to select the matters to be put to the court and if he decides, in the interest of saving time and costs, to weed out parts of the case which could possibly be advanced, he is justified in doing so (*Secretary of State for Trade and Industry v Tillman* [1999] B.C.C. 703). The judge has no power to open the case more widely than the applicant has chosen to present it (*Re SIG Security Services Ltd* [1998] B.C.C. 978). The burden of proof is on the applicant (*Re Verby Print for Advertising Ltd* [1998] B.C.C. 652).

As noted above (see the note to s.1), disqualification proceedings are essentially civil, but they differ from ordinary private law proceedings in many respects: "Significantly, the 1986 Act does not expressly equip the court with a discretion to deploy the armoury of common law and equitable remedies to restrain future misconduct (injunction or undertaking in lieu of injunction), to punish for disregard of restraints imposed by court order (contempt powers of imprisonment or fine), to compensate for past loss unlawfully inflicted (damages) or to restore benefits unjustly acquired (restitution)" (Lord Woolf MR in *Re Blackspur Group plc (No.2)* [1998] 1 W.L.R. 422 at 427D–E; [1998] B.C.C. 11 at 16B–C). However, there is no doubt that the court may, either under the Rules or in its inherent jurisdiction, exercise many powers which are not expressly conferred by the Act, e.g. to grant a stay or suspend an order pending an appeal (*Secretary of State for Trade and Industry v Bannister* [1996] 1 W.L.R. 118; [1995] B.C.C. 1,027; *Re Barings plc (No.4)* [1999] B.C.C. 639).

The legislation does not include any provision which expressly allows the court to make a disqualification order on the basis of a "plea of guilty" or an agreement reached between the Secretary of State or official receiver, on the one hand, and the respondent director, on the other. However, in practice this became possible as a result of the decision of Ferris J in *Re Carecraft Construction Co Ltd* [1994] 1 W.L.R. 172; [1993] B.C.C. 336. As a result, a very significant proportion of disqualification orders were made by this method in the years that followed. However, the power given to the Secretary of State by IA 2000 to accept an undertaking in lieu of making, or continuing with, an application to court provides an even more convenient way of dealing with an uncontested case (see the notes to s.1A, above), and there will be little reason to follow the Carecraft procedure in most instances. One exceptional situation might be where there is no dispute as to the facts, but disagreement on the appropriate length of disqualification.

The Secretary of State has a general power to delegate his functions to an official receiver under IA 1986 s.400, and accordingly he may direct an official receiver to make an application under s.7(1)(a) even where (because the company in question is not being wound up by the court) the case does not come within s.7(1)(b). In such a situation the proceedings should be brought in the name of the Secretary of State and not that of the official receiver; but if an error is made in this respect it can be cured by amendment: *Official Receiver v Pafundo* [2000] B.C.C. 164; not following *Re Probe Data Systems Ltd* (1989) 5 B.C.C. 384.

Other cases of disqualification

Determining unfitness etc: matters to be taken into account

12C—

GENERAL NOTE

Replace the note with:

Section 12C was inserted by SBEEA 2015 s.106(5) as from 1 October 2015. It replaces the original s.9, and brings with it a revised version of Sch.1. Strangely, it has not been enacted as a substitute s.9, but has been given a new number and placed uncomfortably under the heading "Other cases of disqualification", where it does not belong at all. In addition to taking full account of the extension of the disqualification regime to include conduct in relation to overseas companies, and making specific reference to disqualification undertakings, the section in conjunction with the more generally reworded schedule is designed to ensure that the concept of misconduct is not restricted by a narrow or technical approach to construction. Thus, "matters for determining unfitness" is replaced by "matters to be taken into account", and a long list of specific statutory provisions gives way to "any applicable legislative or other requirement". There is also a subtle difference of emphasis when the language is compared with that of the original schedule, with a specific mention of the frequency of any misconduct, and the nature and extent of any loss or harm caused.

Note, that in determining whether to make a disqualification order, the court (or Secretary of State in determining whether to accept a disqualification undertaking) must under s.12C(4) "have regard to" the matters in the Schedule.

According to *Official Receiver v Atkinson* [2020] EWHC 2839 (Ch) (a case on repealed s.9 and the previous Sch.1), this does not require the court to look beyond the matters actually before it, and so, e.g. in an application for a disqualification order, if the applicant has not properly placed before the court a particular matter to which it says the court should have regard, then it is not for the court to choose for itself to make findings on those issues. (The official receiver's sole allegation had been that the defendants had caused the company to operate an unsustainable business model. Yet, only shortly before the proceedings were to be heard did a skeleton argument for the first time introduce allegations as to preferences and breaches of duty mentioned in the previous Sch.1. The court concluded that it would be unfair to allow the official receiver to seek findings in relation to those matters.) At the later disqualification hearing the court took a relatively benevolent attitude toward the position of unpaid non-executive directors of the charitable company concerned: *Re Keeping Kids Co; Official Receiver v Batmanghelidjh* [2021] EWHC 175 (Ch) (see further below).

Like its predecessor, the schedule is divided into two sections, but the grouping is based on different criteria. The first section lists "matters to be taken into account" (replacing "matters applicable") in all cases, but the content of the items grouped under these essentially similar wordings is quite different, reflecting the fact that the additional "matters to be taken into account" (or "matters applicable") which are grouped in the second section apply, under the former schedule, "where the company has become insolvent" but, in the new schedule, "where the person is or has been a director".

Despite these differences, it is probable that there will be little change in the interpretation and development of the concept of unfitness in practice. The discussion of the established case-law which follows necessarily relates to the earlier schedule, but it is likely that, at least in broad terms, it will hold good for the future. In *Secretary of State for Business, Innovation and Skills v Akbar* [2017] EWHC 2856 (Ch); [2018] B.C.C. 448 HHJ Davis-White QC commented (at [98]–[100]) that the new Sch.1 would make little real difference to the position applying under the previous version. See also the note to Sch.1.

Although Sch.1 para.5 refers to "any misfeasance or breach of any fiduciary duty" by a director, in *Re Brooklands Trustees Ltd; Secretary of State for Business, Energy and Industrial Strategy v Evans* [2020] EWHC 3519 (Ch), Deputy ICC Judge Baister stated that breach of duty was neither necessary nor of itself sufficient to find unfitness. He went on to say that it had not been necessary in that case to plead the regulatory duties alleged to have been breached by two directors of a regulated financial services company, as the general statutory duty for a director to exercise reasonable care, skill and diligence (Companies Act 2006 s.174, consolidating the previous common law duty) necessarily entailed compliance with principles of professional conduct.

Schedule 1 para.1 refers to responsibility by a (director) for the causes of material contravention by a company of applicable legislation. In *Re Pure Zanzibar Ltd; Secretary of State for Business, Energy and Industrial Strategy v Barnsby* [2022] EWHC 971 (Ch) where the disqualification allegations included the director causing or allowing a travel agency company to operate in breach of ATOL travel legislation, the court at [40]–[45] discussed the meaning of "caused or allowed".

Schedule 1 is not applicable in competition disqualification cases (s.9A(5)(c)).

In must be emphasised that the Act does not contain any definition of unfitness. The Schedule (unlike the former version) does not list specific instances of unfitness. But even when it did, these were treated only as guidelines for the court, which could treat any other conduct as evidencing unfitness (*Re Amaron Ltd* [1998] B.C.C. 264); and did not consider itself bound by statutory definitions (*Re Sykes (Butchers) Ltd* [1998] B.C.C. 484; *Re Migration Services International Ltd* [2000] B.C.C. 1,095).

In *Re Bath Glass Ltd* (1988) 4 B.C.C. 130 at 133, Peter Gibson J said: "To reach a finding of unfitness the court must be satisfied that the director has been guilty of a serious failure or serious failures, whether deliberately or through incompetence, to perform those duties of directors which are attendant on the privilege of trading through companies with limited liability. Any misconduct of the respondent qua director may be relevant, even if it does not fall within a specific section of the Companies Act or the Insolvency Act". In *Cathie v Secretary of State for Business, Innovation and Skills* [2012] EWCA Civ 739 it was held that in determining the question of unfitness the judge should consider the evidence as a whole, including any extenuating circumstances, and that in this context the use of the term "exceptional circumstances" was better avoided.

In *Re Lo-Line Electric Motors Ltd* [1988] Ch. 477 at 496; (1988) 4 B.C.C. 415 at 419; Browne-Wilkinson VC said: "Ordinary commercial misjudgment is in itself not sufficient to justify disqualification. In the normal case, the conduct complained of must display a lack of commercial probity although I have no doubt that in an extreme case of gross negligence or total incompetence disqualification could be appropriate". (It may be that under the reworded Sch.1 the court would now take a more severe view of cases of negligence.)

In *Re Polly Peck International plc, Secretary of State for Trade & Industry v Ellis (No.2)* [1993] B.C.C. 890 at 894, Lindsay J said that he would "pay regard to the clear thread derived from the authorities that whatever else is required of a respondent's conduct if he is to be disqualified, it must at least be 'serious'".

However, it should be borne in mind that in *Re Sevenoaks Stationers (Retail) Ltd* [1991] Ch. 164 at 176; [1990] B.C.C. 765 at 773 (the leading case on disqualification for "unfitness") Dillon LJ warned against treating such statements as "judicial paraphrases of the words of the statute, which fall to be construed as a matter of law in lieu of the words of the statute".

In *Re Landhurst Leasing plc* [1999] 1 B.C.L.C. 286 at 344, Park J observed that in disqualification cases the relevant standard of conduct "is more frequently described as a standard of 'probity' and 'competence' than stated in the traditional terms of care, skill and diligence". The standard may vary depending upon the nature and size of the company and the role which the defendant played in its affairs. Where it has been established that a defendant's conduct has fallen below the standard of probity and competence, a disqualification order must be made, even though this is not thought necessary in the public interest: *Re Grayan Building Services Ltd* [1995] Ch. 241; [1995] B.C.C. 554. The question for the court to determine is whether the director's conduct, as shown by the evidence, demonstrates unfitness—not whether, at the time of the hearing, the person is or continues to be unfit.

The fact that the director himself honestly believed that what he was doing was not wrong does not excuse him, if on an objective view his conduct justifies a finding of unfitness: *Goldberg v Secretary of State for Trade and Industry* [2003] EWHC 2843 (Ch); [2004] 1 B.C.L.C. 597.

In the leading Scottish case, *Secretary of State for Trade and Industry v Blackwood*, 2003 S.L.T. 120; [2005] B.C.C. 366 the court stressed that a failure to act reasonably (e.g. in deciding to continue to trade) did not necessarily lead to the conclusion that the person concerned was unfit to be a director. In such circumstances directors could not be expected to have wholly dispassionate minds, but might tend to cling to hope. In *Re Smooth Financial Consultants Ltd; Secretary of State for Business, Energy and Industrial Strategy v Broadstock* [2018] EWHC 2146 (Ch), after stressing that it was necessary to assess the conduct as a whole to determine if such made a director unfit, the court added that where a director remained in office while a company was involved in inappropriate activity, it was necessary to consider the merits of his explanation for doing so. If he was aware of such activity and did nothing, he was likely to be in breach of duty. If he remained in office with a view to bringing such activity to an end, however, and could be seen to have attempted to do so, a finding of unfitness by no means followed: it then became necessary to assess what he achieved and set out to achieve together with his explanation for doing so. Conversely, if he was entirely unaware of the relevant activity, it becomes necessary to ask why.

A number of reported cases have been concerned with a particular issue: the failure by a company and its directors to set aside sufficient funds to meet Crown debts for PAYE, NIC and VAT, in effect using this money as working capital as insolvency looms. The views expressed by different judges in these cases have ranged between treating such Crown debts as "quasi-trust moneys" (Harman J, *Re Wedgecraft Ltd* (unreported, 7 March 1986)), on the one hand, to a refusal to draw any distinction between these and other debts (Hoffmann J, in *Re Dawson Print Group Ltd* (1987) 3 B.C.C. 322), on the other. Prior to the ruling of the Court of Appeal in *Re Sevenoaks Stationers (Retail) Ltd* (above), a consensus had emerged among the judges in the Chancery Division which took a middle line between these extremes, holding that the failure to pay such moneys over to the Crown was, though not a breach of trust, "more serious" and "more culpable" than the non-payment of commercial debts (*Re Stanford Services Ltd* (1987) 3 B.C.C. 326; *Re Lo-Line Electric Motors Ltd* [1988] Ch. 477; (1988) 4 B.C.C. 415). However, in the *Sevenoaks Stationers* case passages from the judgment of Hoffmann J in *Dawson Print* were approved, and the ruling given that non-payment of a Crown debt cannot automatically be treated as evidence of unfitness; it is necessary to look more closely in each case to see what the significance, if any, of the non-payment of the Crown debt is. In more recent cases, emphasis has been put on another factor: that the company has pursued a policy of deliberately discriminating between creditors. This may be seen as evidence of unfitness regardless of the status of those who are discriminated against but, in the nature of things, it is very often the Crown which is disadvantaged by such a policy. (See *Secretary of State for Trade and Industry v McTighe* [1997] B.C.C. 224, and contrast *Official Receiver v Dhaliwall* [2006] 1 B.C.L.C. 285, where non-payment was held, in the circumstances, not to amount to unfitness.) Discriminating in not paying Crown debts together with non-validated payments by a director in breach of IA 1986 s.127 (especially payments to himself) was unfitness in *Re St John Law Ltd; Secretary of State for Business, Energy and Industrial Strategy v Murphy* [2019] EWHC 459 (Ch). The fact that there has been correspondence or negotiations with the Revenue authorities may count in the director's favour, and its absence weigh against him: *Re Funtime Ltd* [2000] 1 B.C.L.C. 247; *Re Structural Concrete Ltd* [2001] B.C.C. 578; *Re Amaron Ltd* [1998] B.C.C. 264; *Re Hopes (Heathrow) Ltd* [2001] 1 B.C.L.C. 575 at 581; *Cathie v Secretary of State for Business, Innovation and Skills* [2012] EWCA Civ 739. In the Scots case of *Bradley v Secretary of State for Business, Innovation and Skills* [2016] CSIH 80 divergent views were made on non-payment of Crown debts. In *Re CQH1 Ltd and RTD1 Ltd; Secretary of State for Business, Energy and Industrial Strategy v Steven* [2018] EWHC 1331 (Ch) the director's assertion that he believed business would improve sufficiently to clear the debts to HMRC were too speculative to deflect from the discriminatory treatment of HMRC, particularly given the prolonged trading period over which the discrimination had occurred, and he was disqualified for three years. Discriminating against the Crown, together with unvalidated dispositions by a director in breach of IA 1986 s.127 (especially payments to himself) resulted in an eight-year disqualification order in *Re St John Law Ltd;*

Secretary of State for Business, Energy and Industrial Strategy v Murphy [2019] EWHC 459 (Ch); [2019] B.C.C. 901. In *Official Receiver v Arron* [2021] EWHC 1587 (Ch) the court found that the director's decisions in not paying HMRC were evidence of the director's incompetence and this was sufficient to justify a finding of unfitness even in the absence of any dishonesty. See *Re Ixoyc Anesis (2014) Ltd; Secretary of State for Business, Energy and Industrial Strategy v Zannetou* [2018] EWHC 3190 (Ch); [2019] B.C.C. 403 for a useful summary of cases on discriminating between creditors.

Other types of conduct which have been held to be evidence of "unfitness" include:

- failure to keep proper books of account and/or to make statutory returns (*Re Rolus Properties Ltd* (1988) 4 B.C.C. 446; *Re Western Welsh International System Buildings Ltd* (1988) 4 B.C.C. 449; *Re T & D Services (Timber Preservation & Damp Proofing Contractors) Ltd* [1990] B.C.C. 592; *Re Chartmore Ltd* [1990] B.C.L.C. 673; *Re Carecraft Construction Co Ltd* [1994] 1 W.L.R. 172; [1993] B.C.C. 336; *Re Synthetic Technology Ltd, Secretary of State for Trade & Industry v Joiner* [1993] B.C.C. 549; *Re New Generation Engineers Ltd* [1993] B.C.L.C. 435; *Re A & C Group Services Ltd* [1993] B.C.L.C. 1297; *Re Pamstock Ltd* [1994] B.C.C. 264; *Re Firedart Ltd* [1994] 2 B.C.L.C. 340; *Re Park House Properties Ltd* [1998] B.C.C. 847; *Official Receiver v Stern (No.2)* [2001] EWCA Civ 1787; [2004] B.C.C. 581); *Secretary of State for Business, Innovation and Skills v Jeromson* [2013] ScotSC 26; *Re Artistic Investment Advisers Ltd* [2014] EWHC 2963 (Ch); *Carlson v Secretary of State for Business, Innovation and Skills* [2015] 1 B.C.L.C. 619; *Re Javazzi Ltd; Secretary of State for Business, Energy and Industrial Strategy v Rajgor* [2021] EWHC 1239 (Ch);

- trading or continuing to draw remuneration while insolvent (*Re Western Welsh International System Buildings Ltd* (above); *Re Ipcon Fashions Ltd* (1989) 5 B.C.C. 773; *Re Melcast (Wolverhampton) Ltd* [1991] B.C.L.C. 288; *Re Cargo Agency Ltd* [1992] B.C.C. 388; *Re City Investment Centres Ltd* [1992] B.C.L.C. 956; *Re Synthetic Technology Ltd, Secretary of State for Trade & Industry v Joiner* (above); *Re Firedart Ltd* (above); *Secretary of State for Trade & Industry v McTighe* [1997] B.C.C. 224; *Re Park House Properties Ltd* (above); *Re City Pram & Toy Co Ltd* (above); *Secretary of State for Trade & Industry v Van Hengel* [1995] B.C.C. 173; *Re Amaron Ltd* [1998] B.C.C. 264; *Official Receiver v Stern (No.2)* (above); *Re Vintage Hallmark plc* [2006] EWHC 2761 (Ch); [2007] 1 B.C.L.C. 788);

- purportedly taking into his own hands the liquidation of the company, by-passing the statutory procedure and safeguards (*Re Ipcon Fashions Ltd* (above));

- misleading customers by high-pressure selling tactics (*Official Receiver v Wild* [2012] EWHC 4279 (Ch));

- inadequate capitalisation (*Re Chartmore Ltd* (above); *Re Austinsuite Furniture Ltd* [1992] B.C.L.C. 1047; *Re Pamstock Ltd* (above)); or trading (as a public company) in breach of the statutory minimum capital requirements (*Secretary of State for Trade and Industry v Hollier* [2006] EWHC 1804 (Ch); [2007] B.C.C. 11);

- trading with a succession of "phoenix" companies and/or using a prohibited company name (*Re Travel Mondial Ltd* [1991] B.C.C. 224; *Re Swift 736 Ltd* [1993] B.C.C. 312; *Re Linvale Ltd* [1993] B.C.L.C. 654; *Re Migration Services International Ltd* [2000] B.C.C. 1095);

- issuing false invoices or other financial statements: *Kappler v Secretary of State for Trade and Industry* [2006] B.C.C. 845; *Re Trans Tec plc (No.2)* [2006] EWHC 2110 (Ch); [2007] 2 B.C.L.C. 495;

- making misrepresentations to customers, suppliers of funds and others: *Secretary of State for Business, etc. v Sullman* [2008] EWHC 3179 (Ch); [2010] B.C.C. 500;

- generating fictitious funds by manipulating ("kiting") cheques (*Secretary of State for Trade and Industry v Swan (No.2)* [2005] EWHC 603 (Ch); [2005] B.C.C. 596); *Re City Truck Group Ltd (No.2)* [2007] EWHC 350 (Ch); [2008] B.C.C. 76;

- misapplication of company's funds or property (*Re Keypak Homecare Ltd (No.2)* [1990] B.C.C. 117; *Re Tansoft Ltd* [1991] B.C.L.C. 339; *Re City Investment Centres Ltd* (above); *Re Austinsuite Furniture Ltd* (above); *Re Synthetic Technology Ltd, Secretary of State for Trade & Industry v Joiner* (above); *Re Park House Properties Ltd* (above); *Secretary of State for Trade and Industry v Blunt* [2006] B.C.C. 112); *Re Mea Corp Ltd* [2006] EWHC 1846 (Ch); [2007] B.C.C. 288; *Secretary of State for Business, Innovation and Skills v Doffman* [2010] EWHC 3175 (Ch));

- irresponsible intra-group loans, etc. (*Re Continental Assurance Co of London plc* [1996] B.C.C. 888; *Re Dominion International Group plc (No.2)* [1996] 1 B.C.L.C. 572; *Official Receiver v Stern (No.2)* (above));

- drawing excessive remuneration (*Re Synthetic Technology Ltd, Secretary of State for Trade & Industry v Joiner* (above); *Re A & C Group Services Ltd* (above));

- irresponsible delegation (*Re Burnham Marketing Services Ltd, Secretary of State for Trade & Industry v Harper* [1993] B.C.C. 518; *Re RD Industries Ltd, Secretary of State for Business, Innovation and Skills v Dymond* [2014] EWHC 2844 (Ch));

- continuing to incur liabilities after trading had ceased (*Re McNulty's Interchange Ltd* (1988) 4 B.C.C. 533; *Re Ipcon Fashions Ltd* (above));

- dishonesty, deception and self-dealing (*Re Godwin Warren Control Systems plc* [1992] B.C.C. 557; *Official Receiver v Doshi* [2001] 2 B.C.L.C. 235; *Re Bunting Electric Manufacturing Co Ltd* [2005] EWHC 3345 (Ch); [2006] 1 B.C.L.C. 550; *Re City Truck Group Ltd* (above); it is immaterial whether the director's dishonesty has been towards the company itself or its clients or creditors: *Re JA Chapman & Co Ltd* [2003] EWHC 532 (Ch); [2003] 2 B.C.L.C. 206);

- breach of trust or fiduciary duty (*Secretary of State for Trade & Industry v Van Hengel* (above); *Re Dominion International Group plc (No.2)* (above));

- giving a preference to a particular creditor or paying creditors selectively (*Re Living Images Ltd* [1996] B.C.C. 112; *Secretary of State for Trade & Industry v McTighe* (above); *Re Funtime Ltd* [2000] 1 B.C.L.C. 247; *Re Structural Concrete Ltd* [2001] B.C.C. 578); *Official Receiver v Arron* [2021] EWHC 1587 (Ch);

- failure to co-operate with the official receiver or the FSA [now the FCA], lack of frankness with the court, or dishonesty as a witness: *Re JA Chapman & Co Ltd* [2003] EWHC 532 (Ch); [2003] 2 B.C.L.C. 206 (*Re Tansoft Ltd* (above); *Re Godwin Warren Control Systems plc* (above); *Secretary of State for Trade & Industry v Reynard* [2002] B.C.C. 813); *Ghassemian v Secretary of State for Trade and Industry* [2006] EWHC 1715 (Ch); [2007] B.C.C. 229;

- entering into a transaction at an undervalue, contrary to s.238 or giving financial assistance, contrary to CA 2006: *Re Genosyis Technology Management Ltd* [2006] EWHC 989 (Ch); [2007] 1 B.C.L.C. 208; *Secretary of State for Business, Enterprise and Regulatory Reform v Poulter* [2009] B.C.C. 608;

- failure to ensure VAT returns were filed: *Re CQH1 Ltd and RTD1 Ltd; Secretary of State for Business, Energy and Industrial Strategy v Steven* [2018] EWHC 1331 (Ch); and

- remaining in office whilst failing to protect client funds: *Re Smooth Financial Consultants Ltd; Secretary of State for Business Energy and Industrial Strategy v Broadstock* [2018] EWHC 2146 (Ch). Of course, in many cases several of these features will have been present at the same time. Other considerations, such as the number of companies involved, their size, the extent of their losses, the position of the individual concerned in the managerial hierarchy and his experience (or lack of it), and whether there has been a lack of probity, may also go towards deciding whether unfitness has been established or determining the length of the order to be made:

- causing or allowing a travel agency company to operate in breach of ATOL travel legislation (*Re Pure Zanzibar Ltd; Secretary of State for Business, Energy and Industrial Strategy v Barnsby* [2022] EWHC 971 (Ch)).

Factors which have weighed with the court in deciding that a disqualification order should not be made, or that a reduced period of disqualification would be appropriate, have included the following:

- acting on professional advice (*Re Bath Glass Ltd* (1988) 4 B.C.C. 130; *Re McNulty's Interchange Ltd* (1988) 4 B.C.C. 533; *Re Douglas Construction Services Ltd* (1988) 4 B.C.C. 553; *Re C U Fittings Ltd* (1989) 5 B.C.C. 210; *Re Cladrose Ltd* [1990] B.C.C. 11; *Re Bradcrown Ltd* [2001] 1 B.C.L.C. 547);

- employing a qualified company secretary or finance director (*Re Rolus Properties Ltd* (1988) 4 B.C.C. 446; *Re Douglas Construction Services Ltd* (above));

- absence of dishonesty (*Re Bath Glass Ltd* (1988) 4 B.C.C. 130; *Re Lo-Line Electric Motors Ltd* [1988] Ch. 477; (1988) 4 B.C.C. 415; *Re D J Matthews (Joinery Design) Ltd* (1988) 4 B.C.C. 513; *Re Burnham Marketing Services Ltd* [1993] B.C.C. 518);

- readiness to make a personal financial commitment to the company or the fact that the respondent has sustained heavy personal loss (*Re Bath Glass Ltd* (above); *Re Douglas Construction Services Ltd* (above); *Re Swift 736 Ltd* [1993] B.C.C. 312);

- reliance on regular budgets and forecasts (even though subsequently shown to be inaccurate) (*Re Bath Glass Ltd* (above));

- the fact that events outside the director's control contributed to the company's misfortunes (*Re Bath Glass Ltd* (above); *Re Cladrose Ltd* (above));

- evidence that the same company or other companies have been successfully and properly run by the respondent (*Re D J Matthews (Joinery Design) Ltd* (above); *Re A & C Group Services Ltd* [1993] B.C.L.C. 1297; *Re Pamstock Ltd* [1994] B.C.C. 264);

- the fact that the business was kept going on assurances of help from others (*Re C U Fittings Ltd* (above));

- the respondent's relative youth and inexperience (*Re Chartmore Ltd* [1990] B.C.L.C. 673; *Re Austinsuite Furniture Ltd* [1992] B.C.L.C. 1047);

- the fact that the director was fully occupied as the company's production manager and had left board matters to others (ibid.);

- the fact that the proceedings have been a long time coming to a hearing and that the respondent has already been under a disqualification by reason of bankruptcy (*Re A & C Group Services Ltd* (above));

- the fact that the respondent has admitted his responsibility (*Re Carecraft Construction Co Ltd* [1994] 1 W.L.R. 172; [1993] B.C.C. 336; *Re Aldermanbury Trust plc* [1993] B.C.C. 598).

In *Re Melcast (Wolverhampton) Ltd* [1991] B.C.L.C. 288 the court held that a ten-year disqualification was merited, but reduced the term to seven years on account of the respondent's age (68). Where other directors have also been disqualified, the court may take into account the period of disqualification imposed on them for the purpose of comparison, but should not be over-influenced by this fact (*Re Swift 736 Ltd* (above)).

One or two cases have been reported in which the court has found that the defendant's conduct was not such as to warrant a finding of unfitness. These include *Re Stephenson Cobbold Ltd* [2001] B.C.C. 38; *Re Cubelock Ltd* [2001] B.C.C. 523; and *Secretary of State for Trade and Industry v Creegan* [2002] 1 B.C.L.C. 99.

The wording of Sch.1 appears to be directed primarily at those directors who have taken an active part in the company's affairs, rather than those whose role has been nominal or who have involved themselves only intermittently; but such passive conduct may also in itself justify a finding of unfitness. Even a non-executive director of a small family company is liable to disqualification if he merely stands by, or is content to remain in ignorance, while those who are actively managing the company run up losses or allow accounts, records and returns to fall into disarray: see *Re Peppermint Park Ltd* [1998] B.C.C. 23; *Re Park House Properties Ltd* [1998] B.C.C. 847; *Re Galeforce Pleating Ltd* [1999] 2 B.C.L.C. 704; *Official Receiver v Stern (No.2)* [2001] EWCA Civ 1787; [2001] 1 B.C.L.C. 119; *Re Bradcrown Ltd* [2002] B.C.C. 428; *Secretary of State for Trade and Industry v Thornbury* [2007] EWHC 3202 (Ch); [2008] 1 B.C.L.C. 139; *Re AG (Manchester) Ltd* [2008] EWHC 64 (Ch); [2008] 1 B.C.L.C. 321; *Secretary of State for Trade and Industry v Thornbury* [2007] EWHC 3202 (Ch); [2008] B.C.C. 768; *Secretary of State for Business, Innovation and Skills v Reza* [2013] CSOH 86. In *Re City Truck Group Ltd (No.2)* [2007] EWHC 350 (Ch); [2008] B.C.C. 76 a director who passively acquiesced in a fraud perpetrated by a co-director was disqualified for the same period as the principal offender (12 years). The courts in these cases have stressed that the title "director" is not to be accepted by any person without a corresponding assumption of responsibility—the more so if he is paid remuneration.

On the other hand, it has been a factor counting against a director that he held a high position in the company: the greater the status and its rewards, the higher the standard for measuring its responsibilities (*Re Barings plc, Secretary of State for Trade & Industry v Baker* [1998] B.C.C. 583; *Re Barings plc (No.5)* [1999] 1 B.C.L.C. 433 (affirmed on appeal [2001] B.C.C. 273); and see *Secretary of State for Trade and Industry v Swan (No.2)* [2005] EWHC 603 (Ch); [2005] B.C.C. 596. On similar reasoning individuals whose business consisted of acting as nominee directors of large numbers of "offshore" companies for remuneration have been severely dealt with: see *Re Kaytech International plc* [1999] B.C.C. 390; and *Official Receiver v Vass* [1999] B.C.C. 516. The fact that the respondent relied on his fellow-directors may be relevant, but only if it is shown that he was justified in doing so, and for this purpose evidence on his part of his perception of their reliability is material: *Secretary of State for Trade & Industry v Dawes* [1997] B.C.C. 121. In *Re Landhurst Leasing plc* [1999] 1 B.C.L.C. 286, relatively junior directors were held to have been justified in relying on their more experienced co-directors. The court held that a proper degree of delegation and division of responsibility by the board (not amounting to a total abrogation of responsibility by any individual director or directors) was permissible. An absentee director will not necessarily be excused: *Re Peppermint Park Ltd* [1998] B.C.C. 23. Total abrogation of duties was not proved on the evidence and the disqualification application dismissed in *Secretary of State for Business, Energy and Industrial Strategy v Lord* [2022] EWHC 21 (Ch). The position of a director who dissented from or opposed the course of conduct being followed by his colleagues as disaster loomed has brought a mixed reaction from the judges. Plainly, much depends on the circumstances. In *Re Peppermint Park Ltd* (above) it was said ([1996] B.C.C. 23 at 26) that the director in question should, at least, have resigned his directorship.

However, in *Secretary of State for Trade & Industry v Taylor, Re C S Holidays Ltd* [1997] 1 W.L.R. 407; [1997] B.C.C. 172 the fact that a director whose protests went unheeded did not resign was not held to be fatal.

The courts appear to take a fairly benevolent approach to the position of charity trustees where there is no allegation of dishonesty or wilful misconduct, particularly in relation to unpaid trustee non-executive directors of charitable companies. See *Re Keeping Kids Co; Official Receiver v Batmanghelidjh* [2021] EWHC 175 (Ch) where it was considered that incompetent conduct which might render the director of a commercial company unfit might not do so in a charitable context. Having pointed out that trustee directors of charitable companies have the same duties as other company directors, and the same test for disqualification applied, the court added that the charity sector depended on capable individuals being prepared to take trusteeship roles, and the perceived risk of disqualification proceedings based on wide-ranging but unclear allegations of incompetence might dissuade them from doing so. The court went on to give recommendations for the future on the conduct by the applicant in preparing a wide-ranging application for disqualification as in the current case.

On the topic of unfitness, see further Walters and Davis-White, *Directors' Disqualification & Insolvency Restrictions*, 3rd edn (Sweet & Maxwell, 2010), Ch.5; and Totty, Moss & Segal, *Insolvency*, G1–18 et seq.

Miscellaneous and general

Extent

24—

GENERAL NOTE

Replace the note with:

The disqualification regime in Northern Ireland is contained in the Company Directors Disqualification (Northern Ireland) Order 2002 (SI 2002/3150) (as amended) as supplemented by other measures, primarily including the Insolvent Companies (Reports on Conduct of Directors) Rules (Northern Ireland) 2003 (SR 2003/357) (as amended), the Insolvent Companies (Disqualification of Unfit Directors) Proceedings Rules (Northern Ireland) 2003 (SR 2003/358) (as amended) and the Companies (Disqualification Orders) Regulations (Northern Ireland) 2010 (SR 2010/184) (see the note to IA 1986 s.441 for a full list).

EU Regulation on Insolvency Proceedings 2015

Regulation (EU) 2015/848

Special note
Replace the note with:

The text which follows is the "recast" or replacement version of the Regulation, which came into force on 26 June 2017. Readers who wish to refer to the original EC Regulation are referred to the 19th edition of this work.

Amendments to the Regulation by the Insolvency (Amendment) (EU Exit) Regulations 2019 (SI 2019/146) (as amended by the Insolvency (Amendment) (EU Exit) (No.2) Regulations 2019 (SI 2019/1459) and the Insolvency (Amendment) (EU Exit) Regulations 2020 (SI 2020/647)) as from Brexit IP completion day of 31 December 2020 11pm have not been incorporated into the text of the Regulation immediately below and are not reflected in these annotations, and that version continues to apply in relation to main insolvency proceedings which were opened before the IP completion date (on whether insolvency proceedings have been "opened" in this context, see *Re Mederco (Cardiff) Ltd; Duffy v Mederco (Cardiff) Ltd* [2021] EWHC 386 (Ch); [2022] B.C.C. 597 at [50]–[64]). It is important to note that since the UK left the EU from the latter date, the unamended version of the Regulation no longer applies to the UK to proceedings that commenced after that date (see, e.g. *Barings (UK) Ltd v Galapagos SA* [2022] EWHC 1633 (Ch); [2022] B.C.C. 1113). The radically amended "retained" EU Regulation, in force after the IP completion date appears immediately after this version. The Insolvency Service on 15 January 2021 published *Cross-border Insolvencies: Recognition and Enforcement in EU Member States from 1 January 2021* providing some basic information regarding the applicable frameworks in certain EU Member States (Belgium, France, Germany, Ireland, Italy, the Netherlands and Spain), as a starting point towards seeking recognition for UK insolvency proceedings and dealing with assets in the EU. This was replaced on 24 March 2021 by *Cross-border Insolvencies: Recognition and Enforcement in EU Member States* and updated with further detail and additional notes on the EU Member States which have implemented the UNCITRAL Model Law on Cross-Border Insolvency (Greece, Poland, Romania and Slovenia (the UK was the only other prior to Brexit)) and notes on recognition of insolvency proceedings in the remaining EU Member States. See *https://www.gov.uk/government/publications/cross-border-insolvencies-recognition-and-enforcement-in-eu-member-states/cross-border-insolvencies-recognition-and-enforcement-in-eu-member-states.*

CHAPTER I—GENERAL PROVISIONS

Article 3

International jurisdiction

GENERAL NOTE
Replace the note with:

The Regulation only applies where the centre of the debtor's main interests is located in the EU—although he (or it) need not be an EU national: see the Preamble para.25 and *Re BRAC Rent-A-Car Inc* [2003] EWHC 128 (Ch); [2003] B.C.C. 248 (followed in *Re Buccament Bay Ltd* [2014] EWHC 3130 (Ch)). It also applies only where the debtor has assets (and, usually, creditors) in more than one Member State. And it has nothing to say about assets situated outside the EU, or creditors resident or domiciled outside the Union. In any of the situations not covered by the Regulation, a Member State is free to apply its national law (including, in the case of the UK, the CBIR). It is not essential that the case should involve a cross-border element as between two or more Member States: in *Schmid v Hertel* (C-328/12) [2015] B.C.C. 25 it was confirmed that the Regulation applied where the defendant resided in a non-EU jurisdiction (Switzerland). Article 3 confers jurisdiction on the courts of the Member State of the opening of main proceedings, not only in matters of insolvency law *stricto sensu*, but also in regard to matters "directly derived from and closely related to" the insolvency proceedings: see the Preamble, para.35 and art.6 (confirming the rulings in *Seagon v Deko Marty Belgium NV* (C-339/07) [2009] 1 W.L.R. 2168; [2009] B.C.C. 347 and *Schmid v Hertel* (above); *H v HK* (C-295/13) 4 December 2014 CJEU).

On whether the proceedings in question qualified as "insolvency proceedings" for the purposes of what is now art.3 see *Tunkers France* (C-641/16) EU:C:2017:847. The proceedings in question were concerned with an allegation of unfair competition made against the assignee of a business which was undergoing insolvency were found not to be insolvency proceedings and therefore could not be main proceedings for the purposes of the Regulation.

Article 3(1) deals with the jurisdiction to open "main" proceedings and art.3(2)–(4) with the jurisdiction for "secondary" and "territorial" proceedings. Non-main proceedings are "secondary" if they are opened after the opening of main proceedings, and "territorial" if they precede the opening of main proceedings. If main proceedings are opened at a time when any territorial proceedings are in existence, those proceedings "become" secondary proceedings (art.3(4)). Looking at the picture from another angle, there is no difference between territorial and secondary proceedings apart from the more stringent conditions imposed on the *opening* of territorial proceedings imposed by art.3(4). (Under the former Regulation, territorial proceedings could only be for winding up. This limitation is not continued.)

The court of a Member State with which a request to open main insolvency proceedings has been lodged still retains exclusive jurisdiction to open such proceedings if the centre of the debtor's main interests is moved to another Member State after that request has been lodged, but before the first court has delivered a decision on it, so that the court of the other Member State with which another request is subsequently lodged cannot declare that it has jurisdiction to open main insolvency proceedings until the first court has delivered a decision to decline jurisdiction: *Galapagos BidCo Sàrl* (C-723/20) 24 March 2022 (CJEU). (For important further proceedings in the English court see the General note to the Retained EU Regulation on Insolvency Proceedings 2015.)

The reference in art.3(1) and (2) to "the courts of a Member State" could give rise to difficulties where it is sought to put a company into creditors' voluntary liquidation where the company is incorporated in one State but has its centre of main interests in another. The resolution would have to be passed by the company's shareholders in accordance with the law of the State of incorporation, but even assuming that the meeting was held in the "main" Member State it would call for some ingenuity to construe "the court of that other Member State" as meaning that meeting. Some of these questions arose in *Re TXU Europe German Finance BV* [2005] B.C.C. 90. Two companies registered respectively in Ireland and the Netherlands had their COMIs in England. Being satisfied that the law of both Ireland and the Netherlands made provision for a procedure equivalent to a special resolution and that the counterparts to the registrar of companies in each country were willing to recognise the winding up for the purposes of the dissolution of their companies, Mr Registrar Baister, in exercise of the discretion conferred by IR 1986 r.7.62(5) [IR 2016 r.21.5], made an order confirming resolutions which had been passed for a voluntary winding up of the two companies (which, in the circumstances, was a creditors' winding up). The court accepted that the liquidations would be conducted in accordance with English insolvency law, but did so only on the basis of assurances given by the liquidator that foreign creditors would be treated fairly.

Article 34 provides that the fact that main proceedings have been opened is to be taken as conclusive evidence of the debtor's insolvency in any later secondary proceedings.

On the primacy of art.3 see *Wiemer & Trachte GmbH v Tadzher* (C-296/17) EU:C:2018:902; [2019] B.P.I.R. 252. This case is discussed in the note to art.21 below.

Annexes

GENERAL NOTE TO THE ANNEXES

Replace the note with:

Annexes A and B list (respectively), in each jurisdiction, the insolvency proceedings recognised for the purposes of the Regulation (arts 1(1), 2(4)) and the insolvency practitioners similarly recognised (art.2(5)(i)). In contrast with Annex A to ECRIP, Annex A is declared to be exhaustive, while Annex B is silent on this point. An amending Regulation ((EU) 2017/353) published on 15 February 2017 and effective 26 June 2017, made changes to the Polish entries in Annexes A and B. These have been incorporated in the text below, as have changes to the Belgian, Bulgarian, Croatian, Latvian and Portuguese entries in Annexes A and B made by amending Regulation ((EU) 2018/946), published on 6 July 2018 and effective on 26 July 2018. Note that Ireland has opted out of the application of Regulation 2018/946 (see para.5 of the Preamble). On 17 May 2021 the European Commission commenced a consultation on a Regulation to replace Annexes A and B in light of amendments to domestic insolvency laws in the Netherlands, Italy, Lithuania, Cyprus and Poland, which resulted in EU Regulation 2021/2260 ([2021] OJ L455/4) of 15 December 2021 to replace its Annexes A and B, in force with direct applicability in Member States as from 8 January 2022: the substituted Annexes, which also exclude the United Kingdom, have been incorporated in the text below (again, Ireland did not originally sign into Regulation 2021/2260 from the commencement date, but Ireland's inclusion was confirmed by Commission Decision (EU) 2022/1437 ([2022] OJ L225/3) as from 30 August 2022).

Annex C (which is not reproduced) lists the amendments made to the original Regulation during its lifetime, while Annex D conveniently provides a correlation table between ECRIP and the present Regulation.

(Retained) EU Regulation on Insolvency Proceedings 2015

[Preamble]

GENERAL NOTE

Replace the note with:

Strangely, the Preamble is not mentioned in the Insolvency (Amendment) (EU Exit) Regulations 2019 (SI 2019/146) (as amended, see above) as being amended and thus in theory its recitals would appear still to apply in the UK as part of the retained EU Regulation in the post-Brexit era, albeit that many of the concepts the recital relate to do not form part of the retained provisions.

There is some judicial discussion from ICC Judge Mullin in *Re Investin Quay House Ltd; BUJ Architects LLP v Investin Quay House Ltd* [2021] EWHC 2371 (Ch) on the role of the retained Regulation, which was held to be applicable in this case and a Jersey company was found to have COMI in England. For the perspective of the Jersey court see Investin *Quay v BUJ Architects* [2021] JRC 233.

Issues relating to the application of the recast EU Insolvency Regulation (EURIP) and jurisdiction for main proceedings have been considered in *Barings UK Ltd v Galapagos SA* [2022] EWHC 1633 (Ch); [2022] B.C.C. 1113. The case revolved around whether the centre of main interests (COMI) had been shifted from Luxembourg to England before Brexit and if so whether the UK court could make a winding up order when there were alternative proceedings for restructuring before a German court. The German court referred the matter of jurisdiction to the CJEU which stated that if the COMI had moved to the UK and proceedings in the UK were started first and at a time when the UK was still a member state then the UK proceedings were the main proceedings (*Galapagos* (C-723/20) EU:C:2022:209). The UK court found on the facts the COMI had moved and therefore the recast EURIP did not apply. As such the retained UK version of the EU regulation which was based upon the 2015 regulation not the 2019 regulation applied and the court could order a winding up.

CHAPTER I—GENERAL PROVISIONS

Article 3

Centre of main interests

GENERAL NOTE

Replace the note with:

Heading to art.3 substituted art.3(1) amended and art.3(2)–(4) omitted by the Insolvency (Amendment) (EU Exit) Regulations 2019 (SI 2019/146) reg.2 and Sch. paras 1, 4 as from 11pm on 31 December 2020 subject to saving provisions in reg.4. By these amendments the retained Regulation has been stripped of its international jurisdiction. COMI now relates to domestic proceedings although a domestic court is granted jurisdiction where the debtor's COMI is in a Member State (defined in art.2(1A)) and the debtor has an establishment (defined in art.2(10)) in the United Kingdom; however the automatic recognition by EU Member States (apart from Denmark) of a domestic court's decision in relation to those proceedings is no longer provided by the Regulation since Brexit.

In an early case on the retained art.3(1) and COMI, the court in *Re Investin Quay House Ltd; BUJ Architects LLP v Investin Quay House Ltd* [2021] EWHC 2371 (Ch); [2022] B.C.C. 497 still took a traditional approach to the topic where the relevant retained wording remained similar, citing leading cases from the pre-Brexit era such as the ECJ decision in *Eurofood IFSC Ltd (C-341/04)* [2006] B.C.C. 397. The court concluded that the presumption in relation to a Jersey-registered company was rebutted where, amongst other things, the company's sole economic purpose was to carry on business in the UK by the development of its principal asset in England, its contracts were governed by English law and subject to the jurisdiction of the English courts, head-office functions were carried out not at the registered officer address in Jersey but at offices in Solihull from where the central administrative functions of the company were conducted. The English court thus had jurisdiction to wind up the company. The pre-Brexit approach to the topic of establishing a company's COMI was also applied in *Barings (UK) Ltd v Galapagos S.A.* [2022] EWHC 1633 (Ch); [2022] B.C.C. 1113 (albeit in the absence of any submission that a different approach should be taken), in which Bacon J cited with approval the principles enunciated by Trower J in *Re Swissport Holding International* [2020] EWHC 3556 (Ch).

UNCITRAL Model Law on Cross-Border Insolvency

Note

Replace the note with:

The text of the UNCITRAL Model Law, as formally agreed, is not reproduced here, since it is not part of the law of the UK but has been superseded for this purpose by Sch.1 to the Cross-Border Insolvency Regulations 2006 (below). However, since the Preamble to the Model Law has not been incorporated into Sch.1 and may be relevant for reference as an aid to interpretation of the Regulations, it is set out below.

The total number of jurisdictions which have enacted legislation based on the Model law is now 52 in 49 states. These are Australia, Bahrain, Benin, Brazil, Burkina Faso, Cameroon, Canada, Central African Republic, Chad, Chile, Colombia, Comoros, Congo, Côte d'Ivoire, Democratic Republic of Congo, Dominican Republic, Equatorial Guinea, Gabon, Greece, Guinea, Guinea-Bissau, Israel, Japan, Kenya, Malawi, Mali, Mauritius, Mexico, Montenegro, Myanmar, New Zealand, Niger, Philippines, Poland, Republic of Korea, Romania, Senegal, Serbia, Seychelles, Singapore, Slovenia, South Africa, Togo, Uganda, United Kingdom of Great Britain and Northern Ireland (including the British Virgin Islands, Gibraltar, Great Britain), United Arab Emirates (Dubai International Financial Centre), United States of America, Vanuatu, Vietnam and Zimbabwe.

The Model Law is supplemented by Guide to Enactment and Interpretation of the UNCITRAL Model Law on Cross-Border Insolvency (2013).

On 2 July 2018 UNCITRAL approved and adopted the text of a new model law, the Model Law on the Recognition and Enforcement of Insolvency-Related Judgments, together with a guide to enactment thereto. The 2018 Model Law may be regarded as an attempt to supplement the existing 1997 UNCITRAL Model Law framework for cross-border insolvency cooperation, e.g. by cross-border recognition and enforcement of judgments in addition to the appointments of representatives etc. The 2018 Model Law was approved by resolution 73/200 of the UN General Assembly on 20 December 2018 (see *https://www.un.org/en/ga/search/view_doc.asp?symbol=A/RES/73/200*). To be effective at national level it will need to be adopted into domestic legislation. In a consultation document issued on 7 July 2022 the UK Insolvency Service indicated that it would not propose implementation of the 2018 Model Law in the UK, but was proposing adoption in the UK of the special provision published within the 2018 Model Law named "Article X" which supplements the 1997 Model Law so as to give the court a discretion in the enforcement and recognition of insolvency-related foreign judgments. The *UNCITRAL Model Law on the Recognition and Enforcement of Insolvency-Related Judgments with Guide to Enactment* is available at *https://uncitral.un.org/sites/uncitral.un.org/files/media-documents/uncitral/en/ml_recognition_gte_e.pdf*. See Moss (2019) 33 Insolv. Int. 21 and Walters (2020) 41 Comp. Law. (4) 91 for discussion.

Another insolvency-related Model Law has been adopted in 2019: the UNCITRAL Model Law on Enterprise Group Insolvency together with a guide to enactment thereto, intended to provide effective mechanisms to address cases of insolvency affecting the members of an enterprise group, was approved and adopted by UNCITRAL on 15 July 2019 and formally adopted by the United Nations General Assembly on 18 December 2019. It is available at *https://uncitral.un.org/sites/uncitral.un.org/files/media-documents/uncitral/en/19-11346_mloegi.pdf*. This too would have to be implemented into national legislation to be effective.

UNCITRAL Working Group V (Insolvency Law) is next expected to produce a simplified regime for the insolvency of micro and small enterprises.

Cross-Border Insolvency Regulations 2006

Article 15. Application for recognition of a foreign proceeding

General Note

Replace the note with:

Recognition of the foreign proceeding necessarily involves recognition of the foreign representative and the validity of his appointment. The Model Law aims to avoid the need for any formal "legalisation" of the foreign documents submitted as evidence—an aim endorsed by this article, stipulating for no other requirement than a translation where this is needed. The court is entitled to assume that the documents are authentic without further ado (art.16.2), but is not bound to do so. On the meaning of "foreign representative", see the note to art.2(j).

In *Re 19 Entertainment Ltd* [2016] EWHC 1545 (Ch); [2017] B.C.C. 347 the court accorded recognition to US Bankruptcy Code 1978 Ch.11 protection from bankruptcy proceedings in the United States which took the normal "debtor in possession" format, without any individual office-holder who could be recognised as the foreign representative. The court held that the company itself and each of its directors was the foreign representative. On the basis of the latter decision the English court in *Re Astora Women's Health LLC* [2022] EWHC 2412 (Ch) was content to accept that US Ch.11 proceedings satisfied the description of foreign proceedings, together with further evidence from the company's London solicitors, the UNICTRAL Model Law on Cross-Border Insolvency G to E and UNCITRAL's guide for judiciary, "The Model Law on Insolvency: The Judicial Perspective"; these collectively obviated the need and high cost of employing expert US level evidence as to the nature of Ch.11 proceedings, which in this case were "akin to a liquidation in England".

On the procedure, see generally Sch.2 Pt 2, and on notice, Sch.2 paras 21 et seq. The G to E, para.135 points out that the Model Law does not make the issuance of any form of notice mandatory, but stresses the need for a recognition proceeding to be dealt with expeditiously. Mr Registrar Nicholls has issued a helpful note on various aspects of the procedure under arts 15 and 21, reported as *Re Rajapaske (Note)* [2007] B.P.I.R. 99.

The court was prepared to make a recognition order in relation to bankruptcy proceedings in Brazil of a limited liability partnership in *Mendonca v KPMG Corporate Finance (Sao Paulo, Brazil)* [2020] EWHC 351 (Ch) despite the LLP having been dissolved (and its property vested as bona vacantia) subject to the foreign representatives applying to restore the LLP to the register.

Article 17. Decision to recognise a foreign proceeding

General Note

Replace the note with:

The purpose of this article is to indicate that, if the application meets the requirements set out, recognition should be granted as a matter of course and without delay, so ensuring the effective protection of the debtor's assets. The decision to grant recognition should not involve an examination of the merits of the foreign court's decision or the foreign representative's suitability. The only exception is art.6 (public policy). Although (subject to the art.6 public policy exception) art.17.1 states that the foreign proceedings "shall" be recognised if the requisite conditions are fulfilled, it appears that it is not absolutely mandatory: the Scottish court refused an application in *Chang Chin Fen v Cosco Shipping (Qidong) Offshore Ltd* [2021] CSOH 94 despite the requirements for recognition being met and recognition would not be manifestly contrary to public policy, as the relief could not be achieved under Scots (or English) law (on reliefs see note to art.21 below).

In the unusual case of *Kireeva v Bedzhamov* [2021] EWHC 2281 (Ch) where the Russian court had made a bankruptcy order against the debtor, the CBIR did not apply as the debtor's COMI was not in Russia, Snowden J made a recognition order at common law of the debtor's Russian bankruptcy proceedings as the debtor had submitted to the jurisdiction of the courts of the state (Russia) where the bankruptcy proceedings were opened, and there was no underlying fraud or reason of public policy or natural justice as to why the bankruptcy should not be recognised. But the Court of Appeal ([2022] EWCA Civ 35) overruled this decision on common-law recognition on the basis that recognition should not have been granted where the debtor had alleged that the bankruptcy order had been obtained by fraud and the judge had not been entitled to discount the bankrupt's account without him being cross-examined on the point; the recognition matter was remitted to the High Court for determination.

In *Global Maritime Investments Cyprus Ltd v OW Supply and Trading AS* [2015] EWHC 2690 (Comm) the question at issue was whether recognition of a foreign proceeding constituted a "real and present dispute" for the purposes of a jurisdiction clause. It was held that recognition in itself was not enough, until the office-holder in those proceedings took steps to obtain an order or judgment against the claimant.

A lack of COMI on the part of the debtor in the relevant jurisdiction will render the CBIR regime inapplicable—hence the course of the litigation in *Kireeva v Bedzhamov* [2022] EWCA Civ 35.

On the question of determining COMI of an English registered company which operated in the USA see *Re 19 Entertainment Ltd* [2017] B.C.C. 347. Recognition was granted to the foreign representative pursuant to art.17 and relief in the form of a moratorium was made available under arts 20 and 21. See also *Re Astora Women's Health LLC* [2022] EWHC 2412 (Ch).

Re Dalnyaya Step LLC; Cherkasov v Olegovich [2017] EWHC 756 (Ch); [2019] B.C.C. 1 was concerned with recognition and security for costs (Rose J). An official receiver of a Russian company having been recognised for CBIR purposes was then ordered to provide security for costs in an application under of IA 1986 s.236. Rose J held that the art.6 exception on grounds of public policy came into play due to the difficulty of enforcing a costs order in Russia. For later proceedings see *Cherkasov v Olegovich (the Official Receiver of Dalnyaya Step LLC) (No.2)* [2017] EWHC 3153 (Ch); [2019] B.C.C. 23 where Vos C revoked the recognition order which had been granted under art.17 because there had been a lack of full and frank disclosure.

In *Re Videology Ltd* [2018] EWHC 2186 (Ch); [2019] B.C.C. 195 Snowden J refused to grant recognition under art.17 on the basis of the existence of foreign main proceedings. The US Chapter 11 insolvency proceedings related to the affairs of an English subsidiary of a US parent. In so deciding, he found that the COMI of the company was in the UK (where its registered office was located) and not in the USA. However, he granted recognition on the basis that the proceedings were foreign non-main proceedings and then he also granted relief under art.21(3). For comment see Hawthorn [2018] 11(5) C.R.I. 161.

Bankruptcy in Brazil of a limited liability partnership was recognised as a foreign proceeding in *Mendonca v KPMG Corporate Finance (Sao Paulo, Brazil)* [2020] EWHC 351 (Ch); [2020] B.C.C. 486 despite the LLP having been dissolved (and its property vested as bona vacantia) subject to the foreign representatives applying to restore the LLP to the register. A Hong Kong bankruptcy order was recognised in *Chen v Li* [2021] EWHC 3346 (Ch) as main proceedings (but not non-main proceedings). Compare *Chang Chin Fen v Cosco Shipping (Qidong) Offshore Ltd* [2021] CSOH 94 and [2021] CSOH 95 for a valuable discussion by Lord Ericht on the pragmatic linkage between recognition and relief.

The Australian court held in *Re Hydrodec Group plc* [2021] NSWSC 755 that an IA 1986 Pt A1 moratorium was a "foreign proceeding" but not a foreign "main" proceeding (see note to art.17.2 below).

Debt Respite Scheme (Breathing Space Moratorium and Mental Health Crisis Moratorium) (England and Wales) Regulations 2020

Introductory note to the Regulations

Replace the note with:

These regulations took effect on 4 May 2021. They form part of a policy of assisting distressed debtors by freezing hostile creditor action and giving distressed debtors an opportunity to seek professional guidance on the best way forward. They do not provide a debt resolution per se, but rather facilitate the finding of such a solution. For general background information see "Debt respite scheme" in the Introduction to Vol.1 of this edition.

This breathing space regime has been widely used since its inception. The standard breathing space was triggered on 45,710 occasions up to end of January 2022. The mental health crisis regime was used on 696 occasions in the same period.

As one might have suspected, the widespread usage has not translated into a flood of litigation. The most significant reported decision is that of HH Judge Matthews in *Axnoller Events Ltd v Brake* [2021] EWHC 2308 (Ch). This particular ruling (which builds upon observations in his earlier decision in the case reported at [2021] EWHC 1500 (Ch)) forms but part of a complex web of fiercely contested litigation. It deals with liability for costs and casts light on the mental health crisis element in Pt 3 of the 2020 Regulations by clarifying the effect of the moratorium, the role of the debt adviser, the nature of a qualifying debt and moratorium debt. Regulations 10, 15, 17 and 19 are commented upon. HH Judge Matthews rejected an application by creditors to cancel the moratorium on the grounds of alleged unfair prejudice. A moratorium was obtained in *Lees v Kaye* [2022] EWHC 1151 (QB) to render a landlord's eviction and sale of a flat against the leaseholder null and void under reg.7 and the leaseholder was entitled to an order restoring the pre-eviction position.

Guidance for creditors on the moratorium was reissued as updated on 31 May 2022 and is available at *https://www.gov.uk/government/publications/debt-respite-scheme-breathing-space-guidance/debt-respite-scheme-breathing-space-guidance-for-creditors* and guidance for money advisors is similarly available at *https://www.gov.uk/government/publications/debt-respite-scheme-breathing-space-guidance/debt-respite-scheme-breathing-space-guidance-for-money-advisers.*

Note also the amendments made to the Financial Guidance and Claims Act 2018 by s.35 of the Financial Services Act 2021. For comment on the debt respite regime note Ramsay [2021] 64 Can. Bus. L.J. 123.

The above Regulations represent the first part of the regime for debt respite schemes and on 13 May 2022 HM Treasury published a consultation on statutory debt repayment plans, including draft Debt Respite Scheme (Statutory Debt Repayment Plan etc) (England and Wales) Regulations 2022. Copies of *Statutory Debt Repayment Plan: consultation on draft regulations* and *The Debt Respite Scheme (Statutory Debt Repayment Plan etc.) (England and Wales) Draft Regulations* are available at *https://www.gov.uk/government/consultations/statutory-debt-repayment-plan-consultation* and comments are requested by 5 August 2022.

Ancillary Statutes

Companies Act 2006

Arrangements and Reconstructions: Companies in Financial Difficulty

General Note to Part 26A

Replace the note with:

The scheme of arrangement mechanism in CA 2006 Pt 26, has been a great success in recent years. It has attracted "customers" from across the world, provided they can establish a link with the English jurisdiction. With the City of London being a major hub of global finance that link is often not difficult to establish. Schemes of arrangement can be used for solvent reorganisations as well as for debt restructuring. Such schemes have a debtor-in-possession feature. But the standard scheme of arrangement has its weaknesses. The major problem is that a scheme can be scuppered by one class of creditors refusing to cooperate. This in turn has led to litigation in which certain stakeholders assert that they are part of such a distinct class in order to enjoy a power of veto. This is particularly galling when the dissentient class is out of the money anyway.

The new Pt 26A, introduced into CA 2006 by CIGA 2020 s.7 and Sch.9 and entitled "Arrangement and Reconstructions for Companies in Financial Difficulty", seeks to provide an alternative that eliminates these weak points. But as its name suggests, it can only be used by companies "in financial difficulty". Part 26A consists of ss.901A–901L of CA 2006.

Under s.901A the company must have encountered or is likely to encounter financial difficulties that affect its ability to carry on its business as a going concern. Clearly this is more flexible than requiring proof of insolvency and mirrors a "Chapter 11 type approach" (referring to Ch.11 of the US Bankruptcy Code 1978 (as amended)) to distressed firms. Companies involved in the financial services sector may be excluded by regulations made under s.901B; at the time of writing no such regulations have been made. There are standard provisions (comparable with Pt 26 ss.896–898) for the convening of meetings of members and creditors (ss.901C, 901D and 901E).

As with existing CA 2006 Pt 26, a company wishing to use this new procedure under CA 2006 Pt 26A must obtain the sanction of the court for any scheme which the court can only grant if 75% in value (but without the requirement of a majority in number: cf. Pt 26 s.899) agree to the compromise or arrangement (s.901F). The attraction in this alternative scheme is the ability to cram down (i.e. bind) dissenting classes (s.901G). This is now described as a cross-class cram down and will comply with the EU Restructuring Directive 2019/1023 art.11 (to be implemented by EU Member States by 17 July 2021, but as the UK is no longer a Member State its position on this is as yet unknown). The court can in effect overrule a dissenting class where it would not be any worse off than they would be in an alternative scenario (defined by s.901G(4)). This means that secured and preferential creditors can be brought into line in a way that is not possible at present under either the standard scheme of arrangement or indeed under a CVA. Special provision is made where the scheme is preceded by a moratorium. In such a case the moratorium creditors are debarred from voting on the scheme (s.901H). The court enjoys consequential powers when sanctioning a scheme (s.901J). Note the late insertion of s.901I which is designed to deal with employers operating occupational pension schemes by providing information rights for the Pensions Regulator. Note also the Pension Protection Fund (Moratorium and Arrangements and Reconstructions for Companies in Financial Difficulty) Regulations 2020 (SI 2020/693) (as amended by SI 2020/783). Like many of the provisions in CIGA 2020 the Government minister is given wide power under s.901L to amend associated provisions in CA 2006 in order to facilitate the operation of the new scheme model.

Part 26A retains the debtor-in-possession feature of schemes of arrangement. There was some discussion in earlier consultations about whether a supervisor should be introduced into this restructuring model but the August 2018 proposals rejected this as a mandatory component (see para.5.139).

The Chancellor of the High Court issued a new *Practice Statement (Companies: Schemes of Arrangement under Part 26 and Part 26A of the Companies Act 2006)* [2020] B.C.C. 691 on 26 June 2020. This replaces the 2002

Practice Statement [2002] 1 W.L.R. 1345; [2002] B.C.C. 355. Some discussion of this new *Practice Statement* in the context of a Pt 26 scheme proposal can be found in the judgment of Snowden J in *Re ColourOz Investment 2 LLC* [2020] EWHC 1864 (Ch); [2020] B.C.C. 926.

The Pt 26A procedure is now being used and a burgeoning case law is developing. The first case on it appears to be *Re Virgin Atlantic Airways Ltd* [2020] EWHC 2191 (Ch); [2020] B.C.C. 997 in which the court gave guidance as to the approach to be taken at a convening hearing and went on to make an order convening meetings of creditors to consider a solvent restructuring plan as proposed by the airline company which had been pushed to the brink of collapse as a result of the COVID-19 pandemic and sought to avoid administration. In his judgment Trower J cited various paragraphs of *Practice Statement (Companies: Schemes of Arrangement under Part 26 and Part 26 of the Companies Act 2006)* and some well-known cases on the procedure under Pt 26, including the recent decision of *Re Castle Trust Direct plc* [2020] EWHC 969 (Ch); [2021] B.C.C. 1 that a virtual meeting was the appropriate forum in the circumstances of the pandemic. Snowden J later sanctioned the restructuring plan (*Re Virgin Atlantic Airways Ltd* [2020] EWHC 2376 (Ch); [2020] B.C.C. 997). It has subsequently been held in *Re gategroup Guarantee Ltd* [2021] EWHC 304 (Ch); [2021] B.C.C. 549 that Pt 26A restructuring plans are a form of insolvency proceedings partly because, unlike schemes of arrangement under CA 2006 Pt 26, restructuring plans under Pt 26A are available only to companies facing actual or anticipated financial difficulties. Thus Pt 26A plans are subject to the insolvency exemption from the Lugano Convention whereas Pt 26 schemes will fall under the Convention as civil and commercial matters (in the post-Brexit world the UK has applied (in April 2020) to become a signatory to the Lugano Convention, but it is understood that the European Commission has opposed the application). The gategroup restructuring plan was eventually sanctioned ([2021] EWHC 775 (Ch); [2021] B.C.C. 722).

For the meaning of when members are "affected by" a restructuring plan under s.901C so as to be entitled to be consulted in a convened meeting, see *Re Hurricane Energy plc* [2021] EWHC 1418 (Ch), which involved a cross-class cramdown. The court refused to sanction the latter plan in *Re Hurricane Energy plc* [2021] EWHC 1759 (Ch); [2021] B.C.C. 989 as there was a realistic prospect that the company would be able to discharge its obligations to bondholders, leaving assets with potential for exploitation, which was enough to refute the contention that the dissenting shareholders would be no better off under the relevant alternative so that the threshold condition was not satisfied.

Other early instructive cases on restructuring plans demonstrating a positive approach by the courts include *Re Virgin Active Holdings Ltd* [2021] EWHC 814 (Ch) (convening hearing), [2021] EWHC 911 (Ch) (costs) and [2021] EWHC 1246 (Ch) (sanction granted) in which objections by landlords failed to prevent the plan being approved by the necessary majorities and sanctioned by the court and indicating that this may be an easier way to obtain a rent reduction than a CVA. The latter case involved a cross-class cram down under s.901G where each dissenting class of creditor would be no worse off under the plans than in the relevant alternative of administration and would receive a better return than in an administration. The court in considering its discretion, in parallel with Pt 26 scheme cases, had regard to class creditors "in the money" who had a genuine economic interest in the company, but the objections to the plan of ("out of the money") creditors who opposed the plan and had no such interest carried no weight. But in later separate proceedings, the company's guarantors of the landlords' debts were, under the wording of the plan, still liable for the shortfall resulting to the landlords under the plan as it only applied by operation of law to alter the liability of the plan company under the lease, leaving third-party liabilities of the guarantors unaffected (*Oceanfill Ltd v Nuffield Health Wellbeing Ltd* [2022] EWHC 2178 (Ch)). Further see *Re Smile Telecoms Holdings Ltd* [2021] EWHC 395 (Ch); [2021] B.C.C. 587, where a convening meeting was ordered in relation to a foreign company (registered in Mauritius) as it could be wound up as an unregistered company in England (for further proceedings in relation to convening a single class meeting of creditors to consider and approve a proposed restructuring plan, see *Re Smile Telecoms Holdings Ltd* [2022] EWHC 387 (Ch)). A plan was eventually sanctioned in *Re Smile Telecoms Holdings Ltd* [2022] EWHC 740 (Ch) in circumstances of excluding members and all but one class of creditors and despite opposition, relying on *Re ED & F Man Holdings Ltd* [2022] EWHC 687 (Ch). The first case of an administrator applying for a restructuring plan is *Re Amicus Finance plc (in admin.)* [2021] EWHC 3036 (Ch) which was sanctioned despite strong opposition by a creditor where the court considered that the applicants had shown that the creditor would be no worse off under the plan than under the alternative of immediate liquidation (including antecedent "clawback" claims, albeit that the court at a sanction hearing could not conduct a mini-trial on clawback claims).

Most of the above cases concern restructuring plans for "large" companies, often operating in the international sphere, but an application for convening meetings of creditors members was granted in *Re Houst Ltd* [2022] EWHC 1765 (Ch) concerning a company in the small to medium-sized enterprise (SME) sector which provided property management services for short-term holiday lets. A few weeks later the court ([2022] EWHC 1941 (Ch); [2022] B.C.C. 1143), in a relatively short but illuminating judgment, sanctioned the restructuring plan despite HMRC as the only preferential creditor as a single class creditor did not vote in favour of the plan (all other creditors classes and shareholders as a class voted in favour) but HMRC was—for the first time—subjected to a cram down and the plan was sanctioned because valuation evidence (the judgment was delayed while more evidence was brought) showed that HMRC would be better off than in the alternative and, further, unsecured creditors (excluding HMRC) would receive a dividend under the plan but would receive nothing in a prepack.

Commercial Rent (Coronavirus) Act 2022

Insert new Act:

(2022 Chapter 12)

An Act to make provision enabling relief from payment of certain rent debts under business tenancies adversely affected by coronavirus to be available through arbitration; and for connected purposes.

[24th March 2022]

Contents

Overview

1—(1)　**[Relief from payment of protected rent debts]** This Act enables the matter of relief from payment of protected rent debts due from the tenant to the landlord under a business tenancy to be resolved by arbitration (if not resolved by agreement).

(2)　**[Parts of Act]** In this Act–

(a)　sections 2 to 6 define for the purposes of this Act the terms "protected rent debt", "the matter of relief from payment" and other key terms used in this Act;

(b)　Part 2 provides for statutory arbitration between the landlord and the tenant under a business tenancy in relation to the matter of relief from payment of a protected rent debt;

(c)　Part 3 provides for temporary restrictions on the availability of certain remedies and insolvency arrangements that would otherwise be available in relation to a protected rent debt.

(3)　**[No effect of agreements]** Nothing in this Act is to be taken as–

(a)　affecting the capacity of the parties to a business tenancy to resolve by agreement, at any time, the matter of relief from payment of a protected rent debt (or any other matter relating to the tenancy), or

(b)　preventing an agreement resolving the matter of relief from payment of a protected rent debt from having effect or being enforced.

"Rent" and "business tenancy"

2—(1)　**["Rent"]** "Rent", in relation to a business tenancy, means an amount consisting of one or more of the following–

(a)　an amount payable by the tenant to the landlord under the tenancy for possession and use of the premises comprised in the tenancy (whether described as rent or otherwise);

(b)　an amount payable by the tenant to the landlord under the tenancy as a service charge;

(c)　interest on an unpaid amount within paragraph (a) or (b).

(2)　**[VAT, landlord, "service charge" in s.2(1)]** In subsection (1)–

(a)　a reference to an amount includes any VAT chargeable on that amount;

(b)　a reference to the landlord includes a person acting for the landlord (such as a managing agent);

(c)　"service charge" means an amount–

(i)　which is payable (directly or indirectly) for services, repairs, maintenance, improvements, insurance costs or the landlord's management costs (including management costs of a superior landlord which the landlord is required to pay), and

(ii)　which is a fixed amount or an amount that varies or may vary according to the relevant costs (or a combination of the two).

(3)　**["Insurance costs", "the relevant costs" in s.2(2)(c)]** In subsection (2)(c)–

(a)　"insurance costs" includes costs incurred by the landlord in connection with insuring against loss of rent or in complying with obligations under the tenancy either to insure the whole or any part of–

(i)   the premises comprised in the tenancy, and

(ii)   any common parts of a property which includes those premises,

or to pay the costs of such insurance incurred by any superior landlord;

(b)   "the relevant costs" means the costs or estimated costs incurred or to be incurred by or on behalf of the landlord in connection with the matter for which the service charge is payable, and for this purpose–

(i)   "costs" includes overheads, and

(ii)   costs are relevant costs in relation to a service charge whether they are incurred, or to be incurred, in the period for which the service charge is payable or in an earlier or later period.

(4)   **[Deduction from deposit treated as unpaid rent]** An amount drawn down by the landlord from a tenancy deposit to meet the whole or part of a rent debt is to be treated as unpaid rent due from the tenant to the landlord (and such rent is "paid" where the tenant makes good any shortfall in the deposit).

(5)   **["Business tenancy"]** "Business tenancy" means a tenancy to which Part 2 of the Landlord and Tenant Act 1954 applies.

(6)   **["English business tenancy"]** "English business tenancy" means a business tenancy comprising premises in England.

(7)   **["Welsh business tenancy"]** "Welsh business tenancy" means a business tenancy comprising premises in Wales.

"Protected rent debt"

3—(1)   **["Protected rent debt"]** A "protected rent debt" is a debt under a business tenancy consisting of unpaid protected rent.

(2)   **[When rent due is "protected rent"]** Rent due under the tenancy is "protected rent" if–

(a)   the tenancy was adversely affected by coronavirus (see section 4), and

(b)   the rent is attributable to a period of occupation by the tenant for, or for a period within, the protected period applying to the tenancy (see section 5).

(3)   **[Interest on an unpaid amount s.2(1)(a), (b)]** Rent consisting of interest on an unpaid amount within section 2(1)(a) or (b) is to be regarded for the purposes of subsection (2)(b) as attributable to the same period of occupation by the tenant as that unpaid amount.

(4)   **[Period of occupation]** A period of occupation by the tenant that began, or ended, at a time during a particular day is to be treated as including the whole of that day.

(5)   **[Attribution of part period]** If any rent due under the tenancy is attributable to a period of occupation by the tenant of which only part is of the description in subsection (2)(b), then so much of the rent as can be reasonably attributed to that part of the period is protected rent.

(6)   **[Unpaid rent under s.2(4)]** An amount treated by section 2(4) as unpaid rent is to be regarded as unpaid protected rent if the rent debt that was satisfied (in whole or part) by drawing it down from the tenancy deposit would otherwise have been a protected rent debt.

"Adversely affected by coronavirus"

4—(1)   **["Adversely affected by coronavirus"]** A business tenancy was "adversely affected by coronavirus" for the purposes of section 3(2)(a) if, for any relevant period–

(a)   the whole or part of the business carried on by the tenant at or from the premises comprised in the tenancy, or

(b)   the whole or part of those premises,

was of a description subject to a closure requirement.

(2)   [**"Closure requirement", "relevant period"**] For this purpose–

     (a)   "closure requirement" means a requirement imposed by coronavirus regulations which is expressed as an obligation–

         (i)   to close businesses, or parts of businesses, of a specified description, or

         (ii)   to close premises, or parts of premises, of a specified description; and

     (b)   "relevant period" means a period beginning at or after 2 p.m. on 21 March 2020 and ending at or before–

         (i)   11.55 p.m. on 18 July 2021, for English business tenancies, or

         (ii)   6 a.m. on 7 August 2021, for Welsh business tenancies.

(3)   [**Requirement expressed obligation to close businesses or premises**] A requirement expressed as an obligation to close businesses or premises of a specified description, or parts of businesses or premises of a specified description, every day at particular times is to be regarded for the purposes of subsection (2)(a) as a closure requirement.

(4)   [**Where specific limited activities allowed by regulations**] It is immaterial for the purposes of subsection (2)(a) that specific limited activities were (as an exception) allowed by the regulations to be carried on despite the obligation to close (and accordingly the fact they were permitted or carried on is to be disregarded in determining whether the tenancy was adversely affected by coronavirus).

(5)   [**Where business not carried on solely from premises**] Where the premises comprised in the tenancy were occupied by the tenant for the purposes of a business not carried on solely at or from those premises, the reference in subsection (1)(a) to the business carried on at or from the premises is to so much of the business as was carried on at or from the premises.

(6)   [**"Coronavirus regulations"**] In this section "coronavirus regulations" means regulations–

     (a)   made under section 45C of the Public Health (Control of Disease) Act 1984 (whether or not also made under any other power), and

     (b)   expressed to be made in response to the threat to public health posed by the incidence or spread of coronavirus.

"Protected period"

5—(1)   [**"Protected period"**] The "protected period", in relation to a business tenancy adversely affected by coronavirus, is the period beginning with 21 March 2020 and ending with–

     (a)   where the business tenancy comprises premises in England–

         (i)   if subsection (2) identifies a day earlier than 18 July 2021, that day, or

         (ii)   in any other case, 18 July 2021;

     (b)   where the business tenancy comprises premises in Wales–

         (i)   if subsection (2) identifies a day earlier than 7 August 2021, that day, or

         (ii)   in any other case, 7 August 2021.

(2)   [**Relevant day for s.5(1)(a)(i), (b)(i)**] The relevant day for the purposes of subsection (1)(a)(i) or (b)(i) is the last day on which (or for part of which)–

     (a)   the whole or part of the business carried on by the tenant at or from the premises, or

     (b)   the whole or part of those premises,

was of a description subject to either a closure requirement or a specific coronavirus restriction.

(3) **["Specific coronavirus restriction" in s.5(2)]** In subsection (2) "specific coronavirus restriction" means a restriction or requirement (other than a closure requirement) imposed by coronavirus regulations which regulated any aspect of–

    (a) the way a business, or a part of a business, of any specified description was to be carried on, or

    (b) the way any premises, or any part of premises, of a specified description were or was to be used.

(4) **[What not specific coronavirus restriction]** But for the purposes of subsection (3)–

    (a) requirements to display or provide information on premises (or parts of premises), and

    (b) restrictions applying more generally than to specific descriptions of businesses or premises (or parts of businesses or premises),

are not specific coronavirus restrictions.

(5) **["Closure requirement", "coronavirus regulations" in s.5]** In this section "closure requirement" and "coronavirus regulations" have the same meaning as in section 4 .

"The matter of relief from payment"

6—(1) **["The matter of relief from payment"]** References to the matter of relief from payment of a protected rent debt are to all issues relating to the questions–

    (a) whether there is a protected rent debt of any amount, and

    (b) if so, whether the tenant should be given relief from payment of that debt and, if so, what relief.

(2) **["Relief from payment"]** "Relief from payment", in relation to a protected rent debt, means any one or more of the following–

    (a) writing off the whole or any part of the debt;

    (b) giving time to pay the whole or any part of the debt, including by allowing the whole or any part of the debt to be paid by instalments;

    (c) reducing (including to zero) any interest otherwise payable by the tenant under the terms of the tenancy in relation to the whole or any part of the debt.

PART 2

ARBITRATION

Approved arbitration bodies

Approval of arbitration bodies

7—(1) **[Power of Secretary of State to approve bodies]** The Secretary of State may approve one or more bodies to carry out the functions under section 8 (and a body which is for the time being so approved is referred to in this Act as an "approved arbitration body").

(2) **[Only suitable bodies to be approved]** The Secretary of State may only approve a body which the Secretary of State considers to be suitable to carry out those functions.

(3) **[Power of Secretary of State to withdraw approval]** The Secretary of State may withdraw an approval given under subsection (1) if the Secretary of State considers that the body is no longer suitable to carry out those functions.

(4)   **[Notice to body]** Where the Secretary of State proposes to withdraw an approval given under subsection (1), the Secretary of State must notify the body in question and give the body an opportunity to make representations.

(5)   **[Arrangements regarding fees]** Where an approval given under subsection (1) is withdrawn from a body, the Secretary of State must make arrangements relating to–

    (a)   the repayment of any fees or expenses already paid to the body (if any), and

    (b)   the body's entitlement (if any) to fees or expenses.

(6)   **[Acts done by body before approval withdrawn valid]** The withdrawal of an approval given under subsection (1) does not affect the validity of anything done by or in relation to the body in question before that withdrawal.

(7)   **[List of approved arbitration bodies]** The Secretary of State must maintain and publish a list of approved arbitration bodies.

Functions of approved arbitration bodies

8—(1)   **[List of approved arbitrators]** An approved arbitration body has the following functions–

    (a)   to maintain a list of arbitrators who–

        (i)   are available to act as arbitrators under this Part (whether alone or as a member of a panel of arbitrators), and

        (ii)   appear to the body to be suitable, by virtue of their qualifications or experience, to act as such,

    (b)   to appoint an arbitrator or panel of arbitrators from that list to deal with the matter of relief from payment of a protected rent debt referred to the body for arbitration under this Part,

    (c)   where an arbitrator appointed by the body resigns, dies or otherwise ceases to hold office, to appoint another arbitrator from that list to fill the vacancy,

    (d)   to set, collect and pay its fees and the fees of an arbitrator appointed by it,

    (e)   to oversee any arbitration in relation to which it has appointed an arbitrator or panel of arbitrators, and

    (f)   to remove an arbitrator appointed by it from a case on any one of the grounds in subsection (2).

(2)   **[Grounds for removal from a case]** The grounds for removal are–

    (a)   that circumstances exist that give rise to justifiable doubts as to the impartiality or independence of the arbitrator,

    (b)   that the arbitrator does not possess the qualifications required for the arbitration,

    (c)   that the arbitrator is physically or mentally incapable of conducting the arbitration or there are justifiable doubts as to their capacity to do so, or

    (d)   that the arbitrator has refused or failed to properly conduct the arbitration, or to use all reasonable despatch in conducting the proceedings or making an award, and that substantial injustice has been or will be caused to the parties.

(3)   **[Arbitrators to be independent from parties to arbitration]** An approved arbitration body must ensure that an arbitrator or panel of arbitrators appointed by it under subsection (1)(b) is independent from the parties to the arbitration.

(4)   **[Where arbitrator ceases to hold office]** Where an arbitrator resigns, dies or otherwise ceases to hold office, an approved arbitration body must make arrangements relating to–

(a)   the repayment of any fees or expenses already paid to the arbitrator (if any), and

(b)   the arbitrator's entitlement (if any) to fees or expenses.

(5)   **[Body to report to Secretary of State]** Where requested by, or as agreed with, the Secretary of State, an approved arbitration body must provide a report to the Secretary of State containing details of–

(a)   the exercise by the approved body of its functions under this section, and

(b)   any arbitrations overseen by the approved body under subsection (1)(e), including the progress of, and any awards made in relation to, such arbitrations.

(6)   **[Fees to be published on body's website]** An approved arbitration body must publish on its website the fees payable in relation to arbitrations referred to it under this Part.

References to arbitration by tenant or landlord

Period for making a reference to arbitration

9—(1)   **[Where tenant and landlord are not in agreement]** This section applies where the tenant and the landlord under a business tenancy are not in agreement as to the resolution of the matter of relief from payment of a protected rent debt.

(2)   **[Reference by 23 September 2022]** A reference to arbitration may be made by either the tenant or the landlord within the period of six months beginning with the day on which this Act is passed.

(3)   **[Power of Secretary of State to extend period by regulations]** The Secretary of State may by regulations made by statutory instrument extend the period allowed by subsection (2) for making references to arbitration in the case of–

(a)   English business tenancies,

(b)   Welsh business tenancies, or

(c)   English business tenancies and Welsh business tenancies.

(4)   **[Statutory instrument subject to annulment]** A statutory instrument containing regulations under subsection (3) is subject to annulment in pursuance of a resolution of either House of Parliament.

Requirements for making a reference to arbitration

10—(1)   **[Notification of intention to make reference]** Before making a reference to arbitration–

(a)   the tenant or landlord must notify the other party ("the respondent") of their intention to make a reference, and

(b)   the respondent may, within 14 days of receipt of the notification under paragraph (a), submit a response.

(2)   **[Reference more than 14 days after period for response]** A reference to arbitration must not be made before–

(a)   the end of the period of 14 days after the day on which the response under subsection (1)(b) is received, or

(b)   if no such response is received, the end of the period of 28 days beginning with the day on which the notification under subsection (1)(a) is served.

(3)   **[No reference where tenant subject to CVA, IVA or compromise/arrangement]** A reference to arbitration may not be made, an arbitrator may not be appointed, and no formal proposal under section 11(2) or (4) may be made, where the tenant that owes a protected rent debt is subject to one of the following–

(a) a company voluntary arrangement which relates to any protected rent debt that has been approved under section 4 of the Insolvency Act 1986,

(b) an individual voluntary arrangement which relates to any protected rent debt that has been approved under section 258 of that Act, or

(c) a compromise or arrangement which relates to any protected rent debt that has been sanctioned under section 899 or 901F of the Companies Act 2006.

(4) **[Reference made to be to approved arbitration body]** A reference to arbitration must be made to an approved arbitration body.

(5) **[No appointment of arbitrator]** After a reference to arbitration has been made, an arbitrator may not be appointed, and no formal proposal under section 11(2) or (4) may be made, during any period where the tenant that owes a protected rent debt is the debtor under one of the following–

(a) a company voluntary arrangement which relates to any protected rent debt that has been proposed and is awaiting a decision under section 4 of the Insolvency Act 1986,

(b) an individual voluntary arrangement which relates to any protected rent debt that has been proposed and is awaiting a decision under section 258 of that Act, or

(c) a compromise or arrangement which relates to any protected rent debt that has been applied for and is awaiting a decision under section 899 or 901F of the Companies Act 2006.

(6) **[CVA or compromise/arrangement applicable to LLPs]** This section, so far as relating to a company voluntary arrangement and a compromise or arrangement under section 899 or 901F of the Companies Act 2006, applies to limited liability partnerships (as well as to companies).

Proposals for resolving the matter of relief from payment

Proposals for resolving the matter of relief from payment

11—(1) **[Reference to include formal proposal]** A reference to arbitration must include a formal proposal for resolving the matter of relief from payment of a protected rent debt.

(2) **[Other party's formal proposal in response within 14 days]** The other party to the arbitration may put forward a formal proposal in response within the period of 14 days beginning with the day on which the proposal under subsection (1) is received.

(3) **[Formal proposal accompanied by supporting evidence]** A formal proposal under subsection (1) or (2) must be accompanied by supporting evidence.

(4) **[Revised formal proposal within 28 days]** Each party may put forward a revised formal proposal within the period of 28 days beginning with the day on which the party gives a formal proposal to the other party under subsection (1) or (2).

(5) **[Revised formal proposal accompanied by supporting evidence]** A revised formal proposal must be accompanied by any further supporting evidence.

(6) **[Extension of time periods in s.11(2), (4)]** The periods in subsections (2) and (4) may be extended–

(a) by agreement between the parties, or

(b) by the arbitrator where the arbitrator considers that it would be reasonable in all the circumstances.

(7) **["Formal proposal"]** In this section "formal proposal" means a proposal which is–

(a) made on the assumption that the reference is not dismissed for a reason set out in section 13(2) or (3),

(b) expressed to be made for the purposes of this section, and

(c) given to the other party and the arbitrator.

Written statements

12—(1) **[Application of section]** This section applies to any written statement provided to the arbitrator by a party (whether made by the party or another person) which relates to a matter relevant to the arbitration.

(2) **[Verification by statement of truth]** The written statement must be verified by a statement of truth.

(3) **[Unverified statement disregarded]** The written statement may be disregarded by the arbitrator if it is not so verified.

Arbitration awards

Arbitration awards available

13—(1) **[Awards open to arbitrator]** This section sets out the awards open to the arbitrator on a reference under this Part.

(2) **[When reference to be dismissed]** If the arbitrator determines that–

(a) the parties have by agreement resolved the matter of relief from payment of a protected rent debt before the reference was made,

(b) the tenancy in question is not a business tenancy, or

(c) there is no protected rent debt,

the arbitrator must make an award dismissing the reference.

(3) **[Dismissal if business not viable]** If, after assessing the viability of the tenant's business, the arbitrator determines that (at the time of the assessment) the business–

(a) is not viable, and

(b) would not be viable even if the tenant were to be given relief from payment of any kind,

the arbitrator must make an award dismissing the reference.

(4) **[Dismissal if business viable after assessment]** Subsection (5) applies if, after making that assessment, the arbitrator determines that (at the time of the assessment) the business–

(a) is viable, or

(b) would become viable if the tenant were to be given relief from payment of any kind.

(5) **[Arbitrator to resolve matter of relief from payment]** In that case the arbitrator must resolve the matter of relief from payment of a protected rent debt by–

(a) considering whether the tenant should receive any relief from payment and, if so, what relief, and

(b) making an award in accordance with section 14.

Arbitrator's award on the matter of relief from payment

14—(1) **[Application of section]** This section applies where the arbitrator is considering how to resolve the matter of relief from payment of a protected rent debt as required by section 13(5).

(2) **[Arbitrator to consider any final proposal]** Before determining what award to make the arbitrator must consider any final proposal put forward to it by a party under section 11.

(3)   **[Where both parties put forward final proposals]** Where both parties put forward final proposals under section 11–

    (a)   if the arbitrator considers that both proposals are consistent with the principles in section 15 the arbitrator must make the award set out in whichever of them the arbitrator considers to be the most consistent;

    (b)   if the arbitrator considers that one proposal is consistent with the principles in section 15 but the other is not, the arbitrator must make the award set out in the proposal that is consistent.

(4)   **[Where only party making reference puts forward final proposal]** Where only the party making the reference to arbitration puts forward a final proposal under section 11, the arbitrator must make the award set out in the proposal if the arbitrator considers that the proposal is consistent with the principles in section 15.

(5)   **[Otherwise award arbitrator considers appropriate]** Otherwise, the arbitrator must make whatever award the arbitrator considers appropriate (applying the principles in section 15).

(6)   **[Award]** An award under this section may–

    (a)   give the tenant relief from payment of the debt as set out in the award, or

    (b)   state that the tenant is to be given no relief from payment of the debt.

(7)   **[Payment period where tenant given time to pay]** Where an award under subsection (6)(a) gives the tenant time to pay an amount (including an instalment), the payment date must be within the period of 24 months beginning with the day after the day on which the award is made.

(8)   **["The payment date" in s.14(7)]** In subsection (7) "the payment date" means the day specified in the award as the day on which the amount concerned falls due for payment.

(9)   **[Effect of giving tenant relief from payment]** An award giving the tenant relief from payment of a protected rent debt is to be taken as altering the effect of the terms of tenancy in relation to the protected rent constituting the debt.

(10)   **[Meaning of s.14(9)]** Subsection (9) means, in particular, that–

    (a)   the tenant is not to be regarded as in breach of covenant by virtue of–

        (i)   non-payment of an amount written off by the award, or

        (ii)   failure to pay an amount payable under the terms of the award before it falls due under those terms;

    (b)   a guarantor of the tenant's obligation to pay rent, or a former tenant who is otherwise liable for a failure by the tenant to pay rent, is not liable in respect of anything mentioned in paragraph (a)(i) or (ii);

    (c)   a person other than the tenant who is liable for the payment of rent on an indemnity basis is not liable–

        (i)   to pay any unpaid protected rent written off by the award, or

        (ii)   to pay an amount payable under the terms of the award before it falls due under those terms;

    (d)   any amount payable under the terms of the award is to be treated for the purposes of the tenancy as rent payable under the tenancy.

(11)   **["Final proposal" in s.14]** In this section "final proposal" means–

    (a)   the revised formal proposal put forward by a party under section 11(4), or

(b) if there is no revised formal proposal put forward by a party, the formal proposal put forward by the party under section 11(1) or (2).

Arbitrator's principles

15—(1) **[The principles]** The principles in this section are–

(a) that any award should be aimed at–

    (i) preserving (in a case falling within section 13(4)(a)), or

    (ii) restoring and preserving (in a case falling within section 13(4)(b)),

the viability of the business of the tenant, so far as that is consistent with preserving the landlord's solvency, and

(b) that the tenant should, so far as it is consistent with the principle in paragraph (a) to do so, be required to meet its obligations as regards the payment of protected rent in full and without delay.

(2) **[Viability of tenant's business and landlord's solvency for s.15(1) purposes]** In considering the viability of the tenant's business and the landlord's solvency for the purposes of subsection (1), the arbitrator must disregard anything done by the tenant or the landlord with a view to manipulating their financial affairs so as to improve their position in relation to an award to be made under section 14.

(3) **[Meaning of when landlord is "solvent"]** For the purposes of this section, the landlord is "solvent" unless the landlord is, or is likely to become, unable to pay their debts as they fall due.

Arbitrator: assessment of "viability" and "solvency"

16—(1) **[What arbitrator to have regard to]** In assessing the viability of the business of the tenant, the arbitrator must, so far as known, have regard to–

(a) the assets and liabilities of the tenant, including any other tenancies to which the tenant is a party,

(b) the previous rental payments made under the business tenancy from the tenant to the landlord,

(c) the impact of coronavirus on the business of the tenant, and

(d) any other information relating to the financial position of the tenant that the arbitrator considers appropriate.

(2) **[Arbitrator to regard in assessing landlord's solvency]** In assessing the solvency of the landlord, the arbitrator must, so far as known, have regard to–

(a) the assets and liabilities of the landlord, including any other tenancies to which the landlord is a party, and

(b) any other information relating to the financial position of the landlord that the arbitrator considers appropriate.

(3) **[What arbitrator to disregard]** In making an assessment under subsection (1) or (2), the arbitrator must disregard the possibility of the tenant or the landlord (as the case may be)–

(a) borrowing money, or

(b) restructuring its business.

Timing of arbitrator's award

17—(1) **[Period allowed]** Subject to subsection (2), the arbitrator must make an award under section 14 as soon as reasonably practicable after–

    (a)   where both parties have put forward a final proposal, the day on which the latest final proposal is received, or

    (b)   otherwise, the last day on which a party may put forward a revised formal proposal (see section 11(4)).

(2)   **[Period following conclusion of oral hearing]** Where an oral hearing is held (see section 20), the arbitrator must make an award within the period of 14 days beginning with the day on which the hearing concludes.

(3)   **[Extension of period following conclusion of oral hearing]** The period in subsection (2) may be extended–

    (a)   by agreement between the parties, or

    (b)   by the arbitrator where the arbitrator considers that it would be reasonable in all the circumstances to do so.

(4)   **["Final proposal"]** In this section "final proposal" has the same meaning as in section 14(11) .

Publication of award

18—(1)   **[Application of section]** This section applies when the arbitrator has made an award on a reference under this Part.

(2)   **[Publication of award with reasons]** The arbitrator must publish the award together with the reasons for making it, subject as follows.

(3)   **[Exclusion of confidential information]** The arbitrator must exclude confidential information from anything published under this section, unless the arbitrator has been notified by the person to whom it relates that the person consents to its publication.

(4)   **["Confidential information" in s.18(3)]** In subsection (3) "confidential information" means information which the arbitrator is satisfied is–

    (a)   commercial information relating to a party or to any other person the disclosure of which would, or might, significantly harm the legitimate business interests of the person to which it relates, or

    (b)   information relating to the private affairs of an individual the disclosure of which would, or might, significantly harm that individual's interests.

Arbitration fees and oral hearings

Arbitration fees and expenses

19—(1)   **[References to arbitration fees in s.19]** In this section references to arbitration fees are to–

    (a)   the arbitrator's fees and expenses (including any oral hearing fees), and

    (b)   the fees and expenses of any approved arbitration body concerned.

(2)   **[Power of Secretary of State to make regulations]** The Secretary of State may by regulations made by statutory instrument specify limits on arbitration fees, which may differ depending on the amount of protected rent debt in question.

(3)   **[Statutory instrument subject to annulment]** A statutory instrument containing regulations under subsection (2) is subject to annulment in pursuance of a resolution of either House of Parliament.

(4)   **[Applicant to pay arbitration fees in advance]** The applicant must pay arbitration fees (other than oral hearing fees) in advance of the arbitration taking place.

(5) **[Respondent to reimburse half successful applicant's fees]** When the arbitrator makes an award under section 13 or 14, the arbitrator must (subject to subsection (6)) also make an award requiring the other party to reimburse the applicant for half the arbitration fees paid under subsection (4).

(6) **[Different proportion under s.19(5)]** The general rule in subsection (5) does not apply if the arbitrator considers it more appropriate in the circumstances of the case to award a different proportion (which may be zero).

(7) **[Parties to meet own legal/other costs]** Except as provided by subsection (5) and section 20(6), the parties must meet their own legal or other costs.

(8) **[Legal/other costs not recoverable under term of business tenancy]** Legal or other costs incurred in connection with arbitration (including arbitration fees) are not recoverable by virtue of any term of the business tenancy concerned.

(9) **["Applicant" in s.19]** In this section, "applicant" means the party which made the reference to arbitration.

Oral hearings

20—(1) **[Requested by either or both parties]** An oral hearing must be held where either or both of the parties make a request to the arbitrator.

(2) **[Period for holding hearing]** An oral hearing must be held within the period of 14 days beginning with the day on which the arbitrator receives a request under subsection (1).

(3) **[Extension of s.20(2) period]** The period in subsection (2) may be extended–

    (a) by agreement between the parties, or

    (b) by the arbitrator where the arbitrator considers that it would be reasonable in all the circumstances to do so.

(4) **[Liability for hearing fees]** Where both parties request an oral hearing, the parties are jointly and severally liable to pay the hearing fees in advance.

(5) **[Single party liability for hearing fees]** Where one of the parties requests an oral hearing, that party must pay the hearing fees in advance.

(6) **[Respondent to reimburse half hearing fees to successful applicant]** When the arbitrator makes an award under section 13 or 14 the arbitrator must (subject to subsection (7)) also make an award requiring the other party to reimburse the applicant for half the hearing fees.

(7) **[Different proportion under s.20(6)]** The general rule in subsection (6) does not apply if the arbitrator considers it more appropriate in all the circumstances to award a different proportion (which may be zero).

(8) **[Oral hearing to be held in public]** An oral hearing must be held in public unless the parties agree otherwise.

Guidance

Guidance

21—(1) **[Power of Secretary of State to issue]** The Secretary of State may issue guidance to–

    (a) arbitrators about the exercise of their functions under this Part, and

    (b) tenants and landlords about making a reference to arbitration under this Part.

(2) **[Guidance may be revised]** The Secretary of State may revise any guidance issued under this section.

(3) **[Publication of guidance]** The Secretary of State must arrange for any guidance issued or revised under this section to be published.

Modification of Part 1 of the Arbitration Act 1996

Modification of Part 1 of the Arbitration Act 1996

22— Schedule 1 modifies Part 1 of the Arbitration Act 1996 in relation to arbitrations under this Part.

PART 3

MORATORIUM ON CERTAIN REMEDIES AND INSOLVENCY ARRANGEMENTS

Temporary moratorium on enforcement of protected rent debts

23—(1) **[Content of Sch.2]** Schedule 2 contains–

    (a) provision preventing a landlord who is owed a protected rent debt from using the following remedies in relation to (or on the basis of) the debt during the moratorium period–

        (i) making a debt claim in civil proceedings;

        (ii) using the commercial rent arrears recovery power;

        (iii) enforcing a right of re-entry or forfeiture;

        (iv) using a tenant's deposit;

    (b) retrospective provision in relation to certain debt claims made by such a landlord before the start of the moratorium period for the protected rent debt;

    (c) provision relating to the right of such a landlord during the moratorium period to appropriate any rent paid by the tenant;

    (d) retrospective provision in relation to the right of such a landlord to appropriate any rent paid by the tenant before the start of the moratorium period for the protected rent debt;

    (e) provision connected with certain things mentioned in paragraphs (a) to (d).

(2) **["The moratorium period" in s.23]** In this section "the moratorium period", in relation to a protected rent debt, is the period–

    (a) beginning with the day on which this Act is passed, and

    (b) ending–

        (i) where the matter of relief from payment of the protected rent debt is not referred to arbitration within the period of six months beginning with that day, with the last day of that period, or

        (ii) where that matter is referred to arbitration, with the day on which the arbitration concludes.

(3) **[Extension of s.23(2)(b)(i) period]** Subsection (2) is subject to any extension of the period mentioned in paragraph (b)(i) that–

    (a) is made by or by virtue of section 24, and

    (b) has effect in relation to the protected rent debt.

(4) **[Conclusion of arbitration under s.23(2)(b)]** For the purposes of subsection (2)(b) an arbitration concludes when–

    (a) the arbitration proceedings are abandoned or withdrawn by the parties,

    (b)   the time period for appealing expires without an appeal being brought, or

    (c)   any appeal brought within that period is finally determined, abandoned or withdrawn.

(5)   **["Arbitration" in s.23]** In this section "arbitration" means arbitration under Part 2 .

Alteration of moratorium period

24—(1)   **["Extension regulations"]** In this section "extension regulations" means regulations under section 9(3) extending the period allowed by section 9(2) for making references to arbitration.

(2)   **[Extension of s.23(2)(b)(i) period]** Where extension regulations made by virtue of section 9(3)(a) or (c) extend that period in the case of English business tenancies, the period specified in section 23(2)(b)(i), so far as it applies in the case of a protected rent debt under an English business tenancy, is extended for the same period of time.

(3)   **[Application of s.23(4)]** Subsection (4) below applies where extension regulations made by virtue of section 9(3)(b) or (c) extend that period in the case of Welsh business tenancies.

(4)   **[Power of Secretary of State to make s.23(2)(b)(i) extension regulations]** The Secretary of State may by regulations made by statutory instrument extend the period specified in section 23(2)(b)(i), so far as it applies in the case of a protected rent debt under a Welsh business tenancy, for the same period of time.

(5)   **[What s.23(4) regulations to provide]** Regulations under subsection (4) must provide for the extension referred to in that subsection–

    (a)   to have effect for the purposes of this Part including the purposes of Schedule 2, or

    (b)   to have effect for the purposes of this Part other than the purposes of Schedule 2.

(6)   **[Where consent of Welsh Ministers needed]** The power to make the provision referred to in subsection (5)(a) is exercisable only with the consent of the Welsh Ministers to the extension having effect for the purposes of Schedule 2 other than the purposes of paragraph 3(6) and (7).

(7)   **[Statutory instrument subject to annulment]** A statutory instrument containing regulations under subsection (4) is subject to annulment in pursuance of a resolution of either House of Parliament.

Temporary restriction on initiating certain insolvency arrangements

25—(1)   **[Application of section]** This section applies where the matter of relief from payment of a protected rent debt has been referred to arbitration.

(2)   **[No CVA, IVA or compromise/arrangement]** During the relevant period–

    (a)   no proposal for a company voluntary arrangement under section 1 of the Insolvency Act 1986 which relates to the whole or part of the debt may be made,

    (b)   no proposal for an individual voluntary arrangement under section 256A of that Act, or an application for an interim order under section 253 of that Act, which relates to the whole or part of the debt may be made, and

    (c)   no application for a compromise or arrangement under section 896 or 901C of the Companies Act 2006 (court orders for holding of meetings) which relates to the whole or part of the debt may be made.

(3)   **["The relevant period"]** In this section "the relevant period" means the period beginning with the day on which an arbitrator is appointed and ending with–

    (a)   where the arbitrator makes an award in accordance with section 14, the day which is 12 months after the day on which that award is made,

    (b)   where the arbitrator makes an award dismissing a reference under section 13(2) or (3), the day on which that award is made,

(c) where an award made in accordance with section 14 is set aside on appeal, the day on which that decision is made, or

(d) where the arbitration proceedings are abandoned or withdrawn by the parties, the day of that abandonment or withdrawal.

(4) **[CVA or compromise/arrangement applicable to LLPs]** This section, so far as relating to a company voluntary arrangement and a compromise or arrangement under section 899 or 901F of the Companies Act 2006, applies to limited liability partnerships (as well as to companies).

Temporary restriction on initiating arbitration proceedings

26—(1) **[No arbitration proceedings during the moratorium period]** The tenant or the landlord under a business tenancy may not initiate arbitration proceedings (other than an arbitration under Part 2) in relation to a protected rent debt during the moratorium period for the debt, unless the other party agrees.

(2) **["The moratorium period" in s.26]** In this section "the moratorium period" has the meaning given by section 23(2) .

Temporary restriction on winding-up petitions and petitions for bankruptcy orders

27 Schedule 3 contains temporary provision in relation to winding up petitions and petitions for bankruptcy orders.

Note

Section 27, insofar as relating Sch.3 para.1, in force as from 1 April 2022 by virtue of s.31(5).

PART 4

FINAL PROVISIONS

Power to apply Act in relation to future periods of coronavirus control

28—(1) **[Power of Secretary of State to make regulations]** The Secretary of State may by regulations provide for this Act (apart from this section) to apply again in relation to rent debts under business tenancies adversely affected by closure requirements.

(2) **[Application of regulations]** Regulations under this section may–

(a) be made so as to apply in relation to–

    (i) English business tenancies,

    (ii) Welsh business tenancies, or

    (iii) English business tenancies and Welsh business tenancies;

(b) exclude the provisions mentioned in subsection (10)(a) to (c) from the provisions being re-applied in relation to Welsh business tenancies.

(3) **[Business tenancy adversely affected by closure requirement]** A business tenancy is adversely affected by a closure requirement for the purposes of subsection (1) if–

(a) the whole or part of a business carried on at or from the premises comprised in the tenancy, or

(b) the whole or part of those premises,

is of a description subject to a closure requirement imposed at any time after 7 August 2021.

(4) **["Closure requirement" in s.28]** In this section "closure requirement" means a requirement imposed by regulations as a public health response to coronavirus and expressed as an obligation–

(a) to close businesses, or parts of businesses, of a specified description, or

(b)   to close premises, or parts of premises, of a specified description.

(5)   **["Coronavirus" in s.28(4)]** In subsection (4) "coronavirus" means severe acute respiratory syndrome coronavirus 2 (SARS-CoV-2).

(6)   **[Power exercisable]** The power under this section is exercisable whether or not the closure requirement remains in force when the regulations are made.

(7)   **[Application of s.28(3)–(5)]** Subsections (3) to (5) of section 4 apply for the purposes of this section as they apply for the purposes of section 4.

(8)   **[What provisions may provide for]** Regulations under this section may–

(a)   provide for provisions of this Act to apply with such necessary modifications as are specified in the regulations;

(b)   make different provision for England and for Wales;

(c)   make incidental, supplemental, consequential, saving or transitional provision (including provision amending or otherwise modifying an Act of Parliament).

(9)   **["Modifications" in s.28(8)(a) and when necessary]** For the purposes of subsection (8)(a)–

(a)   "modifications" means omissions, additions or variations, and

(b)   modifications are "necessary" if they appear to the Secretary of State to be necessary for the provisions being re-applied to operate correctly in relation to business tenancies adversely affected by the closure requirements in question.

(10)   **[Consent of Welsh Ministers]** The power under this section is exercisable only with the consent of the Welsh Ministers so far as it relates to the re-application, in relation to Welsh business tenancies, of–

(a)   Schedule 2 apart from paragraph 3(6) and (7),

(b)   section 23 so far as relating to Schedule 2 apart from paragraph 3(6) and (7), and

(c)   Part 1 and this Part, so far as relating to the provisions mentioned in paragraphs (a) and (b).

(11)   **[Regulations by statutory instrument]** Regulations under this section–

(a)   are to be made by statutory instrument, and

(b)   may not be made unless a draft of the statutory instrument containing them has been laid before and approved by a resolution of each House of Parliament.

Concurrent power for Welsh Ministers to apply moratorium provisions again

29—(1)   **[Power of Welsh Ministers]** The Welsh Ministers may exercise the power conferred by section 28, concurrently with the Secretary of State, so far as it relates to the re-application, in relation to Welsh business tenancies, of–

(a)   Schedule 2 apart from paragraph 3(6) and (7),

(b)   section 23 so far as relating to Schedule 2 apart from paragraph 3(6) and (7), and

(c)   Part 1 and this Part, so far as relating to the provisions mentioned in paragraphs (a) and (b).

(2)   **[Effect of s.28 re regulations made by Welsh Ministers]** Section 28 has effect in relation to regulations made by the Welsh Ministers by virtue of this section as if–

(a)   references to the Secretary of State were to the Welsh Ministers,

(b)   subsection (2)(a)(i) and (iii) and (b) were omitted,

(c)   in subsection (8)–

(i)   the references in paragraph (a) to provisions of this Act were references to provisions mentioned in subsection (1)(a) to (c) above, and

(ii) the reference in paragraph (c) to an Act of Parliament included a reference to an Act or Measure of Senedd Cymru,

(d)   subsection (10) were omitted, and

(e)   in subsection (11)(b), for "each House of Parliament" there were substituted "Senedd Cymru".

(3)   **[Amendment of Government of Wales Act 2006 Sch.7B para.11(6)(b)]** In Schedule 7B to the Government of Wales Act 2006 (general restrictions on legislative competence of Senedd Cymru), in paragraph 11(6)(b) (exceptions to restrictions relating to Ministers of the Crown)–

(a)   omit the "or" at the end of paragraph (vi), and

(b)   after paragraph (vii) insert

"; or

(viii) section 28 of the Commercial Rent (Coronavirus) Act 2022."

Crown application

30   This Act binds the Crown (but without prejudice to section 2(5) which secures that the business tenancies to which this Act applies are those to which Part 2 of the Landlord and Tenant Act 1954 applies).

Extent, commencement and short title

31—(1)   **[Parts 1–3 extend to England and Wales only]** Parts 1 to 3 extend to England and Wales only (except as provided by subsections (2) and (3)).

(2)   **[Provisions extended to United Kingdom]** The following provisions extend to England and Wales, Scotland and Northern Ireland–

(a)   in section 25–

(i)   subsections (1), (2)(c) and (3), and

(ii) subsection (4) so far as relating to a compromise or arrangement under section 899 or 901F of the Companies Act 2006,

(b)   Part 1 so far as relating to the provisions mentioned in paragraph (a), and

(c)   this Part.

(3)   **[Provisions extended to England and Wales and Scotland only]** The following provisions extend to England and Wales and Scotland only–

(a)   in section 25–

(i)   subsection (2)(a), and

(ii) subsection (4) so far as relating to a company voluntary arrangement,

(b)   paragraph 1 of Schedule 3 and section 27 so far as relating to that paragraph, and

(c)   Part 1 so far as relating to the provisions mentioned in paragraphs (a) and (b).

(4)   **[Act in force 24 March 2022]** This Act comes into force on the day on which it is passed (except as provided by subsection (5)).

(5)   **[Section 27 and Sch.3 para.1 into force 1 April 2022]** Paragraph 1 of Schedule 3, and section 27 so far as relating to that paragraph, comes into force on 1 April 2022.

(6)   This Act may be cited as the Commercial Rent (Coronavirus) Act 2022.

SCHEDULE 1

Section 22

MODIFICATIONS OF THE ARBITRATION ACT 1996 IN RELATION TO ARBITRATIONS UNDER THIS ACT

1—   Part 1 of the Arbitration Act 1996 has effect in relation to arbitrations under this Act as if the following were omitted–

(a)   in section 14 (commencement of arbitral proceedings), subsections (1) and (2);

(b)   in section 15 (arbitral tribunal), in subsection (1), the words "or umpire";

(c)   sections 16 to 19 (appointment of arbitrators);

(d)   in section 20 (chairman), subsections (1) and (2);

(e)   section 21 (umpire);

(f)   in section 22 (decision-making where no chairman or umpire), subsection (1);

(g)   in section 23 (revocation of the arbitrator's authority), subsections (1), (2), (3)(a), (4) and (5)(a);

(h)   in section 25 (resignation of arbitrator), subsections (1) and (2);

(i)   in section 27 (filling of vacancy), subsections (1) to (3);

(j)   in section 30 (competence of tribunal to rule on its own jurisdiction), in subsection (1), the words "Unless otherwise agreed by the parties";

(k)   in section 37 (power to appoint experts, legal advisers or assessors), in subsection (1), the words "Unless otherwise agreed by the parties";

(l)   in section 38 (general powers exercisable by the tribunal), subsections (1) to (4);

(m)   in section 39 (power to make provisional awards), in subsection (2)(a), the words "or the disposition of property";

(n)   in section 48 (remedies), subsections (1), (2) and (5)(b) and (c);

(o)   in section 49 (interest), subsections (1) to (3), (5) and (6);

(p)   in section 51 (settlement)–

    (i)   in subsection (1), the words "unless otherwise agreed by the parties"; and

    (ii)   in subsection (2), the words "if so requested by the parties and not objected to by the tribunal";

(q)   in section 52 (form of award), subsections (1) and (2);

(r)   in section 58 (effect of award), in subsection (1), the words "Unless otherwise agreed by the parties";

(s)   in section 68 (challenging the award: serious irregularity), in subsection (2)(e), the words "vested by the parties".

2—   Part 1 of the Arbitration Act 1996 has effect in relation to arbitrations under this Act as if –

(a)   in section 20 (chairman), in subsection (3), at the beginning there were inserted "Where there is a chairman,";

(b)   in section 22 (decision-making where no chairman), in subsection (2) for "If there is no such agreement" there were substituted "Where there are two or more arbitrators with no chair-man";

(c)   in section 34 (procedural and evidential matters), in subsection (1) after "matters", there were inserted "(including in relation to oral hearings held in public)";

(d)   in section 35 (consolidation of proceedings and concurrent hearings), in subsection (2), for the words from "Unless" to "has no" there were substituted "The tribunal also has";

(e)   in section 37 (power to appoint experts, legal advisers or assessors), in subsection (1)(a), after "tribunal may" there were inserted ", where agreed by the parties";

(f)   in section 68 (challenging the award: serious irregularity), in subsection (2)(c), the words "procedure agreed by the parties" were substituted by "statutory procedure";

(g)   in section 74 (immunity of arbitral institutions)–

   (i)   in subsection (1), for "appoint or nominate" there were substituted "appoint, nominate or remove";

   (ii)   in subsection (2), for "appointed or nominated", in both places, there were substituted "appointed, nominated or removed".

3   The modifications under paragraphs 1 and 2 are without prejudice to the operation of sections 94 to 98 of the Arbitration Act 1996 in relation to other provisions.

SCHEDULE 2   Section 23

TEMPORARY MORATORIUM ON ENFORCEMENT OF PROTECTED RENT DEBTS

Preliminary: interpretation

1—(1)   This Schedule applies in relation to a protected rent debt under a business tenancy.

(2)   In this Schedule–

(a)   references to "the protected debt" or "the debt" are to the whole or any part of that protected rent debt;

(b)   "the business tenancy" is the business tenancy under which the protected debt arose;

(c)   "the landlord" and "the tenant" refer respectively to the landlord and the tenant under that tenancy;

(d)   "the moratorium period", in relation to the protected debt, has the meaning given by section 23(2);

(e)   a reference to doing something "in relation to" the protected debt includes, where appropriate, its being done on the basis of the debt.

Making a debt claim

2—(1)   The landlord may not, during the moratorium period for the debt, make a debt claim to enforce the protected debt.

(2)   In this paragraph "debt claim" means a claim to enforce a debt in civil proceedings (including by a counterclaim or any other way of claiming payment of a debt in such proceedings).

Debt claims made before the day on which this Act is passed

3—(1)   This paragraph applies to proceedings on a debt claim which–

(a)   is made on or after 10 November 2021 but before the day on which this Act is passed, (b)　is made by the landlord against the tenant, and

(c)　relates to, or to debts which include, the protected rent debt.

(2)　Either of the parties to the business tenancy may apply to the court for the proceedings on the debt claim to be stayed in order to enable the matter of payment of the protected rent debt to be resolved (whether by arbitration or otherwise).

(3)　Where such an application is made in respect of proceedings on a debt claim the court must stay the proceedings (unless it is satisfied that they are not proceedings to which this paragraph applies).

(4)　Sub-paragraphs (5) to (7) apply if judgment on the debt claim is given in favour of the landlord during the period described in sub-paragraph (1)(a).

(5)　So long as the judgment debt so far as relating to the protected rent debt, or any interest on it, is unpaid, then–

(a)　the matter of relief from payment of the judgment debt so far as relating to the protected rent debt, or any interest on it, may be resolved by arbitration under Part 2 of this Act or by agreement (as if that part of the judgment debt and any interest on it were a protected rent debt), despite the judgment having been given,

(b)　the judgment debt, so far as relating to the protected rent debt or any interest on it, may not be enforced or relied on by the landlord before the end of the moratorium period for the protected rent debt, and

(c)　if relief from payment is awarded or agreed, the effect of the judgment debt is to be taken as altered in accordance with the award or agreement.

(6)　Where it comes to the attention of the officer of the court in which the judgment is entered that–

(a)　the judgment relates solely to the protected rent debt,

(b)　relief from payment of the protected rent debt has been awarded under Part 2 of this Act or agreed, and

(c)　the moratorium period for the protected rent debt has ended,

the officer must send a request to the registrar to cancel the entry in the register of judgments under section 98 of the Courts Act 2003.

(7)　Following receipt of a request under sub-paragraph (6), the registrar must cancel the entry.

(8)　In this paragraph–

"debt claim" has the same meaning as in paragraph 2;

"tenant" includes–

(a)　a person who has guaranteed the obligations of the tenant under a business tenancy,

(b)　a person other than the tenant who is liable on an indemnity basis for the payment of rent under a business tenancy, and

(c)　a former tenant who is liable for the payment of rent under a business tenancy.

Using CRAR (the commercial rent arrears recovery power)

4—(1)　The landlord may not, during the moratorium period for the protected debt, use CRAR in relation to the debt.

(2)　This means that during that period–

(a)　an authorisation to exercise CRAR on behalf of the landlord in relation to the protected debt may not be given,

(b) a notice of enforcement may not be given in relation to the protected debt on behalf of the landlord, and

(c) the protected debt is to be disregarded in calculating the net unpaid rent for the purposes of section 77 of the Tribunals, Courts and Enforcement Act 2007 (the rent recoverable using CRAR).

(3) In this paragraph "CRAR" and "notice of enforcement" have the same meaning as in Chapter 2 of Part 3 of that Act.

(4) In section 77 of that Act, after paragraph (b) of subsection (1) insert

";

(c) it is not excluded from recovery using CRAR by paragraph 4 of Schedule 2 to the Commercial Rent (Coronavirus) Act 2022 (temporary moratorium on enforcement of protected rent debts)."

Enforcing a right of re-entry or forfeiture

5—(1) The landlord may not, during the moratorium period for the protected debt, enforce, by action or otherwise, a right of re-entry or forfeiture for non-payment of the debt.

(2) No conduct by or on behalf of the landlord during the moratorium period, other than giving an express waiver in writing, is to be regarded as waiving a right of re-entry or forfeiture, under the business tenancy, for non-payment of the debt.

(3) For the purposes of determining whether the ground mentioned in section 30(1)(b) of the Landlord and Tenant Act 1954 (persistent delay in paying rent which has become due) is established in relation to the business tenancy, any failure to pay the debt during the moratorium period is to be disregarded.

6—(1) This paragraph applies where–

(a) a superior landlord enforces, by action or otherwise, a right of re-entry or forfeiture in relation to a superior tenancy during the moratorium period, and

(b) the tenant applies for relief from forfeiture in relation to its interest in the property comprised in the tenancy.

(2) For the purposes of determining whether to grant the tenant relief from forfeiture and, if so, the terms of such relief, the court must disregard any failure to pay the protected rent debt.

Using landlord's right to appropriate rent

7—(1) This paragraph applies in relation to a payment of rent under a business tenancy which is paid during the moratorium period for the debt at a time when–

(a) the tenant owes the landlord an unprotected rent debt in addition to the debt, and

(b) the tenant has not exercised the tenant's right to appropriate the payment to any particular rent debt owed to the landlord.

(2) The landlord's right to appropriate the payment must be used to apply the payment to meet the unprotected rent debt before it is applied to the protected rent debt.

(3) In this paragraph an "unprotected rent debt" is a debt consisting of–

(a) rent that is not protected rent, or

(b) interest on rent that is not protected rent.

8—(1) This paragraph applies in relation to any payment of rent under a business tenancy which was paid during the period mentioned in sub-paragraph (2) at a time when–

(a) the tenant owed the landlord an unprotected rent debt in addition to the debt, and

(b)   the tenant had not exercised the tenant's right to appropriate the payment to any particular rent debt.

(2)   The period relevant for the purposes of sub-paragraph (1) is the period–

(a)   beginning with the day after the last day of the protected period for the debt, and

(b)   ending with the day before the first day of the moratorium period for the debt.

(3)   During the moratorium period for the debt, the landlord's right to appropriate the payment must be used to apply the payment to meet the unprotected rent debt before it is applied to the protected rent debt.

(4)   If the landlord used that right during the period mentioned in sub-paragraph (2) to appropriate the rent to the debt, then–

(a)   the appropriation of the payment to the debt is ineffective to the extent of the unprotected rent debt, and

(b)   the payment is to be treated for all purposes as having been appropriated to the unprotected rent debt first.

(5)   In this paragraph "unprotected rent debt" has the same meaning as in paragraph 7 .

Using tenant's deposit to apply towards unpaid rent debt

9—(1)   This paragraph applies where a tenancy deposit is available to the landlord for the purpose of applying towards an unpaid rent debt.

(2)   The landlord may not, during the moratorium period for the debt, recover the debt from the tenancy deposit.

(3)   If the landlord has lawfully recovered the debt from the tenancy deposit before the beginning of the moratorium period, the tenant is not required to make good any shortfall in the deposit before the end of that period.

Schedule 3

Section 27

Winding-up and bankruptcy petitions

Prohibition on presenting a winding-up petition solely in relation to a protected rent debt

1—(1)   This paragraph applies where a landlord under a business tenancy is owed a protected rent debt and the tenant is a company.

(2)   The landlord may not, during the moratorium period for the debt, present a petition for the winding up of the company under section 124 of the Insolvency Act 1986 on a ground specified–

(a)   in the case of a registered company, in section 122(1)(f) of that Act, or

(b)   in the case of an unregistered company, in section 221(5)(b) of that Act,

unless the landlord is owed a debt by the company which is not a protected rent debt.

(3)   In this paragraph–

"the moratorium period", in relation to a protected rent debt, has the same meaning as in section 23;

"registered company" means a company registered under the Companies Act 2006 in England and Wales or Scotland;

"unregistered company" has the same meaning as in Part 5 of the Insolvency Act 1986 .

(4)   This paragraph, so far as relating to registered companies, applies to limited liability partnerships.

Note

Schedule 3 para.1 in force as from 1 April 2022 by virtue of s.31(5).

Prohibition on presenting a bankruptcy order petition in relation to a protected rent debt

2—(1)   This paragraph (and paragraph 3) applies where the landlord under a business tenancy is owed a protected rent debt and the tenant is an individual.

(2)   The landlord may not present a petition for a bankruptcy order against the tenant on a ground specified in section 268(1)(a) or (2) of the Insolvency Act 1986 where the demand referred to in those provisions related to any protected rent debt and was served during the relevant period.

(3)   The landlord may not present a petition for a bankruptcy order against the tenant on a ground specified in section 268(1)(b) of that Act where the judgment or order referred to in that provision related to any protected rent debt and the claim for that debt was issued during the relevant period.

(4)   If a petition mentioned in sub-paragraph (2) or (3) is presented, the court may make such order or give such directions as it thinks appropriate to restore the position to what it would have been if the petition had not been presented.

(5)   If it appears to the interim receiver or special manager that the petition is one mentioned in sub-paragraph (2) or (3), the interim receiver or special manager must refer the matter to the court to determine whether to make an order or give directions under sub-paragraph (4).

(6)   Neither the interim receiver or special manager is liable in any civil or criminal proceedings for anything done pursuant to an order made under section 286 or 370 of the Insolvency Act 1986 in relation to a petition that relates to any protected rent debt.

(7)   The "relevant period" is the period which begins on 10 November 2021 and ends with the day mentioned in section 23(2)(b) .

(8)   In this paragraph "claim" includes a counterclaim or any other way of claiming payment of a debt in civil proceedings.

(9)   This paragraph is to be regarded as having come into force on 10 November 2021.

Bankruptcy orders made before the day on which this Act is passed

3—(1)   This paragraph applies where–

    (a)   a court makes a bankruptcy order against the tenant on a petition from the landlord under section 267 of the Insolvency Act 1986,

    (b)   the order was made on or after 10 November 2021 but before the day on which this Schedule comes into force, and

    (c)   the order was not one which the court would have made had this Schedule been in force at the time.

(2)   The court is to be regarded as having had no power to make the order (and, accordingly, the order is to be regarded as void).

(3)   Neither the trustee, official receiver, interim receiver or special manager is liable in any civil or criminal proceedings for anything done pursuant to the order.

(4)   The court may make such order or give such directions as it thinks appropriate to restore the position to what it was immediately before the petition was presented.

(5)   If at any time it appears to the trustee, official receiver, interim receiver or special manager that–

    (a)   a bankruptcy order made by the court is void by virtue of sub-paragraph (2), and

    (b)   it might be appropriate for the court to make an order or give directions under sub-paragraph (4),

the trustee, official receiver, interim receiver or special manager must refer the matter to the court to determine whether to make such an order or give such directions.

Interpretation

4—(1)   In this Schedule–

    "interim receiver" means a person appointed under section 286 of the Insolvency Act 1986;

    "special manager" means a person appointed under section 370 of that Act;

    "trustee" means the trustee of a bankrupt's estate.

(2)   In this Schedule, references to the "tenant" include–

    (a)   a person who has guaranteed the obligations of the tenant under a business tenancy,

    (b)   a person other than the tenant who is liable on an indemnity basis for the payment of rent under a business tenancy, and

    (c)   a former tenant who is liable for the payment of rent under a business tenancy.

Ancillary Statutory Instruments

Insolvency Proceedings (Fees) Order 2016

Interpretation

2

Note
Add new note:

In art.2(a) the deposit of £990 on the presentation of a bankruptcy petition is increased to £1,500 and in art.2(b) the deposit of £1,600 on the presentation of a winding-up petition is increased to £2,600 by the Insolvency Proceedings (Fees) (Amendment) Order 2022 (SI 2022/929) arts 1, 2(a), (b) as from 1 November 2022.

Deposit

4—

Note
Add new note:

In art.4(1)–(9) the word "will", in each place where it occurs, is substituted by the word "must" by the Insolvency Proceedings (Fees) (Amendment) Order 2022 (SI 2022/929) arts 1, 2(c) as from 1 November 2022.

Appendix II: Forms

Companies House Forms

Corporate Voluntary Arrangement

Replace the table of Corporate Voluntary Arrangement forms:

2017	NEW RULE	FORM TITLE	1986
CVA1	2.38	Notice of voluntary arrangement taking effect	1.1
CVA2	2.40	Notice of order of revocation or suspension of CVA	1.2
CVA3	2.41	Notice of supervisor's progress report in voluntary arrangement	1.3
CVA4	2.44	Notice of termination or full implementation of voluntary arrangement	1.4
VAC	2.37	Notice of a court order in respect of a voluntary arrangement	

Appendix IV: Practice Direction: Insolvency Proceedings [2020] B.C.C. 698

General Note

Replace the note with:

This Practice Direction ("PD IP") is the latest in a succession of PDs relating to insolvency proceedings going back to 1999. It was issued on 3 July 2020 with effect from that day (except in respect of proceedings already listed for hearing in the county court: see para.2.2) and succeeded a PD of the same name which came into effect on 4 July 2018 ([2018] B.C.C. 421) to replace another 2018 PD IP which contained drafting errors and some inconsistencies with County Court business. A PD may be amended from time to time and the current version at any time is to be found at *http://www.justice.gov.uk/courts/procedure-rules/civil/rules/insolvency_pd*. For analysis of the 2018 iteration see Catterson (2018) 31 Insolv. Int. 126. PD IP 2020 contains new para.3.3(6), (7) added in light of the introduction of the moratorium contained in s.1 of CIGA 2020 and inserted as Pt A1 of IA 1986.

The PD IP is expressed (para.2.1) to replace all previous Practice Directions, Practice Statements and Practice Notes relating to insolvency proceedings except for the *Insolvency Practice Direction Relating to the Corporate Insolvency and Governance Act 2020* [2020] B.C.C. 694 dated 3 July 2020 (reproduced as App.V to this *Guide*), the *Temporary Practice Direction Supporting the Insolvency Practice Direction* [2020] B.C.C. 686 in force 6 April 2020 to 30 September 2020, replaced by the *Temporary Practice Direction (No.2) Supporting the Insolvency Practice Direction* [2020] B.C.C. 844, in force 1 October 2020 to 31 March 2021, *Temporary Practice Direction (No.3) Supporting the Insolvency Practice Direction* [2021] B.C.C. 199, in force 1 April 2021 to 30 June 2021, *Temporary Practice Direction (No.4) Supporting the Insolvency Practice Direction* [2021] B.C.C. 731, in force 1 July 2021 to 30 September 2021, and *Temporary Practice Direction (No.5) Supporting the Insolvency Practice Direction* [2021] B.C.C. 877, in force from 1 October 2021 until amended or revoked, (and reproduced as App.VII to this *Guide*) and the *Practice Statement (Companies: Schemes of Arrangement under Part 26 and Part 26A of the Companies Act 2006)* [2020] B.C.C. 691 dated 30 June 2020 (reproduced as App.VI to this *Guide*). This IPD does not affect the *Practice Direction: Directors Disqualification Proceedings* [2015] B.C.C. 224. This PD IP must be taken to have replaced *Practice Direction: Order under s.127 of the Insolvency Act 1986* [2007] B.C.C 839 which we still reproduce as App.VIII for information as it contains a useful standard form for an IA 1986 s.127 order but otherwise contains the same material.

Paragraph 3.1 on distribution of court business was applied in *Brittain v Michael Wilson & Partners Ltd* [2021] EWHC 3041 (Ch) where proceedings were pending in the Commercial Court, the company's liquidators' application under IA 1986 s.112 for directions on payment of a dividend in the liquidation was correctly issued in the Insolvency and Companies List and heard by an ICC judge who gave the directions sought.

For the meaning of "all the unsecured creditors" in para.12.8.8 (and presumably 9.11.7) see *Re Hood; Hood v Revenue and Customs Commissioners* [2019] EWHC 2236 (Ch); [2019] B.P.I.R. 1425. Paragraph 12.8.8 of the PD IP was also considered in the bankruptcy validation case of *State Bank of India v Mallya* [2021] EWHC 191 (Ch).

The procedure on full or partial transfer of business under paras 3.6 et seq. should be read in light of IR 2016 r.12.30; these provisions were discussed by the Court of Appeal in *Re Ide (a Bankrupt); HH Aluminium & Building Products Ltd v Bell* [2020] EWCA Civ 1469.

PD IP para.5.2 now provides that CPR Pt 6 applies to service both within and out of the jurisdiction.

On service of statutory demand and petitions other than by personal service in the context of para.12.7.1(4) see *Canning v Irwin Mitchell LLP* [2017] EWHC 718 (Ch); [2017] B.P.I.R. 934. On the effect of substituted service of a bankruptcy petition in light of a predecessor PD, see *Ardawa v Uppal* [2019] EWHC 456 (Ch); [2019] B.P.I.R. 475.

The predecessor provision to what is now para.11.4.4 was discussed by Vos J in *Inbakumar v United Trust Bank Ltd* [2012] EWHC 845 (Ch); [2012] B.P.I.R. 758 at paras [15] and [16]. See also *Jones v Financial Conduct Authority* [2013] EWHC 2731 (Ch); [2013] B.P.I.R. 1033. In *Zafar v Waltham Forest LBC* [2014] EWHC 791 (Ch); [2014] B.P.I.R. 1012 Nicholas Strauss QC confirmed the practice of not looking behind liability orders in bankruptcy proceedings. But at the same time he warned the creditor of the risk in persisting with bankruptcy proceedings where it was known that the liability order was questioned. For a full analysis of para.11.4.4 see *Vieira v Revenue and Customs Commissioners* [2017] EWHC 936 (Ch); [2017] B.P.I.R. 1062 where the court refused to look behind a tax assessment even if it was under appeal.

An appeal was allowed in *Javeri v Zorab* [2020] EWHC 621 (Ch) where the district judge had not considered the guidance and options in para.12.6 of the PD IP covering the position of failure to attend a listed hearing and which empowered the court to re-list (or dismiss) the petition.

Part 6 of PD IP (Applications relating to the remuneration of office-holders) largely reproduces the 2004 Practice Statement of Chief Registrar Baister on "The Fixing and Approval of the Remuneration of Appointees" (see [2014] B.C.C. 525). For background to the 2004 Practice Statement see Baister (2006) 22 I.L. & P. 50. Early cases dealing with this 2004 Statement include *Simion v Brown* [2007] B.P.I.R. 412 and *Barker v Bajjon* [2008] B.P.I.R. 771. The leading case on the significance of the 2004 Practice Statement is *Brook v Reed* [2011] EWCA Civ 331; [2012] 1 W.L.R. 419; [2011] B.C.C. 423. See annotation to IR 2016 r.18.28. The principles embodied in the 2004 Practice Statement were applied in Scotland by Lord Malcolm in *Re Nimmo, Approval of Accounts of Intromissions* [2013] CSOH 4 at [32]. The importance of the guidelines now contained in Pt 6 in all cases where remuneration is being questioned was reiterated by the Chancellor of the High Court, Sir Terence Etherton in *Salliss v Hunt* [2014] EWHC 229 (Ch); [2014] 1 W.L.R. 2402 and were applied in *Hunt (Liquidator of Total Debt Relief Ltd) v Financial Conduct Authority* [2019] EWHC 2018 (Ch); [2019] B.P.I.R. 1495. See *Mowbray v Sanders* [2015] EWHC 2317 (Ch) where Hildyard J supported the right of a trustee to receive remuneration and expenses but expressed some disquiet about the relative high cost involved in the case of a small bankruptcy. An application for a payment to office-holders, partly under the jurisdiction in *Re Berkeley Applegate (Investment Consultants) Ltd* [1989] Ch. 32; (1988) 4 B.C.C. 279, to recover costs from the possible proceeds of sale of freehold properties currently subject to investors' leasehold interests, was refused in *Re CHF 2 Ltd; Jackson v Alshammari* [2020] EWHC 2685 (Ch) where the court applied PD IP paras 21.1 and 21.2(4) that remuneration should be commensurate with the nature and extent of the work undertaken and reflect the value of the service, not simply reimburse the office-holder in respect of time and cost.

Note also the illuminating approach adopted by Chief Registrar Baister in *Re Borodzicz* [2016] B.P.I.R. 24.

Reference is made in PD IP para.8.1 to the Practice Direction 51O, The Electronic Working Pilot Scheme. These PDs give the permission required under IR 2016 r.1.46 for electronic delivery of documents to the court (*Re Keyworker Homes (North West) Ltd; Woodside v Keyworker Homes (North West) Ltd* [2019] EWHC 3499 (Ch); [2020] B.C.C. 223, a ruling of HHJ Hodge QC). Unfortunately this and several other first-instance cases have noted that para.8.1 of this PD contains a drafting mistake. This has been the source of considerable confusion for the courts in those cases relating to notification of appointment of administrators to court by electronic filing out of court hours. In the first case, *Wright v HMV Ecommerce Ltd* [2019] EWHC 903 (Ch); [2019] B.C.C. 887, Barling J identified that PD IP para.8.1, apparently disapplying PD 51O para.2.1 (which normally allows electronic filing), is ambiguous as it is unclear whether it precludes use of the electronic filing scheme altogether in relation to the appointment of administrators out of usual court opening hours or only in relation to the appointment out of hours made by a qualifying floating charge holder (QFCH) to which instead IR 2016 rr.3.20–3.22 apply (allowing filing out of court hours by QFCH only by fax or email), but rr.3.20–3.22 do not apply to appointment by a director or the company. The above *HMV Ecommerce* and *Keyworker Homes* cases both described the wording of para.8.1 as "byzantine" and in need of reform. The principles (some of them conflicting) from the cases appear to be:

- notification of *intention to appoint* administrators can be filed electronically *at any time* by the

154

company, the directors or by a QFCH: *Re SJ Henderson & Co Ltd; Re Triumph Furniture Ltd* [2019] EWHC 2742 (Ch); [2020] B.C.C. 52 (ICC Judge Burton) and *Keyworker Homes* (above);

- notification of *appointment* of administrators by electronic means out of court hours must be in accordance with IR 2016 (rather than PD 51O): and the only such rules are rr.3.20–3.22 which apply only to appointment by a QFCH, by fax or email (see Marcus Smith J in *Re Skeggs Beef Ltd* [2019] EWHC 2607 (Ch); [2020] B.C.C. 43);

- notification of appointment of administrators by electronic means out of court hours by the company or directors does not invalidate the appointment (*HMV Ecommerce* and *Keyworker Homes*) but *SJ Henderson* considered that it was invalid as there was no express power to do so, but the appointment could take effect when the relevant court next opened;

- notification of appointment of administrators by electronic means out of court hours was a procedural defect that could be validated by IR 2016 r.12.64 (*HMV Ecommerce, Re Skeggs Beef, Causer v All Star Leisure (Group) Ltd* [2019] EWHC 3231 (Ch); [2020] B.C.C. 100 and *Keyworker Homes*) or IA 1986 Sch.B1 para.104 (*HMV Ecommerce*). But *SJ Henderson* concluded (at [89]) that it was not a defect that could be so validated.

On one matter the above cases all agree: PD IP para.8.1 (and/or PD 51O) is in urgent need of amendment (according to HHJ David Cooke in *Causer v All Star Leisure (Group) Ltd* this could be done by removing the "carve out" in relation to appointment by QFCH from PD 51O and PD IP para.8.1). In the meantime the courts have been adept in finding ways to validate appointments and to offer reassurance to practitioners who are naturally concerned by the confused legal position. In light of the confusion from the conflicting decisions, Sir Geoffrey Vos C on 29 January 2020 issued guidance, reported as *Practice Note* [2020] B.C.C. 211, directing court clerks to refer a notice of appointment filed through the electronic filing system outside court hours by a QFCH(or by a company or its directors), at the first possible opportunity to a specified High Court judge, who will determine the validity of the appointment and, if appropriate, the time at which the appointment takes effect, either on paper or following a short hearing (for which he or she may request written or oral submissions). Amendments to IR 2016 are anticipated to clarify the position for the future. On the first case reported after the *Practice Note*, Zacaroli J in *Re Symm & Co Ltd* [2020] EWHC 317 (Ch) concluded that an appointment by a company or its directors by way of electronic filing outside court hours is not permissible (but that under r.12.64 the court may declare the appointment effective as from the time when the court office next opens, provided that the irregularity has caused no substantial injustice).

Pending changes to IR 2016 (or PD 51O), *Temporary Insolvency Practice Direction (No.5) Supporting the Insolvency Practice Direction* [2021] B.C.C. 877 (in force from 1 October 2021 and without an end date unless amended or revoked), superseding earlier Practice Directions noted above dating back to 1 April 2020, clarifies that on electronic filing (CE-file) of notice of appointment of administrators:

- in court-opening hours, notice of intention to appoint an administrator filed by a company or its directors, and notice of appointment of an administrator filed by a QFCH or by a company or its directors shall be treated as delivered to the court at the date and time recorded in the filing submission email (paras 3, 4; paras 3.1, 3.2 in the superseded TPDs);

- outside court opening hours of 10.00 to 16.00, notice of intention to appoint an administrator by e-filing by a company or its directors on any day that the courts are open for business shall be treated as delivered to the court at 10.00 on the day that the courts are next open for business (para.5; para.3.3 in the superseded TPDs); and

- outside court opening hours of 10.00 to 16:00 hours, notice of appointment of an administrator by e-filing by a company or its directors on any day that the courts are open for business shall be treated as delivered to the court at 10:00 hours on the day that the courts are next open for business (para.6; para.3.4 in the superseded TPDs).

There are references in para.6.1 to the Chancery Guide, which was rewritten and reissued on 29 July 2022 and is available at *https://www.judiciary.uk/wp-content/uploads/2022/07/Chancery-Guide-2022-28-7-22.pdf*.

New Parts to PD IP include Pt 4 Appeals (clarifying the position) and Pt 7 Unfair Prejudice Petitions,

Winding up and Validation Orders (repeating the point made in *Practice Direction: Order under s.127 of the Insolvency Act 1986* [2007] B.C.C. 839 of the undesirability of asking for a winding-up order in an unfairly prejudicial conduct petition under s.994 of the Companies Act 2006).

Appendix IX: Practice Direction: Directors Disqualification Proceedings [2015] B.C.C. 224

Replace the note with:

This *Practice Direction (PD)* was first issued in 1999 and has since been amended from time to time. A complete revision of the Practice Direction was issued in January 2015 and is reproduced in the text below. The current version at any time is to be found at *http://www.justice.gov.uk/courts/procedure-rules/ civil/rules/disqualification_proceedings*. There are references in paras 10.1 and 10.2 to the *Chancery Guide*, which was rewritten and reissued on 29 July 2022 and is available at *https://www.judiciary.uk/wp-content/uploads/2022/07/Chancery-Guide-2022-28-7-22.pdf*.

Appendix XI: Index of definitions appearing in the Insolvency Act 1986

Insert new Appendix:

This index set out words and phrases defined in the Insolvency Act 1986 (IA 1986) as currently in force and assuming that the Insolvency (Amendment) (EU Exit) Regulations 2019 (SI 2019/146) apply (that is, that no main proceedings in respect of the debtor were opened before the end of the Brexit transition period).

The numbers shown refer to the section of IA 1986, or paragraph of Sch.B1 to IA 1986, in which the definition appears.

An asterisk (*) means that the term has the defined meaning for only a limited part of the legislation. Where a definition applies to bankruptcy, this is shown by *^{b}, and where a definition applies to all the corporate parts of IA 1986, this is shown by *^{c}.

Some words or phrases are given more than one meaning and where this is the case, each reference is shown.

We show definitions in the singular or plural as in IA 1986. Where, however, the word or expression is given separate singular and plural definitions in different provisions of IA 1986 we have used one entry for both definitions and used whichever of the singular or plural seemed to us to be most appropriate.

We have omitted definite articles included in defined words or phrases.

This index omits:

- Definitions in provisions in force only for transitional purposes.

- Definitions set out in schedules to IA 1986 other than Sch.B1. (This is because definitions appearing in schedules other than Sch.B1 are invariably defined only for the purposes of the schedule or paragraph in which the word or phrase appears, and the location of the definition will be obvious. Where, however, the relevant word or phrase is used in the main body of IA 1986 by cross-referring to a definition in a schedule, the word or phrase is included in this index. For example, "eligible company" is included in this index, in the context of a moratorium under Pt A1 of IA 1986, by reference to s.A2, though the substantive definition (as s.A2 makes clear) appears in Sch.ZA1.

- Words and phrases defined in the original Pt 2 (administration) of IA 1986.

- Words and phrases inserted, or which are to be read into, IA 1986 under legislation for entities which would not otherwise be within the ambit of IA 1986 and where additional or amended definitions may apply. For example, definitions added to s.110 for limited liability partnerships under the Limited Liability Partnerships Regulations 2001 (SI 2001/1090).

- Definitions relevant only to Scotland or Northern Ireland, or Scottish or Northern Irish insolvency proceedings.

We have included words or phrases that are not stated as definitions or meanings as such but which we consider have that effect (for example, "net property" in s.176A(6)). We have however excluded some phrases that we assessed as providing, in each case, merely an example, non-exhaustive qualification, inclusion or exclusion, or as explanation rather than definition. Examples include:

- Fine imposed for an offence (s.281(4A)).

- Property comprised in a bankrupt's estate (s.283(5)).

- Appointment of an administrator (Sch.B1 para.100(1)).

- Action (Sch.B1 para.111(3)).

Statutory definition	Provision
acceleration or early termination clause	s.174A(11)*
acquired property	s.A31(6)*
	Sch.B1 para.70(3)*
acquiring or receiving property	s.359(5)*
action	Sch.B1 para.111(3)*
acts as an insolvency practitioner	s.388
adjudicator	s.385(1)*[b]
administration application	Sch.B1 para.12(1)*
administration order	Sch.B1 para.10
administrative receiver	ss.29(2)*, 72A(3)*, 251*[c], 388(4)*
	Sch.B1 para.111(1)*
administrator	Sch.B1 paras 1(1), 75(5)*, 101(2)*, 101(3)*, 111(1)*
affairs [of a person]	s.385(2)*[b]
agency worker	s.A21(6)*
agent	ss.A48(10)*, 7A(8)*, 19(3)*, 251*[c]
appeal against a conviction is pending	s.277(3)*
appears to be unable to pay a debt	s.268(1)*
appears to have no reasonable prospect of being able to pay a debt	s.268(2)*
appointed day	s.436(1)
application date	s.251X(1)*
appointment of a receiver or manager under powers contained in an instrument	s.29(1)(b)*
appropriate amount	s.342D(9)*
appropriate authority	ss.A48(3)*, 7A(2)*
appropriate number	ss.246ZF(6)* c, 379ZB(6)*[b],
appropriate regulator	ss.A49(13)*, 4A(5A)*
approved intermediary	ss.251U(2)*, 251X(1)*
approved pension arrangement	s.342A(8)*
arbitration agreement	s.349A(4)*
articles	s.436(2)
assignee	s.215(3)*
assignment	s.344(3)*
associate	ss.249*, 435, 436(1)
assurance	s.190(1)*
attachment	s.128(3)*
attachment completed	s.346(5)
authorised deposit taker	Sch.B1 para.9(4)*
bankrupt	s.381(1)*[b]
bankrupt obtaining credit	s.360(2)*
bankruptcy application	s.381(1A)*[b]
bankruptcy debt	s.382*[b]
bankruptcy level	s.267(4)*
bankruptcy order	s.381(2)*[b]
bankruptcy petition	s.381(3)*[b]
bankrupt's estate	s.283*[b]
body corporate	s.436(1)
books and papers	s.251*[c]
building	s.72DA(3)*

Index of definitions appearing in the Insolvency Act 1986

Index of definitions appearing in the Insolvency Act 1986

Index of definitions appearing in the Insolvency Act 1986

Index of definitions appearing in the Insolvency Act 1986

Statutory definition	Provision
property comprised in the bankrupt's estate	s.351*
property of the company	s.42(2)(b)*
property or goods of the bankrupt	s.285(6)*
property possession of which is required to be delivered up	s.351*
proposal	ss.1(2)*, 253*
proposed monitor	s.A6(1)*
proprietor	ss.180(1)*, 319(1)*
prosecuting authority	ss.A48(10)*, 7A(8)*, 262B(3)*
public company	s.436(2)
public-private partnership project	s.72C(2)*
purpose of administration	Sch.B1 para.111(1)*
qualified person	s.A54(1)*
qualifying debt	s.251A(2)*, 251X(1)*
qualifying floating charge	Sch.B1 para.14(2)*
qualifying decision procedure	ss.246ZE(11)*c, 251*c
qualifying liability	s.44(2A)*
reasonable prospect that debtor will be able to pay a debt	s.271(4)*
reasonable replacement	s.308(4)*
receiver	ss.A52(3)*, 72(2)*, 251*c
receiver or manager of the property of a company	s.29(1)(a)
recognised professional body	s.391*
records	s.436(1)
recovery provisions	ss.342C(7)*
redundancy payment	ss.A18(7)*, 174A(11)*
register	s.251X(1)*
registrar of companies	s.436(2)
regulated activity	s.A49(13)*
regulated business	s.72D(2)(b)*
regulated company	s.A49(13)*
regulations	ss.342C(7)*, 342F(9)*
regulator	s.A49(13)*
regulatory arrangements	s.391D(6)*
regulatory functions	s.391C(2)*
regulatory objectives	s.391C(3)*
regulatory principles	s.391C(4)*
relative of an individual	s.435(8)*
relevant accelerated debt	s.174A(4)*
relevant circumstances	s.425(3)*
relevant contributions	s.342A(5)*
relevant contributories	s.246ZF(8)* c,
relevant country or territory	s.426(11)*
relevant creditors	ss.246ZF(7)*c, 379ZB(7)*b Sch.B1 para.98(3)*
relevant date	ss.131(6)*, 387*
relevant day	ss.166(6)*, 372(1)*
relevant debts	s.217(3)*
relevant documents	ss.A6(1)*, A49(1)*
relevant financial institution	s.387A
relevant information about status of person	ss.360(4)*, 360(6)*
relevant insolvency procedure	s.233B(2)*

Appendix XII: Index of definitions appearing in the Insolvency (England and Wales) Rules 2016

Insert new Appendix:

This index set out words and phrases defined in the Insolvency (England and Wales) Rules 2016 (SI 2016/1024) (IR 2016) as currently in force and assuming that the Insolvency (Amendment) (EU Exit) Regulations 2019 (SI 2019/146) apply (that is, that no main proceedings in respect of the debtor were opened before the end of the Brexit transition period).

The numbers shown refer to the rule or the paragraph of the indicated schedule to IR 2016 in which the definition appears.

An asterisk (*) means that the term has a special meaning for only a limited part of IR 2016.

Some words or phrases are given more than one meaning and, where this is the case, each reference is shown.

We show definitions in the singular or plural as in IR 2016. Where, however, the word or expression is given separate singular and plural definitions in different provisions of IR 2016 we have used one entry for both definitions and used whichever of the singular or plural seemed to us to be most appropriate.

We have omitted definite articles included in defined words or phrases (except in the case of "the chair", "the insolvent" and "the IP", where we considered the inclusion helpful).

This index omits:

- Definitions in provisions in force only for transitional purposes.

- Words and phrases inserted, or which are to be read into, IR 2016 under legislation for entities which would not otherwise be within the ambit of the Insolvency Act 1986 (IA 1986) and where additional or amended definitions may apply, for example in relation to limited liability partnerships.

- Definitions relevant only to Scotland or Northern Ireland, or Scottish or Northern Irish insolvency proceedings.

We have included words or phrases that are not stated as definitions or meanings as such but which we consider have that effect (for example, "claim form" in Sch.4 para.1). We have however excluded some phrases that we assessed as providing, in each case, merely an example, non-exhaustive qualification, inclusion or exclusion, or as explanation rather than definition. Examples include:

- Former bankrupt (r.8.36(4)).

- Property and debtor's property (r.9.8).

- Determination period (r.10.40).

- Creditors (r.14.26(2)).

- Last date for proving (r.14.30).

Where a term is not defined by IR 2016, the Interpretation Act 1978 s.11 (Construction of subordinate legislation) will operate to attribute to it any meaning assigned to that term in IA 1986.

No account is taken of notes appearing in IR 2016 that purport to add explanation or definition. This is because the status and authority of notes is unclear and they do not appear to be the subject of updating or amendment by later legislation even where amendment might have been expected.

For example:

- A note in r.1.2 (defined terms) appears after the definition of "document" to indicate that the phrase "EU Regulation" is "…defined for the purposes of these Rules by section 436 of the Act as Regulation (EU) No 2015/848 of the European Parliament and of the Council". (Note, IR 2016 r.1.2).

  In fact, the definition in IA 1986 s.436 has now (for all practical purposes) been modified following Brexit. Further, "EU Regulation" is in fact defined in the body of the definition of "Article 1.2 undertaking" in the same rule 1.2.

- The note appearing before r.1.2 states that "the terms which are defined in rule 1.2 include some terms defined by the Act for limited purposes which are applied generally by these Rules. Such terms have the meaning given by the Act for those limited purposes". (Note, IR 2016 r.1.2).

  The meaning of this is not entirely clear, but suggests that, notwithstanding the definition of any particular term in r.1.2, that defined term may nevertheless bear a different meaning (being the meaning attributed to it by IA 1986) in certain contexts.

Index of definitions appearing in the Insolvency (England and Wales) Rules 2016

Index of definitions appearing in the Insolvency (England and Wales) Rules 2016

Pilkington on Creditor Schemes of Arrangement and Restructuring Plans, 3rd
edn   *Christian Pilkington; Will Stoner*
ISBN: 9780414100022   Publication date: September 2022
Formats: Hardback/Westlaw UK/ProView eBook
This authoritative legal text offers provides in-depth guidance on the legal
principles, formal procedures and practical issues which underpin the use of
schemes of arrangements and the new 'restructuring plan' option as used in
complex financial restructurings. The expert author team at White & Case, cover
the subject in full, taking in its development and the fundamental principles of its
use as a restructuring tool, alongside key subjects such as jurisdiction, class
composition issues and foreign recognition. Practical in its focus, the book
provides not only diagrams and flowcharts which summarise complex processes
but also case studies to illustrate different types of schemes of arrangement and
explain some of the most high-profile international restructurings of recent
years.

Insolvency Litigation: A Practical Guide, 3rd edn   *Adam Deacock; Josh Lewison*
ISBN: 9780414090491   Publication date: December 2021
Formats: Hardback/Westlaw UK/ProView eBook
This comprehensive text focuses on the process, procedure and issues faced by
practitioners conducting insolvency related litigation. Offering specific practical
guidance to the most important court applications in insolvency practice and
guidance to different aspects of litigation, including litigation against an insolvent
defendant, limitation, costs and funding issues, litigation by office holders and
their approach to litigation and the types of application that arise in insolvency
cases. This new third edition has been completely updated in line with the
Insolvency Rules 2016 as amended and after the Corporate Insolvency and
Governance Act 2020 as well as containing two new chapters – one explaining the
structure of CVAs, the other providing an overview of insolvency litigation in the
Caribbean (Cayman Islands, Bermuda, and the BVI)

Contact us on: Tel: +44 (0)345 600 9355
Order online: sweetandmaxwell.co.uk